"This Blue Hollow"

**Co-winner of the 1999 Colorado
Endowment for the Humanities Publication Prize**

The CEH Publication Prize was created in 1998, and the first
awards were made in 1999. The prize annually supports publication of outstanding nonfiction works that have strong humanities content and that make an area of humanities research more
available to the Colorado public. The CEH Publication Prize
moneys are shared by the University Press of Colorado and the
author whose works are being recognized.
The Colorado Endowment for the Humanities is a statewide,
nonprofit organization dedicated to improving the quality of
humanities education for all Coloradans. In 1999, CEH is
celebrating 25 years of people, programs, and ideas.

"This Blue Hollow"

~

Estes Park, the Early Years, 1859–1915

James H. Pickering

University Press of Colorado

Copyright © 1999 by the University Press of Colorado
International Standard Book Number 0-87081-528-8

Published by the University Press of Colorado
P.O. Box 849
Niwot, Colorado 80544

Printed in the United States of America.

The University Press of Colorado is a cooperative publishing enterprise supported, in part, by Adams State College, Colorado State University, Fort Lewis College, Mesa State College, Metropolitan State College of Denver, University of Colorado, University of Northern Colorado, University of Southern Colorado, and Western State College of Colorado.

The paper used in this publication meets the minimum requirements of the American National Standard for Information Sciences-Permanence of Paper for Printed Library Materials. ANSI Z39.48–1984

Library of Congress Cataloging-in-Publication Data
Pickering, James H.
    This blue hollow : Estes Park, the early years, 1859–1915 / James H. Pickering.
    p. cm.
    Includes bibliographical references and index.
    ISBN 0-87081-528-8 (alk. paper)
    1. Estes Park (Colo.)—History. I. Title.
F784.E85P53   1999
978.8'68—dc21

08 07 06 05 04 03 02 01 00 99   10 9 8 7 6 5 4 3 2 1

Contents

~

Figures

∼

Preface

〜

Although the Estes Park region has been inhabited by white men barely more than half a century, marks of the pioneers are being obliterated so fast by the enormous development of the country as a summer resort that within another year or two the last vestiges of the region's early history will have disappeared completely, and one of the most romantic chapters in the story of Colorado's development will have become only a memory.

—Denver Post, November 26, 1916

This history began more than a decade ago when I set out to celebrate a lifelong interest in Estes Park and Colorado by publishing new editions of works by Frederick Chapin, Enos and Joe Mills, Samuel Bowles, and Ernest Ingersoll. In each case I was asked to prepare an introduction and a set of explanatory notes that would be helpful for the contemporary reader. In so doing, it quickly became clear that the nineteenth- and early-twentieth-century history of Estes Park was difficult to reconstruct in many of the particulars with which I was most concerned.

To their credit, the residents of the Estes Park valley have always been interested in their own history and over the years have sought to perpetuate it in a variety of ways. The Estes Park Public Library provides easy access through its well-kept Colorado Collection to most of what has been published about Estes Park and maintains valuable collections of photographs and oral histories. The Estes Park Area Historical Museum through its permanent displays and special exhibitions does an excellent job of educating visitors and residents alike about Estes Park as it was in earlier days. Other resources, including photographs, are available at the Rocky Mountain National Park's Library in McLaren Hall.

But aside from a small number of full-length monographs—books like Curt Buchholtz's *Rocky Mountain National Park: A History* (1983) and Alex Drummond's *Enos Mills: Citizen of Nature* (1995), both of which focus primarily on the twentieth century—the historical treatment of Estes Park, especially the early years, remains partial and incomplete and is not infrequently inaccurate in detail and emphasis. Almost without exception, the narratives that do exist take the form of short pamphlets illustrated by period photographs, which provide information of interest to first-time visitors and casual students of history. Heavily dependent, as they are, on secondary sources (and on each other), these brief accounts—which include June Carothers's *Estes Park Past and Present* (1951), Caroline Bancroft's *Trail Ridge Country: The Romantic History of Estes Park and Grand Lake* (1968), Dave Hicks's *Estes Park From the Beginning* (1976), Ruth Stauffer's *This Was Estes Park: Historical Vignettes of the Early Days* (1976), Anne Canning's *Early Estes Park* (1990), and Kenneth Jessen's *Estes Park: A Quick History* (1996)—not surprisingly tend to perpetuate many of the myths, misinformation, and mistaken impressions that have long since gathered around such important historical figures as Joel Estes, Griff Evans, Isabella Bird, Rocky Mountain Jim, and the Earl of Dunraven. Though surely not intentionally, such publications have helped to transform real men and women into standardized folkloristic representations that contemporaries, much less the originals themselves, would be hard pressed to recognize.

The work of more established historians such as Marshall Sprague does not serve us much better. Though Sprague includes sprightly and highly readable chapters on Isabella Bird and Rocky Mountain Jim ("Love in the Park") and the Earl of Dunraven ("The Dude from Limmerick") in his 1966 book *A Gallery of Dudes*, his narratives are flawed by the author's failure to question either the motives or the accuracy of his principal sources, the published writings of Isabella Bird, Dunraven, and the Earl's personal physician, Dr. George Kingsley. Sprague, for example, characterizes Rocky Mountain Jim as "an English [sic] desperado . . . who had 'black fits' and a tendency to commit mayhem during sprees in the grog-shops of Denver." Such statements—for which there is little or no historical justification—serve only to reinforce the histrionic view of the hunter-rancher for which Isabella Bird herself was largely responsible. Moreover, Sprague's account of Dunraven's land dealings and the subsequent shooting of Mountain Jim is skewed by the completely erroneous assertion that William Haigh, the young Englishman who stood beside Griff Evans at the time of the shooting, was Dunraven's hand-picked "purchasing agent."

The secondary source most often cited by Marshall Sprague and his companions is Harold Marion Dunning's monumental *Over Hill and Vale*, published in three volumes between 1956 and 1971. Yet *Over Hill and Vale* is not a history in the formal sense at all. Rather it is a compilation of historical vignettes, interesting bits and pieces of information, that a dedicated antiquarian from Loveland, pursuing a labor of love, picked up over a lifetime. In short, as a source of historical fact Dunning's volumes, though fascinating in their own way, are neither definitive nor always reliable.

The accounts of early Estes Park most helpful to the contemporary historian, by contrast, are those by its pioneer residents. These include Enos Mills's small 105-page history of 1905, *The Story of Estes Park and a Guide Book*, Elkanah Lamb's two volumes of memoirs, *Memories of the Past and Thoughts of the Future* (1906) and *Miscellaneous Meditations* (c. 1913), as well as the extremely valuable series of articles that Abner Sprague began to contribute to the *Estes Park Trail*, beginning in 1922, and which he apparently originally intended to publish in book form. Though not without their own biases and inaccuracies, these narratives have a decided advantage: they were written at a time much closer to the events they relate and by individuals who witnessed, and even participated in, those events.

Fortunately, as I have discovered over the years, there are ample primary materials from which to reconstruct the early history of Estes Park. They take the form of letters, journals and diaries, autobiographies, directories, land and census records, legal documents, travel narratives, monographs, and, of course, newspaper and magazine articles, most of them widely scattered, hard to access, and unindexed. Newspapers have proven to be a particularly valuable resource. Though Estes Park lacked its own year-round newspaper until 1921, the newspapers of Denver and the towns along the Front Range contain a great deal of useful (and previously untapped) information about Estes Park, which I found I could ferret out by working my way through them, issue by microfilmed issue. Beginning in the 1870s, and then with increasing frequency and interest, these papers carried news of a young Estes Park. They did so not only because their residents were finding the park an attractive and accessible place to visit, but because of the growing recognition by their business communities that local economic interests were clearly and inevitably linked to the "gem of the Rockies."

The history of early Estes Park that has emerged is primarily the story of individuals: literate, strong-willed, self-reliant, entrepreneurial men and women who came to visit and then to make their home in Joel Estes's valley. Though the stay of Estes and his family was relatively brief and their isolated world relatively tranquil, others followed: hunters and fishermen, prospectors, government surveyors and geologists, homesteading settlers, lumbermen, mountaineers, artists and writers, and vacationers. They came for many reasons—first for exploration, exploitation, and settlement, later for escape, health, recreation, and renewal. It is their collective experiences and accomplishments—their successes as well as their failures—that make up the history that follows.

For settler and visitor alike Estes Park has always been a special place—psychologically and, particularly in its early days, physically isolated and remote, a world apart. Nevertheless, in reconstructing its early years I have tried to make it clear that the story of Estes Park is part of the unfolding story of pre– and post–Civil War America and particularly the discovery by a westering people of the value of leisure and recreation. As we shall see, the pioneers of Estes Park, most of whom initially came to ranch and farm, discovered very early that survival depended on their ability to cater to tourists and to adapt their own lives and interests to America's growing preoccupation with nature and the outdoors. In relatively short order the geography of the region—what historians are fond of calling the "genius of place"—forced upon these early residents the kind of recognitions and concerns that in our own time have been identified with environmentalism.

The title of my book comes from the pages of Isabella Bird's *A Lady's Life in the Rocky Mountains* (1879). "For, in truth," she writes, "this blue hollow, lying solitary at the foot of Long's Peak, is a miniature world of great interest, in which love, jealousy, hatred, envy, pride, unselfishness, greed, selfishness, and self-sacrifice can be studied hourly. . . ." In three short words, Isabella Bird manages to capture the physical description of Estes Park that anyone who has visited it will immediately and vividly remember. And the remainder of the sentence reminds us that Estes Park, for all its beauty, apparent tranquility, and sense of remoteness, is but a microcosm of the larger world beyond the mountains to which its history is very much connected.

The debts I have contracted over the past decade are enormous, both to those who have contributed by way of answering questions and providing information and to those who through their interest have encouraged a project that at times seemed never ending. I have tried to acknowledge these individuals, many of whom have long since become correspondents and friends, in the prefaces of my earlier books. I will not repeat their names here (at the risk of both redundancy and omission), though in choosing not to do so it is important to underscore the obvious: that studying and writing history is a cumulative process. Without their help this book could not have been completed. I would, however, like to thank the staffs of the following institutions and libraries where I spent so many hours during the fall, winter, and spring of 1995–

1996: the Colorado Historical Society, the Western History Department of the Denver Public Library, Norlin Library of the University of Colorado, the Rocky Mountain National Park Library, and the public libraries in Boulder, Longmont, Loveland, Fort Collins, Greeley, and, of course, Estes Park. The interlibrary loan department of the University of Houston's M. D. Anderson Library, on whose services I have heavily relied, has proven to be an invaluable asset.

I owe a continuing debt to Alex Drummond of Ward, Colorado, the author of *Enos Mills: Citizen of Nature*, the sensitive and clearly definitive biography of the writer-naturalist whose efforts on behalf of Estes Park are so much a part of the story I have tried to tell. What began as correspondence between two individuals living far apart, but interested in the same subject, has developed into an important friendship and source of encouragement, culminating in the autumn of 1995 in a never-to-be-forgotten three-day backpacking and camping excursion over Hagues Peak to visit Rowe Glacier. I have learned from Alex Drummond a great deal about the world of Estes Park and Colorado that any historian who writes about place needs to know—not facts and dates, but sensitivity and respect. His eyes and spirit have taught me not only how to focus on nature and the wilderness but how to understand better those who once made that wilderness their home.

I would also like to thank Dr. Patrick Sartorius of East Lansing, Michigan, and Terrell Dixon, my colleague at the University of Houston, both of whom have remained interested in my work over the years and have actually offered to read my manuscripts. Pat Sartorius is a physician by training, but his proofreading abilities and literary sensitivities match those of the best of editors.

Finally, there are the members of my family: my wife, Patricia; my son, David; my daughter, Susan; my son-in-law, Rick; and their (and my own) circle of friends. They have endured, with a patience and good humor far greater than my own, not only my absences from home but years of stories and anecdotes (foisted upon them in front of the fireplace, on the porch, or on the trail) growing out of my researches and idiosyncratic enthusiasms. Special recognition is due as well to my father and mother, who years ago brought a boy all the way from suburban New York to a turn-of-the-century cabin on the slope of Twin Sisters Mountain and by so doing initiated me into "this blue hollow." My only hope is that I have produced a book that all of you who have been part of my world—and this world of Estes Park, Colorado—will find enjoyable and rewarding.

"This Blue Hollow"

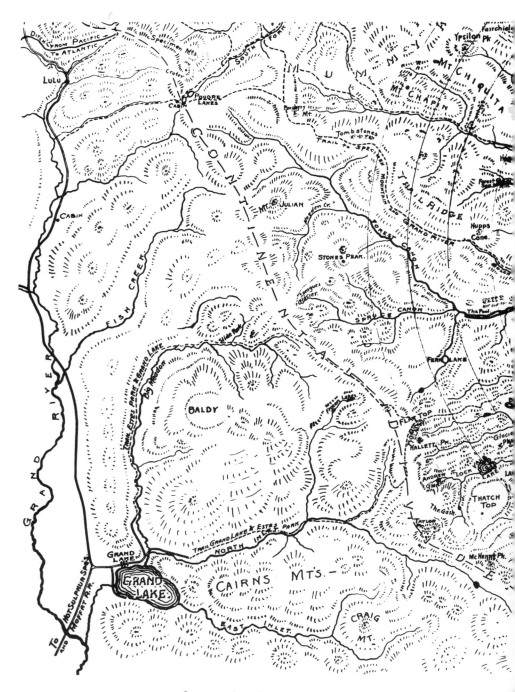

Figure 1.1. Map of Estes Park and surroundings, 1905. Courtesy Elizabeth M. Mill

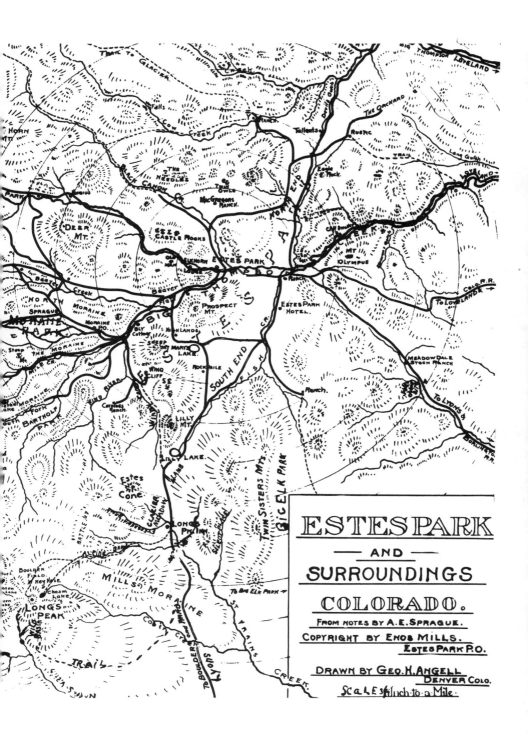

ESTES PARK
— AND —
SURROUNDINGS
COLORADO.
FROM NOTES BY A.E.SPRAGUE.
COPYRIGHT BY ENOS MILLS.
ESTES PARK P.O.

DRAWN BY GEO.H.ANGELL
DENVER COLO.
SCALE ⅜ inch to a Mile.

Chapter 1

~

Loomings

On a day in mid-October of 1859, fifty-three-year-old Joel Estes and his nineteen-year-old son, Milton, having followed the Little Thompson westward into the mountains on a hunting and exploring trip from their ranch at Fort Lupton, cleared the top of the ridge now known as Park Hill. From there they gazed down upon the grassy, tree-fringed upland valley (or "park," in the parlance of the mountains) that would soon bear their name. "I shall never forget my first sight of the Park," Milton Estes later wrote.

> We stood on the mountain looking down . . . where the Park spread out before us. No words can describe our surprise, wonder and joy at beholding such an unexpected sight. It looked like a low valley with a silver streak or thread winding its way through the tall grass, down through the valley and disappearing around a hill among the pine trees. This silver thread was Big Thompson Creek. It was a grand sight and a great surprise.
>
> We did not know what we had found. . . . We were monarchs of all we surveyed, mountains, valleys and streams. There was absolutely nothing to dispute our sway. We had a little world all to ourselves.[1]

Though the valley they had stumbled upon lay empty, theirs for the taking, others had surely preceded them. Stories persist that Estes Park had been visited and even briefly occupied by earlier generations of hunters, trappers, and prospectors, including the legendary Kit Carson himself. Many of these stories, including the one about Kit Carson, are apocryphal,[2] and few if any can be fully substantiated.[3] Yet well before the gold rush of 1858–1859 brought Colorado to the attention of the nation, its interior network of mountains and parks was well known, and the principal valleys and streams along the Front Range had been entered. Longs Peak, which the French trappers called "Les Deux Oreilles," or "Two Ears," was clearly visible from the plains. Active trading posts on the South Platte were in equally close proximity: at Fort St. Vrain, Fort Vasquez, Fort Jackson, and Fort Lupton, all dating from the 1830s and all connected with Taos, New Mexico, by a well-worn trail running up the Platte. It thus is virtually certain that well before the time of Joel Estes other white men had wandered in and out of Estes Park, leaving the valley as they found it, without visible sign or written record of their having been there. In competition as they were with one another, such visitors tended to follow the self-reliant tradition of mountain men and kept what they had seen and heard largely to themselves.

All of this changed with the discoveries of gold in Cherry Creek and up Clear Creek Valley. By 1859 prospectors had moved back into the hills of nearby Boulder County, making discoveries at Gold Hill, fol-lowed a year later by equally promising strikes at Ward and Jamestown. The Estes family may well have had Estes Park to itself, but not far away the hills and valleys of Boulder County were already crawling with thou-sands of their countrymen equally eager to establish new beginnings.

Fortunately for the landscape all about them, as well as for the peace and tranquility of Joel Estes and later residents, the great mineral belt of northern Colorado did not extend into Estes Park. To be sure, prospec-tors periodically wandered in to try their luck, and in various places, particularly in the Tahosa Valley in the vicinity of Longs Peak, one en-counters the remnants of their efforts. But with the exception of the Cudahy-Norwall, or Eugenia, Mine on the lower slope of Battle Moun-tain, which dates from 1905 and operated for more than a decade, these would-be miners did not stay. As a result Estes Park was spared the in-dignities of active mining, which elsewhere in Colorado left mountain slopes denuded, scarred, and ugly almost beyond belief.[4]

The Indians had known Estes Park well. Native Americans used the park for seasonal hunting and camping, and though their annual visits had been suspended by the time Joel Estes arrived, evidence of their presence was everywhere. The first trails leading from the plains into Estes Park, including the one followed by Joel Estes along the ridges east of Muggins Gulch, were of Indian origin. In more recent times evidence of Indian encampments and activity—Ute, Shoshoni, Arapaho, Chey-enne, Kiowa, and Comanche in origin—has been discovered in widely scattered places over the entire region: near Little Prospect Mountain, along Deer Ridge and in Beaver Meadows, in Moraine Park, at Marys Lake (many of which are now covered by the lake itself), at Tuxedo Park, at Granite Pass, at Timberline Spring at the head of the south fork of Mill

Creek, on Flattop Mountain, on Forest Canyon Pass and Specimen Mountain above Poudre Lakes, in the Wind River drainage, down along Cabin Creek in the Tahosa Valley, and at Thunder Lake and on Mount Orton deep in the remoteness of Wild Basin. High in the tundra, close by what is now Trail Ridge Road, as well as on Flattop Mountain, there are the remains of game-drive systems, low-walled structures used to herd animals to waiting hunters in terrain lacking natural cover or camouflage.[5]

Perhaps the most interesting material evidence of all lies in the five deposits of Indian artifacts—potsherds, projectile points, broken knives and tools, and obsidian flakes—found at separate locations on the western and southeastern slopes of Oldman Mountain, the conical granite knob overlooking Fall River at the western end of the town of Estes Park. These artifacts, together with similar ones discovered on the south-facing hillside at Beaver Point, eight-tenths of a mile to the south, suggest that Oldman Mountain with its panoramic view was used by Native Americans some three thousand years ago, and for a period of eight hundred years and perhaps longer, as a sacred fasting place and vision quest site. The concentrations of artifacts suggest the presence of way stations where individuals stopped to smoke, pray, and make offerings while climbing to the summit, the place of fasting. Many of these artifacts, particularly the shards of glazed pottery, confirm the existence of a complex trading network between the Indians of the Front Range and the Colorado Plateau and those living farther to the southwest dating back to the late seventeenth and early eighteenth century.[6]

According to tradition Estes Park had been the site of spirited skirmishes between tribes, presumably involving the Arapaho and Utes. The Arapaho were the latecomers. They arrived on the Great Plains from the northeast about 1790, only to be forced by the Sioux into the country along the South Platte and the Front Range, where they inevitably came in contact with the Utes. The Utes had preceded them. They were the long-standing inhabitants of western Colorado and eastern Utah, including the Salt Lake basin, and considered the mountains and parks of Colorado their own. The coming of the Arapaho, together with their traditional allies, the Cheyenne, and their gradual movement from the high plains into the mountain parks ushered in a short, but intense, state of perpetual war. For evidence of their conflict early residents of Estes Park pointed out rocks on a low knoll in upper Beaver Meadows, west of the old Hondius ranch house. These, they said, had once formed the crude breastworks of an Indian fort used during a three-day skirmish in the 1850s between bands of Arapaho and Utes. Projectile points had been found in the vicinity.

Much of the important ethnological work in Estes Park, including the work done at the Oldman Mountain site, is of comparatively recent vintage. The National Park Service, after a flourish of activity in the 1930s by chief naturalist Dorr Yeager, assistant superintendent John Preston, and ranger Jack Moomaw, has placed most of its emphasis on nature interpretation and recreation, leaving others to discover, explain, and display the rich material culture that connects Native Americans to the high country of Colorado's Front Range.

One such effort came in 1914, at a time when the park bill was making its way slowly through the Congress. That year, as part of its campaign for the park, the nomenclature committee of the Colorado Mountain Club, chaired by Harriet Vaille, daughter of the president of the Colorado Telephone Company, set out to research the original names given by the Indians to landmarks in the Estes Park region.[7] When professional anthropologists proved unavailable, Vaille and her colleagues turned to the Indians themselves, raising enough funds (thanks to Harriet's father) to bring to Estes Park three members of the northern Arapaho from the Wind River Reservation in Wyoming.

About noon on Tuesday, July 14, 1914, the three Arapaho arrived by train at Longmont. The oldest, at seventy-three, was the taciturn Gun Griswold, a retired judge. His younger and more animated companion was Sherman Sage, age sixty-three, dressed for the occasion in his blue-cloth chief-of-police uniform and carrying a roll of blankets under his arm. Griswold's only luggage, by contrast, was an eagle-feather fan. With them was a much younger man of mixed blood, named Tom Crispen, their interpreter, for neither Griswold nor Sage could speak English. The Longmont Ledger tried to capture the spirit of the occasion: "It suggested," it said, "dream land, fairy land and Leather Stocking Tales. . . ."[8] The three were promptly placed in cars and taken to Longs Peak Inn, where they were greeted by its proprietor, Enos Mills. The well-scripted plan for their visit called for a two-week pack trip outfitted and led by the noted guide Shep Husted, during which Griswold and Sage would be asked to recall the names and the history of places they had not visited for some fifty years.

Their trip began two days later, on the sixteenth, at Marys Lake. There Griswold and Sage examined an old Indian camp and then rode over to the Hondius ranch in Beaver Meadows to inspect the remains of the Indian fort and battle site, whose combatants they identified (somewhat improbably) as Arapaho and Apache. That night Sage favored the group with a war dance and song. From the Hondius ranch they went up Windy Gulch to Trail Ridge, following it west to

Figure 1.2. Visit of the Arapaho, 1914. Standing, *left to right*, Shep Husted, Gun Griswold, Sherman Sage, Tom Crispen, and Oliver Toll; sitting, David Hawkins. Courtesy National Park Service—Rocky Mountain National Park.

a campsite at the Poudre Lakes. The next day they climbed the crater of Specimen Mountain and then descended to Beaver Creek and Squeaky Bob Wheeler's guest ranch on the North Fork of the Grand (now the Colorado) River, where they spent the night of the twentieth. The party then followed the North Fork up past the remains of the old 1880s mining camp of Lulu City, returning to Estes Park and Lester's Hotel on the rim of Devils Gulch by way of the North Inlet trail, Flattop Mountain, and Mill Creek Basin.

Though Sherman Sage could recall Denver as it existed in 1861—"a group of houses standing, resting on posts, on sand spits in bottom of Cherry Creek"—he was less helpful when it came to the mountains. "The Indians seemed to enjoy locating historic places," the young collegian Oliver Toll recorded in his field notes, "but did not attempt to pose as authorities."[9] Their frequent reply to questions was simply "I don't know" or "That was before my time," and much of the information they did provide was vague or redundant. Plainly uncomfortable when subjected to the scrutiny of tourists and their cameras, the Arapaho became less communicative as the days went by and the novelty of their visit wore off. They were also eager to go home.

What they did provide, though far from conclusive, was a helpful and badly needed reminder of an ancient indigenous culture that by 1914 had already been largely forgotten by Coloradans. As a result of the trip some thirty-six original Indian names were added to the map of the new park. As Abner Sprague later explained, "the Indians had names for each arm of the Park and for many of the streams and mountains . . . ; usually . . . entire sentences; impossible to spell, and harder to pronounce; one locality, Glacier Basin, was known, as nearly as can be translated, as the Place-of-the-big-trees, or Where-the-large-trees-are."[10]

In addition, Griswold and Sherman identified and named old trails to and from the park and within the park itself, including three crossings from Estes Park to Grand Lake. They also told stories of the olden times, about a buffalo herd trapped by winter snows and slaughtered on Thatchtop Mountain and about an eagle trap big enough to conceal a man that Griswold's father, Old Man Gun, had built on the summit of Longs Peak. Oliver W. Toll would not publish his field notes for forty-eight years, until 1962, when his account would read like a voice from the ancient past.

Early settlers like Joel Estes did not need to be reminded about the Indians. They were a daily fact of life. They were also, most white Coloradans had long since decided, both a nuisance and a hindrance to settlement. Nonetheless, during the first years of territorial status after 1861, race relations remained more or less cordial. For their part, the local tribes, the Arapaho, Cheyenne, and Utes, had been content to watch the influx of prospectors streaming into Denver, the Clear Creek area, and the mountains beyond with an interest bordering on amazement, and there was little conflict between them. Moreover, under the terms of the Fort Wise treaty of 1861, the Cheyenne and Arapaho, the two tribes occupying Colorado's plains, had ceded their lands east of the mountains in exchange for a small reservation along the Arkansas, leaving that area relatively quiet.

By 1863, however, the year Estes moved his family to the park, the situation had begun to deteriorate. The traditional hunting grounds of the Plains Indians, with its herds of buffalo, antelope, and deer, lay directly across the emigrant routes. This encroachment was exacerbated by the coming of the railroad, first by the advance of the Union Pacific Railroad across the plains from Omaha, and later by Union Pacific's Eastern Division, building northwest from Kansas City. The result was the ongoing series of violent incidents known as "the Indian wars." For several years they provided almost constant fodder for Indian-thumping newspapers like William Byers's *Rocky Mountain News*, which regularly carried such inflammatory headlines as "Indians, Murder and Depredations," "Indian Outrages," or "More Indian Murders," producing and then heightening a sense of tension and alarm. Much of this highly colored journalism simply reflected an existing deep-seated bias and hostility toward the Indian. But it was also aimed at influencing the government to send more soldiers into the West, enriching local merchants in the process.

Misunderstanding and the clash of cultural differences inevitably led to violence. White willingness to coexist became transformed into highly emotional calls for "active extermination of the red devils," culminating in such tragic events as Sand Creek, where Colonel John Chivington and his Colorado Volunteers slaughtered and mutilated some 150 Cheyenne and Arapaho, mostly women, children, and old men. Acts of reprisal followed, initiating full-blown warfare that extended from Missouri across the plains into Wyoming and westward toward Nevada. Isolated farms were pillaged and burned, not infrequently with loss of life and tales of survivors led into captivity by the "hostiles," livestock run off, and stages and wagons attacked. For a time emigrant travel and the delivery of mail along the Platte River road all but ceased. At one point in 1864 it was estimated that there was not more than six weeks' food supply left in all of Colorado.

Indian warfare in eastern Colorado, at least of the sporadic variety, with all its attendant rumors and alarms, would last until the summer of 1869. By then accommodation had been reached not only with the Arapaho and Cheyenne but with the seven tribes of the Utes. Though the Utes had traditionally gotten along fairly well with whites, in time they too became a target for removal. The treaty that was signed by all parties in Washington on March 2, 1868, was a fair one by the standards of the day. Following some additional diplomacy by Colorado's territorial governor, Alexander H. Hunt, who was forced to return to Middle Park that summer to persuade the various Ute tribes to acquiesce to changes demanded by the Senate prior to ratification, the Utes finally agreed to accept resettlement in western Colorado south of the fortieth parallel and west of the seventieth meridian.

The northeastern Front Range of Colorado had been fortunate. The last recorded battle between Indians in Larimer County, a skirmish between hunting parties of Arapaho and Pawnees, occurred in the latter part of August 1858. Thereafter, thanks, in part, to the presence of a garrison of soldiers at Camp Collins beginning in May 1864, early settlers in the Boulder, Big Thompson, and St. Vrain valleys seldom found the Indians much more than a nuisance. The last Indian incursion in the area took place the year that Camp Collins was established, when a small party raided settlers along the foothills of the St. Vrain and Little Thompson, destroying property and running off cattle and horses. David Lykins, a native of Indiana and veteran of the gold fields, who in 1859 had taken up ranching in a gulch between the St. Vrain and Left Hand Creeks, was elected captain of a group of settlers sent in pursuit. Lykins and a companion intercepted the retreating Indians in a small canyon of the Little Thompson, killing one and wounding another. According to Abner Sprague, Lykins backtracked this band along the top of the ridge east of Muggins Gulch to the head of Emmons Gulch (on what is now the Crocker Ranch), down through the site of the future town of Estes Park and through the northern end of the Park. "From there it was supposed they were making for the Laramie Plains and the chase was given up."[11] Though other incidents would take place, the pioneer settlers of Larimer County were for the most part allowed to concentrate on the problems of earning a living in a new and undeveloped country.

Among the earliest of these pioneers was Kentucky-born Joel Estes. Like so many other frontier Americans of the nineteenth century, Estes was a wanderer, unlikely to remain anywhere very long if opportunities and adventure beckoned. Even as a young married man with a growing family, his penchant for new places was well developed. In 1833, at the age of twenty-seven, with his wife, Mary Ann ("Patsy"), expecting the fifth of their thirteen children, Joel left his farm near Liberty, Clay County, Missouri, to prospect and trap around Santa Fe with his father, Peter, and a party of some seventy others, traveling along the Front Range and visiting Laramie before returning by way of the Black Hills two years later. In 1849, by now a resident of Andrew County, Missouri, he again went west, this time to the gold fields of Grass Creek, California, in the company of his son Hardin, where they reportedly made some thirty thousand dollars by striking a rich vein. Returning to his family in 1850, Joel decided to move once again, to a farm in Holt County in northwestern Missouri. There he built a large, two-story stone house, doubtless financed with the funds brought back from California. Six years later, in 1855, Joel and Hardin came west for the third time, following the Oregon Trail to Baker City in the Powder River country of eastern Oregon, where Hardin would eventually settle. A fourth trip west, inspired apparently by recent discoveries of gold, brought him to the future site of Denver in the early summer of 1859, then a crude community consisting of a few wooden buildings surrounded by shacks and tents.

This time Estes's western travel took on a note of permanency. Ten-

Figure 1.3. Milton Estes shared his father's wanderlust and in 1858 engraved his name on Register Cliff, Wyoming. Courtesy National Park Service—Rocky Mountain National Park.

sions in antebellum Missouri were increasing, and when he started across the plains for Colorado he was accompanied by Patsy and the five children still living at home, other relatives and friends, and a herd of cattle and horses. Their five mule-drawn wagons arrived safely at Auraria, on the banks of Cherry Creek, on June 15. They then camped near the mountains, in and around the future site of Golden, until late summer while Joel inspected opportunities for placer mining in the Clear Creek region. Not liking what he found, Joel took his family and cattle to a place on the Platte River northeast of Denver known as Fort Lupton Bottom (now Platteville), where he could ranch and cut wild hay. There they built two houses and corrals, taking full advantage of the wild hay that grew luxuriantly along the bottom lands as well as the short buffalo grass nearby on the gently rolling prairie—altogether a fine place for raising cattle. That October came his memorable trip into the mountains.

Joel's first thought, Milton recalled, was that they had stumbled on North Park, the only park in that part of the Rockies that the newly arrived Estes had heard about. A few days of exploration changed his mind, for whereas they found Indian lodgepoles in two different places, there were no signs of previous white habitation. Joel and another son, Francis Marion,[12] camped in the park during the winter of 1859–1860, constructing a shelter cabin located on the north side of the Big Thompson about half a mile above its canyon.

March of the next year found Joel and twelve-year-old Joel Estes Jr. crossing the plains on their way to Missouri to bring out more supplies and cattle. They were back in Estes Park by summer, however, where, encouraged by the mildness of the preceding winter, Joel had decided he would try to make a living raising stock, hunting, and fishing. With one or more of his sons, he built two substantial log houses and several corrals on lower Willow Creek (now Fish Creek), brought in whatever household goods could be packed on animals, and then drove up cattle from their claim on the Platte, fencing the trail at the entrance to the park to prevent the animals from returning to the valley.

Estes had expected to move his family to the park the following year, 1861. But the Civil War intervened, and instead Estes once more headed back to Missouri to look after his property and affairs, which, so family tradition has it, included a number of slaves. He did not remain long, for much of the following winter, 1861–1862, was spent in the park looking after his growing cattle business. The events of 1862 are somewhat hazy, but by 1863 Joel Estes was sufficiently enthused by the prospect of raising stock in Estes Park that he completed preparations to move his family from Fort Lupton Bottom. With him came Patsy, four sons (Wesley Jasper, twenty-six; Milton, twenty-three; Francis Marion, seventeen; and Joel Jr., fifteen), and a daughter, Sarah, twenty-one. Milton, now married, brought with him his wife of two years, Mary Louise, and their two small sons, Newton and George. A third son, Charles F. Estes, arrived on February 19, 1865, the first white child born in the park.

For the next three years Joel Estes and his family were the park's principal occupants. Life was never easy. However idyllic the park seemed in summer and in the golden days of autumn, the winters were long and the isolation severe. The nearest ranch was located on the upper St. Vrain some twenty-five miles distant; the nearest post office was farther downstream at Burlington, a stage stop on the Overland Express. With the last provisions packed in for winter came the last mail until spring.

By the very fact of its remoteness, Estes Park was a hunter's and fisherman's paradise. Joel Estes was an expert shot who very much enjoyed the chase. It was not long before he and his sons were taking dressed skins and hindquarters of deer, elk, and sheep by cart down through the foothills to Denver to be sold. One year, Milton claimed, he killed a hundred elk all by himself. He also recalled a memorable deer hunt of April 1864, when he shot thirteen deer with a muzzle-loading rifle in the northern part of the park. On another occasion, he shot and killed a large moose that had wandered in with a herd of elk. Milton also remembered hunting mountain sheep on the rocks near Marys Lake and a bear so large that it took Joel Estes, two of his sons, and a visitor to finally bring it down. Fish were equally abundant. Lured by grasshoppers or a variety of homemade artificial flies, "they would bite as fast as we could pull them out." A byproduct of hunting were skins, which could be made into clothing. "We must have looked like real Robinson Crusoes," Milton recalled, "but we were warm and comfortable."[13]

Getting cattle and game to and from the park required that the Esteses construct and maintain a cart road. The trail Estes used, as Abner Sprague later noted, was but an extension of one of the wood roads into the lower hills. These roads were used by early settlers to obtain the timber they needed to build and fence their claims and, in turn, probably followed much the same routes used by an even earlier generation of hunters and prospectors on their forays back into the mountains.[14] The Estes road entered the mountains about halfway between the St. Vrain and Little Thompson and followed the Little Thompson up through the foothills, staying whenever possible close to the mountainsides in order to avoid the inevitable underbrush encountered at stream crossings and in ravines and gulches. Reaching Little Elk Park (now Pinewood Springs) from the south, the trail passed down a steep draw to the Little Thompson and then up and over a ridge to Muggins Gulch. Though they worked at the road at odd times throughout their stay, it was never anything more than a fair trail for pack animals, and a loaded cart had to be helped over many places just to keep it upright. It remained in this condition, scarcely usable at times, throughout the decade of the 1860s and well into the next.

The Esteses were not without company. Joel apparently hired additional help as needed, and other visitors wandered in, hunting, prospecting, or, in the case of William N. Byers, founding editor of the *Rocky Mountain News*, intent on climbing mountains. One of those Estes hired was a young man named Dunham Wright, who spent the winters of 1860–1861 and 1861–1862 in the park. His second winter was a particularly memorable one, for he brought with him thirty-one-year-old Henry M. Teller, the future United States senator from Colorado, who was recovering from a bad case of mountain fever. Wright had been working at a quartz mill in Central City that summer, where he discovered Teller, a lawyer who had arrived in late April from his native New York, lying in "a dingy cabin." Wright, nineteen at the time, nursed Teller into the fall and then in the first week of November took him down to the Platte, where a family, neighbors of Joel Estes, had agreed to take him in as a boarder. Once he arrived at Fort Lupton Bottom, Wright found word that Estes, who had already left for the park, taking supplies and sixty head of cattle, needed him for the winter. Over everyone's protestations, Teller insisted upon going too, a journey that took three days to complete. They encountered Estes living in a "big wall tent" whose floor was covered with five or six inches of rye grass. There was also a storehouse "filled with all the food that three stalwart yoke of oxen could haul in."[15]

Teller and Wright were not the only ones in residence with Joel Estes during those two winters. In a letter written in April of 1927, Wright specifically mentions the names Marion Estes, George W. Smith, John Dickson, and John Heaston as well.[16] Teller, on his part, regained his strength quickly. The highlight of his visit was the taking of a big-horn sheep, which Wright shot for him, whose horns and upper jaw weighed forty-five pounds. Teller later mounted this trophy on a board and displayed it in his office in Central City, where he became one of Colorado Territory's foremost experts on mining law.[17]

"Mr. Estes was a typical frontiersman of the Daniel Boone style," Dunham Wright recalled. "A generous, kindhearted, good natured man. To know him was to admire him. . . ."[18] Wright remembered evening chats around the campfire after a day of hunting and meals of broiled sheep. There was also the inexplicable behavior of a full-blooded grey-hound hunting dog that "absolutely quit us and took up with a band of large grey timber wolves" and had to be killed the following winter. Stock raising, however, was the focus of their activity: "Mr. Estes drove quite a number of cattle into the Park each winter we were there. They wintered and did well on the grass that grew in the Park. I milked some of the cows so we had plenty of good milk in camp in that far off land at that day. . . ."[19]

In the years following their establishment in the park, the number of visitors increased. Joel and Patsy Estes did what they could to make them welcome. John T. Prewitt, who stayed at the Estes ranch during a three-day hunting expedition in April 1864, reported:

> We got in somewhat after dark. He had big fires in the fireplaces. It was cold in there. And he had a beaver tail supper. We had sent him word we were coming. He was wonderfully pleased to see us. The woman had hot biscuits and plenty of good coffee, and we enjoyed a fine supper. However, I didn't enjoy the beaver tail as much as he thought I did. He had some hay for our horses, and good warm stables. After supper we talked and he told us more hunting stories than I ever heard in my life. . . .
>
> Mrs. Estes was such a nice clean motherly lady and she told us we were the first people she had seen since she went in there. . . . I forgot to mention their

nice log house, four of them in fact[,] set together and it was so neat and clean. He had a mine there too and some days took out as much as three dollars, other days nothing.[20]

That same year, during the month of August, saw the arrival of William Byers, who, though still a comparative newcomer to the Colorado Territory, had already become one of its most vigorous promoters. His enthusiasm for Colorado was based on firsthand experience, and when adventuring was to be done, Byers invariably insisted on being part of the doing. The events in which he participated also made good news stories, and earned him the reputation of being, as the late Wallace Stegner so aptly put it, "a pioneer, an opener, a pass-crosser of a pure American breed, one for whom an untrodden peak was a rebuke and a shame to an energetic people."[21] Several of his more notable trips of reconnaissance brought Byers to Estes Park and mark the beginning of its mountaineering history.

By 1864, as the mountain historian William M. Buehler has noted, 14,256-foot Longs Peak had become "the chief climbing goal in Colorado territory,"[22] and Byers was determined to try. For his companions he chose the English-born botanist Charles C. Parry, who three years earlier had recorded several first ascents of mountains along the Front Range,[23] the zoologist Jacob W. Velie, and George Nichols of Boulder. The first night out of Denver was spent in Boulder with Nichols, after which they traveled north by wagon to the homestead of Benjamin F. Franklin on the St. Vrain, where they camped out. By the evening of August 18, after having followed a trail so rough and choked with timber and brush that they were forced "in disgust" to leave their wagon behind, the Byers party reached the Estes ranch. "We had met the old gentleman and one of his sons ten or twelve miles back on the road on their way to the valley," Byers would later write,

> but we found a ready welcome at the hands of the remainder of the family— Mrs. Estes, a pleasant old lady of forty-five or fifty years, a grown up daughter and a boy of twelve or fifteen. We were the first visitors they had seen this year, and they seemed overjoyed to look upon a human face more than their own. It must be lonely living so far from any other human habitation. Though only twenty-four miles it seemed a hundred, and for ease of travel, might better be two hundred on the plains.[24]

The daily rigors of life in the park were apparently starting to tell, for Byers went on to observe that "they are getting tired of the solitude and we suspect they would like a change. The picturesque will do for a time but like everything else grows monotonous."[25]

The next day, August 19, piloted by Joel Jr., who took them to the foot of the mountain, Byers and his companions, accompanied by pack animals, began their ill-fated attempt to climb Longs Peak. In the absence of a well-defined trail, they laboriously picked their way "through the obstruction of fallen timber," over "precipitous rocks" and "tangled mazes of wooded thickets."[26] By evening they had reached and crossed the Boulder Field as far as the Keyhole, from where they briefly looked down into the wilderness to be known as Glacier Basin. Camp that night, Parry recalled in the account he published the next month in the *Chicago Evening Journal*, "was devoted to a discussion of routes and probabilities for the following day, before a blazing campfire; the night was rendered brilliant by twinkling stars in the serene atmosphere . . . undisturbed by dyspeptic nightmare or outside intrusions. . . ."[27]

The next morning the explorers tried a new tack. Rather than retracing their way to the Keyhole, they turned south and by 9 A.M. had succeeded in climbing "the summit of the east peak [13,911-foot Mount Meeker] as high as anyone has ever gone." Though they had the satisfaction of adding their names "to the five who had registered before," Byers and his companions could only stare in frustration across an abyss at the summit of Longs Peak, "some three hundred feet above them," concluding, in Byers's words, that "not a living creature, unless it had wings to fly, was ever upon its summit, and we believe we run no risk in predicting that no man will ever be, though it's barely possible that the ascent can be made."[28] Before returning to the Estes ranch, where Byers paid Joel $2.20 for food and lodging, Parry and Velie climbed and measured the height of nearby Storm Peak, which for a number of years would be known as Velies Peak.

Byers published a two-part account of the trip in the *Rocky Mountain News* the following month. In so doing, he not only gave Estes Park its name but, with typical enthusiasm, predicted that "eventually this park will become a favorite pleasure resort. Probably by another season the road will be so improved that a carriage can go from Denver directly to the foot of the snowy range, and the drive will be but a day and a half to reach such magnificent prospects and surroundings as the imagination can hardly paint."[29]

Though it is generally believed that Joel Estes and his family were the only residents until the time of their departure, they apparently shared the park, at least at times, with others. An August 1873 article by E. R. Painter, the cofounding editor of Greeley's *Colorado Sun*, states that "in 1862 Sowers & Blanton, of Texas, took up residence in the Park, and were the first parties to settle there. . . . Estes, the man after whom the

Park is named, took possession in 1863...."[30] Painter's remark (though wrong on the date of Joel Estes's arrival) finds confirmation in Milton Estes's later statement that

> we named all the mountains and streams; but they were renamed after we moved out of the Park, except the Gulch at the east of the Park, called Muggins Gulch, . . . which . . . was named for George Hearst, whose nickname was "Muggins." He was given this name by Dan Grant, who with a man called Sowers, had some cattle in the Park, and "Muggins" was their herder. Muggins built a cabin at the head of the Gulch, so he could watch the cattle, lest any should try to leave and go back to the valley.[31]

Unfortunately Sowers, Blanton, Dan Grant, as well as George Hearst, the colorful "Muggins," have all vanished from Colorado history.

The winter of 1864–1865 caused Joel Estes and his family to reassess their present and future prospects. Until that time, despite the all too short growing seasons, the winters, including those that Joel spent in the park without his family, had been mild. They had been able to cut enough meadow grass for the cattle simply by using a common scythe. That winter, however, the snows came early, two and a half feet in November, and continued to lie on the ground, badly drifted, until spring, testing and retesting the cracks and crevices in cabin roofs and walls and making winter grazing all but impossible. When the hay ran out, it was necessary to move the cattle down into the foothills. The heavy snow only increased the sense of "solitude," "monotony," and forced intimacy that William Byers had sensed the summer before. In addition, the ever restless Estes wanted to expand the scale of his stock raising, which meant finding a lower elevation and a milder climate.

Because his land had not been surveyed, Joel Estes had little more to offer than squatter's rights. He nonetheless got what he could and on April 15, 1866, moved out, never to return. The family then parted ways, Wesley Jasper, Francis Marion, and Sarah turning east to Iowa, while Joel and Patsy, both now sixty, Joel Jr., and Marion and his family headed south into New Mexico, where they would eventually settle.[32] Their stay in the park had been brief. Yet in managing to eke out a living by ranching, hunting, and the taking in of tourists, Joel Estes and his family established a pattern that would be frequently repeated in the decades ahead.

Chapter 2

Griff Evans's Estes Park

Though often forgotten, there was a period of nearly a decade between the time that Joel Estes and his family left Estes Park in April of 1866 and the arrival in 1874 and 1875 of the valley's first permanent settlers. During this interlude, as the Earl of Dunraven recognized during his first visit of December 1872, Estes Park in its pristine, unblemished state was a bucolic paradise well worth the time and trouble of making one's own. To be sure, hunters and prospectors continued to make their way into the valley, as did at least one other rancher who, like Estes, found the climate surprisingly conducive to raising cattle on a year-round basis. Each summer also brought an increasing number of summer vacationers who pitched their tents along the streams and otherwise "roughed it" for the season. Throughout these years, there was, however, only one prominent resident in the park, the jovial, curly-headed Welshman Griffith J. Evans.

After the departure of Estes, a series of rights swaps followed in quick succession. Estes turned the park over to John Hollenbeck, who since the fall of 1865 had been herding cattle on a squatter's claim on the St. Vrain just west of the present town of Lyons. The price, Enos Mills, Estes Park's first historian, later maintained, was "fifty dollars, a yearling steer, or a yoke of oxen. It is impossible to say which. . . ."[1] After helping to move the Estes family back to Fort Lupton, using a big, two-wheel cart and a yoke of oxen, Hollenbeck, like Estes, used the park to graze cattle. Some nine months later he too sold out and moved back to the valley, where he purchased a homestead relinquishment. Estes Park next passed into the hands of a Mr. Jacobs and then to a character remembered only as "Buckskin."

Griff Evans (1832–1900) arrived in the fall of 1867, moving into Estes's two rude log cabins on the site of what is now Lake Estes. The known facts of Evans's life prior to his arrival at Estes Park are relatively few and scattered. What we do know, however, squares pretty well with the brief biographical sketch titled "Evans of Estes Park" that appeared in the August 26, 1874, issue of the *Rocky Mountain News*:

Captain G. J. Evans, the well-known pioneer of Estes Park, is described by campers-out as a strong, well built man of Welsh descent, and now about forty years old, possessing pleasant manners, a kind heart, and a strong sense of humor and honesty about men. He came from Michigan to Colorado in 1863, and was soon successful in accumulating a small fortune, but lost it through a dishonest partner. His sense of honesty compelled him to settle all claims against the firm, and not only his money, but his last team went this way. In this destitute condition, with his wife and their little children, he went to Estes Park some eight years ago. The journey was made on pack mules and when these returned, for he did not own even them, he was left in that wilderness with his gun and less than a dollar in money. Game was plenty, but he had no way of getting it to market. He frequently performed the rough trip to the nearest settlement, some forty miles, for bread, and as hunters began to go in sold them deer and elk which his steady rifle brought in abundance, and in this way got a team, and a start in raising cattle. He struggled on, entered upon his land and gained property generally, until this summer, when he sold his possessions to Earl Dunraven & Co. for a handsome sum.[2]

Arthur Pendarves Vivian, a British member of Parliament, the Earl of Dunraven's brother-in-law, and an incorporator and shareholder of the Estes Park Company, Limited, fleshes out this portrait in his account of his hunting trip to Estes Park in 1877, published two years later as *Wanderings in the Western Land*. He notes that Griff, who "loved Wales and everything Welsh," had emigrated to Wisconsin with his family "when a mere child." His father had worked as a miner in the Penrhyn slate quarries at Llanberis in northwest Wales, and for a time Griff, who for many years would list his occupation as "miner,"[3] seemed destined to follow that career. In Wisconsin, however, Evans turned to farm work and also became a "capital shot" and an experienced hunter. There he met Jane Owen, also Welsh by birth. They were married in Elba, Dodge County, Wisconsin, on June 29, 1855. Coming west to Colorado in 1863, they settled for a brief time at Golden City, before moving north to the St. Vrain. "Whatever his failings may have been," Vivian concluded, "he was certainly a cheerful companion, most thoroughly well-informed in all matters connected with a western life, and one of the best hunters I came across in my trip."[4]

Figure 2.1. Griffith J. Evans. Courtesy Richard M. Evans.

To these accounts can be added the recollections of Evans's friend and partner, Captain George Brown, about the circumstances surrounding Griff's removal to the park:

Mrs. Griff Evans came to me . . . to tell me of such a splendid opportunity they had to go up to Estes Park and care for the Ranch of Jacobs. Those were the days when a job was a job, but she said they had no way of getting there. As I had never visited the place, I offered to take them. I had a good stout wagon and team doing nothing just then. My offer was enthusiastically accepted, so the following morning I went over to see what they would have to move in the way of household goods. The list was short—a broken cook stove, two chairs, past using, a table with one leaf gone, and a few pieces of bedding making up the entire list. After loading these onto the wagon I said, "Now for the Provisions." Mrs. Evans said, "We haven't any." It was the truth, they had nothing, and were ready to start to that lonely place at the beginning of winter with no supplies. I asked Griff what he meant to do. "Ain't there deer and

Figure 2.2. Jane Owen Evans. Courtesy Richard M. Evans.

fish?" was his answer. "Have you a gun?" I asked. "Yep." "Any powder?" "No." "Any anything?" "No." . . . So we passed our camp and I divided my supplies with them, a sack of measly little potatoes and one of smutty flour, a little powder and lead and salt. Thus replenished, we started for the famous Estes Park. I think I mentioned the condition of the furniture as none too good at the start. But after being rescued from three turnovers, and finally deposited in the little shack that comprised the only house in Estes, it was some worse. We found quite a lot of cattle about the place, and succeeded in catching two young calves. By putting them in the corral over night we were able, after quite some difficulties, to get some milk from their mothers for the young-sters' breakfast. After a day or two of inspection of the Park, I left the first Lyons family that ever moved to Estes to manage as best they could.[5]

The best description we have of Griff Evans comes from Isabella Bird, who spent two months at the Evans ranch in the fall of 1873. "'Griff,' as Evans is called," Bird subsequently wrote, is short and small, and is hospitable, careless, reckless, jolly, social, convivial, peppery, good-natured, "nobody's enemy but his own." . . . He is a splendid shot, an expert and successful hunter, a bold mountaineer, a good rider, a capital cook, and a generally "jolly fellow." His cheery laugh rings through the cabin from the early morning, and is contagious, and when the rafters ring at night with such songs as "D'ye ken John Peel?" "Auld Lang Syne," and "John Brown," what would the chorus be without poor "Griff's" voice? What would Estes Park be without him, indeed? When he went to Denver lately we missed him as we should have missed the sunshine, and perhaps more. . . . Free-hearted, lavish, popular, poor "Griff" loves liquor too well for his prosperity, and is always tormented by debt. He makes lots of money, but puts it into "a bag with holes." He has fifty horses and 1,000 head of cattle, many of which are his own, wintering up here, and makes no end of money by taking in people at eight dollars a week, yet it all goes somehow.[6]

Miss Bird was equally impressed by Jane Evans, a "most industrious," if overworked, wife, and their five musical children (Jennie, sixteen; Llewellen, ten; Evan ["Eph"], seven; Katherine Ellen ["Nell"], four; and George, two). "Mrs. E. is such a nice Welshwoman," she noted in one of her original letters, "and brings up her children beautifully."[7] Throughout most of Bird's visit Jane was indisposed by the impending birth of their sixth child, Florence ("Floss"), who arrived early the next

Figure 2.3. The Evans children: (*left to right*) Llewellyn, Jennie, Nell, George, and Evan—about the time of Miss Bird's arrival. Courtesy Richard M. Evans.

year. For her middle name the Evanses, significantly, chose "Isabella." A seventh, and last, child, John, would be born in 1876.

During his first few years in the park Griff supported the family almost entirely by hunting, sending the meat by wagon down to Denver and selling it for what it would fetch in the open market. Over a period of two months, working with a partner, Vivian reported, Evans killed 112 deer, 17 elk, and 26 mountain sheep.[8] He also entered the cattle business.

By the time of Isabella Bird's visit, Evans had added to Joel Estes's original ranch. Bird recalled her first impressions vividly. Dashing down the hill from Muggins Gulch "over a mile of smooth sward at delicious speed," she suddenly came upon "a small lake, close to which was a very trim-looking log cabin, with a flat mud roof, with four smaller ones." The central cabin was occupied by the Evans family. Bird describes its appearance:

> I saw a good-sized log room, unchinked, however, with windows of infamous glass, looking two ways; a rough stone fireplace, in which pine logs, half as large as I am, were burning; a boarded floor, a round table, two rocking-chairs, a carpet-covered backwoods couch; and skins, Indian bows and ar-

Figure 2.4. Griff Evans's ranch. Courtesy City of Greeley Museums, permanent collection.

rows, wampum belts, and antlers, fitly decorated the rough walls, and equally fitly rifles were stuck up in the corners.[9]

The room also contained, as it turned out, Evans's prize possession, a type of reed organ known as a harmonium. Bird then expands upon her description to include the rest of the ranch:

> The chinks should be filled with mud and lime, but these are wanting. The roof is formed of barked young spruce, then a layer of hay, and an outer coating of mud, all nearly flat. The floors are roughly boarded. The "living-room" is about sixteen feet square, and has a rough stone chimney in which pine-logs are always burning. At one end there is a door into a small bedroom, and at the other a door into a small eating-room, at the table of which we feed in relays. This opens into a very small kitchen with a great American cooking-stove, and there are two "bed closets" besides. Although rude, it is comfort-able, except for the draughts. The fine snow drives in through the chinks and covers the floors, but sweeping it out at intervals is both fun and exercise. There are no heaps or rubbish-places outside. Near it, on the slope under the pines, is a pretty two-roomed cabin, and beyond that, near the lake, is my cabin, a very rough one. My door opens into a little room with a stone chim-ney, and that again into a small room with a hay bed, a chair with a tin basin on it, a shelf and some pegs. A small window looks on the lake, and the glories of the sunrises which I see from it are indescribable. Neither of my doors has a lock, and, to say the truth, neither will shut, as the wood has swelled. Below the house, on the stream which issues from the lake, there is a beautiful log dairy, with a water-wheel outside, used for churning. Besides this, there are a *corral*, a shed for the wagon, a room for the hired men, and shelters for horses and weakly calves. All these things are necessaries at this height.[10]

Though Bird found the family's prosperity tenuous, it is also clear that by 1873 Evans had made substantial progress in reestablishing his place in the world.

Evans did not own most of the cattle under his care. Rather, he made use of other men's capital, taking on partners and hired hands as cir-cumstances demanded. His operation was nonetheless a sizable one. In the summer of 1871, the earliest date for which we have evidence, Evans was overseeing six hundred head of cattle, mostly Texan, belonging to Captain George Brown and his partner, Wilbur C. Lothrop, of Denver.[11] Though the following winter of 1871–1872 was a severe one, Evans apparently increased the size of his herd, for early the next spring he bragged to the editor of Longmont's *Colorado Press* that he had success-fully wintered eight hundred head without hay, losing "only two or three," "and those by accident," and had already brought seventy-five head down to market.[12] Two months later Evans came through Boulder with eighty head of cattle on his way to Golden to fulfill a contract that Brown had made with the Colorado Central. In passing, Griff noted that Estes Park had suffered its worst snowstorm of the winter on May 4th and that as a result "the grass is backward."[13]

Isabella Bird, whom Griff pressed into service to round up cattle the following year, claimed that two thousand head "of half-wild Texan cattle" were scattered throughout the canyons of the park, eleven hundred of which were in the care of Evans. Bird also noted that Evans had fifty horses. The total number of cattle sounds high, but it may well not be inflated. In September 1874, the *Central City Daily Register* noted, in describing the "warm and pleasant climate" of the park, in which "stock does well summer and winter," that "about four thousand head have been kept there for some years . . . ,"[14] and in the summer of 1876 the *Boulder County News* reported that "fifteen hundred sleek cattle roam the meadows and crop the luxurious grass and its smooth uplands and craggy heights."[15] By the time of Bird's arrival, or perhaps a little later, Griff Evans had also established some kind of working relationship with the park's only other year-round resident, James McLaughlin, who occupied a squatter's claim a mile farther up Fish Creek, where he raised potatoes and barley and experimented with timothy.[16] Just how many of these cattle were under McLaughlin's control, however, is uncertain.

Stock raising, like hunting, is an inherently lonely occupation, and from the beginning of their Estes Park years, Griff and Jane Evans were only too happy to have visitors. There was also, they discovered, money to be made in lodging and feeding them. As their number increased, additional cabins were added, and it was not long until the Evanses were also outfitting their guests, renting horses, giving fishing and hunting directions, and otherwise helping outsiders to enjoy the place. Griff prided himself on his expertise as a mountaineer and, as time permitted, personally guided visitors to the summit of Longs Peak or to other places in the park. The cash income from these efforts greatly augmented what could be earned from raising cattle.

Success in the tourist business, even if one enjoyed a virtual monopoly, then as now depended on word-of-mouth reputation. The genial Evans knew the value of making his hospitality known. As early as August of 1871, Griff told a correspondent for the *Chicago Tribune* that "he and others contemplate putting up a cheap hotel for the next season, to accommodate visitors who wish a change of air, fresh trout, and restored health."[17] These intentions were reiterated the following spring by Longmont's *Colorado Press*, which announced on April 10, 1872, that "Mr. G. J. Evans of Estes' Park, is fitting up a house, preparatory to keeping a hotel this summer. There will undoubtedly be a large influx of visitors to the mountains this season, and if it is known that good hotel accommodations can be had Estes' Park will come in for a large share of them."[18]

Two months later, on May 22, following another visit by Evans, the *Press* again reported that "Mr. G. J. Evans . . . has fitted up in the park a public house, where all the wants of the inner man can be supplied and strength gained for the task of scaling the heights."[19] Evans's good press continued. Two years later, the editor of the *Fort Collins Standard* was positively effusive in his praise:

> We had the pleasure of meeting the genial landlord of the Estes Park Hotel, Mr. G. J. Evans in town last week, who was down looking after his taxes, etc. Mr. Evans says there is no snow in the park, that the feed is short, but that eleven hundred head of cattle wintered there for several winters. . . . The reputation of Estes Park as a resort is world wide. Its cool and limpid waters, its splendid carriage drives, grand and awe inspiring scenery, luscious trout, and last but not least, the genial smiling face of mine host, makes it a general favorite with all who have the good fortune to cast off the cares and worries of business, and seek shelter within its invigorating shades for a few weeks during the summer days. . . . A semi-weekly hack will be run from Longmont, and it is said once a week from Greeley. Mr. Evans will keep a full stock of saddle animals, carriages, etc., and will spare no pains to make the visits of his numerous friends pleasant and agreeable. . . . Mr. Evans' table, like the park itself, is far famed.[20]

Those who took such advice and stayed for any length of time were invariably touched by the place. For the thirty-three-year-old Bostonian Henry Adams, for example, his brief stay at the Evans ranch in 1871 turned out to be a defining moment. Having accepted an invitation from one of the field parties of Clarence King's Fortieth Parallel Survey, Adams found himself camped on the flank of Longs Peak under the watchful eye of geologist Arnold Hague. Deciding to go fishing, he rode off into the valley, lingering by the stream until, unexpectedly overtaken by darkness, he became lost without "prospect of supper or of bed." "Estes Park was large enough to serve for a bed on a summer night for an army of professors," Adams subsequently wrote (characteristically in the third person) in his *Education* (1907),

> but the supper question offered difficulties. There was but one cabin in the Park, near its entrance, and he felt no great confidence in finding it, but he thought his mule cleverer than himself, and the dim lines of mountain crest against the stars fenced his range of error. The patient mule plodded on without other road than the gentle slope of the ground, and some two hours must

have passed before a light showed in the distance. As the mule came up to the cabin door, two or three men came out to see the stranger.

One of these men was Clarence King on his way up to the camp. Adams fell into his arms. As with most friendships, it was never a matter of growth or doubt. Friends are born in archaic horizons. . . . King had come up that day from Greeley in a light four-wheeled buggy, over a trail hardly fit for a commissariat mule, as Adams had reason to know since he went back in the buggy. In the cabin, luxury provided a room and one bed for guests. They shared the room and the bed, and talked till far towards dawn.[21]

The next day the two men celebrated what would become a lifelong friendship by climbing Longs Peak.

Another visitor that summer was the agricultural correspondent of the Chicago Tribune, who on August 15, 1871, just ten days after Clarence King had driven his buggy up from Greeley, filed a lengthy report for his readers detailing his trip to Estes Park with a party consisting of three ladies, four gentlemen, and a four-seat springboard wagon loaded with "cooking utensils, bedding, commissary stores, guns, etc." After toiling uphill and down, during which time the wagon had to be frequently emptied of its passengers, they reached the park and its "only residence, that of Mr. G. J. Evans, who has made this his house for the past four years. His house consists of five stories placed horizontally, made of mountain-pine, and covered with adobe, or, in plain English, the soil mixed with water into a mortar, and put on poles that have been first covered with hay."[22] Though editor and party preferred to camp in tents, they did secure Evans's service as guide for a tour of the park. "I see no reason," his subsequent story concluded, "why this cannot be made a most popular resort, worth a dozen of Saratogas, for the invalid, especially delicate women, and those troubled with lung complaints. . . ."[23]

During these early years, as the Tribune reporter suggested, Evans had to contend with much the same road conditions that bedeviled his predecessor. "Estes Park has attractions for such as wish to ascend Long's Peak," the Greeley Tribune noted on September 13, 1871, "but others hardly will be recompensed for the weariness arising from the exceedingly, the almost impassable road, while but few fields are to be seen."[24] What maps there were tended to be inaccurate. Four months earlier the Tribune had complained of one that "represents Este's [sic] Park as lying south of Long's Peak" and locates timber "where none was ever known."[25] This situation had not materially improved by the time of Isabella Bird's visit two years later; in fact, her first attempt to find the trail into the park, with the help of a homesteader on the Big Thompson who claimed to know the way, met with failure. Winter travel posed a special problem.

Although Bird became used to riding in and out over the mountain trail even in inclement weather, she noted that one of Evans's wagons, containing six elk, had gone over in a ravine some six miles from the ranch, falling sixty feet, escaping total destruction only because it lodged against a pine.

The guests at the Evans ranch were a predictable, if varied, lot. Though the Evanses entertained a number of celebrities—William Byers, Henry Adams, Clarence King, the Earl of Dunraven, Albert Bierstadt, Anna Dickinson, Ralph Meeker, members of the Hayden Survey, and Isabella Bird among them—most visitors were the typical summer tourists of the day, men and women adventurous enough to be attracted to the mountains by the charms of their scenery and by the variety of their recreational activities. During August of 1873, for example, a reporter for the *Larimer Press* noted that he had found at the Evanses', "representatives of Chicago, Philadelphia and New York, and our own towns of Denver, Longmont and Greeley." There were also "numerous parties . . . encamped about the park, enjoying the fishing, sight-seeing &c. . . ."[26] "It would be difficult to find jollier parties than at Evans's," an English visitor who identified himself only as "G. W." wrote home to *The Field, the Country Gentleman's Newspaper* that same month:

> Evans . . . keeps a very comfortable house, and is always full all summer, as hundreds of people come from the States (please bear in mind that Colorado is not in the States) every summer for the shooting, fishing, and scenery. . . . All the summer there are lots of saddle ponies at the door—somebody going fishing, or someone going for a mountain sheep with a fine old dog, who understands the business and "trees" his sheep every time. . . .[27]

All this changed in the fall when the summer tourists went home. When Isabella Bird arrived at the Evans ranch, she found not only Griff Evans and family, his current partner, Edwards, with his wife and his son Sam, but a most heterogeneous collection of boarders. They included Mr. and Mrs. Dewey, "a very intelligent and high-minded American couple," drawn to the mountains because of Mr. Dewey's lung disease, presumably consumption; "a young Englishman, the brother of a celebrated African traveller," called "The Earl" because of his "insular peculiarities" (which included an insistence on riding on an English saddle); a miner prospecting for silver; a young man "whose health showed consumptive tendencies when he was in business, and who is living a hunter's life here"; "a grown-up niece of Evans";[28] and a "melancholy-looking hired man."[29]

In the days that followed others arrived, including elk hunters, "two

Englishmen of refinement and culture" on their way to prospect for gold in North Park, and a miner named Cavanaugh. Cavanaugh was apparently working for Evans and well enough known as a resident for the *Denver Tribune* to report on November 23, 1873, that "Cavanaugh, of Estes Park, killed two deer, and broke the leg of a third one, at one shot."[30] Bird also mentions a Mr. Buchanan, a young man "here for his health," and a Mr. Allen, a nineteen-year-old theology student from St. Louis with literary pretensions, who was trying to restore his health through "the panacea of manual labor." An odd mix of people, indeed, but one no doubt fairly representative of those who sought refuge during fall and winter in such outposts of the Colorado Territory as Estes Park.

By 1873 the park ("the most lovely spot I ever saw in my life—like a nest surrounded by snowclad mountains") was being advertised as a hunter's paradise as far away as London. "An Englishman stayed here last winter," G. W. noted in his letter to the editor of *The Field*;

> and I advise any of your readers who want good shooting, lovely scenery, and mountain air, and withal to be thoroughly comfortable, within sixteen days of *The Field* Office, to try a winter with Griff Evans, Este's [sic] Park, via Longmont, Colorado. Buy a good horse in Denver, and ride up. . . . Have your luggage sent to Longmont, and Evans will fetch it in a waggon [sic]. Buy your shot gun in England, and rifle in America.[31]

Though the Reverend Elkanah J. Lamb is generally regarded as the first professional guide to Longs Peak, that honor probably belongs to Griff Evans, who claimed to have made the second recorded ascent following Major Powell. Just how many trips to the summit Evans actually made, or when he began to guide others, is unclear. The *Colorado Press* refers to him on June 19, 1872, as "the guide to Longs Peak,"[32] and we know that the following year, in September of 1873, he guided Anna Dickinson, Ralph Meeker, and their party of nine up from the ranch to rendezvous with Ferdinand Hayden and members of his survey at the base of the peak. Evans then presumably accompanied them the next day as they completed their climb. We also know that he declined a similar honor the following month, allowing Rocky Mountain Jim to pull and drag Isabella Bird to the summit. By contrast, Elkanah Lamb, who made his first climb of Longs Peak during the summer of 1871, did not begin his guiding career until after he had established his squatter's claim in the Tahosa Valley in 1875.

Life in Estes Park, for all its charms, was never easy, even after the coming of the Earl of Dunraven, to whom Evans sold his squatter's interest and for whom he worked for a time as foreman. The exact date and conditions of Evans's arrangement with Dunraven, undoubtedly consummated through the earl's soon-to-be resident agent, Theodore Whyte, is unclear. Alexander MacGregor, in a letter of July 1881, gives the date as February 1873;[33] and Abner Sprague sets the amount received at five thousand dollars.[34] Horace Ferguson, another early settler, who arrived in 1875, later placed the purchase price at twice that sum.[35] Whyte also purchased Brown and Lothrop's herd of cattle, thus securing for Dunraven the entirety of Griff Evans's Estes Park operation.

MacGregor's date of February 1873, though it seems early, since it precedes by a year the actual surveying of the park, is corroborated by other evidence. It also seems logical that, before Dunraven would invest heavily in any plan to acquire the park, he would deal definitively with those who might conceivably stand in his way or actually oppose him. Evans had the right of first possession, and that fact alone would have been sufficient for him to obtain title either by homesteading or preemption once the survey and platting had been completed.[36]

Interestingly enough, Dunraven was not the only citizen of the British Isles to entertain the possibilities of owning Estes Park. When G. W. visited in mid-July 1873, Evans told him, rather disingenuously, that he and his partner (presumably James McLaughlin) were co-owners of the park and that it was "for sale, price £3000." The Englishman, who had arrived in America from Lincolnshire the previous July and knew something of farming, laid out in his August letter to The Field the cost of turning the park into "the most valuable stock or sheep ranch I have seen in America after a year's inspection." The figures, which may well have come from Evans, whom G. W. pronounced "a first-rate fellow and an Old-Countryman," included

a United State [sic] Government title to the property, it is estimated, would cost £2000; to fence in the whole park, portions being already fenced, and build a good house, lumber and stone being on the spot, £1000; to stock it with 1000 head of cattle or 10,000 head of sheep, £6000—total £12,000 . . . There is water power enough for a saw mill, and abundance of fine timber. They churn by water power, and have about 1200 cattle and forty horses in the park, all of which are in fine condition, and get nothing but the grass. Oats will grow well near the streams, and a great portion is easily irrigated. I should like to see it in the hands of an English company, as lots of money is to be made by stock and sheep farming in Colorado.[37]

G. W.'s words about ownership by an English company proved, of course, to be prophetic.

As far as Griff Evans was concerned, the money and security of working for the rich Irishman undoubtedly proved attractive, especially after his trying experiences of the summer and fall of 1874 when he faced trial in the shooting death of Rocky Mountain Jim. Evans's newfound wealth gave him the chance to broaden his business interests with the purchase in the summer or fall of 1874 of the St. Vrain Hotel in Longmont, whose acquisition he duly celebrated with "a grand dinner."[38] This hotel, opened in 1872 and operated by the genial Captain William Sigley, had become a favorite stopping place for those going to and from the park. It was a good investment. Longmont, which since April 1873 had been served by the railroad, was a fast-growing town, rapidly outgrowing its original identity as an agricultural colony. Because of "his popularity at Estes Park . . . in former seasons,"[39] Evans's ownership and improvements were greeted with enthusiasm despite the lament from Fort Collins that "to go to Longmont, and not receive a cordial welcome from Capt. Sigley, would seem strange enough."[40] Evans operated the St. Vrain Hotel, the "Best Hotel in Northern Colorado," from November 1874 to August 1875, while still making his home in Estes Park. During this period the hotel's surviving register contains the names of such early park settlers as William E. James, Alexander MacGregor, Hank Farrar, and Hugh McDermot, as well as Theodore Whyte and the Earl of Dunraven.[41]

By the fall of 1878, however, the Evans family finally had enough of Estes Park.[42] On November 7 Evans turned over to Theodore Whyte and the English company his residual holdings of 160 acres[43] and moved his family back to the St. Vrain Valley. It is said that when he left the park Griff Evans took with him eighteen thousand dollars.[44]

What finally compelled the Evanses to move out is unclear. Perhaps it was the schooling needs of the children, perhaps just a desire to do new things. It was certainly not that the popular Welsh couple were no longer welcome. Any stigma initially attached to Griff's shooting of Mountain Jim in June 1874 was short-lived. And just a year earlier, on March 21, 1877, Jane Evans had exercised her new commission as Estes Park's postmistress and transferred the post office from the MacGregor Ranch to their own. That same fall, Griff entertained Vivian and then accompanied the Englishman, his Scottish stalker, Sandie Macdonald, and the celebrated local hunter Israel Rowe on an enjoyable interlude of hunting around the ranch and into Horseshoe Park, climaxed by a spirited and successful bear hunt up over "the Range" (presumably in the direction of Lawn Lake).

Griff Evans moved to Lyons, bought a house just west of town on the North St. Vrain, and went into the quarry business. The house subsequently served as a stage stop and inn for travelers on the road to Estes Park.

During the early 1880s Evans and his Evans Townsite and Quarry Company had a hand in opening the first of the great stone quarries at Lyons in partnership with Hiram F. Sawyer and Edward S. Lyon, for whom the town was later named.[45] Evans also developed mining interests at Leadville in Lake County, where in the summer of 1882 he was badly injured when a body of rock and earth fell on him.[46] Hospitality, however, remained the outgoing Welshman's true calling. After giving up his quarrying operation about 1883, Griff, Jane, and their unmarried children moved back to the mountains to Jamestown (or Jimtown as it was often called), an old mining camp in the hills of Boulder County. There, in a town once called Elysian Park, they managed the Evans House in Central Gulch for well over a decade, with Jane at various times operating a confectionery and general merchandise store and serving as town postmistress. At Jamestown, which was then being touted as "just ready to blossom out into the richest mining camp in Boulder County and probably the richest in the state,"[47] Griff ripened into old age, becoming the town's first "resident father Christmas" because of his long white beard. When the local church split its congregation, leaving the new group to holds its services in a tent on the east side of town, with no music of their own, Griff stepped in with his melodeon, "because no church should be without it!"[48] On July 6, 1900, Griff Evans died at Jamestown, where both he and Jane, who died in 1926, are buried.

Chapter 3

~

Land Grabbing in Estes Park:
The Arrival of the Earl of Dunraven

Of the early visitors to Estes Park none left his stamp more visibly upon the place than Windham Thomas Wyndham-Quin (1841–1926), the fourth Earl of Dunraven, the master of forty thousand acres in Ireland and Wales. In attempting to secure the whole of the Park for himself, he set a pattern for land development that lasted into the twentieth century. The Irish-born, Oxford-educated Dunraven, whose twin passions were hunting and sailing, had more than enough money to pursue his dreams. And for a while at least, Estes Park seemed to be a nearly idyllic place to do so.

By the time that the tall and slender Dunraven first visited Estes Park in December of 1872, he had seen much of the world. Besides covering the British military expedition to Abyssinia (Ethiopia) in 1867 and the Franco-Prussian War in 1870 as a correspondent for the London Daily Telegraph (writing under the name of Viscount Adare, after his home, Adare Manor, in the county of Limerick), he traveled extensively to the Holy Land, Rhodes, Constantinople, Greece, Sicily, and North Africa. He also tried to visit the United States on a honeymoon trip in 1869, only to succumb to sunstroke in Richmond, which forced him to return home. Three years later, in August 1872, Dunraven was back in America, again in search of sport, adventure, and investment opportunities, bringing with him his personal physician, George Henry Kingsley, and carrying a letter of introduction to General Phil Sheridan, then commanding the Department of Missouri. From Chicago (where in Sheridan's office the Earl saw the head of his first elk) Dunraven and Kingsley traveled the Union Pacific to North Platte. There they were met by their guides, Buffalo Bill Cody and Texas Jack (John Baker) Omohundro, who accompanied them

Figure 3.1. Windham Thomas Wyndham-Quin, the fourth Earl of Dunraven. Courtesy Estes Park Area Historical Museum.

to Fort McPherson from where they spent better than a month hunting elk and buffalo north along the North Platte and south along Medicine and Red Willow Creeks. Dunraven found Cody, already well celebrated by dime novelist Ned Buntline as "King of the Border Men," "a pleasant young fellow."

By December 5, 1872, Dunraven and Kingsley reached Denver, a town whose population already contained a number of Englishmen. The center of social activity for well-to-do foreigners was the exclusive Corkscrew Club on 18th Street near Broadway, and it was there one evening that Dunraven first heard of Estes Park and its hunting opportunities. Kingsley had another engagement, and so Dunraven, in the company of his Scottish gillie, Sandie, decided to go on alone, taking the

Colorado Central thirty miles north to Longmont, then switching to horse and wagon.

What happened during and after that visit is well known: Dunraven became so enamored with Estes Park that he set out to acquire as much of it as possible for his own. Though it is often said that the Earl wished to turn the valley into a private game preserve, that motive seems unlikely. By 1873 Estes Park and its excellent hunting were generally well known and, unless ownership of the entire park could be somehow secured, the difficulty of keeping unauthorized hunters out would have been enormous. In time Dunraven would build a hunting lodge some fifteen miles away in a remote spot up the North Fork of the Big Thompson (long since known as "Dunraven Glade") that would inspire fanciful stories about lost caches of the Earl's whiskey. Yet, when serious hunting was to be done, Dunraven would continue to travel to Wyoming, Montana, Newfoundland, and Nova Scotia rather than confine himself to Estes Park.

It seems more likely that what primarily motivated Dunraven was what motivated so many of his English contemporaries: the prospect of investing in an enterprise that would pay.[1] Like other British citizens, Dunraven saw overseas investments in places like America as a means of securing an estate for his children. In Dunraven's case, the problem was accentuated by the fact that he was the father of three girls. Under the rules of entailment and primogeniture, he faced the prospect (which eventually did occur) that his property in Great Britain and Ireland would not only not be divided among his daughters but, for lack of a male heir, would pass from the immediate family entirely. Dunraven held interests in railroads and mining. Most of his income came, in fact, from coal mines in Glamorganshire, in southwestern Wales, which he leased to others. Cattle ranching represented another opportunity. His decision to purchase Brown and Lothrop's herd and then to expand it suggests that Dunraven, like so many other wealthy Britons, saw stock raising as an attractive means of earning a substantial return on invested money. The fact that the Earl so quickly announced plans for a hotel in the park, as well as for a halfway house for travelers somewhere between Longmont and the valley, suggests that Dunraven also believed that catering to tourists, and building upon what Griff Evans had so successfully begun, offered still an additional possibility.

The whole enterprise never paid, or if so only briefly and marginally. But this probably says less about the wisdom of Dunraven's initial strategy than it does about the changing economics of the western cattle business and the difficult, if not impossible, task of trying to manage it from across the Atlantic. In 1873–1874, however, the Earl of Dunraven was certainly prepared to try.

How to acquire the land once it was surveyed and opened for settlement presented a major problem. American citizens could claim up to two quarter sections or 320 acres through homesteading and preemption. Foreigners, like Dunraven, on the other hand, were barred by law from directly purchasing public land. The obvious strategy was to obtain land that American citizens had already preempted and/or homesteaded, and for that Dunraven needed help. Undoubtedly lawyers were consulted on just how he might proceed. He then retained the services of Theodore George William Whyte (1846–1903), a young Irish·Canadian mining engineer raised in North Devon, the son of a colonel in the Seventh Hussars, who had come to Colorado in 1871 as agent for a Liverpool mining firm after trapping three seasons for the Hudson's Bay Company.[2] These arrangements were apparently made before Dunraven left New York for home in late July of 1873.

The second step, in which the capable and energetic Whyte must have played at least an indirect role, was to have the land in Estes Park

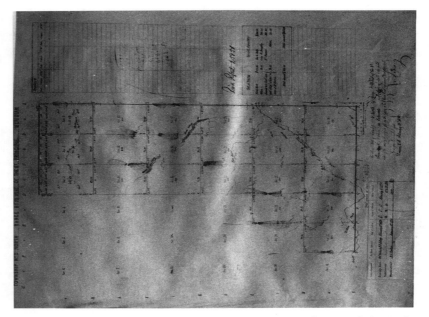

Figure 3.2. Kellogg and Oakes's original 1874 survey map of Estes Park (Township 5 North, Range 73 West), showing the confluence of Fall River and the Big Thompson. Courtesy National Park Service—Rocky Mountain National Park.

surveyed and platted so that it could be opened for filing. On January 12 and February 4, 1874, contracts were signed between the government and the Denver surveyors Daniel C. Oakes and Edwin H. Kellogg (covering Townships 4 and 5 North, Range 73 West) with the provision that the work be completed and the land be ready for preemption and homesteading by May. Usually prospective settlers, or those already occupying the land, would jointly request such a survey. In the case of Estes Park, Abner Sprague contended, "The survey was . . . asked for by men who had never been in the Park, more likely, names without owners."[3]

As might have been expected, the newly available land in Estes Park quickly attracted attention. During the month of May alone, twenty-five individuals filed on slightly more than 4,000 acres. In June and July there were six more claims, each for 160 acres. In every case a warranty deed was immediately (and secretly) filed in Arapahoe County, conveying the property to Theodore Whyte in trust. The price paid by Whyte to the May claimants ranged between $700 and $2,000, with a median of $1,200. The total cost of these thirty-one purchases came to $38,100. A look at the list of names, dates, and amounts paid provides graphic evidence of Whyte's efficiency:

Date	Filer	Price	Acres	Date of Trans.
1. May 5, 1874	James B. Haines	$1,500	160	May 6, 1874
2.	Alfred H. Hord	1,000	172.58	
3.	James Thorne	1,200	170.61	
4. May 9	Andrew Brown	1,300	160	May 10
5.	Henry B. Brown	1,500	160.55	
6.	John L. Henry	1,800	160	
7.	Benjamin A. Williams	1,500	160	
8. May 12	Thomas C. Carpenter	1,000	169.88	May 13
9.	George Robinson	2,000	160	
10. May 18	Charles Aubrey	1,000	171.64	May 19
11.	John Goff	1,500	160	
12.	Samuel Peyton	2,000	160	
13.	Robert S. Rogers	1,200	172.78	
14.	Andrew D. Winslow	1,400	160	
15. May 22	Lyman B. Hooper	1,200	160	May 29
16.	Thomas Pogue	1,000	160	May 23
17.	Joseph Putnam	1,300	160	
18.	Samuel Sumner	800	160	
19. May 23	Charles S. Graham	900	160	May 25
20.	Morris Wilson	700	160	
21. May 27	James Dunn	1,000	160	May 29

22.	John W. Sibley	900	160	
23. May 28	Joseph S. Boyer	800	160	May 30
24.	Wilson H. James	1,800	170.23	
25.	William Tempest	1,400	170.34	
26. June 27	James L. Daly	1,200	160	June 29
27.	John W. Dogherty	1,000	160	
28.	William Haines	1,000	160	June 28
29. July 6	James B. Dalton	1,100	160	July 10
30	George S. Harvey	900	160	
31.	William Kellogg	1,200	160	

The Estes Park Company Limited was incorporated on August 19, 1876, with capital stock of thirty-three thousand pounds. Less than a month later, on September 14, 1876, Whyte filed these warranty deeds, and a number of others that he had subsequently acquired in Larimer County, and then transferred them to what became known as the "English Company."

As Theodore Whyte was well aware, the initial filings had been done in haste and were far from perfect. To make the warranty deeds in his possession public was thus to invite public scrutiny and possible challenges. Accordingly, the methodical Whyte obtained the services of an obscure Englishman named Frederick G. Cornish. On September 4, 1876, for the sum of five dollars, Whyte transferred to Cornish the deeds in question. The next day, for the same amount, Cornish executed a deed of trust conveying jointly to Whyte and David H. Moffatt, Dunraven's Denver banker, "for the use and benefit of the Estes Park Company Limited," most of the original thirty-one claims (whose locations, in some instances, had been changed and corrected). This deed was filed with Larimer County on September 14, 1876. On the very same day Whyte filed with the county the warranty deeds that he had been holding. A letter written by Alexander MacGregor from Estes Park on July 23, 1881, to John A. Jones, special agent in the Interior Department, at Laramie, asking that he continue to investigate Dunraven's land acquisitions in Estes Park, throws additional light on what was obviously a complicated transaction. "It appears," MacGregor wrote,

> that White [Whyte] after he got the deeds deeded to a Mr. Fred Cornish. Now Cornish is well known here. He is a hanger on at the Estes Park Cat. Ranch—working a little at times for wages during haying, potato digging &c, at other times stopping there—loafing about—riding around a little & helping enough for his board, at other times boarding himself at one of the houses. [H]e has a small ranch on the Platt [sic] River which he rents on shares—brings him in a little—but not enough for a living. He is an Englishman—& friend of

Whytes—He it appears redeeded to Whyte & Dave Moffatt. Now the First Natl Bank of Denver has been from the first the Banking house of the Earl of Dunraven and it is through that bank that all businesses is done. . . .

The transfers seem irregular on their face—first from the Deed from Whyte to Cornish for a nominal consideration absolutely conveying it to Cornish then Cornish gives a *Trust Deed* to Whyte & Moffat (and in it referring to the Earl of Dunraven) then Whyte & Moffat give a *quit Claim Deed* to Estes Park Co. of which the Earl of Dunraven is the Company & this same Theo Whyte the Manager.

Trusting that right and justice will be done in this matter I remain

Yours &c

A. Q. MacGregor[4]

MacGregor's facts were substantially correct, for all the deeds referenced were duly filed in Larimer and Arapahoe Counties. They include Whyte and Moffat's quit claim deed of February 4, 1879, conveying to the Estes Park Company, Limited, for the price of one dollar, all "lands, tenements and hereditaments mentioned and described in a deed executed by Frederick G. Cornish . . . dated September 5, 1876" because "the said property is in fact owned and possessed by the said Estes Park Company, Limited." Significantly, his assignment completed, Fred Cornish vanishes from Estes Park history.

Just who the original thirty-one filers were is unclear, for when the office of the U.S. Marshal later attempted to serve them with summonses for perjury and the subornation of perjury (for many had signed as witnesses for each other) the men were not to be found. Doubtless, as was said at the time, they were drifters, of which Colorado and the West was full—men more than willing for a few dollars to follow the instruction of Theodore Whyte, or those in Whyte's employ, to sign their names to the documents placed before them.[5]

Though it is probable that from the beginning Whyte and Dunraven saw Griff Evans as a potential ally rather than as an impediment, they were shrewd enough, as indicated in the previous chapter, to settle with him early on, well before they had begun to implement their larger plans. They also apparently reached a similar accommodation with James McLaughlin. Evans's only attempt to secure direct title to land in Estes Park came four years later, in 1878, when he filed on the land beneath Mount Olympus where the Charles Denison house was located—a tract that he had never occupied. McLaughlin, on his part, subsequently entered a quarter section claim adjacent to the land on Fish Creek where his buildings were located. In retrospect, the actions of both men are perfectly clear. Both had already sold out their income-producing properties to the

Dunraven interests. Their subsequent purchases and sales, made shortly before they decided to leave the park, only confirm that Evans and McLaughlin were smart businessmen able to make money on property that Dunraven and Whyte had initially overlooked or had been unable to secure.

As other would-be homesteaders arrived, they quickly discovered that Dunraven's acquisition of land had been far from piecemeal. Rivers, creeks, and springs were critical for anyone seeking to ranch or farm. A contemporary map of Estes Park, had there been one, would have shown that Dunraven and Whyte, in checkerboard fashion, had secured most of the land for two miles south of the Evans ranch on both sides of Fish Creek, a strip as much as a mile wide along five miles of the Big Thompson and something less than a mile up Fall River from its point of confluence. Also in their possession was another mile-long strip up the Black Canyon, as well as four miles of rich grazing land out along Dry Gulch. For all practical purposes the Earl of Dunraven had achieved control of some ten thousand acres of the best land in Estes Park.

In 1874 British investment in western lands was hardly new, and, thanks to the abundance of vacant land in the West, was accepted, more or less, as a matter of fact. "There is no doubt but lands in America are considered good investments by English capitalists," the *Greeley Tribune* observed as early as December 27, 1871.

> During the last two years many thousand acres have been repurchased between Denver and Colorado City, mainly with English money, and agents are still scouring the country beyond Colorado City, picking up all the choicest pieces of government lands, whether remarkable for scenery, or valuable for timber, springs and streams. Where so much land is taken up in a country, the only effect will be to retard settlement for many years. . . .

Rather than seeing such activity as particularly threatening, the Greeley paper adopted an attitude of bemusement, predicting that after a few years British buyers would find their investments "ill advised." "If these capitalists were wise," the *Tribune* cautioned, bowing in the direction of the traditional yeoman farmers who were its readers, "they would avoid large tracts and buy small ones, here and there, in the midst of settled districts. But they are so set on being large landed proprietors, and of emulating those of their class at home."[6]

As the tone of the *Tribune* article suggests, British residents and visitors were more than welcome throughout the Colorado Territory. When it came to the Earl of Dunraven (who, it was later said, came to own sixty thousand acres in America),[7] the Colorado press greeted his presence with an attitude that mixed genuine respect and deference with the kind of good-natured and humorous treatment of titled aristocracy that one would expect in democratic America. Dunraven and Kingsley's arrival in Denver in December 1872, for example, was announced succinctly by the *Denver Tribune*: " 'Mi Lud' Dunraven and Dr. Kingsley are registered at Charpiot's."[8] When they returned to Colorado in June 1874, the press again took notice and in much the same vein. "The Earl of Dunraven's baggage has arrived in Denver," the *Pueblo Daily Chieftain* reported on the seventeenth. "He has only a thousand pounds of it, and some of the trunks are said to be almost as large as the boots of the city editor of the *News*."[9] The Earl's retinue also attracted attention. The following notice appeared in the August 1, 1874, issue of the *Colorado Springs Gazette*, addressing a community whose large British population could be counted on to appreciate the intended humor: "When Lord Dunraven's darkey gives a party to his colored brethren, the Denver reporters write up the affair for their papers. It's a rare thing for Denver to be honored by the presence of the 'colored attendant' of a real live Earl, you know."[10]

The Earl and the doctor continued to attract notice as they set out for the mountains. Leaving Denver on June 22, Dunraven and his party arrived at the station fifteen minutes after the departure of the Colorado Central train. An engineer from the Boulder Valley Railroad, rushing to the aid of nobility in distress, quickly offered to take the Earl through to Boulder in time to connect with his original train to Longmont. Dunraven "was very profuse in his thanks, and it is said offered the conductor a handsome gift, which was politely but firmly declined."[11]

Though their visit to Estes Park that summer was interrupted by Griff Evans's shooting of Rocky Mountain Jim, an event in which both Kingsley and Dunraven found themselves involved, the Colorado press was far more interested in Dunraven's hunting adventures. "The Earl of Dunraven and party, among whom is Dr. Kingsley, brother of the Canon, have been cutting up high jinks in Estes Park and enjoying all sorts of hair breadth escapes," the *Rocky Mountain News* reported on July 22, 1874:

A reliable correspondent writes us that they have been particularly successful in following the pet pursuit of good old Isaac Walton, and that scores if not hundreds of speckled beauties overload their baskets daily. They have also killed any number of "beasties" of various sorts, and the Earl had a pitch battle with a female mountain lion not long ago, that came very near to causing much weeping and wailing at Dunraven castle.[12] He was alone, having separated from the rest of the party, when he observed the leonine mountaineer about to spring upon him from an overhanging rock in the vicinity. He had just time to raise his gun to his shoulder and fire when the creature went for him. The

ball hit her fairly in the belly, but did not stop her career. She lit on the nobleman, overturning him, and was just about to spring at his throat, as he lay
prostrate at her mercy, when a timely shot from Dr. Kingsley brought her
down. The Earl arose much flustered at his narrow escape, but otherwise none
the worse for it, although he privately told our correspondent that "those
mountain lions were blasted nasty things to meet when alive, you know."[13]

Allegations of "land grabbing," on the other hand, were a far more
serious subject and did not amuse the Colorado press. By the spring of
1874, men other than Dunraven were interested in obtaining land in
Estes Park. Led by the feisty Alexander MacGregor, a lawyer who was
elected to a term as Larimer County judge during the early 1880s, a
number of claimants—Marshall Bradford, David Miller, and (interestingly enough) Griffith Evans among them—registered formal complaints
with the federal authorities in Denver. Shortly thereafter a man named
Thorn, staying in the park for reasons of health, sent a letter alerting the
papers in Denver. By mid-August, stories began to appear. "We are informed from reliable sources," the Fort Collins Standard reported on August
12, 1874,

> that one of the most villainous land steals ever perpetrated in Colorado has
> been enacted in Estes' Park within the last few months, by some Englishmen,
> who through the perjury of various parties, have succeeded in gaining pos-
> session of some 6,000 acres of land lying, on either side of, and controlling
> the different streams in the Park. We expect to be able to give the full particu-
> lars of the swindle next week.[14]

The promised details proved difficult to come by, perhaps because
the case had already (or would shortly) be delivered to a grand jury, and
those in a position to know were not talking. During the two weeks that
followed, papers like the Standard and the Greeley Tribune kept the story
alive, while acknowledging their inability "to get the full particulars."[15]
Then, on August 26, the following article, bristling with outrage and
signed by "Veritas," appeared in the Tribune.

> While standing here, surrounded by all these beauties, and feeling that they
> were a part of my inheritance, a wealthy gentleman, in a broad English accent,
> with whom I had been conversing, said:
> "Yaas—we shall allow all the campers and tourists that are a mind to to
> come to in the park this year, you know. Next year, however, we propose to
> have all the cattle out, the blarsted heifers, and shall then reserve the park for
> our hunting and fishing, you know. Of course, we caan't let common people
> come in then, you know, blast 'em."
> I heard but could hardly realize the impudence and audacity of my noble
> associate. What! An English "Milord," to lay claim to all the most valuable land

of Este's [sic] Park that he and a few of his foreign bobs and nabobs, counts and no-accounts might have a convenient place to hunt and fish. All the American pioneers and frontiersmen, too, to be excluded by these dem foin [sic] foreigners, the idea seems too preposterous. The more so when I remember the laws relating to public lands. And yet "My Lord" thought he had his property right, and that all the valuable portion of Este's [sic] Park was his. I knew, too, that some of the land-sharks who infest Colorado had done their best to get up a "Land Grab" of Titanic dimensions, and that they had operated with the party who now boldly claimed the "proprietorship of Este's [sic] Park."

Let us look into this business. The only way the public land can be obtained under the law, is by homestead or pre-emption. And no single American sovereign is entitled to more than 160 acres. This, too, to hold, the said "sovereign" must reside upon, improve, etc., etc.

But to Este's [sic] Park. The first survey of the land therein was made last January. About the middle of the month there was filed upon, or entered (nominally) 3,500 acres.

In March ensuing the survey was completed; and there was then entered or pre-empted over 3,000 acres. (!)

I have seen a map of the survey, on which was checked, or marked, the land entered, made by an officer in the Denver Land Office. I found that all the land in the Park proper, Black Canyon, Fall River bottom, and the land on the upper waters of the Big Thompson, is included in this "Grab."

The fact therefore remains that if the few Land Grabbers who have thus technically gobbled up all of these broad acres, are permitted to complete their "airy titles," they will have possession of some 38,000 acres, embracing, too, all the smaller and richer parks, canyons and gulches leading out of or into the park proper.

In the face of this audacious claim of a dozen, more or less, Land Grabbers, it must be remembered that there is not now, nor ever has been, more than five persons in the park occupying land, and making it their home. This fact is well known by the government surveyors who surveyed the park, and is, or certainly should have been known, by some of the officers in the land office of Denver.

It was only last January, when Griffith J. Evans—backed by a Denver land firm—marshalled his rag tag and bob-tail band of "legitimate settlers" in the land office at Denver, and then and there it was that oath was made (and what swearing!) to have lived on and improved all the property described.

It is possible that the Land Office official before whom this vast amount of "blasphemy" was practiced, was ignorant of all "goings on." We certainly hope so. But still the proper papers were made out and forwarded on to the National Capital.

The Land Grabbers who have put up this latest "gobble" are confident of receiving their patents from the U.S. Government. The English purchasers are so confident that they already consider Este's [sic] Park as their own. They have also made more or less advances of money.

The question then arises whether the people of Colorado will permit one of the richest and most attractive portions of the Territory to be set apart for the exclusive benefit and behoof of a few English aristocrats, or whether the Government itself shall keep its title to the park, pass stringent laws relative to the fish and game, and so have this broad and lovely domain, forever kept as a National "Institution," of a general benefit to the people of Colorado.

Anyway or anyhow the days of Land Grabbing in this Territory are about over![16]

H. C. Alleman, the U.S. territorial attorney, who had arrived in Denver from Philadelphia the previous year with considerable fanfare, went to work with surprising alacrity.[17] Within a matter of weeks of the original complaints, he was able to parade a number of Estes Park residents, including James McLaughlin, David Miller, Hank Farrar, Hugh McDermot, and Dexter Smith, before an assembled grand jury. Three of these individuals, interestingly enough, had close connections with Griff Evans: McLaughlin was his sometime partner, McDermot his hired man, and eighteen-year-old Dexter Smith in January 1878 would become his son-in-law by marrying Jennie, his oldest daughter. Well before the end of September Alleman had secured the indictment of thirty-one individuals for "committing perjury and subornation of perjury in making and filing false proofs in the Este's [sic] Park." The names of all thirty-one were promptly published in the press.[18]

With the possible exception of William Byers's *Rocky Mountain News*, which earlier that summer had staunchly defended David Moffat Jr.'s controversial role in securing land titles at Las Animas,[19] the territorial press was delighted with the outcome of Alleman's investigation, particularly papers like the *Denver Tribune*, *Rocky Mountain Herald*, *Fort Collins Standard*, and *Greeley Tribune*, which had jockeyed with one another for the honor of leading the original exposé.[20]

It was common knowledge that Englishmen (or at least "foreigners") had been the "land grabbers" in Estes Park. Yet the role played by Dunraven himself, "in purchasing land from certain well known land grabbers,"[21] seems to have by and large escaped public notice, much less public wrath. There were exceptions. On August 19, 1874, for example, the *Greeley Tribune* ran the following item from the *Larimer County Express*, citing the involvement of not only Dunraven but Griff Evans and his two partners in the cattle business (whose names they managed to confuse and roll into one):

We are credibly informed that the late reported purchase of six thousand acres of land in Estes' Park, embracing all the most valuable portion of that grand domain, by the Earl of Dunraven, is one of the most barefaced land steals of this land-stealing age.

We are informed that Griffith Evans and Lothrop Brown [sic] were principally concerned in manufacturing titles to consummate this sale, and we now bring the attention of the U.S. Attorney Alleman to this matter, for his investigation. We have taken measures to get at the more important facts in this transaction.[22]

A month later, on September 26, at the time of the indictments, the *Greeley Tribune* reprinted with obvious satisfaction the assertion of the *Denver Tribune* that

"Milord" Dunraven, instead of having his *patents* in his pocket would seem to be very far from getting them at all. And hence Dunraven and his suite are without anything to show for the money they have advanced to certain well-known Denver land sharks, unless it may be such "sports of the chase" as these "mighty Nimrods" have managed to secure in their summer hunt. As pelts and furs are unusually low at present, we fear our English Earl will have to submit to something of a pecuniary loss. But even this may prove to be advantageous, as it will teach our English cousins to think twice before again making advances to land sharks on hypothetical land claims, and particularly those of Denver.[23]

Even more curious was the fact that the very issue—and page—of the *Fort Collins Standard*, which spread the alarm about the "villainous" land grab, carried without comment, and without any indication that it sensed a contradiction, news that "the Earl of Dunraven has purchased 8,000 acres of land in Estes' Park and he proposes to make it a summer resort of the first magnitude."[24] The following story, which appeared in August 1874 in papers in Arapahoe, Weld, Clear Creek, and El Paso Counties, was even more explicit about Dunraven's plans:

A NEW company, of which the Earl of Dunraven is the principal stockholder, has purchased all available lands in Estes Park, embracing some 6,000 acres. The company proposes making extensive and costly improvements. Among these will be a large hotel, a sawmill, new roads through the park, a hotel at Longmont, and a half-way house on the road between that place and the park.[25]

Whyte (or perhaps even Griff Evans) was probably the source of these stories, for by late July the Earl had gone off on a three-month first visit to Yellowstone and a series of adventures he would chronicle in *The Great Divide: Travels in the Upper Yellowstone in the Summer of 1874*, published in London in 1876.

In the end, Alleman's victory in securing the original indictments proved a Pyrrhic one. In every case the government marshal, whose job it was to locate and serve the indictees, reported his inability, despite a diligent search, to find them. Alleman had no choice. The indictments were dropped, leaving Whyte free to exercise on Dunraven's behalf control over lands to which he already held the deeds. As noted above, a very determined Alexander MacGregor would continue to pursue the issue of land fraud into the early 1880s, "trusting that right and justice will be done," and apparently did succeed in having the question reopened during the period he was serving as Larimer County judge.[26] In the end, however, Dunraven's purchases remained secure. Moreover, as one of Dunraven's British contemporaries observed in 1879, the Earl "had picked up . . . a park in the western hemisphere which laughs to scorn the beauties of home ones," and he had done so " 'for a song.' "[27]

Given the sensational nature of the charges and the press's well-known ability to inflame public ire, particularly at the expense of anti-democratic foreigners, why so little sustained hue and cry? And, given the fact that his agency was well known, why should Dunraven's role go largely unchallenged? Several answers suggest themselves. One is the fact that land grabs and land grabbing (and charges thereof) were an accepted part of the history of America's expanding frontier. As William Byers explained to his readers in July 1874, there were "many instances, all over the country, [of] false swearing . . . or the purpose of effecting entries," and "so notorious has [sic] these violations and evasions of those laws become, that their practice had almost ceased to attract attention."[28] Another reason had to do, certainly, with the determination of Estes Park's other early settlers—the Spragues, MacGregors, Jameses, Fergusons, Hupps, Farrars, Lambs, and one or two others—who, coming on the scene in 1874 and 1875, found ways to locate and establish claims of their own. In future years their involvement in the tourist industry would complement (rather than be dominated by) Dunraven's Estes Park Company.

Whyte, acting on behalf of Dunraven, quickly went to work to implement the Earl's plans, much in the way that the Colorado press had described. The hotel to be established at Longmont was, undoubtedly, the St. Vrain Hotel, which Griff Evans took over in November of 1874, quite possibly with Dunraven's direct financial backing. While the halfway house, either at Lyons or somewhere up the North St. Vrain road, never materialized (or, at least, not one owned and operated by the English Company),[29] the hotel in Estes Park most certainly did, though its construction took longer than originally expected.

The spot selected for the Estes Park Hotel was along Fish Creek south of the Evans ranch. Credit for locating the site is generally given to Albert

Bierstadt, founder of the Rocky Mountain School of landscape painting, who accompanied the Earl to Estes Park in 1876, in order to paint on commission the 5-by-8-foot canvas *Long's Peak, Estes Park, Colorado,* which for many years adorned the walls of Glin Castle in the county of Limerick.[30] That same summer the promised sawmill, operated by steam, was brought in. For building lumber Whyte and his foreman, John Cleave, an Englishman from Cornwall, chose a particularly fine grove of yellow pine not far from the ranch near the foot of Park Hill. Many of their efforts in 1876, however, were directed toward building post and plank fences to enclose pastures and hanging gates at the crossings of roads and pathways. They also constructed several cottages, including an octagonal Queen Anne style cottage just to the north of the proposed hotel site to serve as Dunraven's home when he was in the park. While the hotel was being built, the Dunraven cottage served as a convenient place to house Cleave's workers.

The Estes Park Hotel, built of wood, brick, and stone at a cost of some fifteen thousand dollars, was opened for business on July 9, 1877, under the watchful eye of its resident manager, C. H. Hinman. Theodore Whyte and his wife marked the occasion by giving a formal ball, with guests coming from as far away as Denver.[31] The white, 40-by-100-foot, three-story hotel, with its rooms for cards, billiards, and lounging, and with 14-foot verandas on the south and west from which to view

Figure 3.3. The original Estes Park, or English, Hotel. Courtesy Hazel E. Johnson collection, City of Greeley Museums, permanent collection.

Figure 3.4. The Estes Park Hotel with its new roof. Courtesy Estes Park Area Historical Museum.

Longs Peak and the Mummy Range, was an imposing structure. The building, which had twelve front-facing windows on each story, was originally wrapped on three sides with a second-story open-railed balcony covering a columned porch below. This balcony was later converted to a roof, perhaps as a means of reducing after-hours festivities. In 1908 a wing to the north containing twenty rooms was added, bringing the total number to fifty and extending the veranda to a full 170 feet. That same year the old oil lamps were replaced by gaslights.

In front of the hotel, as a place for guests to wander, was a well-manicured lawn, and close by to the west an artificial lake, large enough for small boats, made by the damming of Fish Creek. The hotel had its own tennis courts and nine-hole golf course, as well as a dairy, blacksmith shop, and butcher shop. These outbuildings, in contrast to the frame hotel, were built of logs. To the north, along Fish Creek, was the livery. Guides were provided, among them Hank Farrar, known throughout the region for his expertise as a hunter, as well as for his greyhound dog, the "Old Man," who frequently accompanied him. The British engineer Daniel Pidgeon, who engaged Farrar in conversation on the hotel piazza during July 1880, found him a "guide, philosopher, and friend of every stranger who comes to Estes Park in search of sport." It "was pleasant," Pidgeon wrote, "to listen to his slow good-humored talk of elk and elk-hunting, and to admire his word-pictures of chase and camp."[32]

Figure 3.5. The Dunraven ranch, c. 1890 (on the site of the original Evans ranch). Courtesy National Park Service—Rocky Mountain National Park.

During the late 1870s and well into the decade that followed the "exquisitely furnished and admirably kept" Estes Park Hotel (or English Hotel, as it was locally known) provided the most fashionable accommodations in the park. Time, lack of continuity in management, and competition, however, eventually took their toll. Between 1888 and 1902, for example, the hotel ran through a succession of at least ten managers. On August 4, 1911, in its thirty-fifth season, the Estes Park Hotel was destroyed by fire, fortunately without loss of life or serious injury. The fire broke out about 8 A.M. as most guests were at breakfast, starting in the attic and burning through the hotel so quickly that only six or eight trunks of clothes were saved. The loss, estimated at seventy-five thousand dollars, was only partially covered by insurance. Rumor later had it that the fire was the work of a disgruntled employee who had been dismissed the day before.[33]

As for the Earl of Dunraven, his enthusiasm for Estes Park began to wane. There were visits in 1876 with Albert Bierstadt and others, and he presumably returned in 1877 to see at first hand his newly opened hotel. By the time of Dunraven's visit of 1879, however, his attitude toward the place had decidedly changed. There is a note of unmistakable ennui in his letter of October 4, 1879, to Lord Bernard Fitzpatrick: "Mr. & Mrs. Whyte & I are living in the hotel with the yard boy as cook &

Charlie to wait on us & that is all the establishment—with music & books & writing the time passes pretty well—at least it w^d certainly be worse without them!! but it wouldn't exactly break my heart if I was never to set eyes on Estes Park again."[34] It was an honest sentiment, for Dunraven apparently never returned.[35]

Dunraven's grand design for Estes Park proved to be unworkable. As Abner Sprague explained,

> Estes Park did not furnish grazing lands sufficient to make the cattle business pay; the settlers confined the company to their own lands by surrounding them with their claims, thus cutting off the larger part of the pasture lands of the region. The Company used the North Fork range for several years, which was a better stock country than the Park; still the stock business could not be made to pay expenses. The addition of revenue derived from the rentals of the Estes Park Hotel and cottages did not help matters much. After repeated calls for money to carry on the business, and the Earl's original ideas being defeated, Mr. Whyte was told the place would have to be self-supporting; the establishment was toned down; yet it ran behind, debts were contracted, and finally the property was leased under option, and Theodore Whyte passed out of the history of Estes Park.[36]

In his two-volume autobiography, *Past Times and Pastimes*, published years later in 1922, Dunraven offered a somewhat different explanation, compressing rather disingenuously nearly forty years of history into a single paragraph:

> After a time people began to wander in. The first I well remember. I was sitting smoking at the door of a little one-room shanty when to me appeared a queer little old chap on a pack horse, and says he, "Say, stranger, is this a good place to drink whiskey in?" I said it was if only there was whiskey. He looked disappointed and wandered off. It became evident that we were not to be left monarchs of all we surveyed. Folks were drifting in prospecting, fossicking, pre-empting, making claims; so we prepared for civilization. Made a better road, bought a sawmill at San Francisco, hauled the machinery in, set it up, felled trees, and built a wooden hotel, and did pretty well with a Chinese cook who could make venison and anything else out of bogged cow beef. Neither I or my chum stayed there long. People came in disputing claims, kicking up rows; exorbitant land taxes got into arrears; we were in constant litigation. The show could not be managed from home, and we were in danger of being frozen out. So we sold for what we could get and cleared out, and I have never been there since.[37]

The final selling out did not occur, however, until June of 1908, when after a series of protracted negotiations, Dunraven agreed to relinquish the rights of the English Company to Burton D. Sanborn of Greeley and Freelan O. Stanley of Estes Park. From that time on the Earl of Dunraven severed completely his relationship with Estes Park.

"Land grabbing" notwithstanding, Dunraven and his pioneer neighbors were soon enough living amicably side by side in Estes Park, raising cattle, farming, and catering to the hunters, fishermen, and vacationers who wandered in to visit. In the end, the hope that "Veritas" had expressed in August of 1874 proved to be prophetic. Though it would take over forty years to establish Rocky Mountain National Park, the U.S. government did at length retain title to much of the region, "pass stringent laws relative to the fish and game, and so have this broad and lovely domain, forever kept as a National 'Institution,' of a general benefit to the people of Colorado."

Chapter 4

⌣

Isabella Bird's "Desperado":
The Life and Death of Rocky Mountain Jim

This gulch, with the euphonious title, is a fair, prairie-like dale between rugged mountains, forming the dwelling place of Mountain Jim, whose little log cabin still stands in the edge of the willows near a small brook; but the intrepid mountaineer has gone on an endless journey in the wondrous country "over the range."

—Boulder County News (1876)

Close by the gates of the park we discovered an open cabin. It was built of unhewn logs, and covered with earth. The door and window were gone, and the paths that once led to it were overgrown with bramble. We learned that this had once been the home of Mountain Jim, who, during his life, had been known as a trapper, hunter, fisherman, ranchman, and guide. . . . The desolate cabin still serves as a monument to his memory; and, as it is pointed out to strangers, the thrilling events of his strange life and tragic death are related; all of which have become historically associated with the park.

—S. Anna Gordon, Camping in Colorado (1879)

The history of Colorado and the Rocky Mountain West is filled with stories of bigger-than-life men and women whose lives and exploits yielded legend and romance. One of these is James Nugent of Estes Park—or "Rocky Mountain Jim" as he was widely known. Jim's activities between 1871 and 1874, particularly those that culminated in his death at the hands of Griff Evans in September 1874, were well reported in the territorial press of the day, and, as Anna Gordon's comment suggests, quickly became part of the early history of Estes Park.[1]

Rocky Mountain Jim was a man in search of notoriety, and Isabella Bird (1831–1904) became his Boswell. Bird made her emotion-charged relationship with Jim the center of the original letters that she sent home to her younger sister, Henrietta, and then edited and published in 1878 in the British periodical *Leisure Hour* and a year later in book form as *A Lady's Life in the Rocky Mountains*. Her book, long since a classic, not only publicized and popularized Mountain Jim's short but colorful career, but provided the prism through which subsequent generations would come to view and understand him. That the historical James Nugent was an interesting and complex human being is clear. But in the hands of Isabella Bird, Rocky Mountain Jim became a melodramatic figure who could just as easily have stepped from the pages of one of Erastus Beadle's popular dime novel Westerns. Isabella Bird's book offers one view of James Nugent. A fresh and comprehensive look at the historical evidence offers quite another.

When Isabella Bird rode up through Muggins Gulch on her way to Estes Park in the early days of October 1873, the first sign of human life she came upon was Jim's "rude, black log cabin." She then encountered Jim himself. She recalled the occasion for Henrietta in graphic detail:

> . . . it was the home, or rather den, of a notorious "ruffian" and "desperado." . . . The big dog lay outside it in a threatening attitude and growled. The mud roof was covered with lynx, beaver, and other furs laid out to dry, beaver paws were pinned out on the logs, a part of the carcass of a deer hung at one end of the cabin, a skinned beaver lay in front of a heap of peltry just within the door, and antlers of deer, old horseshoes, and offal of many animals, lay about the den. Roused by the growling of the dog, his owner came out, a broad, thickset man, about the middle height, with an old cap on his head, and wearing a grey hunting suit much the worse for wear (almost falling to pieces, in fact), a digger's scarf knotted round his waist, a knife in his belt, and "a bosom friend," a revolver, sticking out of the breast pocket of his coat; his feet, which were very small, were bare, except for some dilapidated moccasins made of horse hide. The marvel was how his clothes hung together, and on him. The scarf hung round his waist must have had something to do with it. His face was remarkable. He is a man about forty-five, and must have been strikingly handsome. He has large grey-blue eyes, deeply set, with well-marked eyebrows, a handsome aquiline nose, and a very handsome mouth. His face was smooth-shaven except for a dense mustache and imperial. Tawny hair, in thin uncared-for curls, fell from under his hunter's cap and over his collar. One eye was entirely gone, and the loss made one side of the face repulsive, while the other might have been modeled in marble. "Desperado" was written in large letters all over him. I almost repented of having sought his acquaintance. His first impulse was to swear at the dog, but on seeing a lady he contented himself with kicking him, and coming to me he raised his cap, showing as he did so a magnificently-formed brow and head, and in a cultured tone of voice asked if there were anything he could do for me? I asked for some water, and he brought some in a battered tin, gracefully apologizing for not having anything more presentable. We entered into conversation, and as he spoke I forgot both his reputation and appearance, for his manner was that of a chivalrous gentleman, his accent refined, and his language easy and elegant. I inquired

about some beavers' paws which were drying, and in a moment they hung on the horn of my saddle.[2]

According to Bird, Nugent wasted little time in explaining the reason for his strange appearance: "He told me that the loss of his eye was owing to a recent encounter with a grizzly bear, which, after giving him a death hug, tearing him all over, breaking his arm and scratching out his eye, had left him for dead."[3]

Bird concludes her introduction by offering her readers a summary portrait of the man who is (or, by the time of the book's publication, had been) James Nugent:

> This man, known through the Territories and beyond them as "Rocky Mountain Jim," or, more briefly, as "Mountain Jim," is one of the famous scouts of the Plains, and is the original of some daring portraits in fiction concerning Indian frontier warfare. So far as I have at present heard, he is a man for whom there is now no room, for the time for blows and blood in this part of Colorado is past, and the fame of many daring exploits is sullied by crimes which are not easily forgiven here. He now has a "squatter's claim," but makes his living as a trapper, and is a complete child of the mountains. Of his genius and chivalry to women there does not appear to be any doubt; but he is a desperate character, and is subject to "ugly fits," when people think it best to avoid him. It is here regarded as an evil that he has located himself at the mouth of the only entrance to the Park, for he is dangerous with his pistols, and it would be safer if he were not here. His besetting sin is indicated in the verdict pronounced on him by my host: "When he's sober Jim's a perfect gentleman; but when he's had liquor he's the most awful ruffian in Colorado."[4]

Bird prefaces this paragraph with the following footnote, juxtaposing Jim's life and death:

> Of this unhappy man, who was shot nine months later within two miles of his cabin, I write in subsequent letters only as he appeared to me. His life, without doubt, was deeply stained with crimes and vices, and his reputation for ruffianism was a deserved one. But in my intercourse with him I saw more of his nobler instincts than of the darker parts of his character, which, unfortunately for himself and others, showed itself in its worst colours at the time of his tragic end. It was not until after I left Colorado, not indeed until after his death, that I heard of the worst points of his character.[5]

Such dramatic passages, freely alluding to Nugent's dark character and notoriety, are presented throughout the book. What is remarkable about them is how confidently, not to mention how quickly and finally, Bird was willing to assert the verdict of history upon James Nugent. She calls him a "ruffian" and a "desperado"—a man guilty of (unspecified) crimes and misdeeds whose "fame for violence and ruffianism preceded him into Colorado."[6] These two words and all they resonate have shaped Nugent's reputation from Bird's time until our own.

This was not, however, the view of the great majority of Jim's contemporaries. That Jim was known in northeastern Colorado as a hunter, fisherman, and mountaineer, as well as a man with a mysterious and colorful past, is clear. But "ruffian" and "desperado," as those terms are usually understood in the lexicon of the West, he assuredly was not. Nor was his reputation as widespread as Bird would have us believe. Her statement that "one can hardly take up a newspaper without finding a paragraph about him, a contribution by him, or a fragment of his biography" simply is not true.[7]

The reasons for Isabella Bird's treatment of Jim are not hard to divine. One surely had to do with her own psychological needs; a second with what her Victorian contemporaries were prepared to tolerate in the way of romance. The relationship that developed between these two most dissimilar individuals—a relationship that Bird's book tries to mute but scarcely conceals—was intense and deeply felt. It was also a relationship that no "lady" could permit to continue, especially a spinster going home to the drawing rooms of Edinburgh and London. For such an audience, as well for the readers of her book, how better explain away such an implausibility than by reducing James Nugent to the melodramatic stereotype of the western "desperado" whom any woman might be attracted to, and even love, "but no sane woman would marry"?

There was also the matter of writing a book that would sell. Here, too, Jim served her well. "I need money and a book," she had confided to Henrietta in one of her original letters, "though not [one that at a] risk of losing, might produce nothing."[8] *A Lady's Life in the Rocky Mountains* succeeds, like all great works of travel literature, because of its author's ability to combine vivid physical descriptions of scenery with vibrant, colorful, and convincing human portraits. In Rocky Mountain Jim, Isabella Bird found a subject only too willing to conform his appearance and behavior to her literary needs.

Given the extravagance of Isabella Bird's representation, it is surely ironic that James Nugent's intrusion into the pages of Colorado's recorded history is confined to a period of only three years, 1871 to 1874. The period begins with the hyperbolic account of his encounter with a "monstrous" bear in Middle Park that appeared in the July 11, 1871, issue of William Byers's *Rocky Mountain News*:

> Last Thursday morning as "Rocky Mountain Jim" was making his way up the Grand to the lake, he left his night camp to visit a deer-lick near by. He left his gun and carried only a large revolving pistol. As he was crawling up upon

several deer that he found at the lick, his dog which had followed along, came howling out of some bushes near by, followed by a monstrous cinnamon bear and two cubs. The dog ran to his master, and the bear, paying no more attention to the brute, rushed upon the man. Jim knew what was coming and began firing, lodging four balls in her carcass before she reached him. She seized him by the left arm at the elbow, biting it through and through and mangling it fearfully, hurled him to the ground and shook him as a dog would a rat. Jim still held on to his pistol, and placing the muzzle against her body fired the fifth shot. The sixth refused to go. She then let go the arm and seized him by the head, ripping the scalp to the bone along the right side and across the forehead. Her weight settled upon his chest and he became insensible.

When he recovered consciousness he found himself in a pool of clotted blood, but no bear in sight. His clothes were nearly all torn off; fifty wounds scarred his body from head to foot; his right eye was entirely hidden under the torn scalp; his left thumb bitten off, and his strength exhausted by loss of blood. Most men would have given up and died, but Jim groped his way to his mule, saddled it and started for Grand Lake, eight miles distant. He heard shoutings and calls on the way, and answered them, but no one came, because they were only the creation of his bewildered brain. Once he came to and found himself in the grass beside his mule from which he had fallen. He reached the lake and hallooed for help. The two men there were at the further shore, but they came as soon as the two miles distance could be rowed. As they neared the shore one said, "The Indians are upon us sure this time, for here is a man scalped." They cared for him the best they knew and then one started out into the great park in the dim hope to find a doctor. Fortunately there was one by merest chance fifteen miles away at the new mining camp—Dr. Pollock, en route to the lake—and at 10 o'clock in the night he came, sewed up his wounds and partially relieved his intense suffering. . . .

Jim has been a mountaineer for twenty-eight years and has roamed over all this western region and British America. He has seen many adventures and suffered many wounds from Indians and wild beasts, but he says this was the worst, and his thought when the old bear seized him that he "was going under." Of late years he has been most of the time in the employ of the army, as guide, scout, and spy. Recently he took up a rancho in Estes park, and settled down to engage in stock raising.[9]

The *News* was Colorado's most influential newspaper, and Nugent emerged from his escapade in Middle Park with a widely circulated, larger-than-life reputation and public persona that would have done credit to any frontiersman. Maimed for life, he was now "Rocky Mountain Jim, the bear fighter," a man with a story to tell.

It is also clear that the details Nugent offered about his past life, here as elsewhere, were not only embellished but largely, if not entirely, self-fabricated. Efforts over the years to substantiate the facts of Jim's life story have proven both frustrating and fruitless.[10] To his credit, however, he was remarkably consistent in their retelling.

In July of 1873, for example, two months before Isabella Bird descended upon Estes Park, Nugent provided Editor Painter of the Colorado Sun with a life story virtually identical with the one he had furnished the Rocky Mountain News. Painter and a small party of Greeley men had come to Estes Park to climb Longs Peak. "Our second day in camp," Painter subsequently wrote,

> we met the famous ROCKY MOUNTAIN JIM, who has traveled these parts for lo, these many years. His proper name is James Nugend [sic], and he hails from Montreal, Canada, from whence he started as a trapper in the service of the Hudson Bay Company on the 25th of August 1842. He remained with the company nine years, but not having a particular liking for the tyranny which the company then exerted over their trappers and hunters, he abandoned them and roamed the plains and mountains as an independent trapper till the year 1863, when he went in the employ of the United States as an Indian scout and spy, which business he pursued for about three years. After that he again occupied his time hunting and trapping in the Rockies till the 4th of July, 1871, which natal day he celebrated by having a fearful encounter with a huge she cinnamon bear in Middle Park, and out of which he came minus his right eye. He, however, got the best of the cinnamon, and confidently expects to "get the drop" on many another bear before he is gathered unto his fathers. This encounter disabled Jim so badly that he is just now fully recovering from the effects, and has not been able to pay much attention to game since. He intends, however, to present his compliments to the bear family this fall. When we last met him, he had just made a wager with an Englishman that he would bring in a bear, dead or alive, within the next three days. If Jim loses that wager it will be because bears are scarcer than skunks were when, as the story goes, the boy's family was out of meat.
>
> James Nugend [sic] was styled Rocky Mountain Jim by the Indians while scouting among them, and as there was Jim Baker, Jim Beckwith, Jim Long, Jim Bridger, and a host of other mountain trappers all floating under the cognomen Jim, his Indian title clung to him to distinguish him from the many trappers of the same name.
>
> Rocky Mountain Jim has also had many a hair-breadth escape from the Indians, and can tell a multitude of stories of the warm and unhealthy places he has passed through, which makes the listener's hair stand on end and quiver while it stands. Jim now has in his mind's eye several scalp-lifters that have tried to play it. Lo! on him, and if they ever give him an opportunity he will take extreme pleasure in giving them a thorough ticket to the happy hunting grounds, per Rifle Ball's Express. He doesn't intend to follow hunting and trapping for a livelihood any more, as it doesn't pay, but will indulge occasionally for his own amusement, and make stock raising his main business. Our mountaineer now owns considerable stock, and has a beautiful place

in the mountains a few miles east of the park. He first visited the park as early as nineteen years ago, and has in his day traveled with all the famous hunters, from Kit and Bob Carson down. In stature Jim is about five feet, ten inches; is well proportioned and slightly inclined to corpulency; beard and hair, light auburn, with the latter worn in curls hanging to his shoulders; Grecian nose, with a round, full and well-shaped face, and notwithstanding he has but one eye, is what would generally be considered a good-looking man. He is exceedingly friendly, kind and accommodating, and for the kindness extended to us, if for nothing else, we can heartily exclaim: Long live Rocky Mountain Jim.

A CHANCE FOR THE FAIR SEX By the way, Jim is quite a ladies' man, and if any of our lady readers yet single are matrimonially inclined, they might do well to take a trip to the vicinity of Jim's tramping ground and cultivate the trapper's acquaintance. We feel confident he would make a good husband, and to help the matter along there is a minister now stopping hard by that Jim would be glad to favor with a job, for says he of the divine in question: "He is the most respectable gospel-slinger I have ever met in these parts." In behalf of Jim's morality, we can say he never played a game of cards, and looks as though his lips had never touched the intoxicating bowl.[11]

Though its somewhat jaunty tone introduces a note of skepticism, Painter's account is particularly valuable. Not only does it provide an excellent physical description of Nugent, but it confirms and extends (with some very precise details) the earlier account in the *Rocky Mountain News*. It also anticipates much of what Jim himself would tell Isabella Bird several months later during their memorable ride up Fall River. Significantly, the editor of the *Sun* did not find Jim a particularly threatening figure, recommending him to "our lady readers yet single" as a man who appeared to neither play cards nor drink.

The version of his life story that Jim gave Isabella Bird offers little new information. What is different is the highly emotional tone with which it is reported. "There was no choice," Bird later wrote, "as we rode up the canyon, and I listened to one of the darkest tales of ruin I have ever heard or read."[12] To the story of his Canadian youth Jim added the fact that his "father was a British officer quartered at Montreal, of a good old Irish family," and that "he was an ungovernable boy, imperfectly educated." He also told Isabella Bird that, "maddened" at eighteen by the death of a girl "of angelic beauty" (a girl, he confessed, he had seen but three times and "scarcely spoke to"), he had run away from home and entered the service of the Hudson's Bay Company.

Jim rambled that day. His three-hour narrative, "told with a rush of wild eloquence that was truly thrilling," "seemed to lack some link,"

for I next found him on a homestead in Missouri, from whence he came to Colorado a few years ago. There, again, something was dropped out, but I suspect, and not without reason, that he joined one or more of those gangs of "border ruffians" which for so long raided through Kansas, perpetrating such massacres and outrages as that of the Marais du Cygne. His fame for violence and ruffianism preceded him into Colorado, where his knowledge of and love of the mountains have earned him the sobriquet he now bears. He has a squatter's claim and forty head of cattle, and is a successful trapper besides, but envy and vindictiveness are raging within him. He gets money, goes to Denver, and spends large sums in the maddest dissipation, making himself a terror, and going beyond even such desperadoes as "Texas Jack" and "Wild Bill"; and when the money is done returns to his mountain den, full of hatred and self-scorn, till the next time. Of course I cannot give details. The story took three hours to tell, and was crowded with terrific illustrations of a desperado's career, told with a rush of wild eloquence that was truly thrilling.[13]

Though Isabella Bird apparently saw no reason to question the facts underlying such pyrotechnics, much less the sincerity of their delivery, many who encountered Rocky Mountain Jim were rather more skeptical. One of these was Dr. George Kingsley, the English physician who accompanied the Earl of Dunraven to Estes Park in 1873 and 1874 and attended Nugent after he was shot. Kingsley, writing with the slightly supercilious tone of the worldly outsider, concluded early on that Jim was pretty much "a humbug and a scoundrel" and nicknamed him the "Mountainous One" "on account of the extraordinary altitude of his lies."[14] Others, equally convinced that Nugent was largely a poseur, simply tried to humor him along. "Miss Bird was quite taken with Jim," Platt Rogers recalled in 1905. Rogers was one of the two young men who brought Isabella Bird to Estes Park in 1873 and then, with Jim showing the way, accompanied her to the top of Longs Peak. On the eve of that event, "we spent the evening before the camp fire," Rogers wrote,

> very much after the matter described in her book. Jim was resourceful, romantic and reminiscent. His adventure with the bear in Middle Park, which cost him his eye, was elaborated for Miss Bird's benefit, and all the doggerel which he had composed in the loneliness of Muggins' gulch was recited by him. The principal theme of his poems was himself, varied by references to a fair maiden, of whom he seemed enamored, and who, we afterwards learned, was Griff Evans' daughter.[15]

Isabella Bird sensed their amusement and disbelief. "She was disposed," Rogers noted, "to resent our want of faith in him and the jollying we felt compelled to give him." Abner Sprague, the Estes Park pioneer who spent an evening in camp with Nugent in 1872, later observed that Jim "gave me the impression that he talked mostly to astonish his audience."[16] Sprague had come up from his home on the Big Thompson in late July or early August with a party of young people bound for Estes Park. They encountered Jim in Little Elk Park, "herding a bunch of sheep to keep the lions from getting them." It "was scandalous how the girls flirted with him," Sprague recalled from a distance of half a century, and perhaps not without envy. "They would not look at us; they ogled him, admired his long hair, and even pretended to believe his very best 'wild and wooly stories.' "[17]

Nugent recovered from his battle in Middle Park quickly. Only three weeks later he was up and around, and, mindful of the debt he owed the press, chose to pay his respects at the offices of the *Central City Register* and the *Rocky Mountain News*. Both papers passed on to their readers word of Jim's recovery, gratitude, and future plans:

> "Mountain Jim," who was so terribly mangled by a bear, in the Middle Park a few weeks ago, made us a call on Thursday. His left arm is yet in a sling, entirely helpless, his right eye bandaged, and his face shows he has suffered a great deal. He is now on his way to Estes' park where he has a grazing ranch and considerable stock. He has heard that tourists have left his gates open and that his cattle are scattered. He takes a man along with him to look after them . . . .
>
> Jim desires us publicly to express his hearty thanks to all who have assisted him, since his misfortune with the bear. He says he did not know he had so many friends. Dr. Adudell won't take a cent. . . . In particular he desires to thank those who so kindly cared for him in the Park, mentioning Mr. Byers, Dr. Potlock [sic], and Mr. Hurd, and particularly Mrs. Potlock and Mrs. Hurd, who, he says, with a moist eye and a trembling lip, cared for him as if he were a prince. Mountain Jim's heart is evidently in the right place.[18] (*Central City Register*, August 5, 1871)
>
> Rocky Mountain Jim came in, to-day, from Middle park. He says he is covered all over with honorable scars and gaping wounds received in that bear fight over there a few weeks since, and, judging from his appearance, I should think he was. His right eye was in total darkness, by reason of a carbuncle over it, about the size of a hen's egg. His left arm was torn and mangled in a manner not pleasant to look upon. The thumb of his left hand had been bitten off down to the first joint. Some of his scalp was scratched off, and the back of his neck showed bloody marks of beastly viciousness. Dr. Adudell is tinkering the old hero up, and thinks he will be able to make him half to two-thirds of a man of him yet. Jim says if he don't peg out this time, he will make himself a terror to the whole bear family. He has sworn eternal enmity to the race; and will devote the remainder of his days to the bear business.[19] (*Rocky Mountain News*, August 5, 1871)

During the next two years, Nugent virtually drops from sight. Until July of 1873, when he talked to the editor of the Greeley paper, we hear little about Rocky Mountain Jim and his activities. Presumably, as promised, he returned to Muggins Gulch and resumed his ranching. When he did make an appearance, Jim seems to have chosen his entrances and exits carefully and in ways that commanded attention and were likely to enhance his reputation.

Just when James Nugent took up his squatter's claim in Muggins Gulch is not clear. Milton Estes, Joel's oldest son, does not mention Jim in his memoirs.[20] Nor is he mentioned by William Byers, who came up the gulch in 1864 on his way to attempt Longs Peak. It is also not clear whether Jim was yet in residence when Griff and Jane Evans arrived in the fall of 1867. Presumably he was not, for Captain George Brown does not mention encountering anyone in bringing the Evans family to the park. Mountain Jim is also absent from the account written by the Earl of Dunraven (a fellow Irishman) of his first trip to Estes Park in the days following Christmas of 1872. Dunraven does mention coming up "a long valley rejoicing in the euphonious title of 'Muggin's Gulch'": "I do not know who Muggins was—no doubt an honest citizen; but he should have changed his name before bestowing it upon such a pretty spot."[21] But he does not mention passing Jim's cabin or meeting the trapper-hunter.

Jim's cabin stood at the junction of Muggins Gulch and the gulch coming down from Hermit Park, on the hillside just below the buildings and spring of the old Meadowdale Ranch. Then as now, Muggins Gulch was largely treeless, in Bird's words, "a long gulch with broad swellings of grass belted with pines," and Jim's "den" was located "not far from the track." Jim's cabin, in short, would have been difficult, if not impossible, to miss by anyone passing by on foot or horseback. The fact that this obvious sign of habitation at the mouth of the park is not mentioned by visitors prior to Isabella Bird is difficult to account for, if indeed Jim had taken up residence there at an early date.

During the summer and fall of 1873, on the other hand, Rocky Mountain Jim was very much in evidence. Not only did he talk to the editor of the *Colorado Sun* but he made it a point to engage—and impress—two famous women visitors: the celebrated lecturer Anna Dickinson and Isabella Lucy Bird.

Jim was there and in top form in September when Anna Dickinson and her party arrived to climb Longs Peak. Rocky Mountain Jim was not a member of the climbing party. But he made himself available, almost as if on cue, when they returned to the Evans ranch to spend the night of September 13 following their successful ascent. There, Dickinson recalled, they enjoyed a celebratory evening in front of "a crackling wood fire" with

> time a plenty for confabulation, a confabulation that was made more "pecooliar" by the presence of "Rocky Mountain Jim," who, having peregrinated up to see us, sat contentedly and looked at us with his one bright eye, finally in quaint language and with concise vividness narrating many a tale of bear and other desperate fights, one of which had two years before nearly ended his days—had broken his right arm, stove in three ribs, torn out his left eye, and "chawed" him up generally, and yet left spirit and grit enough to tell a good story well and to get through a close shave bravely.[22]

Rocky Mountain Jim was also impressed, and quickly let it be known, that he intended to write up Anna Dickinson's adventures for publication. "Mountain Jim has furnished us with an account of life in Estes' Park, and an ascent of Longs Peak with Anna Dickinson and party, which shall have our attention next week," the *Boulder County News* reported on August 26.[23] By October 11, when Jim's old editor acquaintance, Mr. Painter of the *Colorado Sun* (citing as his source the *Central City Register*), took notice of Jim's project, the promised "account" had become a book:

> The *Central Register* says that James Nugend [sic], of Estes Park, better known as Mountain Jim, is about to write a book. Those who know Jim will be most inclined to favor the enterprise, and few of his friends would fail to buy from one to a dozen copies. Of course, although it would treat a variety of subjects and contain a great deal of mountain lore, its author could not help but be the central figure in his narrative, nor would this prove objectionable. Mountain Jim has been through enough in his eventful life to fill a dozen books, but he is no "blow-hard," whose talk of himself can prove offensive.
>
> In his long residence in the mountains Jim has met many celebrated characters, and it was his ascent of Long's Peak in company with Anna Dickinson which suggested the book in question. Perhaps Anna herself suggested the idea. She could not have talked with Jim ever so briefly without discovering the "genuine man" under the rough hunting suit, and no doubt she felt interested in the story of his life. But apart from this purely romantic interest, the book would very likely prove invaluable as a guide to Estes Park and Long's Peak—two great attractions of our mountains, neither of which is sufficiently known. The Park is Jim's pride, and he could describe its manifold beauties in effective and glowing terms. The Peak is a subject more difficult to handle, but nothing could be more interesting than the mere geography of Long's Peak by one who understands it so perfectly. We hope Mr. Nugend will write this book.[24]

A week later, on October 17, the *Boulder County News* picked up the news of Jim's book: "James Nugent, otherwise known as Mountain Jim, is talking of writing a book. Jim has, under a rough crust, no mean abilities, coupled with a heart that beats about right, and if he writes a book we predict it will not be tedious and unreadable."[25]

No "account," much less a book, was forthcoming. Nor, Isabella Bird's assertion to the contrary, is there evidence that *any* of Jim's compositions made their way into print. In this case the reason may have been the fact that Jim had not actually made the climb he promised to write about. But it may also have had to do with his preoccupation with yet another and, as it turned out, even more intriguing, female visitor. Anna Dickinson left Estes Park on the morning of September 14. Less than three weeks later her place around the Evans fireplace was taken by Isabella Bird.

She was, by any standard, a remarkable woman. The daughter of a clergyman, Isabella Bird was an adventuresome, free-spirited soul, who

Figure 4.1. Isabella Bird in her later years. Courtesy Denver Public Library, Western History Department.

enjoyed the physical life of camp and saddle as well as any man (qualities that made her a decided anomaly among her Victorian contemporaries). She was also a most unlikely candidate for strenuous travel. Frail and weak from the time she was four, at age forty-two Isabella Bird suffered from nervous tension (or "nervous debility" as they then called it), insomnia, headaches, depression, and a chronic back pain, for which she was forced to wear a brace. It was, in fact, the search for improved health that brought her to Colorado by way of the Sandwich Islands, having set out from home in July of 1872 at her doctor's suggestion on a journey of recuperation.

The trip itself, even to the point of finding Estes Park, had not been easy. But once arrived and settled at the Evans ranch, Isabella Bird embraced the world of the mountains with gusto. Though the golden fall weather was turning to winter and she would soon find herself snowed in, Bird made the most of her experiences. Her stay in Estes Park would last a little more than two months—punctuated by an arduous six-hundred-mile, month-long trip by horseback to Denver, Colorado Springs, South Park, and the mining towns along Clear Creek. She hurried back to the Evans ranch because she was homesick.

Rocky Mountain Jim presented a paradox: here was a man of grace, culture, and wit living the solitary life of a hunter-trapper. His literary talents, for all Platt Rogers's obvious contempt, struck her as genuine. Bird enjoyed Jim's songs and recitations and felt strongly enough about "the taste and acumen of his criticism" to take him her essay "The Ascent of Long's Peak," which she had promised to J. E. Liller of Colorado Springs for his monthly magazine, *Out West*. ("He made excellent criticism on the style," she told Henrietta, "and pointed out repetitions of the same words."[26]) To encourage Jim's own writing, Bird presented him with "a very nice Russian leather diary."

In this "strikingly handsome" and "fascinating" man, with his "low musical voice and slight Irish brogue," Isabella Bird found a life worth unraveling and, if possible, redeeming, providing he would let anyone reach beneath his rough, well-protected persona. Isabella Bird tried. They both tried, for Jim's feelings clearly matched her own. At times, Jim's black moods frightened her; at times he simply left her puzzled. "I don't know how much of his dark ways and dark language were assumed," she wrote, "he is such a consummate actor and so strange altogether."[27] Though Bird records with surprising candor their halting attempts to reach one another, it was, finally, a challenge too great for either. Jim's hold upon her, however powerful, was plainly disturbing, for any loss of emotional control threatened her Victorian sense of order and propriety.

The original, unedited text of Bird's letter in which she describes for Henrietta her November ride with Jim through the snow to the beaver dams along Fall River is particularly revealing:

> We had not ridden more than two miles when a blinding snow quall [sic] came on and I had to turn back and he turned back a little way with me to show me the trail. Then came a terrible revelation that as soon as I had gone away [on her month-long trip to other parts of Colorado] he had discovered he was attached to me and it was killing him. It began on Longs Peak, he said. I was terrified, it made me shake all over and even cry. He is a man whom any woman might love but who no sane woman would marry. Nor did he ask me to marry him, he knew enough for that. A less ungovernable nature would never have said a word but his dark, proud, fierce soul all came out there. I believe for the moment he hated me and scorned himself though he could not even then be otherwise than a gentleman. *My heart dissolved with pity for him and his dark, lost, self-ruined life.* He is so loveable and fascinating yet so terrible. I told him I could not speak to him, I was so nervous, and he said if I would not speak to him he would not see me again, he would go and camp out on the Snowy Range till I was gone. He said such fearfully bitter things. I could not bear to think of him last night out in the snow, neither eating nor sleeping, mad, lost, wretched, hopeless. It is really terrible. For 5 minutes at the camping ground on Long [sic] Peak his manner was such that for a moment I thought this possible, but I put it away as egregious vanity unpardonable in a woman of 40 and afterwards he explained his emotion satisfactorily and never showed a trace of it again. I miss him very much. He is so charming and can talk on all subjects and has real genius. It takes peace away.[28]

Interestingly enough, Isabella Bird used only the one sentence italicized above in her published book. Even then she changed the word "heart" to "soul."

Her original letter to Henrietta of November 23 was equally explicit:

> We rode a little and then got off and sat under a tree I dare say for 2 hours. He was perfectly calm and rational and entered into the fullest explanation of his circumstances. I told him that if all circumstances on both sides had been favourable and I had loved him with my whole heart I wd. not dare to trust my happiness because of Whisky [sic]. I told him he must not be angry and I told him what I had heard of him from the first and he admitted everything. He said he would never say another word of love.[29]

Given her emotional turmoil, made more difficult by Jim's behavior, Bird could not stay. He accompanied her to the milling hamlet of St. Louis on the Big Thompson, where she caught the Greeley stage and began her journey home. As it drove away, Isabella Bird watched

"'Mountain Jim,' with his golden hair yellow in the sunshine, slowly leading the beautiful mare over the snowy plains back to Estes Park."[30]

The final chapter of Rocky Mountain Jim's story began even before Bird took her leave. On the evening of December 3, at the home of Dr. Francis Blake Hutchinson, an English physician living near the mouth of the Big Thompson Canyon, Bird was introduced to his boarder, "a very rich Englishman who had come out for the winter to hunt," a man named William Haigh. Haigh, whom Bird identifies by name in her original letters, "kindly" gave her the use of his room. It was "a dreadful night of cold"—eight degrees below zero: Haigh, "who had never slept on the floor before and thought it would be fun, never slept."[31]

Seven months later it was William Haigh, then living in Estes Park, who stood next to Griff Evans as the Welshman fired the shots that mortally wounded James Nugent. By the time Isabella Bird reworked her originally letters into book form, she was well informed of these tragic events. As a result she invented for the final pages of *A Lady's Life* a face-to-face encounter between the two men, transforming William Haigh into a "Mr. Fodder":

> When the Greeley stage-waggon [sic] came up, Mr. Fodder, whom I met at Lower Canyon, was on it. He had expressed a great wish to go to Estes Park, and to hunt with "Mountain Jim," if it would be safe to do the latter. He was now dressed in the extreme of English dandyism, and when I introduced them, he put out a small hand cased in a perfectly-fitting lemon-coloured kid glove. As the trapper stood there in his grotesque rags and odds and ends of apparel, his gentlemanliness of deportment brought into relief the innate vulgarity of a rich *parvenu*.[32]

In order to underscore the obvious irony, Bird added in a footnote to her text: "This was a truly unfortunate introduction. It was the first link in the chain of circumstances which brought about Mr. Nugent's untimely end, and it was at this person's instigation (when overcome by fear) that Evans fired the shot that proved fatal."[33]

Bird departed, and Mountain Jim trailed her horse back to Muggins Gulch to pursue his solitary life. We hear about him only twice more that year, the first in the form of a brief note in the November 14 issue of the *Boulder County News*: "Mountain Jim came down from Estes' Park last Tuesday, bringing along 300 pounds of trout, for a share of which he has our thanks. Jim never forgets a friend, nor enemy, neither."[34]

The final appearance of Rocky Mountain Jim in 1873 took place the following month, when he made his literary debut in a series of humorous newspaper articles in the *Greeley Tribune* under the running title "Mac

Smith in the Mountains." "Smith" had begun to write for the Tribune two years earlier, on August 9, 1871, with a letter to the editor, giving an account of a trip to Estes Park ending with a visit to "Evans' ranche."[35] When Smith wrote to the Tribune again on Wednesday, December 3, 1873, it was to tell about his own mountain ranch and to introduce Rocky Mountain Jim, "a prospector and hunter," who arrives "loaded with a pick and shovel, and a rifle," and asks to spend the night. Smith's Jim, who speaks in the vernacular of the frontier, is plainly intended to be a comic figure. He wore

> buckskin clothes, the seams of which were ornamented with fringe of the same material; his beard had not been trimmed for years, and his long hair was braided in many little tags. His eyes were blue and clear, and he had every appearance of being kind-hearted, as is the case with most of the old mountaineers. . . . After he had eaten, he said, in answer to questions by my wife and girls, that he lived on one of the little parks near Long's Peak, and that for more than ten years he had been prospecting around this great mountain, from Middle Park back to the head waters of the St. Vrain. He had sunk many prospect holes, but none of them amounted to anything, and that the gold he did get came from washings in the vicinity of Gold Hill, on a branch of the Boulder. He [words missing] in early days, from the Indians, and he had fought with bears. Of course he had scars and old wounds to show.[36]

In subsequent letters Jim settles in at Smith's ranch, agreeing to do the "milking and hunting."

Not all of the Tribune's readers were impressed. One of them, C. E. Cline, writing to the editor from Marion, Illinois, on December 23, 1873, objected to the portrait:

> "MacSmith [sic] in the Mountains" is good, only he makes "Mountain Jim" use language such as Jim never uses. I have known Jim in the mountains. I once found him there, nearly dead, and was with him a number of times after that; and he is a man of some education. I think he uses quite as good English as Mac displays. "Heard on it," "larned," "scrouger," "seed," etc., never came from Jim, they had their origin in Mac's brain, unquestionably.[37]

Smith responded to Cline's complaint, somewhat lamely, in the same issue: "Mr. Mac Smith sends word that his is another Rocky Mountain Jim, not the one living on the borders of Estes Park. The mountains overflow with Rocky Mountain Jims, Sams, Bills and Jakes, and some of them are certainly men of intelligence, who long ago left home and friends, to forget some great sorrow."[38]

Smith's columns, numbering more than twenty, continued to appear regularly until May 27, 1874, the very eve of Jim's shooting. We then hear no more from Mac Smith until December 3, 1874, when he reappears in the *Tribune* with a new hero, "Chickasaw Bob." Noting that Jim "got shot," Smith's column begins, "The death of Rocky Mountain Jim was a great loss to me, because he generally came around when I needed help. . . ."[39]

The late winter and early spring of 1874 were busy ones in Estes Park. In January, using Theodore Whyte and probably others, Dunraven moved ahead with plans to control the valley by having the land surveyed and platted. How much James Nugent knew of what was taking place below Muggins Gulch we do not know. But what Jim did know—particularly about the incursion of English (and Irish) men and their money and the threat they posed to both his livelihood and his land—he did not like.

If Jim's relationship with Griff Evans had ever been on a good footing, it had degenerated over the past year. Platt Rogers, in remembering his trip up Longs Peak with Isabella Bird, observed that "the only guides to the peak in those days were Griff and Jim and each held in contempt and derision the trail used by the other in making the ascent."[40] What Rogers observed may have been only professional jealousy. But Bird sensed something deeper and more sinister.

Given the events soon to transpire, it is tempting to regard the following sentences from *A Lady's Life in the Rocky Mountains* as Bird's penultimate statement on the relationship between the two: "He hates Evans with a bitter hatred, and Evans returns it, having undergone much provocation from Jim in his moods of lawlessness and violence, and being not a little envious of the fascination which his manners and conversation have for the strangers who come up here."[41] Her suggestion that Evans resented Jim's increasing notoriety rings true, for, as Rogers observed, the two were in direct competition as Longs Peak guides. But it also must be remembered that Bird's letters first appeared in print four years *after* the shooting had taken place, and by then their author had a personal stake in understanding and explaining not only what happened but why.

A better guide to the state of relations between Evans and Jim in the days immediately before her departure are her original unedited (and hence unvarnished) letters home to Henrietta. Here one does, in fact, find confirmation that tensions between Jim and his world had increased. In her letter of November 21, for example, she notes that Nugent "has never come here armed before and yesterday he had 2 revolvers in his belt."[42] On December 1 she passes on, without comment, the remark of the "usually reticent" miner Cavanaugh: "What's wrong with that man! He'll shoot himself or somebody else."[43] Bird was equally explicit in her original letters about Evans's behavior: "Evans is simply killing himself by hard drinking. I have told him so over and over again and he admits [sic] it, but seems driven to it by his lavish social genial nature. No doctor can do him any good unless he gives it up and I don't think he will live two years anyhow."[44]

Just when William Haigh moved up from the Big Thompson Valley and took up residence in the small one-room cabin at Evans's ranch previously occupied by Isabella Bird is uncertain. It was later reported that Haigh had been interested in buying property "in the vicinity of Estes Park" and had hired and then fired Jim as a guide, having found the mountaineer "dissipated and worthless."[45] If true, this would account for Haigh's presence. So would the explanation originally provided by Bird herself (and subsequently confirmed by Dunraven's physician, George Henry Kingsley) that Haigh "had come out for the winter to hunt," an activity that might well have brought him, as it brought so many others, to Estes Park.

Whatever the reason, once Haigh arrived affairs between Evans and Nugent and Haigh and Nugent apparently worsened. The climax came on Monday, June 29, 1874, as Nugent, in company with a man known as William Brown, leisurely rode up along Fish Creek toward the Evans ranch, coming from McLaughlin's where Brown had been staying. They were heading for Muggins Gulch over Park Hill. As Abner Sprague later told the story—a story that he said William Brown told him only "three or four days after it occurred":

> There was no bridge over Fish Creek, the crossing being a ford. The Evans house and the one occupied by Hague were about a hundred yards beyond the crossing, and only about one-third that distance from the road where it made a right angle turn to pass the building. The horses stopped at the ford to drink; Jim's horse only took a swallow or two, then started on ahead. Jim was nearly to the turn of the road in front of the buildings, when Brown followed. Just as Jim turned to pass along the road, Brown saw Hague and Evans come out of the little cabin occupied by Hague, Evans with a double-barreled shot gun in his hands, and Hague urging Evans to shoot. . . . Evans threw up the gun and fired, missing both Jim and his horse. Being urged to shoot again, he fired the other barrel and Jim fell from his horse.[46]

On this sequence of events there is more or less agreement. What is far from clear is the immediate motive or motives for the deed itself. Any number of explanations, each plausible enough in its own way, have been put forth over the years. Isabella Bird later said that she herself received five.[47] According to the Larimer County historian, Ansel Watrous, in a story never corroborated, Jim had fired on Evans some days before and missed.[48] Both Evans and Haigh would later maintain in court that Nugent had threatened them. Jim, Haigh said, had "punched him in the face and eyes with a rifle at full cock, and had used every endeavor to drive him from the Park."[49] Evans claimed that Jim held a grudge against him and that he had so "annoyed" Evans and his family "that it was dangerous for them to travel back and forth." "Several times during the past month," it was reported, Jim had taken "particular delight in coming up to Evans' house during his absence and making threats on his life."[50] On these later occasions, it was later sworn to, Mountain Jim had taken to "the habit of . . . rushing into Mr. Evans' house brandishing a cocked revolver, and insulting everybody present. He would call them all the names he could lay his tongue to, not sparing the ladies, whom he kept in constant terror."[51]

Other motives and provocations were offered as well. According to Abner Sprague, Haigh and Jim had had a falling-out and a heated exchange of words (which ended with Jim poking Haigh off his horse with the muzzle of his cocked rifle and forcing him "to take back what he had said") over Jim's refusal to procure a female companion for the Englishman after having been paid by Haigh to do so.[52] The Earl of Dunraven and Platt Rogers both repeated the story that Jim had made advances to Evans's seventeen-year-old daughter, Jennie.[53] The Reverend Elkanah J. Lamb, who had little use for "English snobs and aristocrats," believed that Jim's death resulted from his opposition to the plan by Dunraven and his allies to take over the park and from their attempt to get rid of a nuisance whose cabin in Muggins Gulch strategically straddled the only way in and out.[54]

This final explanation is the one offered to the press by Mountain Jim himself, as he lay "enfeebled" in Fort Collins awaiting examination by the grand jury.[55] "Rocky Mountain Jim, who was shot some time since by a person considered a creature of the Earl of Dunraven," the *Pueblo Daily Chieftain* (echoing a charge made a week earlier in Greeley's *Colorado Sun*) reported, "declares that the nobleman's in question recent so called purchase of Estes park, was a fraudulent transaction, and that he was ordered by him to be shot for the purpose of getting him out of the way."[56]

Evans was either a poor shot, had been drinking, or both, or he deliberately shot to miss. Jim was apparently so taken by surprise that he made no attempt to move his rifle from across the saddle in front of him. Clearly, he was in no position to do so. As Dr. Kingsley later pointed out, lacking vision in his right eye, Jim could only shoot from his left shoulder, a difficult thing to do, especially when on horseback using a military rifle with its hammer on the right side—a complication that later, when the issue had moved into court, seemingly occurred to no one.[57] The second load of buckshot fired by Evans did the damage. It glanced off the wheel, or some other iron part, of an old broken-down wagon that stood by the side of the road behind Jim. Its ricochet caught Jim in the back of the head below the brain, several pieces of metal penetrating the skull and, as it turned out, the brain. Jim would later insist implausibly, given the nature of his wounds, that the second shot was fired as he lay on the ground.[58]

Dr. Kingsley had been in the park with the Earl of Dunraven for about a week. That day, out bear hunting "in one of the wildest lateral branches of Estes Park," he heard "fearful yelling and howlings" coming from the vicinity of the Evans ranch. Kingsley found Jim prostrate but quiet ("as plucky as any man I ever saw in trouble"), stretched out under a grove of silver-stemmed aspens with five small bullet wounds in his head and face. All the bullets (large, round shot called "blue whistlers"), Kingsley noted, had "gone through," except for one that was embedded in the bony process under the left ear and one that, it would turn out, had passed into the brain. Another had gone right through the bones of the nose, splintering them at its entrance and exit. A sixth bullet, Kingsley discovered a few days later, had passed cleanly through the biceps of Jim's left arm.[59]

Carrying Jim to a nearby hut, Kingsley dressed Jim's wounds as best he could. Not finding the shot that had entered Nugent's brain, thereby misdiagnosing the severity of the wound, Kingsley pronounced that Jim would be up and around in a few days. Prognosis of an early recovery apparently scared Evans and Haigh (both of whom Jim had by now threatened to kill just as soon as he was able). Evans mounted a horse and rode down to Burlington, a small community south of Longmont on the St. Vrain, where he obtained the services of the lawyer John H. Wells. The two men then proceeded to Big Thompson, a stage stop on the river, where Evans gave himself up. He was promptly bound over to the district court, with bail set at one thousand dollars.

In the summer of 1874, Fort Collins, the Larimer County seat, to which the final events of Rocky Mountain Jim's life now moved, was a treeless, dusty town of four hundred, in which goats, hogs, and pigs ran freely in the streets. To the extent that there was other news during the weeks and months that followed, it focused on the fortunes of the local baseball club, the Standards, Collins's "annual attack of railroad fever" (a report that a new line would be built from Longmont through Fort Collins to Cheyenne), and the town's attempt to raise a thousand dollars to fund its share of a new agricultural college by holding a "Floral Festival to the Goddess Flora" at the Masonic Hall on July 4. There was also a well-founded concern about the appearance of grasshoppers on the upper Thompson, "doing great damage to the crops."

By the time Jim arrived in Fort Collins by way of Burlington after several weeks of convalescence in Estes Park, the territorial newspapers had begun to circulate news that Mountain Jim had rallied and would recover.[60] In the words of the *Boulder County News*, "Nothing short of a nitro-glycerine explosion will ever kill Jim."[61] Nugent took up residence at the seventeen-room, three-story Collins House on Jefferson Street. For several weeks he was out and about the streets and, though he appeared feeble, "apparently was getting well."[62]

On July 15, 1874, the district court convened in the Grout Building. District Attorney Byron L. Carr, of Longmont, filed an information with the clerk, charging Evans with assault with intent to kill. He entered a similar accusation against Nugent. Jim himself swore out a warrant against William Haigh as an accessory to the shooting. As a result of this hearing, in which the judge instructed the jury to pay attention only to capital crimes, "Griffith J. Evans was held to bail in the sum of $2500 on the charge of assaulting James Nugent (Rocky Mountain Jim) with a deadly weapon, to await the result of injuries inflicted."[63] Haigh was released without bond or penalty. The press would later complain that Jim's two warrants "cost the county $500."[64]

Nugent also began to tell his side of the story. Initially, at least, what he had to say seemed to sway public opinion. "James Nugent, or as he is more familiarly known, 'Rocky Mountain Jim,' is in town," the *Fort Collins Standard* reported on August 12. "He tells a very different story of his little unpleasantness up in Estes' Park to that published in the territorial papers, and says he will establish its veracity in the courts."[65] The same issue of the *Standard* carried a lengthy letter by Jim, published with the title "Rocky Mountain Jim's Story." Referring to himself as "a law-abiding American citizen," this letter, written in a polished, educated style, set forth the thesis that he was the innocent victim of a "hell-born plot to deprive a man of his life."[66] He also complained that Carr had sought his indictment "without even coming to see me" and "without hearing my story."[67]

By the time Haigh's trial on the warrant sworn by Nugent took place on Saturday, August 29, whatever public sentiment had existed on behalf of Mountain Jim had largely shifted. Presumably William Brown, Henry Farrar, and Dexter Smith all appeared as witnesses for Jim, for they had registered at the Collins House on the previous Monday for that purpose.[68] Nugent himself, however, was noticeably absent. During the past week his condition had deteriorated rapidly. Visitors found Jim's "manner and style" changed—his eagerness to talk had given way to "melancholia" (the nineteenth-century term for depression). On the day of the Haigh trial Rocky Mountain Jim was in fact lying comatose, or nearly so, in his bed at the Collins House under the continuous care of physicians.[69]

William Haigh's own hour had come. The Englishman was talking, and with good effect, as far as his own reputation and the reputation of Griff Evans were concerned. Even before his trial began, the Fort Collins Standard had reprinted a piece from the Denver Tribune in which the editor, on the basis of a face-to-face meeting and Haigh's "detailed version of his difficulties in Estes' Park with Mountain Jim," had decided that "Mr. Haigh himself was the party chiefly abused." Between Evans and Nugent the editor would not take sides. But, he concluded, "we know Mr. Haigh to be all that he assumes—a traveling English gentleman of wealth and leisure, and the last person in the world to seek or create unnecessary trouble." The Tribune hoped that "his annoyances may not disgust him with our territory, as he belongs to a class of men that are an honor to any community, even though they be devoid of the rank and wealth that Mr. Haigh enjoys."[70]

To the surprise of no one, Haigh's trial, before Justice of the Peace Howe, resulted in the discharge of the defendant. "The only ground of complaint against Mr. Haigh," the Standard reported the following Wednesday,

was that when Mr. Evans had shot Jim the first time he (Mr. Haigh) said, "Give him the other barrel." His reason for desiring Evans to give Jim the benefit of the other barrel were very good, inasmuch as Jim had threatened his life on divers occasions, and at one time punched him in the face and eyes with a rifle at full cock, and had used every endeavor to drive him from the Park. It was but natural that Mr. Haigh should be of the opinion that the other barrel would be a benefit, if not to Jim, to the rest of the community, and on the impulse of the moment gave the good advice to Evans, which that gentleman says he did not hear. In fact there was only one witness out of the five or six present who did hear the remark of Mr. Haigh.

It appears that Mountain Jim was in the habit of frequently rushing into Mr. Evans' house brandishing a cocked revolver, and insulting everybody present. He would call them all the names he could lay his tongue to, not sparing the ladies, whom he kept in constant terror. Mr. Evans very naturally got tired of this kind of business, and concluded to put a stop to it, which he did in a very effectual manner. Besides all this, Jim made several threats to kill both Evans and Haigh, and either of them were justified in shooting him on sight in self-defense.[71]

Judge Howe, in delivering his decision, left little doubt where his own sympathies lay. He

> said that had he been placed in a position as perilous as that in which Mr. Haigh had been, he should, himself, have used language similar to that attributed to the defendant, but not proven. Mr. Haigh was fully released from all legal responsibility in the matter, while Mr. Evans is under bonds to await the results of the wounded man's injuries. The decision in the case seemed to meet the approval of the people of Ft. Collins and others who attended the legal investigation.[72]

Nine days later, about 3 o'clock in the afternoon of Monday, September 7, 1874, Mountain Jim died. A coroner's jury of six was quickly impaneled and a postmortem examination held to determine the exact cause of Jim's death. The autopsy was performed by a trio of local physicians, led by Dr. James Stratton Harlow, who had treated Jim during his final days, Dr. L. T. Glenn, and Dr. George P. Taylor. Harlow, who seems not to have been impressed by the notoriety of his patient (for his surviving diary mentions Jim not at all),[73] later testified at the coroner's hearing that, at the time of his arrival in Fort Collins, Jim's wounds, which were two in number, "were entirely healed" and that there was no evidence that anything "had entered the cavity of the skull." The autopsy proved otherwise, offering an unmistakable explanation for both Jim's recent behavior and the cause of his death. Once the skull was removed, it was not only clear that there was a fracture "corresponding with the wound at the back of the head," but that the brain itself had become inflamed. Further examination revealed a large piece of lead that "had completely softened and broken down . . . the brain in that vicinity." This evidence, the report concluded, was "sufficient to satisfy the Coroner, or any other man, as to the cause of his death, and the only wonder is that he lived as long as he did."[74]

There, on September 12, 1874, the matter ended. James Nugent was promptly buried in an unmarked grave in Fort Collins, now long forgotten. Griff Evans was brought down from Estes Park on a coroner's warrant for trial before Justice of the Peace John E. Washburn of Big Thompson and just as promptly "discharged on the grounds of justifiable homicide."[75] Except for the inevitable tidying up, the "Mountain Jim Affair," as it had become known, was over. Nugent, it appears, had already disposed of his squatter's claim in Muggins Gulch on May 7, 1873, to one William H. Cushman for one thousand dollars.[76] His horse, "Tex," "said to be one of the best trained horses in the west," which had been displayed in Fort Collins shortly before Jim's death, was given to Carrie Moore, the infant daughter of one of the owners of the Collins House. Nugent's twenty head of cattle up in Estes Park went to Frank D. Morrison, the barber who shaved him.[77] The bill for burial came to ten dollars.[78]

In its final commentary upon the whole affair, the Fort Collins Standard tried to lay to rest the "discussion throughout the Territory as to whether Evans was justified in shooting him or not." Whatever sympathy there might have been for James Nugent, the facts of the case argued differently:

> Those who heard the trial of Mr. Haigh are satisfied that the shooting was justifiable, but others who have a faculty of seeing corruption and fraud in every act of a man who happens to hold an office of trust, assert that Mountain Jim was terribly abused, couldn't get justice because he was poor, and all that sort of thing. Now, we believe that Mr. Haigh had a fair and impartial trial, and that had he been a pauper he would have been discharged. Those who are trying to create sympathy for Jim, either did not attend the trial, and are ignorant of the facts in the case, or do so maliciously.
>
> We have the evidence as it was adduced in court, and as it is too long for publication it will be shown to any person who takes enough interest in the affair to read it. We are sure that to any unprejudiced, fair-minded man, the decision of the court will appear just, when he has read the evidence in the case. If Mountain Jim had confined his abuse to Evans and Haigh alone, we might have a little sympathy for him, but when a man's family is insulted as was that of Mr. Evans, he can hardly be blamed for not sitting down and figuring out the probable expense to the county before taking some action.[79]

This hardening of public opinion reduced James Nugent to a figure who drank whiskey to excess and thereby "made himself very obnoxious" to friend and enemy alike. The appearance of Isabella Bird's A Lady's Life in the Rocky Mountains simply finished the process of Jim's "apotheosis." By turning a colorful and eccentric human being into a cardboard stereotype conforming to popular imagination, she created a figure easy enough to understand and just as easy to dismiss. In the final analysis, Abner Sprague was undoubtedly correct: "Only for the way he 'strung' Miss Bird ["with his tale of woe"], to which she gives considerable space in her book, and his tragic ending, he would have been forgotten long ago. . . ." The "only thing proven," Sprague concluded, "was Jim's bad character and record, together with his many threats when drunk, which was the only time he was a bad man as nearly as I have been able to find out."[80]

Intriguing stories often have intriguing epilogues. The story of James

Nugent and Isabella Bird is no exception. Bird's attachment to Jim did not end with her departure from Colorado. They corresponded for some months, and as spring turned to summer and then to fall, others kept her abreast of events in Colorado.

The years that followed proved difficult for Isabella Bird. Her beloved sister Henrietta ("Hennie," as she called her) died of typhoid in early June of 1880. Nine months later, on March 8, 1881, at the age of fifty Isabella married her sister's physician, Dr. John Bishop, a man ten years her junior. Bishop was devoted to Isabella (he had proposed as early as 1877), and their marriage, however missing in ardor, was a calming and tranquil one. But Bishop's health soon declined, and, following a lengthy and debilitating series of illnesses, he died on March 6, 1886, two days short of their fifth anniversary. Bird's biographers agree that her response was one of overwhelming grief and despondency, to "the verge of total emotional collapse."[81]

Two months later, in May of 1886, without warning, the editor of the Fort Collins Express received a letter from a man named C. Burke, dated April 16, 1886, bearing the address 21 Dewhurst Road, Brook Green, West, London. Burke made a very specific request:

> Sir:—The society mentioned in the enclosed circular is desirous of obtaining for literary purposes, a newspaper account with full dates, of the *death* of "Mountain Jim," who was shot at Fort Collins in September, 1874. I believe he was not killed instantaneously, but it is the date of his *actual death* which is important to us. I am instructed to say that the society will be glad to give a sovereign (£1) for a copy [printed] of the newspaper containing the account, or for a written copy of the account certified to as correct by some responsible witness, say yourself as editor of the Fort Collins Express. If any of your employees would hunt the matter up, I should be glad. If not, will you kindly insert the appended advertisement in your paper. The matter is very pressing, and I am hoping to get a reply by return mail. Therefore, if any of your staff would help us, it would be the preferable way. If you find it necessary to advertise, please do so at once, and let me know, and I will remit the cost of two insertions.
>
> Your kind assistance will be esteemed a favor, and your prompt and speedy help will forward a question of literary research.
>
> Awaiting the favor of your reply at your earliest convenience, I am sir.
>
> Yours Obediently,
> C. Burke[82]

Just what was this matter of "literary research," a matter so "very pressing" that Burke asked for "speedy help" and a response by return mail? The circular enclosed with his letter suggested the beginnings of an answer. It described the work of the Society for Psychical Research, an organization founded in 1882 by a group of scientists and philosophers connected with Trinity College, Cambridge. Its purpose, in the language of the circular, was to examine that "important body of remarkable phenomena which are *prima facie* inexplicable in any generally recognized hypothesis," including "any reports, resting on strong testimony, of apparitions occurring at the moment of death or otherwise." His interest aroused, the editor of the *Express* not only consulted three of Fort Collins's "old timers"[83] but paid a visit to the county clerk's office to inspect the records.

In its issue of Friday, May 8, the *Courier Express* published Burke's letter in its entirety, together with an excerpt from the society's circular and a short account of Rocky Mountain Jim's life and death. "In 1874, when Colorado was yet a territory and Fort Collins was still in its swaddling clothes," the account began, using the language of fairy tale and legend, "there lived in Estes Park James Nugent, better known as 'Mountain Jim,' a professional hunter, trapper and mountain guide. He was the typical 'leather legs' of earlier days. . . ." It was fairly easy to conjure up a reason for Burke's letter, and the editor did so in the headline of his front page story: "The Death of 'Mountain Jim'—Has His Ghost Arisen in England?" "It is thought," he concluded, "that something has lately occurred in the psycho-spiritualistic circles of London that has caused this inquiry for proof to be made by the society." There was a follow-up story a week later, indicating that "the article in last week's *Express* on the death of 'Mountain Jim' has aroused much interest in the event which many remember, and reminiscences are rife."[84] But there, as far as the people of Fort Collins were concerned, the matter rested.

The reason for the society's interest was soon clear enough. That same year three of its members, Edmund Gurney, Frederic W. H. Myers, and Frank Podmore, produced *Phantasms of the Living*, a two-volume collection of more than three hundred cases of reported incidents of telepathic communication. Case 197, in which "a visual phantasm first appears, and then words are heard which, in the mind of both agent and percipient, were probably of all others the most significant of the bond between them,"[85] involved Isabella Bird and James Nugent.

Though the society had received a secondhand version of the case in March 1883 from a source that it chose not to identify, the request for a formal inquiry had come directly from Isabella Bird herself. Within days of the death of Dr. John Bishop in March of 1886, Isabella had written the society from abroad, in an emotional state described as one of "very great pressure,"[86] submitting the details of an event that had taken place almost a dozen years before:

> On the day in which I parted with Mountain Jim, he was much moved and much excited. I had a long conversation with him about mortal life and immortality, and closed it with some words from the Bible. He was greatly impressed, but very excited, and exclaimed, "I may not see you again in this life, but I shall when I die." I rebuked him gently for his vehemence, but he repeated it with still greater energy, adding, "And these words you have said to me, I shall never forget, and dying I swear that I will see you again."
>
> We parted then, and for a time I heard that he was doing better, then that he had relapsed into wild ways, then that he was very ill after being wounded in a wild quarrel, then lastly that he was well, and planning revenge. The last news I got when I was at the Hotel Interlaken, Interlaken, Switzerland, with Miss Clayton and the Kers. Shortly after getting it, in September, 1874, I was lying on my bed about 6 A.M., writing to my sister, when, looking up, I saw Mountain Jim standing with his eyes fixed on me, and when I looked at him he very slowly but very distinctly said, "I have come, as I promised"; then waved his hands towards me, and said, "Farewell."
>
> When Miss Bessie Ker came into the room with my breakfast, we recorded the event, with the date and hour of its occurrence. In due time news arrived of his death, and its date, allowing for the difference of longitude, coincided with that of his appearance to me.[87]

As with other cases reported to it, the society accepted Isabella Bird's account with great seriousness and proceeded to mount as thorough an investigation as distance and circumstance would permit. That Isabella Bird believed that she had been visited by Rocky Mountain Jim or his apparition was beyond dispute. The question to be resolved was whether or not the visitation appeared at the precise moment of Jim's death. The society's first steps were to have Mr. Burke write to Fort Collins and to forward a series of questions to Isabella. Her responses were both prompt and emphatic: "Mrs. Bishop says that she has never had any other hallucination of the senses; that she had last seen Mountain Jim at St. Louis, Colorado, on December 11th, 1873; and that he died at Fort Collins, Colorado."[88]

Two other valuable pieces of evidence were also ultimately obtained: Bessie Ker's diary for the night of September 5–6, 1874, and the letter that Isabella had written to her sister Henrietta a few days later. Miss Ker's entry is brief and to the point: "On this night Isabella saw Jim vividly appear as if dead."[89] Isabella's letter to Hennie is a bit more expansive:

> Hotel Interlaken, Wednesday. A few days ago, about seven in the morning, I had lain down again after drawing up my blind to let in the beautiful view of the

rose-flushed morning, when I saw an appearance of Mountain Jim, looking just as he did when last I saw him. There was an impression on my mind as though he said: "I have come as I promised. Farewell." It was curious, and if I had not heard that he was getting well and going about, I should have thought he was dead.[90]

The letter to Henrietta, though it contained no date, was judged particularly important, for unlike "an entry in a diary, which sometimes allows of the hypothesis that it was written later than the day under which it figures,"[91] it left no doubt "as to the record of the hallucination having been written and sent away before the news of the death arrived."[92] Equally significant was the information received from Fort Collins and Mountain Jim's inquest indicating "that the death took place on Sept. 7, 1874, between 2 and 3 P.M."[93]

The conclusion reached by the authors of *Phantasm of the Living*, which was reinforced the next year by an article in the *Proceedings* of the American Society for Psychical Research, was that Jim's appearance before Isabella Bird at Interlaken had not coincided with the moment of his death. In a verdict that by no means discounted the reality of the experience itself the society concluded that the case "if telepathic, is one in which the telepathic impulse coincided not with death, but with a time of exceptional danger and probable excitement on the side of the agent."[94]

Isabella Bird, we are told by her best modern biographer, was not, as she herself had insisted, "in the least subject to visions."[95] Yet it is clear that her request to the Society for Psychical Research came precisely at a time when she was in the throes of a deep emotional crisis. For the first time, the seemingly self-reliant and intrepid Isabella Bird found herself without the support of any of the three individuals who had given her life direction and meaning: Bishop, Henrietta, and Rocky Mountain Jim. If her vision at Interlaken, and the subsequent attempt to seek its verification, suggest nothing more, they suggest just how powerful a hold Mountain Jim continued to exert upon the imagination and emotions of Isabella Bird. How fitting, yet how ironic, given the legacy she bestowed upon him, that this sturdy Victorian world traveler who had bravely adventured to the Sandwich Islands, Japan, Persia, Korea, China, and Morocco, should, at the time of her greatest instability and loss, seek support from her strong-shouldered, golden-haired Colorado "desperado."[96]

Chapter 5

The Pioneers of '75

By summer of 1874 the Earl of Dunraven and Theodore Whyte had secured most of Estes Park. But they did not have all of it. To Whyte's chagrin, they had overlooked well-watered land in Black Canyon, Willow (Moraine) Park, and Beaver Meadows, out along Wind River, and in the valley at the base of Longs Peak. They had also misfiled on certain pieces. Others quickly seized upon this opportunity to make the park their home. They included Alexander MacGregor, William James, Horace Ferguson, Abner Sprague, Elkanah Lamb, and John Hupp, all of whom came with families, as well as the celebrated hunters Hank Farrar and Israel Rowe, and a young German named George Bode. Though relatively few in number, the impact of these early settlers upon the future development of the park was substantial. Intent on "honest settlement," as Abner Sprague put it, these "pioneers of '75" stuck it out through "all the petty annoyances put upon them by the management of the English Co. to drive them out."[1] With the exception of John Hupp and George Bode, they also discovered at an early date that the way to earn a living in Estes Park was by serving the needs of tourists and other visitors.

The first to arrive was Alexander Quiner MacGregor (1846–1896), who together with his wife, Clara (1852–1901), established a 160-acre claim in the Black Canyon in late 1873 or early 1874. Though both were natives of Wisconsin and were married there in 1873, Alex and Clara apparently had met in the West during the summer of 1872, when she had come to Colorado on a sketching trip organized by Henry Crawford Ford, founder of the Chicago Academy of Design. That trip took her to Colorado Springs and South Park. Somewhere between there and Estes Park, where Clara also spent time sketching and painting, she met twenty-six-year-old Alex MacGregor.

MacGregor was an ambitious and tough-minded man. Raised in Milwaukee by a widow (his father had drowned four months before his birth), Alex MacGregor developed a strong work ethic at an early age. A newsboy by the age of eight, he entered the office of the *Daily Evening Wisconsin* in Milwaukee at age fourteen, where he learned the trade of job printer. In 1867 he founded *La Belle Mirror* at Oconomowoc, Wisconsin, which he published until August of 1870. Arriving in Denver in late 1870 or early 1871, MacGregor was appointed clerk for the probate judge of Arapahoe County and shortly thereafter began to study law with Judge Henry P. H. Bromwell. He was admitted to the bar in 1872 and a year later formed a legal partnership with Judge Westbrook S. Decker, which lasted until the MacGregors moved to Estes Park.[2]

Alexander MacGregor had first visited Estes Park on a camping trip in 1872, and, given the fact that his homestead predated the government survey, he must have initially taken up what amounted to a

Figure 5.1. Alexander Quiner MacGregor, c. 1872. Courtesy MacGregor Trust.

Figure 5.2. Clara Heeney MacGregor, c. 1870. Courtesy National Park Service—Rocky Mountain National Park.

squatter's claim.[3] The spot selected was nearly idyllic: a low, sloping hillside above Black Canyon Creek facing Longs Peak. Georgianna Heeney, Clara's mother, soon joined them in the Black Canyon, entering on October 5, 1875, a preemption claim of her own on adjacent land and building a log cabin in a wooded section east of the creek.[4] Through astute use of preemption and homestead claims and equally shrewd acquisitions, the MacGregors would eventually acquire within their lifetimes a substantial amount of additional land.[5] By the time of the death of their granddaughter, Muriel, in 1970, MacGregor Ranch holdings had reached 2,931 acres and a value of 4.25 million dollars.

Correctly foreseeing that the physical beauty and location of the park would inevitably attract both tourists and settlers, the entrepreneurial MacGregor deferred completion of his claim cabin and turned his attention to building a wagon road. On September 11, 1874, taking advantage of legislation that allowed private citizens to build and operate toll roads, MacGregor, together with Georgianna Heeney and Marshall Bradford, filed papers of incorporation for the Park Road Company,

> to commence on the Northwesterly banks of the St. Vrain Creek in Boulder County . . . thence running Northwesterly through Timber Gulch . . . to the Little Thompson Creek thence up the said Little Thompson Creek and through Elk and Moose Parks to the source of the branch . . . upon which Mountain Jims Ranche is situated[.] Thence in a Northwesterly direction and down the gulch which heads on the opposite side of the Divide between the Little and Big Thompson Creek and heads near the head of the said branch of the Little Thompson Creek aforesaid to the Easterly side of the Big Thompson Creek in Estes Park. . . .[6]

As affirmation of the future, as well as of the business sense of her son-in-law, Mrs. Heeney put ten thousand dollars of her own capital into the project. Work on the road began at once and continued into the next year, with MacGregor settling his wife and his mother-in-law in Denver for the winter so that he could personally supervise the road crew of nearly a dozen men. The road, which terminated at the MacGregor Ranch, was completed and opened at noon on July 28, 1875. Initially the toll was collected near its eastern end, near where the road entered the foothills; later the toll gate was relocated in the vicinity of what is now Pinewood Springs (then Little Elk Park). The charge was $1.00 a team each way, with a negotiated rate of $.50 to $.60 for frequent users. During the road's first three days of business $31.95 in tolls were collected (a total reduced to $7.00 by the time MacGregor paid his workers and tollkeeper).[7] For a period of years MacGregor also conducted a freight business over the road, using a pair of big mules named "Dutch" and "Honesty."

MacGregor employed as assistant foreman Israel Rowe (1844–1884), who would be remembered as a hunter and guide and as the discoverer of Gem Lake and Rowe Glacier.[8] Rowe's wife, Harriet, accompanied him as the road camp moved westward into the mountains, cooking food for the crew over an open fire while taking care of their two small children, Charles Judson and Dora. After the completion of the road, the Rowes (or Rows, as the name is often spelled) moved into a log cabin in Black Canyon and then to a site on the hill in front of what is now the Stanley Hotel.[9] It was during this period that Rowe earned his reputation as a hunter, transporting the game he shot to Longmont and Denver where the meat could be sold or exchanged for

Figures 5.3 and 5.4. Scenes on the MacGregor Toll Road. Courtesy MacGregor Trust.

flour and other necessities. For several years the Rowes also homesteaded at the foot of Mount Olympus, where in 1877 they built a third cabin on what later became the Crocker Ranch, gradually transforming the place into a ranch with a large herd of cattle.[10]

MacGregor completed his pole-and-bough-roofed homestead cabin with the help of Hank Farrar on February 26, 1875, after nine days of work. That May, with work on the toll road nearing completion, he brought Clara, who had given birth to their first son, George, on January 22, 1875, up to Estes Park. MacGregor then turned his attention to completing the infrastructure for a ranching operation. By 1876 he had not only constructed a series of log buildings that included a milk house, meat house, and ice house, but had put in a water-powered sawmill. By collecting water in a penstock above Black Canyon Creek, from where it was allowed to drop thirty feet upon a Leffel wheel, MacGregor could produce eighteen horsepower to operate the mill. While most of the lumber and shingles produced were used on the ranch, MacGregor also sold them to others. In addition to raising cattle, MacGregor cultivated the land, growing crops of hay, wheat, barley, and oats, as well as vegetables. In the winter he harvested ice. Oats proved to be the best investment because it could be threshed on the ranch, whereas the wheat, though of excellent quality, had to be transported down to Longmont for milling. Noting during the summer of 1876 that his trout population had been decreased by "sportsmen," MacGregor began building a series of dams along Black Canyon Creek "with a view to the formation of lakes, and the establishment of an extensive trout hatchery."[11]

Beginning that same summer, on June 2, 1876, the first post office in the park was established on the MacGregor Ranch in a small cabin on the hillside north of Black Canyon Creek, with Clara serving as postmistress. This cabin eventually housed a small store where settlers and visitors could purchase flour, corn meal, sugar, salt, butter, baking powder, soda, potatoes, bacon, fat pork, tea, coffee, candles, and kerosene, all brought in over the MacGregor Toll Road from Longmont, and butter and potatoes produced locally.[12] The post office remained at the ranch until March 21, 1877. On that day, as Clara noted in her diary, "Mrs. Evans came over and presented her commission as postmaster of Estes Park and demanded the key."[13]

At an early date, the MacGregors also began to provide for the needs of tourists, for whom they constructed a series of log cabins of varying sizes and a dining hall among the trees on the hillside to the north of the creek. New cabins were being added as late as 1895. Visitors were also given permission to pitch their tents in a grove of trees across from the MacGregor house. The going rate for boarders in 1876 was $7.00 a week for room, meals, and washing; stabling a horse cost $.50 a day without feed. For those wishing to build their own cabins—like the Washington McClintock family of Denver—MacGregor was willing to provide long-term leases on his Black Canyon property.[14] By the summer of 1881, MacGregor had torn down his original ranch house and built a new one with rooms "fixed up in the latest style."[15]

One of the early visitors to the MacGregor Ranch was Carrie Adell Strahorn, who has left us a charming account of her 1878 stay with her journalist husband Robert (or "Pard," as she called him) during their fifteen-thousand-mile tour of the West. "There were many people here on pleasure bent," she recalled, "some in tents or small cottages, and some in the main home building. The refined atmosphere of the house was most attractive. . . . Mr. MacGregor had about twelve hundred acres in his ranch, from which the table was supplied with fresh vegetables, eggs, butter, cream and other tempting viands."[16] Others were just as enthusiastic. "Descending into the park," noted a correspondent for the *Boulder County News* in August 1877,

Figure 5.5. MacGregor Ranch from the south. Courtesy Denver Public Library, Western History Department.

a road to the left leads to Evans, a group of some half a dozen little houses, quite attractive from the fact that mail is deposited there Wednesday, and departs Thursday. Half a mile beyond is the new [Dunraven] hotel, a substantial building finely appointed, and furnishing its guests with an abundance of trout and trouting. . . . On the other side of the stream, two or three miles up we find McGregor's [sic], a pretty romantic spot where one can find "Rest for the weary soul," in a fine piano perfectly tuned, a guitar, violin, chest of Homeopathic medicines, arm chairs, and other luxuries of civilization. Near McGregor's, above the saw mill, are quite a field of campers. . . . The great rivalry seems to be in the matter of camp fires, each party strives to create the largest blaze. . . . The white tents and wide awnings gleam through the dark pines, and the blaze of the crackling camp fire throws into bold relief the rustic seats and picturesque groups of men, women, and children. . . .[17]

What seemed to surprise many was the obvious culture and refinement that Clara brought to her rustic environment, as evidenced not only by the "hum of the sewing machine and the silvery notes of the piano," but by the paintings adorning the walls of the MacGregor house. "A natural artist," one visitor applauded, "this lady finds in a wondrous mountain retreat much to satisfy a cultured and innate love of the sublime and the beautiful."[18] MacGregor Ranch, in short, proved to be a success, even though MacGregor himself was often an absentee landlord while he pursued the practice of law in Fort Collins and in Denver.

When MacGregor brought the diminutive Clara back to the park in May of 1875, they had a new neighbor. The month before, Horace

Willis Ferguson (1826–1912) had moved his family from Namaqua to a waiting cabin near Marys Lake. Born in Kentucky, but raised in Memphis, Tennessee, Ferguson had been a merchant, farmer, and miller in Otterville, Missouri, before coming west in April 1871 with his wife and five children to the new agricultural community of Evans, south of Greeley. Purchasing five acres from the St. Louis–Western Colony in September of that year, Ferguson tried both ranching and farming, with equally disastrous results. During the winter of 1871–1872, many of his ninety-four head of cattle drifted away. "It took me four years to get back half . . . ," he later recalled, "and the rest I never got."[19] The next summer he planted fifteen acres of vegetables only to have the grasshoppers destroy the entire crop before it could be harvested. In 1873, hoping to improve his wife's health and his own fortunes, Ferguson left his farm at Evans in the hands his twenty-one-year-old

Figure 5.6. Horace Willis Ferguson. Courtesy Edward B. Reed.

Figure 5.7. William Hunter Ferguson. Courtesy Edward
B. Reed.

son, Hunter, took out a loan, and rented a ranch on the upper Thompson, three miles west of Namaqua. There for the next two seasons he
again tried to make a go of it, putting in crops of wheat and oats, while
raising stock. Each year the grasshoppers descended, as they did throughout much of Colorado, "devouring everything in sight."

By the fall of 1874, Ferguson's situation was desperate. Heavily mort-
gaged and without the means to discharge his debt, he "had reached the
jumping-off-place." Then fate intruded in the unlikely form of the Earl
of Dunraven. Ferguson was one of those who had followed the stories
in the Denver press about Dunraven's activities in the park and the legiti-
macy of the Earl's titles. Sensing potential opportunity, Ferguson decided to go up and have a look around. There he came across Hank
Farrar and two or three others hunting and fishing for the Denver
market.

Farrar was then only twenty-five, but he and his brothers Clint and Ike were already widely known throughout northeastern Colorado for their prowess with a rifle.[20] Meeting Ferguson, he proposed a partnership. Farrar had been having difficulty getting his game to market, a round trip that often required a full six days, barring delays or accidents. He told Ferguson that if he would let Hunter haul his meat and fish by wagon down to Denver, Farrar would give Ferguson two-thirds of whatever purchase price they obtained. Ferguson could also sell what he shot and caught on his own. Hunter was sent for, and in only three days the elder Ferguson had shot 11 deer with his muzzleloading rifle and taken 720 trout. In addition to the chance to make a living, the mountain air of Estes Park offered relief for his wife's chronic bronchial asthma. Horace Ferguson decided once again to relocate.

The land containing a fine spring that Ferguson identified half a mile northwest of Marys Lake had been overlooked by the Dunraven interests (or so Ferguson thought at the time). In February 1875, with the help of Hunter and a hired man, he began work on a two-room, mud-chinked, dirt-roofed log cabin with a good stone fireplace. By April, Ferguson was ready to bring his family up from the valley. They came in three wagons, and the trip proved to be an ordeal. One wagon, loaded with poultry, went over a fifty-foot precipice, killing a dozen or so chickens. Ferguson himself almost broke an arm getting a wagon over the rocks. Steep hills posed their usual problem, the family having to walk behind, while the horses from all three wagons were teamed together to get just one of them to the top of the grade. Ferguson wisely had his livestock brought in by another trail.

Sallie Ferguson, their sixteen-year-old daughter, remembered the trip vividly:

> We were four days coming from Namaqua to the Park. We followed the Little Thompson and stopped at the half way house the first night. Here the wagon backed off the road and scattered our fowls, injuring some so we had to take time out to kill and dress them. The second night we were taken in by hospitable people living in Muggins Gulch. The next morning we proceeded but the snow was too much for heavily loaded wagons and they were left behind. That evening after dark as we reached the hill north of Mary's Lake, we saw in the snowy distance the dim but very welcome glow of a lamp in our homestead window.[21]

It was April 21, 1875, and there were eight inches of snow on the ground.

As in so many other cases, homestead slowly evolved into resort. In 1876, with the establishment by Ferguson and Abner Sprague of a sawmill on the slope of Steep Mountain where they rived and shaved shingles

from a fine stand of Englemann spruce, the original sod roof was replaced with shingles and the next year four rooms were added. "This
was the beginning of our boarding career," Sallie recalled years later,

> although the summer before one eastern lady stayed with us sleeping in a tent
> and having her meals in the kitchen with the family. Visitors from Denver,
> many eastern states and foreign countries began to come at this time, some
> for health—many for rest and pleasure. . . . Most of the tourists brought tents
> and camped on those beautiful rippling streams as the boarding houses or
> hotels were not sufficiently developed to take care of them. However, within
> the next two years Elkhorn Lodge, Sprague's hotel in Moraine Park, Lamb's at
> the foot of Long's Peak and our resort . . . as well as the English Hotel were all
> caring for visitors. Tents were not so popular. Room and board at these places
> ranged from $8 to $14 a week and we made money.[22]

With the help of his family Horace Ferguson enthusiastically entered upon the tourist business. "I . . . met H. W. Ferguson, of Estes Park,"
a correspondent for the *Boulder County News* reported from Longmont on
May 4, 1877, "who will be prepared to entertain all those who may give
him a call at his ranch."[23] Enlarged again in 1878 with the addition of

Figure 5.8. Ferguson's Highlands. Courtesy Denver Public Library, Western History
Department.

a kitchen and a large dining hall attached to the main building, "the Highlands," as the Fergusons named their ranch, would eventually accommodate some sixty paying guests through the summer months in its main building, five three-room cottages, and five tent houses. The site proved a most attractive one. "From the cabins around Ferguson's ranch," mountaineer Frederick Chapin wrote of his visit of 1887, "a magnificent view is obtained of the great Mummy Range; and the sunset lights on the cliffs of Lily [Twin Sisters] Mountain, to the east, are indescribably beautiful."[24] As time permitted, Ferguson would accompany his guests on expeditions into Horseshoe and Willow (Moraine) Parks to fish the Fall River and the Big Thompson.

One of those Ferguson guided left a memorable record of his experiences. Ferguson moved his family into their new cabin in April. That July he was visited by forty-two-year-old Lewis Brown France, together with his wife and son. France, a Denver lawyer, spent his leisure hours either enjoying the natural world or writing about it. A well-published author, it was his series of sketches celebrating the joys and comradery of fishing, *With Rod and Line in Colorado Waters* (1884), that, it has been said, "did more to make readers aware of Colorado fishing than any publication to that time."[25] In Horace Ferguson, who in 1875 still had ample time to indulge himself in the fresh enthusiasm of the newly arrived, France found a most willing companion and teacher.

As France wrote in an essay, "The Lure," published in 1883, the two anglers wasted little time in sharing their mutual passion. A late supper disposed of, his son stowed away in bed, France and Ferguson fell "talking at his broad fire-place about Horse Shoe Park and Fall River," and the prospects for fishing them. At 8 A.M. the next morning, the two rode out toward the beaver dams in Horseshoe Park. An hour later they had reached the divide to the west of Deer Mountain. "Before and below us," France later wrote,

> lay a beautiful park, three miles in length, by a mile in width toward its upper end, where it rounded at the base of the mountain range, giving it the shape of a horse shoe, which no doubt suggested its name. To the north it is guarded by an immense mountain of rocks, where towering and impenetrable cliffs stand out against the background of blue sky, as though the Titans had some time builded there, and mother earth had turned their castles into ruins, and left them as monuments of her power. To the south a long low-lying, pine-covered hill, while from the range in the west with its snow covered summit and base of soft verdure, comes a limpid stream winding down through the grass-covered park, its course marked by the deeper green of the wild grass and the willows. A mile away a band of mountain sheep are feeding; they have

evidently been down to water and are making their way back to their haunts in the cliffs, and whence we know they will quickly scud when they see or wind us. Ferguson longed for his rifle; it was just his luck; he had the "old girl" with him the last time, but "nary hoof" had he seen. To me they were precious hints of man's absence, and the wilderness.[26]

Reaching the stream, they picketed their ponies in mountain grass that rose to their knees, and France rigged his tackle. Within minutes of sending "my favorite gray hackle on its mission," he had "snatched a ten-inch trout from its native element." A second and third followed. Ferguson was nowhere in sight, though France could clearly hear the "swish" of his old cane pole "above the music of the waters." Following the sound of the cane, France "discovered the old gentleman round the edge of the pool, and that old rod going up and down with the regularity of a trip hammer." By noon France had his filled his creel. Ferguson on his part had "his sixteen pound lard-can filled, beside a dozen upon a stick."

France was an urbane and witty man, as well as a writer of ability. But he was also something more: a dedicated nature writer with the soul of a poet. Like so many sportsmen who have come to Estes Park over the years, France not only fished but in so doing meditated on the peace and beauty of his surroundings. Given his appreciation, it is not surprising that in September, when the time came to "break camp and go back to the brick and mortar and the realities of civilization," France did so with the kind of regret that so many have felt—a regret consoled by the thought "that another season will come, and with hope in my heart [that] I am better prepared for the work awaiting me. . . . We gather together our lares of nomadic life, and with a regretful farewell to those I cannot bring away, we make the journey home, a better man and woman, with a nut-brown, healthy boy, for much of which I give credit to the artificial fly, and the beautiful denizens of the mountain streams."[27]

Lewis France had a soft place in his heart for both fishing and children. In concluding *With Rod and Line in Colorado Waters*, he would write: "And here I am moved to say that ours is a noble fellowship; it is a gentle craft we cultivate, one that should beget brotherly love and all things charitable; and if any of you have, as I hope you have, a little white-haired tot who seems inclined to follow you down stream upon summer days, do not say nay, but let your prayer be: 'Lord, keep my memory green.'"[28]

Horace Ferguson's own love of fishing did not wane with age. More than one visitor to Estes Park recalled a white-bearded figure wander-

ing down the hill in the evening to fish the Big Thompson on horseback because he was bothered by arthritis in his legs. In 1876 Ferguson's
ranch became the site of an important milestone, when on December
26 Anna Ferguson married the Longmont merchant Richard M. Hubbell
in the first wedding ceremony to be celebrated in the park. Officiating
was the Reverend C. E. Coffman of Longmont; Abner Sprague and John
Buchanan, another neighbor, served as witnesses.

William E. James (1842–1895), who settled on Fall River, also first
came to know Estes Park as a hunter. Like Ferguson he first visited the
park in the fall of 1874, having recently arrived in Denver from upstate
New York, where his grocery business had failed during the hard times
of 1873. The following May, James returned with the intention of making his home in the park, bringing with him his wife, Ella, and their
three small boys, Homer, Charles, and Howard. A fourth child and only
daughter, Eleanor, was born later. James initially built a small, one-room,
dirt-roofed hunter's cabin near what is now known as McCreery Springs,
out Dry Gulch, about three miles from the present town of Estes Park. A
year later, he built a second cabin on eighty acres in the Black Canyon
above the MacGregors on which he had filed a preemption claim. That
claim was contested by Georgianna Heeney, Clara's mother. The ensuing
dispute was ultimately resolved in the MacGregors' favor and created an
animosity between the two families that would take years to resolve.
Well into the twentieth century MacGregor remained "that pettifogging
lawyer."[29]

William James could have found other property in the Black Canyon, but his land would have been cut off from access to grazing by
mountains to the west and private land to the east, and James wanted to
ranch. He wisely chose another course of action. In November 1876
James swapped his original 1874 claim along Lumpy Ridge for a tract of
land on Fall River, just west of Dunraven's property, owned by the Reverend William H. McCreery, a missionary from Pennsylvania who had
come up from Loveland in 1875 and homesteaded. There James proceeded to construct a modest frame cabin consisting of a living room,
dining room, kitchen, and two bedrooms. One of the attractions of his
new location was that still farther to the west in Horseshoe (then Cascade) Park was unsurveyed land that promised to remain open for grazing for years to come. In time James would purchase a tract there. James
moved his family to Fall River on April 2, 1877. Three days later, perhaps to
spite his old neighbor, James set fire to his barn in the Black Canyon.[30]

Though at the time of the 1880 census the thirty-eight-year-old
James still considered himself a farmer and stockman, the family had

already begun to take in summer boarders. A series of cabins and tent houses was added, and by the summer of that year the Elkhorn Lodge, as they had named their ranch, could accommodate between thirty-five and forty guests. Ultimately the Elkhorn would consist of a small village of thirty-three cabins surrounding a new central lodge. As their daughter, Eleanor Hondius, later wrote, "Every summer people came to the ranch and begged to be allowed to stay, and each winter another cabin would be built on the ranch to house them. Father and Mother soon found there was more money in caring for summer tourists than in raising cattle."[31] In time Elkhorn Lodge would became the largest tourist resort in the park.

Abner Sprague (1850–1943) and his family also found that making a living in Estes Park inevitably required a more than casual involvement with tourists. Born in Dundee, Kane County, Illinois, Sprague came to the Big Thompson Valley in 1864 with his parents, Thomas and Mary Sprague, his brother Fred, and his sister Areanna (Arah). They settled on a squatter's claim Thomas had purchased that straddled the Larimer-Weld county line. Home was a sixteen-by-twenty-four-foot, one-room pine and cottonwood cabin with a fireplace at one end, whose roof was constructed of wide boards thatched with hay and covered with dirt.

Figure 5.9. Elkhorn Lodge, summer 1889. Courtesy National Park Service— Rocky Mountain National Park.

As Sprague grew older, so did the lure of the mountains. He paid a
first visit to Estes Park with two school friends during the summer of
1868. Taking with them ten days' worth of supplies, the three young
men simply rode their ponies westward, eventually coming upon cart
tracks, which they followed up through the foothills and into the mountains until they reached the park. There they came upon and briefly
talked with Griff Evans and Rocky Mountain Jim, who were setting poles,
and then camped for the night. The next day they began to make their
way home, following the North Fork. In 1872, Sprague returned on a
pack trip with his future brother-in-law, Alson Chapman, to climb Longs
Peak. He was also in the park two summers later, arriving in time to hear
William Brown's account of the shooting of Mountain Jim.

When Abner Sprague came again in 1875, it was with the intention
of staying. On May 9 of that year, after a series of exploratory trips,

Figure 5.10. Abner E. Sprague. Courtesy National Park Service—Rocky
Mountain National Park.

Abner and his partner, Clarence Chubbuck, the son of the county superintendent of schools, squatted on unoccupied land in Willow Park containing a spring. Before returning to the valley, they staked out two claims
"in the usual fashion" by laying four logs on end to form a foundation.
Sprague and Chubbuck had planned to come back as soon as possible to
complete their cabins and then summer in the park, but fate intervened.
A month later young Chubbuck was murdered at a round-up near St.
Louis on the Big Thompson by one John Phillips, whom he had accused
of stealing cattle.

Abner Sprague returned that June, bringing with him his father.
Together they completed a twenty-four-by-sixteen-foot, rough-hewn
homestead cabin roofed with poles and covered with eight inches of
peat dug from a swampy area nearby. (The roof worked well, Sprague
recalled, unless there was more than an inch of rain—then clear water
leaked through freely.) Early the next month Mary Sprague arrived with
a small herd of livestock. In staking his claim in Willow Park, Sprague
was fully prepared to defy the Dunraven interests. He knew that the land
on which he proposed to settle had already been filed on and paid for,
but assumed, naively as it turned out, that since the original claim had
been fraudulent, Whyte would simply allow him to stay rather than start
trouble. What Sprague shortly discovered was that Whyte himself had
erred. Due to a mistake in the original platting, the land to which Whyte
held title lay not in Willow Park itself but on its south lateral moraine.

Though the Spragues intended nothing more elaborate than a small
farming and ranching operation, they, like the others, soon found themselves drifting into the tourist business. As Arah Sprague Chapman would
recall in 1931, their first boarders were a party from Dunraven's Estes
Park Hotel who, in passing the Sprague ranch on a trip up Windy Gulch,
told Mrs. Sprague that if she would prepare a chicken dinner they would
return to eat it. Others were soon stopping for dinner, and then two
people asked to be allowed to spend the winter.[32] Thomas Sprague began adding cabins (by 1881 there were a dozen) and built a main lodge
containing guest rooms, a dining room, and a kitchen. The lodge was
later expanded to a full three stories. One of the attractions that the
Spragues offered on hot summer days was their springhouse. "In Willow Park," Carrie Adell Strahorn wrote of her visit of 1877, "we were
invited into a spring-house for a drink of milk, or of water from a fine
spring which was harnessed to do the churning by means of wheel and
shaft. On one side stood a freezer of ice-cream, most tempting to warm
and tired scenic enthusiasts, and close by were saddles of two fine elks.
There was scrupulous neatness in every pan and board."[33]

By the late 1870s Mary Sprague was also operating a small general store on the north side of the road east of the bridge over the Big Thompson, offering "provisions, canned goods, cigars, etc." as well as "a good stock of fishing tackle suitable for the place . . . for sale or hire."[34] The back of the store housed Estes Park's second post office, which opened on March 22, 1880, with Mary Sprague as postmistress, a role she occupied until 1908 when she resigned the position in favor of her daughter, Arah. Fred Sprague also homesteaded in Moraine Park, locating in October 1881 on 160 acres east of his brother's claim where he built a log and lumber house in a small meadowlike area near a spring.

Though originally designated Willow Park, the name of the area (including its post office) was soon changed to Moraine, apparently at the suggestion of Abner Sprague. The name confused some, and *Longmont Ledger's* special Estes Park correspondent noted in 1891, tongue in cheek, that "the post-office at Willow park is called Moraine, because they have much rain there. I have heard this given as the reason."[35] The name was changed to Moraine Park in 1902.

As guide and hunter, prospector, mill operator, locating engineer, surveyor, resort owner, and a most able historian, Abner Sprague was destined to play a leading role in Estes Park's development for well

Figure 5.11. Abner Sprague's homestead cabin in Willow [Moraine] Park. Courtesy National Park Service—Rocky Mountain National Park.

over sixty years. In the course of a long and durable lifetime he came to know the park and its geography intimately. As early as 1877, he began his career as guide, taking Washington McClintock and two others into the wild and untraveled country west of the Continental Divide to visit Middle and North Parks. Until that time Sprague himself had never been west of Estes Park. Using Hayden's drainage map of northern Colorado, Sprague and his companions rode up Windy Gulch to Trail Ridge and then descended to the headwaters of the Cache la Poudre at Poudre Lakes. He later wrote that they encountered no sign of a human trail, and that if the route had ever been crossed by Indians, all signs of it had long since been obliterated.[36] Other trips followed, and by the early 1880s, when mines at Lulu City and in North Park were opening up, Sprague and his uncle Jacob Wolaver were regularly crossing and recrossing the Divide to prospect by means of a pack trail originating in Moraine Park, taking as long as seven days to cover the twenty-five-mile distance.

The remaining prominent early settler was the Reverend Elkanah Lamb (1832–1915), who in 1875 took up land at the base of Longs Peak in what was then known as Longs Peak Valley. The son of a farmer, Lamb was born near South Bend in Indiana and first came to Colorado from Kansas in the spring of 1860 in the company of his cousin Enos Mills Sr. (father of the future naturalist), Mills's wife, the former Ann Lamb, and two other relatives to prospect for gold. The party traveled by way of Lawrence, Topeka, and Manhattan to Kearney, Nebraska, and then came west to Denver along the much used Platte River road. They first prospected, without much success, in the Tarryall district of South Park and then crossed over to Breckenridge, where they found just enough gold to replenish their supplies. Enos Mills soon came down with mountain fever, leaving his wife, Ann, to drive their mules and wagon over the mountains to Denver and home to Kansas. When Lamb returned to Colorado in 1871, it was as an itinerant minister for the Church of the United Brethren engaged in organizing churches along the South Platte and in the valleys of the Poudre and Big and Little Thompson.

In August of that year, Lamb made his first visit to Estes Park, where he climbed Longs Peak twice and, while boarding at Griff Evans's ranch, spent "several days . . . wandering up and down the Fall River and the Big Thompson, fishing, prospecting, and enjoying primitive life in its fullness and freshness."[37] He visited the Park again in 1873 while continuing his missionary work in the towns of the St. Vrain Valley. In 1875 Lamb returned with his wife, Jane, and his son Carlyle and constructed both the twelve-by-fourteen-foot pole, brush, and dirt cabin that would become their home and a number of other "crude buildings."

That fall and the following spring, Elkanah and Carlyle cut a wagon road through thick timber from the lower end of Estes Park to the valley. Its route, which followed an older hunting trail into the park, ascended the western side of Twin Sisters Mountain (then called Lily Mountain) and passed directly in front of the later site of Baldpate Inn, before turning south through the hydrographic divide known as Lamb's Notch into the Tahosa Valley.[38] On August 25, 1877, Elkanah Lamb, John McMarble, and Walter A. Buckingham incorporated the Longs Peak Toll Road Company and began charging tolls.[39] The toll gate was located near the Lambs' cabin at the south end of the road. As Abner Sprague recalled, somewhat wryly, "To make it inviting, the gate was left open so you could drive up to the house and not turn back on account of the closed road. When you had made your call, or received the information that you were at the end of the road, and started on the return trip, you would find the gate closed and would be asked to pay toll both ways. This was not the usual way to run a toll gate, but it was the only way in this case."[40]

The reason for a minister to bother with such a toll road once again had to do with tourists. Though he would continue his ministry for many years, Father Lamb was soon augmenting his preacher's salary by raising his own cattle and chickens and pasturing cattle for others, operating a dairy, collecting tolls, putting up tourists, and guiding parties to the summit of Longs Peak for five dollars a trip. "If they would not pay for spiritual guidance," Lamb later quipped, "I compelled them to divide for material elevation."[41]

Adding more cabins, Lamb was soon running Longs Peak House, a way station to the peak, which became known for its "homelike" atmosphere and for the cordiality of its owners, "who never seem to tire in their efforts to render their guests contented and happy."[42] With increasing help from Carlyle, who took over day-to-day management in the 1890s, Longs Peak House would remain in the Lamb family until 1901. That year Carlyle, who held actual title to the land, sold it to Enos Mills, who renamed the Lamb resort Longs Peak Inn. Elkanah and Jane Lamb then moved two miles to the north to Lamb's Notch, where they built a two-story cabin among a grove of trees called "Mountain Home" (later the site of Wind River Ranch).

For their first two years in the mountains the Lambs stayed only during the summer months. In the spring of 1878, however, the ranch became their permanent home, winter and summer, and would remain

Figure 5.12. Lamb's ranch, 1878. Courtesy Colorado Historical Society.

so until the fall of 1881 when the elder Lambs began to spend winters at Fort Collins. It was a lonely existence. "When we remember," Carlyle later wrote, that "for four or five months of the year, it was not possible to go to Estes Park Village, except on horseback, and for months at times it was not possible to go to Loveland with a team, it is not difficult to understand that life at Long's Peak those early years was such as to develop hardihood, resourcefulness and initiative in the natures of our women."[43]

When the younger Lamb married Emma Batchelder of Denver in 1890, he brought her directly to the ranch. "We spent our honeymoon cutting logs, burning brush, looking after our stock, and getting acquainted with the wild life of the region."[44]

What united all these early settlers, as dissimilar as they were in background, temperament, and ambition, was the need to deal with Theodore Whyte and his cowboys. Though Whyte had arrived in the park as manager of the Dunraven interests late in the summer of 1874, it was not until the following year that he began to make his presence felt. Initially, Sprague and his fellow settlers were put off as much by Whyte's lifestyle—he came equipped with race horses, dogs, guns, and "all the paraphernalia of an English gentleman"—as by the attitude and "antics" he adopted toward those who challenged his authority. Whyte himself was an excellent horseman, and Sprague and others watched with something akin to amazement as he used the gates as hurdles,

leaving his trailing hands either to follow his lead or dismount and
open and close them.[45]

For a while the settlers thought the activity of Whyte and his five
or six hard-riding American cowboys was "all show," as Abner Sprague
subsequently put it, rather than a way to occupy their time and "keep all
hands in condition" "against a time of need." The policy that Whyte
adopted in dealing with the pioneers of 1875 was to ignore their rights
and to annoy and harass them. Dismissing Horace Ferguson's claim out
of hand, Whyte simply ordered him to leave, asserting that he owned
the land. Ferguson remembered the experience years later. "I had no
trouble with the English Company," he recalled,

> except that they tried to bluff me off, and treated me in surly, bull dog fashion.
> Theodore Whyte came over and said: "Now, Ferguson, I've got nothing against
> you. I'd as lief have you here as any other man; but, really, you know, you can't
> get a living on this little forty acres, and that's all you've got here you know.
> Our land shuts you off on each side so that forty acres is all you can get onto
> anyway, and really, you know, that won't give you a living. I'd hate to see you
> sitting down here to starve; and, really, you know, you'd better move on."
> "Well," says I, "Whyte, I'm much obliged to you for your good will, but I
> shan't move on just the same. And I shan't ask the English Company to help
> me when I get down to starvation, I've come to stay; and I reckon I can stick
> it out somehow."[46]

When Ferguson investigated the title, he discovered that most of the
land upon which he had settled had been previously filed on by Alfred
H. Hord, one of the thirty-one indictees, and since May 16, 1874, had
been firmly in Whyte's possession. He also discovered that he had erected
his buildings on land still available for entry. Ferguson immediately filed
claim to that land. The issue was finally resolved by offering Whyte another tract near Marys Lake previously claimed by his daughter, Mildred
Frances. Dunraven's agent accepted.

John Hupp, another of the original settlers, was more easily co-
erced. Hupp, his wife, Eliza, and their seven children had come to the
park in August 1875 from Otterville, Missouri (where he and Horace
Ferguson had briefly operated a flour mill together),[47] locating initially
some three quarters of a mile from Beaver Point. The following year
Hupp moved his family two miles farther west where he built a homestead cabin near a spring at the lower end of Beaver Meadows. At age
fifty-five Hupp wanted nothing more than to farm his land without
trouble or interference. Whyte ordered him off. It was soon established,
as in the case of Ferguson, that although Hupp's buildings were on vacant land, the land where the spring was located had already been

Figure 5.13. The Hupp homestead in Beaver Meadows, on the slope of Deer Mountain. The original three-room house measured thirty-eight by forty-six feet; a fourteen-by-sixteen-foot one-room structure was later added at the rear. Courtesy Ray M. Davis.

entered upon and that Whyte had the title.[48] Hupp did not contest the finding. In the spring of 1876, he simply moved his family to vacant land on Beaver Creek to the west. Though Hupp died the following year, Eliza and her children remained on the land where her husband, and later Eliza herself, were buried.

Abner Sprague had a similar experience in Willow Park. Though he and his father, as noted above, had discovered that there had been no filing on the 320 acres they had taken up as squatters and had quickly filed claims of their own, Whyte nonetheless tried to get them to leave. Riding up with two of his cowboys, Whyte summarily ordered Sprague off the land, citing his own ownership. Sprague later recalled that he took great pleasure in telling Whyte that he "had better inform himself as to the location of the land entered by fraud, before he ordered people to move. I pointed to the Moraine, and told him if he would hire a survey made would find it there."[49] After a new survey resolved the question of ownership in Sprague's favor, Theodore Whyte "turned his attention to other annoying methods."

The tactic Whyte next employed was to have his men drive cattle onto the lands of the settlers. In the case of Sprague, Whyte had about two hundred head driven over to Willow Park, where he salted them on the meadow land along the Big Thompson. Sprague refused to be so easily intimidated. As soon as Whyte and his men left, Sprague, with the aid of his shepherd dog, simply guided the offending cattle over the moraine and down to Beaver Creek. Whyte repeated the incursion. Once again Sprague drove the cattle off, but this time he rode over to the Evans ranch where he and Whyte engaged in "quite a wordy row." "I told him we were in the Park to stay," Sprague later wrote, "and expected to treat him, and be treated, as neighbors; and that if he would let the stock alone, those that were running in Willow Park we would not bother, until we had a fence to keep them out."[50] Confronted, Whyte backed off, and Sprague had no further difficulty with errant livestock.

Hank Farrar had his trouble with Theodore Whyte as well, though in his case it was trouble largely of Farrar's own making. Farrar had erected his one-room log cabin near the center of what is now the town of Estes Park, on land which he knew had been claimed and paid for by one of Whyte's hirelings. When, predictably, Whyte showed up and ordered him to move, Farrar responded that he intended to live there until Whyte himself could prove just how he had come by the land. As Farrar knew, the land, which extended to the west as far as the future site of Elkhorn Lodge, had been entered under the name of William Kellogg, who had made no attempt to comply with the land laws before selling out to Whyte.[51] Farrar also knew that with the legality of the original claims still being contested in some quarters Whyte was unlikely to summarily eject him. The matter dragged on without final resolution for some time, until Farrar simply told Whyte he did not care to own the land, that all he wanted was a place to live, and that he intended to stay were he was indefinitely. To resolve the matter with the contrary squatter, Whyte deeded Farrar forty acres along Fall River. Farrar promptly moved his cabin onto his new land.

The only settler with whom Whyte seems to have had a physical altercation is George I. Bode, a thirty-eight-year-old German woodcarver by trade, who in 1876 homesteaded in meadow land at the north end of the park, where he maintained a small number of cattle.[52] Bode had the courage to fence his property to keep Dunraven's cattle out. Not long afterward he found his fence down and his meadows covered with Dunraven cattle. Several days later, Bode, Abner Sprague, William James, and other settlers were helping to build a bridge across the Big Thompson. Bode was standing on the boulder-filled center crib across which lay two horizontal logs, or stringers, with a third log lying unsecured on top of them. Whyte rode up, dismounted, and, crossing to the crib, confronted Bode. Words were exchanged. Bode then grabbed Whyte around the neck with his left arm and forced him down across the unsecured stringer. Sprague and James jumped to the ends of the log to keep it from rolling on top of either Bode or Whyte. After a minute, Bode, losing his nerve, let go, picked up Whyte's cap up from his side of the log, and politely handed it to him. Whyte took it, mounted his horse, and rode away. In Sprague's retelling of the event, he makes it perfectly clear that all of the onlookers were disappointed that Bode had not summarily thrown Whyte into the creek. Bode subsequently transferred his claim to Dunraven on February 8, 1881, though by then he and his wife were living at Freeland, a quiet and short-lived mining community near Idaho Springs.

Bode notwithstanding, Whyte's attempts to encourage settlers to sell their lands and leave met stiff resistance. Ironically, Sprague later confessed, he might well have succeeded had it not been for the increasing number of visitors in the park, who, only too glad to pay for accommodations, were forcing these very same settlers into the tourist business, thus giving them reason enough to stay on.

Whyte made one last attempt to force the issue. During the winter of 1875–1876, he threatened to fence in totally Dunraven's land, close off the roads, and thereby keep the settlers from reaching their own property. What Whyte did not understand was that in America such access could be protected by law. The settlers immediately petitioned the Larimer county commissioners to lay out three public roads in the park. At a meeting in March 1876 three petitions signed by Estes Park landowners were presented. The first, signed by Horace Ferguson, Hank Farrar, and ten others, requested a road across the north end of the park; the second, signed by Hank Farrar, Abner Sprague, and nine others, requested a road up Fall River to Horseshoe Park. The third petition, signed by Abner Sprague, John Buchanan, and eleven others, asked for a road from the east end of the park to Marys Lake, and from there across the Big Thompson and west into Willow Park. In each case Abner Sprague was appointed to notify the landowners along the line of the proposed road and to report any "grievances" back to the commissioners.[53] When Whyte learned of the proposed roads, he consulted lawyers in Denver. He was told that such roads could indeed be made legal highways that would have to be left open to the public.

Whyte gave in. Prior to the July 1876 meeting of the county commissioners, Whyte offered to permit the settlers open access to the roads over Dunraven's land if they would allow gates to be placed where the roads entered and left the property and would try to keep them closed. The settlers were more than willing to accept Whyte's offer, for it meant that their own livestock would be secure. The gates and fences also allowed arriving tourists to secure their horses without fear of having them wander away.

The resolution of the road issue (followed a year later, in October 1877, by the ability and willingness of a number of settlers to obtain a criminal indictment of Whyte and Griff Evans over the alleged misappropriation of some thirty head of cattle[54]) finally brought peace to the valley of Estes Park. Whyte and his fellow settlers decided that they could in fact live together profitably, if not always happily, side by side. As Sprague put it, "We began to neighbor, as our jawing back and forth made us better acquainted, and as much friends as possible under the circumstances. We all began to see that the holding of so much of the Park by one company, even if it had been secured unlawfully, was the best thing for the place, particularly after it was proven that the place was only valuable on account of its location and its attraction for lovers of the out-of-doors. . . ."[55]

That an era of better relations between Dunraven's manager and the settlers of Estes Park had been reached is made quite explicit in comments attributed to James McLaughlin, Griff Evans's sometime partner, which appeared in the June 17, 1876, issue of the *Boulder County News*:

> Mr. James McLaughlin, a stockman from Estes Park, is in town. He reports on the operations of Mr. Theodore Whyte, one of the proprietors, with Earl Dunraven, of large land interests. They have a saw mill at work and are fencing hundreds of acres of mountain meadow. Sawed posts and plank are used. At the crossing of all the roads and pathways, good gates are hung, so that tourists and neighbors are alike pleased and commoded. Mr. Whyte is spoken of as a very kindly, agreeable and popular gentleman. The large hotel contemplated for the accommodation of Summer visitors, will be built next year, the lumber being cut this season. . . .[56]

Once Theodore Whyte came to accept the fact that his new neighbors were there to stay, accommodation followed. For the better part of twenty years Whyte remained on in Estes Park, raising families by two wives, and earning the respect of his neighbors, who elected him on a number of occasions to public office. Years later Abner Sprague would write that "for my part I can say that I would not ask for a better neighbor than Theodore Whyte was to me after we made allowance for each other's faults."[57] Whyte, on his part, no doubt would have agreed.

Chapter 6

The Uses of Scenery: The 1880s and 1890s

And now a word as to how you reach this land of loveliness. Leaving Longmont any day at 10 A.M. you find the stage waiting, and Mr. S.W. Nott [sic], the owner of the stage, on hand, to see that you are comfortably "fixed." There is an outside seat with the driver, and if you are fortunate and sensible you will take it, and then, as the stage starts off, prepare for a ride through the clouds, or at least through cloudland. Longmont and the cultivated and pretty country adjoining are soon left behind and the foothills appear. Then these are passed, and you rush over hills, through vales, across streams, until the eye is wearied and you turn to the driver and ask: "How far from the park now?" He laughs and tells you, "The half-way house will soon be reached," and you stop and eat a dinner with that keen relish that only mountain air can bring. After a short rest you start again, the horses are fresh, the sun beginning to grow less and less and the driver says: "'Fraid 'twill rain,'" and soon his fears are verified and down it comes (for an afternoon shower is a feature of the ride) and the clouds fall so low that you seem to be driving straight through them. Perhaps it rains an hour, perhaps more, and the road gets a trifle muddy, but what of that. The stage loads are usually jolly, and "water won't hurt and mud won't kill." So, on you go, past and through scenery that must be seen to be appreciated, and finally, just as night is falling (unless the shower has detained you), the park is reached, and with your mind full of pictures that shall long hang in "memory's halls," you descend from your sightly seat to partake of supper, and afterward to sleep, soundly and sweetly, to awaken only when the sun bids old Jove good morning.

—Rocky Mountain News (1881)

Abner Sprague, as usual, was correct. The principal value of Estes Park had very much to do with "its location and its attraction for lovers of the out-of-doors." "The hotel business was forced on us," Sprague would later write of himself and the other pioneer resort owners. "We came here for small ranch operations, but guests and visitors became so numerous, at first wanting eggs, milk, and other provisions, then wanting lodging, and finally demanding full accommodations, that we had to go

Figure 6.1. Estes Park, looking west from Mount Olympus, December 1881. Courtesy Hazel E. Johnson collection, City of Greeley Museums, permanent collection.

into the hotel business or go bankrupt from keeping free company!"[1] In short, whatever else Estes Park might become, its permanent residents would have to learn to accommodate and take advantage of a transient and seasonal population: they would have to find ways to make use of scenery. It was a lesson quickly learned.

The major advantage that Estes Park enjoyed, as compared, say, to Yellowstone or Yosemite, lay in its proximity to Denver and the east and to the growing towns of Boulder, Longmont, Loveland, Fort Collins, and Greeley along the Front Range. Its popularity among those seeking a refuge from the summer heat also had very much to do with the fact that the park and its resorts catered from the very beginning to people who were happy with the modest facilities of a guest ranch or willing to "rough it" in the out-of-doors. For those who desired—or required— greater amenities, there was Dunraven's Estes Park Hotel, but even then Estes Park did not begin to truly cater to the well-to-do leisure traveler until the completion of the Stanley Hotel in 1909. Newspaper attention helped. Tentatively at first, but then with increasing pride, newspapers in Denver and the valley towns began to report on and promote Estes Park, "the gem of the mountains"[2] to their readers. By the early 1880s there was sufficient regional interest to justify weekly columns of "Estes Park Items" during the summer months and, later, on a year-round basis.

By 1880 the foundations of the Estes Park tourist industry were well in place. "As a general answer to the many inquiries in regard to Estes Park," a correspondent for the *Fort Collins Courier* had noted in August a year earlier,

> we will here say that the hotels and boarding houses are all full, there being more boarders than we found in the Park on our visit there two summers ago. There are not so many campers as there were at that time; fishing about the same—good opportunities for cultivating one's social nature. There is a dance in the Park every week which the gentlemen can take part in for the small sum of 25 cents. Ice cream is 15 cents per dish. There are several stores there at which campers can replenish their larders at a cost but little in advance of valley prices, with the addition of cost of transportation. Those who have the inclination and the needful can put on style to the tune of "come down with the stamps," at the Estes Park Hotel, where everything is served in first class style, and as complete a bill of fare as will be found in any city in the State.[3]

In Estes Park, in other words, there was something for everyone, and, moreover, the price was right.

In this respect a comparison between Estes Park and Manitou Springs, Colorado's most popular mountain resort of the period, is instructive. In Estes Park tourists and vacationers of modest means were made to feel welcome and at home. This was not nearly so true of Manitou Springs, five miles west of Colorado Springs. There in 1871 William Jackson Palmer, the president of the Denver and Rio Grande, founded a community that he hoped would become "a first class Colorado Watering place & spa,"[4] a status it quickly achieved. By the mid-1870s, at a time when the pioneer families of Estes Park were still arriving, Manitou was taking full advantage of the business of tourism and health seeking that had become so much a part of post–Civil War America. The town consisted of a complex of hotels, boarding houses, bath houses, dance pavilions, bowling alleys, and a bottling plant surrounding soda springs that local physicians such as Dr. Edwin S. Solly claimed could cure everything from consumption and asthma to kidney disease and alcoholism.[5] Nearby were such attractions as Rainbow Falls at the foot of Ute Pass, the Garden of the Gods, Monument Park, Crystal Park, and, after 1880, the Cave of the Winds in Williams Canyon. There was also, of course, Pikes Peak and its summit, increasingly reachable by foot, horse, or burro over improved trails and roads.

Thanks to its easy access from the growing tourist center of Colorado Springs, Manitou flourished. The "Saratoga of the West," it was called—"an appellation," *Harper's* would tell its readers in March 1880, "which pleases Manitou, and does not hurt Saratoga."[6] Here in a picturesque mountain setting was to be found a fashionable social scene, complete with visiting celebrities, that those who pretended to know compared favorably with what could be found anywhere in the East or, for that matter, in Europe. Life in Manitou, a visitor from England remarked, "seems more frivolous, not to say faster, than at similar places in the Old World. . . . The ladies breakfast toilets are good enough for the dinner table, while for dinner they dress as we do for the opera."[7] As with nearby Colorado Springs, the "social affiliations" of Manitou "were with Boston, Philadelphia and New York. The Middle West said little to us."[8]

Though Manitou's aura of luxury and exclusivity would be tempered in the years that followed, its accommodations, like those in Colorado Springs, remained relatively expensive and its social rituals remained intact. The majority of tourists continued to be of the well-to-do sort, even at a time when residents like Dr. William Bell, the Englishman who for some two decades served as the social leader of the sizable British enclaves at Colorado Springs and Manitou, had begun to complain that the place was too touristy and that the "primitive beauty of Manitou had disappeared and been replaced by poor and unsightly structures, very different in character from those castles in the air which we imagined in our mind's eye."[9]

It was very different in Estes Park. Though its visitors certainly included easterners and Europeans who could afford to vacation anywhere, life during the summer months remained by and large a simple and inexpensive affair, with little of the kind of pretentiousness reported at Manitou. Part of this had to do with the continuing remoteness of the Estes Park valley—a circumstance that also retarded the development of a summer resort industry across the Divide in Middle Park, even with the mining activity of the 1880s. But there was also a major difference in the lifestyles and expectations of the owners of Estes Park's guest ranches and resorts. Almost without exception these pioneers had come to Estes Park not to operate resorts but to ranch, farm, and make a life for themselves and their families. The income from housing, feeding, and attending to the needs of visitors provided a welcome (if increasingly necessary) supplement to what they could earn from other activities, and there was little or no incentive (or need) to charge more than what their visitors could comfortably pay.

The history of Estes Park during the eighties and nineties can best be described as one of continuity with only modest growth and change. With the question of landownership and the role of the English Company largely resolved, these years were comparatively tranquil ones. As the 1880s began, the MacGregors, Jameses, Fergusons, Spragues, and

Lambs, together with Theodore Whyte, formed the nucleus of the park's small resident population. While other individuals like Peter J. Pauly Jr., Samuel B. Hart, William D. Ewart, and Julian Johnson would take up sizable tracts and join them, it was the "pioneers of '75" and their families who would continue to play the dominant role in the life of the valley until the turn of the century and, in some cases, well beyond. Though there was considerable interest in raising cattle and to a lesser extent in farming, particularly through the 1880s, the major concern of the resident population was how best to meet the needs of the summer tourists, upon whose satisfaction their livelihoods depended.

The subject that dominated all others during these years, understandably, was transportation: the condition of the roads into the park and the agitation for new ones. By 1880 tourists could easily reach Denver, Longmont, and Loveland from any part of the nation. By 1885 the St. Vrain extension of the narrow-gauge Denver, Utah & Pacific brought them directly to the new town of Lyons. But from those points of transit access to Estes Park remained difficult, if not often problematic. Hattie Carruthers, coming over the original Estes-Evans road in 1874, later remarked, not untruthfully, that it "was called a road only by courtesy. The rocks, streams, and steep ascents made any trip to the Park something of an adventure."[10]

Residents of Fort Collins and the Big Thompson and Poudre Valleys wanted their own road to Estes Park. On October 5, 1875, within months of the opening of MacGregor's toll road to the St. Vrain, the Larimer County commissioners approved the extension of the existing road over Bald Mountain and Pole Hill to Estes Park and appropriated $250 for the purpose. Those funds, not surprisingly, were inadequate, and additional donations were requested—either in labor or in money—from those interested in having the road.[11] In a cash-short world most people preferred to donate their time and energy. County and private funds were used to hire a foreman and pay for supplies.

This new free road, which was accepted by the county as "completed" on January 2, 1876, entered the mountains west of Namaqua, three miles south of the Big Thompson Canyon. Ascending westward through the foothills, the road came over Bald Mountain, through a small picturesque valley with the ominous name Rattlesnake Park, and then proceeded up Pole Hill along a precarious ridge to a place called Diamond Spring. At Diamond Spring this new route turned to the left, took a steep and narrow descent, and wound its way into Muggins Gulch. Following Muggins Gulch to its head, around and across Solitude Gulch, the road then ran up the steep ridge overlooking Estes Park. From there it followed the ridge as far to the right as possible before dropping rather precipitously through Emmons Gulch into the park. The major problem was Emmons Gulch itself, the deep gully that runs down through what is now Crocker Ranch (named for A. J. Emmons, who purchased Israel Rowe's claim at the foot of Mount Olympus). Rumbling down the gulch was easy, if frightening and somewhat dangerous. Going up, on the other hand, required a good team, and even then the driver had to leave his wagon, walk behind, and be prepared to apply the brake when the team stopped to rest.

By 1884, for an outlay of two thousand dollars, the grade over Pole Hill was reduced, and in 1887 an alternative route with an easier grade was located at the Estes Park end. At Park View a turn was made to the left along the ridge that led in the direction of the park. Opposite Park Hill the road began its descent, winding down the side of the mountain until it connected with MacGregor's toll road below. Two years later the county commissioners, again with local help, improved the road both near the eastern foot of Bald Mountain and from Park View west, establishing an easier grade from the head of Emmons Gulch to its connection with the toll road. Even then, however, as one user noted in 1895, this final segment of the road was "only wide enough for teams going one way with an occasional place where there is barely space enough to pass one you meet" and it was necessary to hug the hillside for fear of going over.[12]

Even in its new and "improved" state the Bald Hill–Pole Hill road—whose grade averaged 11 percent and ranged as high as 20 percent—was never good. Bald Mountain, one traveler of 1893 commented, is "the worst climb you have experienced in a public road, and Pole Hill may be a sort of near relative—half brother or first cousin. . . ."[13] Two years later, one member of a party of five collegians from Fort Collins, who gave themselves the names "Jayhawker," "Yankee," "the Hoosier," "the Englishman," and "the Guide," described for the *Fort Collins Express* with good humor their encounter with Bald Mountain, an experience doubtless shared by many.

> All took to the ground now and tried to walk for a change. In order to divide up the labor the Guide drove, the Hoosier managed the brake, the Yankee walked ahead to warn teams coming down and the remainder pushed and held wheels. Long before the top was reached all had declared such hills to be public nuisances and averred that they would petition the county commissioners to run a tunnel through the hill.[14]

The only solace for such travelers was the fact that the tops of both Bald

Mountain and Pole Hill offered fine views: "all the Big and Little Thompson valleys and portions of the Cache la Poudre and St. Vrain valleys . . . with the many lakes used for storing water and for raising fish."[15] Despite complaints about "horrible conditions," which were invariably followed by assurances that "the road is being greatly improved," the Bald Mountain road provided visitors coming from Loveland, Fort Collins, and Greeley with their major access to Estes Park until the road up the Big Thompson was completed in 1904.[16]

MacGregor's toll road presented similar problems. While its completion and opening improved travel for a time, the road soon fell into a chronic state of disrepair because of rock slides and washouts, becoming all but impassable during certain seasons of the year. Alexander MacGregor and his partners had invested heavily in the project and not surprisingly wanted to recoup their investment with as little additional outlay of funds for maintenance and improvement as possible. From the point of view of many of its users, on the other hand, MacGregor was simply guilty of neglect. As a result the toll road was never popular. Settlers and teamsters alike were soon openly grumbling about both the condition of the road and the fairness of the tolls. Dissatisfaction led to vandalism, and between October 1876 and January 1877 the gate was torn down twice. Among those most concerned were resort owners like William James, Abner Sprague, and Horace Ferguson whose yearly income was directly related to access to the park. They alerted the county commissioners, who for a time during the summer of 1882 actually suspended the collection of tolls because of the road's condition.[17]

The long-simmering issue came to a head in the spring of 1883, following a particularly snowy winter, when a group of Estes Park residents, including William James, newcomer Peter J. Pauly Jr., and their hired men volunteered their own time to make the needed repairs. They were soon joined by a number of Longmont residents, who contributed between $150 and $200 to the project. While the work went on, MacGregor was content to allow the men free access to his road. But once it was completed, the tollgate was again put up. Henry S. Gilbert, a liveryman who drove a stage to the park and had worked to improve the road from the Lyons end, was particularly angered at MacGregor's response. Approaching the tollgate in his stage and being asked to pay, Gilbert hitched his rig to the gate, tore it down, and dragged it off.[18] Gilbert was arrested, and a lawsuit followed.

Though MacGregor knew a good deal about his rights under the law, he soon had had enough. The following winter he sold the franchise to a group of Longmont men, which included George N. Atwood,

Joseph N. Boyd, and Byron L. Carr. MacGregor's decision was no doubt
a wise one. Owning and operating a toll road, however sound an investment in theory, almost always proved difficult in practice, particularly
once its users forgot that private, rather than public, monies had originally financed the project. To the extent that this lesson needed rein-
forcement, MacGregor had only to watch from his office in Fort Collins
as a similar controversy involving the four-mile toll road up nearby Rist
Canyon unfolded during the late winter of 1883. There the owners argued that they had only stepped in to operate the road because the
county commissioners had been unwilling to tax the community, and
that the toll charged—$.35 a trip—was "only . . . enough to keep it in
repair." These arguments were brushed aside. Much to the delight of the
Fort Collins press, local settlers forced the owners to open the tollgates
and make the road once again free.[19] Interestingly enough, the widespread unpopularity of MacGregor's toll road may well have led to his
reelection defeat as county judge that November. Of the twenty votes
cast in the Estes Park precinct, where he was of course well known,
Alexander MacGregor received only five.

The Estes Park Road Company, as the new owners named it, made
immediate changes beginning at the mouth of St. Vrain Canyon, three
miles west of Lyons, and extending as far as Little Elk Park (Pinewood
Springs), creating what in effect was a new road. These alterations, which
shortened the distance between Estes Park and Lyons by three miles,
remained substantially in effect until 1907, when F. O. Stanley reconstructed the North St. Vrain road from Lyons to Estes Park to facilitate
the use of his auto stage line. Despite these improvements, the road
continued to need maintenance and repair, especially in the spring, when
travelers reported "mud holes of unfathomable depths." For a time residents at both ends were willing to pitch in and help. Less than a year
after its purchase, on July 3, 1884, the *Fort Collins Courier* reported that
"the Estes Park toll road has been put in good repairs by the citizens of
Estes park, aided by Longmont business men and the county commissioners of Boulder county. The people are compelled to do it in order to
be ready for tourist travel."[20]

The original twenty-year charter on the toll road would have expired in 1895. Before that date, however, its Longmont owners decided
that the road still represented a good investment and moved to have it
rechartered. The charter of the new Longmont and Estes Park Road Company[21] brought with it new trouble, and this time the agent was none
other than Abner Sprague, who as a civil engineer and surveyor prided
himself on firsthand knowledge of mountain roads. In Sprague's retell-

ing, the changes and repairs promised by the owners at the time of the recharter were at best only "slight." The major change, one that affected everyone and infuriated many, was to increase the round-trip toll charge to $1.80 and to refuse to reduce it for those who used the road regularly to make a living.[22]

The case of *Abner E. Sprague v. the Estes Park Toll Road Company* reached the district court in Fort Collins in June 1899. Sprague asked that all of the company's rights, privileges, and franchises be revoked and that the corporation itself be dissolved, arguing that the company had failed to "construct a toll road as its incorporation called for, but occupied lands already built and had been charging toll without a legal right to do so."[23]

Sprague and James Blair, a stock rancher living in Muggins Gulch who had torn down the tollgate as an act of protest and had been arrested and acquitted, hired Denver lawyers to argue the case. The company retained the services of Sylvester Downer of Boulder, one of the "rude young men" who had accompanied Isabella Bird to Estes Park and then up Longs Peak more than two decades before. In April of 1900 the veteran judge Jay Boughton found against the company. Three of the five charters that the company used in defending its right to levy tolls were found to have expired, and the court declared its right of franchise forfeited and the toll road corporation dissolved. The way the decision was rendered, however, virtually guaranteed an appeal. Moreover, Boughton angered the plaintiffs by speaking "very kindly of the road, and said the company was guilty of nothing but keeping it in good repair."[24]

The fact that Boughton allowed the company to continue collecting tolls during the process of appeal did nothing to reduce existing tensions. Tempers ran particularly high in Lyons among a group of teamsters and workers from the sawmill above the town, who of necessity were regular users of the road. Two months later, in June 1900, several of these men appeared at the tollhouse armed with guns, and over the protests of its keepers, destroyed the gate.[25] Making things worse, a little more than a week later, the gatekeeper Charles Knapp brandished a cocked revolver to keep three of the teamsters, John and Otis Walker and Norman Billings, from passing through without paying. In the aftermath, the *Lyons Recorder* reported on July 5, Knapp claimed that he had "instructions to collect toll or keep parties from going over the road even should he be compelled to shoot them at the gate."[26] "Though the argument enforced by the gun was convincing and [the] toll . . . promptly paid,"[27] further retaliation was predictable. On July 16, a group of eleven armed men once again tore down the gate. They were promptly arrested for "malicious mischief" and taken to court, where on August 13, after a lengthy hearing involving a large number of witnesses on both sides, the men were "discharged by the court; the judge saying the company made no case against them" because the toll road had not been "duly incorporated."[28] William Laycock, one of those arrested, scored the final point. On the evening of August 31, he calmly hitched his wagon to the gate with a heavy log chain and "dragged it quite a distance down the road."[29]

When the case reached the state supreme court, the company was finally beaten. "The Lyons and Estes Park Toll road is a thing of the past . . . ," the Lyons Recorder enthused on December 13, 1900. "The old gate is now lying chopped to pieces at the side of the road and teams pass through unhindered. . . . Let's all give thanks and praise to the boys who have brought about this condition by their pluck and sticktoitiveness."[30] Abner Sprague had his vindication. Estes Park now had a free road to Longmont, Boulder, and Denver, but even Sprague, who had sued over the issue, was forced to admit that "this road was poorly kept up until the coming of the auto and auto stage lines."[31]

The first stagecoach line from Longmont to Estes Park was established by Walter A. Buckingham, Elkanah Lamb's toll road partner, in 1878. In 1880 Franklin W. Knott took over the route for a year, followed by Henry S. Gilbert and a man named White who operated it for the next three. Gilbert, who lived in Estes Park and was one of those who led the protest against MacGregor's toll road, turned the business over to William N. Hubbell and his partner, George Eastwood, during the 1885 season—a season that, Elkanah Lamb estimated, brought between eight hundred and one thousand tourists to the park.[32] Hubbell had the greatest longevity. He ran stages to and from the park from 1885 to 1902 when, because of failing health, he sold the business to William F. Cantwell.

Cantwell promptly replaced Hubbell's equipment with eight-horse spring coaches, which offered a better ride and cut almost a full hour from the scheduled time. Despite his success, Cantwell sold half his interest to Charles W. Childester of Leadville, an engineer on the Denver and Rio Grande, in 1904. Three years later, he purchased and then enlarged the eleven-bedroom Burlington Hotel in Lyons, where he continued in the stage and freight business until late 1908. That year, no doubt understanding that change in the transportation industry was decidedly in the air, William Cantwell sold out completely and moved to Denver.

From 1884 to 1893 Abner and Fred Sprague operated a stage line from Loveland to Moraine Park (the end of the mail route and the site of the family guest ranch) and then shifted their route to the Lyons road, where Fred Sprague continued to haul both freight and passengers, in direct competition with William Hubbell, until at least the summer of 1898. The Spragues later sold their equipment to Hubbell and turned to other pursuits. In 1895, and until after the turn of the century, the Loveland stage was in the hands of J. B. Middleton, who made his home at Pinewood on the Bald Mountain–Pole Hill road.

Because of the generally "fearful" condition of the road over Bald Mountain, Loveland did not become the long-desired "natural outlet for the Estes Park trade"[33] until after the opening of a new road up through the Big Thompson Canyon in 1904. In fact, despite Middleton's efforts, stage service from Loveland to the park remained in some years an undependable and decidedly seasonal affair. During the summer of 1900, for example, and much to the chagrin of both arriving tourists and the Loveland business community, there was apparently no regular coach transportation at all.[34] Beginning in May of 1905, however, the Johnson brothers took advantage of the new Big Thompson route by inaugurating scheduled service between Loveland and the Estes Park post office, employing wagons "of the latest pattern, especially designed for the comfort of passengers," over a route already being touted as "unsurpassed for magnificent scenery."[35]

Traffic by stage nevertheless increased each year, particularly after the railroad reached Lyons, and by 1900 three four-horse stage loads of passengers each day were going up the St. Vrain Canyon on the four-and-a-half-hour trip to Estes Park. The fare was two dollars. Competition could be stiff, and costly. In 1901, E. R. March and J. A. Hoover directly challenged Hubbell by establishing a new stage line from Lyons to Estes Park and cutting the fare in half, from two dollars to one. Hubbell promptly countered by lowering his own to fifty cents. This misguided rivalry did not last long; March and Hoover were forced to sell their stages and horses to satisfy creditors.[36]

Good roads were a visible sign of progress, and Coloradans, like most westerners, prided themselves on their ability to build them. During the last three decades of the century, no natural barrier was deemed too great for a road, or railroad, for that matter, to overcome. In January 1880, for example, a small group of enthusiastic Loveland citizens obtained a charter for the Loveland and Estes Park Toll Road Company, which was to pass up through the Sprague ranch in Moraine Park and from there go up through Mill Creek, past the old Hill and Beckwith sawmill, and over the Continental Divide to Grand Lake, a distance of some fifty-five miles.[37] As the *Fort Collins Courier* confidently reported,

"This road will open up the finest body of timber in the state, and . . . will be the favorite route for tourists. . . . The pass on the main range is considerably below timber line, and the estimated ascent to be over-come in going from Estes Park to the summit of the main range is less than 1500 feet."[38]

Spurred by the mining boom of the early 1880s, which created the short-lived town of Lulu City, hopes for building a good wagon road linking Estes Park with Colorado's two other major northern parks per-sisted. An 1893 visitor from Fort Collins reported seeing a wooden sign made of a piece of cracker box at the end of the road up Fall River that optimistically read: "Line of the People's toll road to Middle and North Parks—when we get it finished."[39] There were also dreams of railroads. In 1904, at a time when the road up the Big Thompson remained in-complete, William A. Riley, Greeley Whitford, Frank Bartholf, and others incorporated the Loveland and Estes Park Electric Railway and hired Abner Sprague to survey a route up the canyon.[40] There was also a rumor in 1900 of an electric line to be put through to Copeland Lake at the foot of Mount Meeker and Longs Peak.[41]

Given his unusual set of experiences, including that of citizen-liti-gant, Abner Sprague understood far better than most the significance of transportation and its impact upon the development of mountain com-munities like Estes Park. In Sprague's later years transportation, which he wrote about extensively over the years, became a metaphor for progress and change: for just how much the peaceful and practically uninhabited valley that he first visited in 1868 as a boy of eighteen had become transformed during his own lifetime. Reflection on that fact brought its own kind of nostalgia. "Those old days of the four and six-horse drawn stages are still remembered by many," Sprague wrote in 1928,

without doubt bringing back the prickle along the spine by recalling to mind the wild stories of the driver, when during the telling with a flourish of his long whip-lash, he would cause the leaders to lunge toward the edge of the road as though they were going over into the rushing water of the stream or roll down a mountain side. Or tearing down the steep hills and around sharp bends, the lead team on a gallop, heavier wheel horses on a fast trot, passen-gers gripping each other, or hanging on to anything to keep themselves from "following the laws of moving bodies and flying out into space at a tangent" to light away down below on the rocks. It was no tame thrill.

But mostly it will bring back the taste and smell of dust—dust in your eyes; dust in your mouth; dust in your lungs, up your nose, and all through your baggage, besides your body would be gritty with it from head to heels. Auto tourists may think this overdrawn, but ask any old-timer that has made the trip under those conditions. The traveler reached his hotel too worn out and tired to take a bath in a wash basin (those days were before the freighting in of even the old tin bath tub), but to supper, sometimes too tired to eat, and bed, after only trying to get the taste of dust out of your mouth, and the smell from your nose, declaring before going to sleep, that too much of such fun was plenty; that if ever civilization was reached again, they would never leave a railroad when traveling. After a month's stay in the Park, they came again the next year.[42]

Return they did, and until the first decade of the next century, when there was a sudden flurry of resort and cottage building accompanying the platting of the village of Estes Park, such travelers found the same ranch resorts there to greet them. The MacGregors, Jameses, Fergusons, Spragues, and Lambs continued to do business in much the same way, expanding a bit each year, enlarging or adding a dining room, building a new cabin or two. By so doing, they kept the tourist business almost exclusively to themselves. As might be expected, there were generational changes within each of these families, but as far as the world at large was concerned, the summers in Estes Park seemed unchanged and unchanging in the passage of the years.

Rates during the early 1880s were reasonable. The MacGregors, Fergusons, and Jameses each charged between nine and twelve dollars a week for room and board, with saddle ponies a dollar or two extra. The Estes Park Hotel, of course, was more expensive, posting rates of four dollars a day and fifteen to seventeen dollars a week. All the ranches offered saddle horses for one to two dollars a day, while "fine double carriages with drivers" were available for a daily fee of six dollars.[43] Vacationists who came for a month, or even for the whole season, were not uncommon. That season was a short one, beginning at the end of May and lasting only until the beginning of September, accommodating itself to the weather, school vacations, and the available supply of summer help.

There were, of course, changes. By 1885 William James had completed a new addition to his dining room and could seat eighty guests. That same year, because for several seasons he had "been compelled to turn away parties that desired to stop," James constructed two new cottages, one of three and the other of four rooms "to be used as lodging houses for his boarders."[44] The Elkhorn continued to grow in size and capacity—there were nine cottages by 1891. But major expansion did not occur until 1900, with further additions in 1902, 1908, and 1912, giving the main lodge a frontage of some hundred feet and bringing its total capacity to 180 guests. These changes came after the death of William E. James in 1895, during the period when his widow, Ella, and her two sons, Homer and Howard, were running the lodge.

During his lifetime, much of the success of the Elkhorn was attributable to the "gentlemanly ways and kindly disposition" of its landlord, who was only too willing to indulge his guests in his own twin passions, hunting and fishing. William James also personally presided over the friendly evening bonfire in front of the lodge, where the guests entertained themselves with songs, stories, and recitations: "Mr. James' hunting stories . . . form[ing] not a little part of the evening's entertainment."[45]

Then as now the Elkhorn's distinctive piles of horns, the result of its owner's hunting prowess, attracted the attention of guests and lent themselves to conversation. One newcomer during the summer of 1895, the local correspondent for the *Longmont Ledger* took delight in reporting, made the mistake of asking "what sort of roots they were." When told they were horns, not roots, the inquirer "gave me a look of amusement, no doubt thinking I wanted to give him a western sell. I asked him if he ever heard of an animal called the elk. If I had told him they were Wapiti horns he may have believed it."[46]

Visitors also reported the excellence of James's table: "mountain sheep, venison, trout, raspberries, fresh milk and butter being served in abundance."[47]

Figure 6.2. The Elkhorn Lodge and its famous piles of elk antlers. Courtesy Denver Public Library, Western History Department.

Ferguson's ranch—which during the early 1890s became "Highland House" or simply "The Highlands" (because Horace Ferguson claimed to trace his Scottish roots to King Fergus)—was equally successful as a family enterprise. Described in 1882 as "a regular old-fashioned homestead, where hospitality creeps out every door and window,"[48] its log cottages and tent houses were full throughout the season. When Ferguson's wife, Sally, died suddenly in January 1887, after a thirty-year struggle with acute asthma, other members of the family, particularly his daughter Mildred Frances (Fanny) and youngest son, James, stepped into the breach. Between 1898 and 1902, after being closed for several years, the Highlands was managed by Sallie and her husband Charles L. Reed, who subsequently built and successfully operated for many years the Brinwood Hotel and Ranch in Moraine Park. When the Reeds left, Horace Ferguson, who had remarried in 1888 and was then living in Moraine Park, briefly put the place up for sale, then decided to rent it to others.[49] From 1881 on, as Frederick Chapin discovered, the Highlands offered a special attraction for active mountaineers. As the *Fort Collins Courier* succinctly put it in June of that year: "[William] Hallett has built a neat summer cottage near Ferguson's boarding house."[50]

Sprague's ranch had its devotees as well, particularly those who were looking for a "spot with good fishing and hunting and quiet surround-

Figure 6.3. The Highlands and William Hallett's house, c. 1883. Courtesy Denver Public Library, Western History Department.

ings." Here were to be found "large airy rooms, nicely furnished and carpeted," and a dining room with "a large bay-window in one end of the room, a handsome sideboard, . . . walls adorned . . . with beautifully stuffed birds, and house plants of every variety."[51] As if the nearby Big Thompson and its abundance of trout were not enough, by 1881 Abner and his father had built "an artificial lakelet of the purest spring water" some twenty feet square in "which may be seen from six to seven hundred mountain trout." The pond, one of the Spragues explained, was an experiment in trout farming. If successful, they proposed to enlarge it into "a lake covering fifteen to twenty acres."[52]

Thomas Sprague died on December 6, 1882, and for many years, until 1893, Sprague's ranch was operated by Mary Sprague with the help of her younger son, Fred, with periodic help from Abner and her widowed daughter, Areanna (Arah) Chapman. From the middle 1890s until 1902, when Abner went into partnership with a relative, James D. Stead of Chicago, the hotel business was handled jointly by Abner and Fred Sprague with the help of Abner's wife, Mary Alberta. The name Sprague Brothers was also attached to a stage line from Loveland to Moraine over the Bald Mountain–Pole Hill route that Fred established in 1884, as well as to a sawmill. During the brief period of the Sprague-

Figure 6.4. The Hallett house with friends and family. William Hallett is standing center left. Courtesy Colorado Historical Society.

Figure 6.5. Six-horse stage arriving at the Spragues, 1890s. Courtesy National Park Service—Rocky Mountain National Park.

Stead partnership, which lasted only until the spring of 1904 when Stead purchased the entire property for twenty-five thousand dollars, a new central hotel building was completed (capable of seating 150 at dinner) and several houses and cottages were added. Arah Sprague Chapman, who had filed her own homestead claim in Moraine Park, helped her mother operate the small general store near the river. Aided by her two sons, Alson Jr. and Charles, she also rented out cottages—one of which was occupied in the summer of 1889 by a William Allen White, the future Emporia, Kansas, journalist, and a group of his fellow students from the University of Kansas.[53]

The ranches offered their guests and visitors a wide variety of activities. During the day, in addition to quiet lawn games, there were horseback and carriage rides to points of interest throughout the park, berry picking (one "enterprising family of Greeleyites [vacationing in 1881] put up almost a barrel of raspberry jam"), as well as guided fishing, hunting, and hiking trips; in the evening there were ice cream and cake socials, candy pulls, masquerade balls, dances and lawn parties, musical events, charades, and an occasional amateur theatrical. There was also the ubiquitous bonfire, with guests and hosts alike furnishing the entertainment. By the summer of 1881 visiting ministers were holding Sunday church services on a more or less regular basis. But most of all there was peace and quiet for rest and relaxation: "The departing and arriving of the stage are the grand daily events of life; no telegraph wire tells of the rise and fall in stocks, nor of the temperature of the president; one forgets there is a world of rush and hurry and sits content to gaze upon the wonderful cloud pictures that nature in her thoughtfulness is continually changing."[54]

Most visitors were hard pressed to choose among the guest ranches, though some tried. A Dr. Finks, writing to the editor of the *Fort Collins Courier* in 1880, began by extolling the view from MacGregor's ranch only to conclude that "you should go to Ferguson's or Sprague's, if you want the best the mountains can afford. Here the rich cream and milk, sweet and cold, the ice cream that is *solid cream*, the good cooking and well covered tables, the comfortable rooms—these make one's stay truly enjoyable."[55]

What mostly eluded guests like Dr. Finks and newspaper correspondents from the valley towns was how difficult it could be to succeed at a business that was not only seasonal but subject to the vagaries of transportation, the ability to secure and retain help, the goodwill of one's neighbors and competitors, and, of course, the weather. Sallie Ferguson Reed, the daughter of the founder of the Highlands, in a series of letters written to her husband, Charles, has left a valuable record of just what it was like to manage a resort in Estes Park during the waning years of the century.

The Highlands had enjoyed great popularity during the 1870s, 1880s, and early 1890s thanks to the efforts of Horace Ferguson and his children, who conducted their resort above Marys Lake very much as a family enterprise. By the mid-1890s, however, with his adult children occupied elsewhere, Horace Ferguson, now approaching seventy, closed the Highlands in favor of his ranching and farming interests, particularly those in Moraine Park west of the Spragues. The Highlands remained closed until the spring of 1898, when Sallie, leaving her husband in Longmont where he was serving as city clerk and water commissioner, brought her children, including seven-year-old Charles Jr. and three-year-old Roland, up to the park to reopen the Highlands with the help of a hired man named Spence. (Horace's main contribution that summer was to provide fresh trout for the breakfast table.) Her letters to Charles, written over the months that followed, demonstrate that operating a resort, let alone a resort that would pay, was no simple undertaking, particularly for a woman with young children who also demanded her attention.

Though Sallie was no stranger to the resort business in Estes Park, the trials and tribulations of that summer proved daunting. The first requirement was getting the main house and outlying cottages ready to receive visitors. Not only did the buildings require extra "scrubbing," but Sallie had to contend with deferred maintenance. "I never was so tired of cleaning & seeing things torn up," she wrote Charles shortly after her arrival, adding, "everything here needs repairing." Still, "if the wind don't blow a gale all week then we will get most through. . . ."[56] There was also the garden to attend to (she raised lettuce, radishes, onions, peas, and potatoes for her own table), as well as a small menagerie of farm animals—pigs, chickens, and dairy cows—to take care of. Selling milk, butter, and bread to local residents was a source of additional income. By July Sallie was milking eleven cows and churning and packaging twenty-five pounds of butter a week.

Her central concern, of course, was the hotel and the need to attract a sufficient number of paying guests. That meant building (or in many cases rebuilding) a network of relationships interrupted by the years of closure that included competing stage operators, grocery suppliers in Lyons and Longmont, over whose prices Sallie continually fretted, and her fellow resort owners, with whom there was always at least a hint of rivalry.

Stage operators Fred Sprague and William Hubbell each wanted the Highlands's business, which included not only the delivery of passengers but of food and other supplies. Sprague courted Sallie early on, offering, she told Charles, not only a fixed price on freight goods but "a free pass over the road whenever we wished to go, [even] if it was two or three times a week after he commences running daily which will be the 1st of July." In return Sprague wanted the Reeds "to build platform down at the corner" for the convenience of his passengers. "He also said," Sallie continued in her letter of June 12, "he would bring any passengers for the Highlands right to the door. I didn't commit myself at all but I rather think that I'll give him our patronage. I believe he is more reliable than Hubbell. We'll talk it over when you come up." Sallie had to contend with the same kind of overtures from competing grocers from the valley. "The Gold Rule store at Lyons [operated by a Mr. Decosta] is trying to get the Park trade & offer some great inducements," she reported on July 3. "Are going to take orders here every other day & deliver the goods next day."

Just what she decided with respect to Sprague and his various offers is uncertain. What is clear is that Sallie quickly discovered the need to be on good terms with his competitor, William N. Hubbell, as well. Paying guests were agonizingly slow in arriving, and Sallie began to suspect that this was at least partly due to the favoritism and preferential treatment shown by the stage lines. "I would simply ask him," Sallie suggested to her husband on July 10 with respect to Hubbell, "how much he wanted to run his stage to our door & offer him the same to work for us that he gets from Mrs. James [of Elkhorn Lodge]. Just approach him in a business way. He certainly gives her every advantage & she must pay him something or he wouldn't do it."

With the arrival of her first boarders in mid-June, Sallie experienced still another lesson of resort management: the vagaries of taste. "These people," she wrote Charles on June 22, "don't seem to eat veal very much. Cooked a lovely lot of veal steaks for breakfast Wed morning & Nan was the only one who took any. Felt disgusted." Other guests were more appreciative. Ten days later she reported that she had furnished dinner for fifty cents apiece to three guests from the Estes Park Hotel, who were subsequently quoted as having "said that they were fortunate in coming here as it was the best place in the Park & they had been all around."

July found Sallie Reed still gamely fighting "the battles of boarding house life, which are very discouraging at times." "It looks as if this place is *voodooed*," she wrote Charles on the fourteenth.

> I hate to come down any lower on my prices but begin to think I'll have to. Mrs. James is nearly full. Two ladies came here today from the Hotel looking for board & lodging. Said Mr. Lester [manager of the Estes Park Hotel] sent them here & Dr. Bonnie [sic] recommended this place (one is consumptive). They wanted a room apiece & I offered it for $40.00 per month but they didn't decide whether they would come or not. Said Mrs. James wanted $10 or $12 per week but desirable rooms were taken. Everybody seems to want board at the very lowest rates, but want you to set a first class table. . . .

Rates, Sallie discovered, had a great deal to do with capturing trade, particularly since the Highlands, having been closed, could not count on guests who simply returned through force of habit. A case in point was a Mr. Merrill, his wife, and two sons, whom the Highlands lost as boarders to Harry Cole's resort ranch on Cabin Creek up in the Tahosa Valley. "They would have stayed here," Sallie told Charles,

> but Cole came down on the board so low that it knocked me out. Takes the two boys, 12 & 14 years old, at half price. . . . I offered all the inducements possible to have them remain here, but am afraid Cole's cheap rates will catch them. He offered them room & board for $6.00 per week for each of those large boys. I told him I couldn't come down to that.

It was not that Sallie did not understand the competitive nature of the resort business, for she soon reluctantly reduced her board and lodging rates because "it will be better than not having anyone."

Business remained disappointing throughout July, and Sallie was resentful. "A load of people came up to James's last eve," she reported on the thirty-first, "& they couldn't accommodate them, so hitched up & took them to the [Estes Park] Hotel. I think she might [have] sent them to me. Looks to me like everybody up here is against this house." By August, however, the situation had improved appreciably, and so much so that Sallie told Charles on the seventh that "I have been on the jump all day, had six people come yesterday & two the day before, which makes me 18 now & there is two more coming tomorrow from the Estes Park [Hotel] which will make 20. So you see I am doing better."

Several weeks later the summer season of 1898 ended. For all her early discouragements and frustrations Sallie Reed remained remarkably resilient. She had experienced at first hand a great deal about the day-to-day business of late-nineteenth-century resort life—knowledge that she and Charles would put to good use at the Highlands during the next three years and after 1911 when they opened their own hotel, the Brinwood, in Moraine Park.

Many of those who sought the bracing climate of Estes Park did so for reasons of health. Colorado with its pure, dry air and warm sunshine was widely advertised throughout the 1870s and 1880s as a panacea for those with weakened constitutions and "debilities" of every kind, particularly for those with pulmonary diseases such as consumption. Lured by special guidebooks to its growing number of health resorts and spas, health seekers came in such numbers that by common estimate a full third of the population during these decades was composed of recovered or recovering invalids.[57] Consumptives were received without prejudice at Colorado's resorts, including those in Estes Park. Sadly—at a time when a change of scenery and climate was the only known treatment—many arrived in the final stages of their disease. One such individual was Alice Chapin, the wife of Frederick Chapin, who accompanied her mountaineer husband from their home in Connecticut to Ferguson's ranch during the summer of 1888. Within weeks of their return to Hartford, Alice Chapin was dead.

All too typical, perhaps, is the story of a young woman named Jennie Tryon, who came to Denver from Cleveland in 1888 "in the hope that the change of climate would retard the progress of pulmonary disease from which she was suffering." For a time she worked as a copyist in the county clerk's office in Denver. By May of 1892, however, her health had worsened, and she left her job to spend eight weeks at the Carlton Hotel in Longmont. On July 6, "under the impression that a higher altitude might be better for her," she came to Estes Park, spending two weeks at

Sprague's before seeking the even higher elevation of Lamb's ranch. There Jennie Tryon died on July 27, 1892, at the age of twenty-five.[58] Her case, unfortunately, was by no means unique, and deaths in Estes Park under similar circumstances were reported from time to time. One such death, which occurred at Ferguson's in 1893, provided the occasion for the Estes Park correspondent for the *Longmont Ledger* to deliver the warning that, conventional wisdom notwithstanding, "persons who are suffering in the last stages of lung disease (tuberculosis) are not likely to derive any benefit in this particular locality. Those suffering as above mentioned, had better go to a lower altitude."[59]

Treating tuberculars in Colorado was nonetheless a tourist industry. This was true even in Estes Park where as early as the summer of 1880 the British visitor Daniel Pidgeon reported that Dunraven's Estes Park Hotel had "a resident doctor and a regular *clientele* of invalids, who . . . derive great benefit from the air of this mountain sanatorium. . . ."[60] During the mid-1890s Dr. Carl Ruedi operated a tent camp for consumptives near the hotel, drawing a number of his patients from the Reverend J. S. Flory's Walnut Grove Sanitarium in nearby Hygiene.[61] All this changed, however, after the turn of the century when it became recognized that tuberculosis was a contagious disease and sympathy was replaced by dread. When Enos Mills, who had himself come to Colorado to improve a sickly constitution, purchased the Lambs' Long's Peak House in 1901, he made it clear in his advertisements that "no consumptives [are] taken."

Of the early guest ranch owners, the MacGregors alone were content to be absentee landlords. They continued to welcome summer visitors into the Black Canyon and to operate their ranch year-round, but the lives of Alex and Clara MacGregor during the eighties were focused elsewhere. During the early part of the decade, they made their home on College Avenue in Fort Collins, where Alexander MacGregor served as county judge from May 1882 to January 1885 and then practiced law. In 1886 MacGregor moved his law practice and family to Denver. Through it all the ranch in Estes Park, which both Alex, Clara, and their children visited regularly, continued to flourish. By 1884 it had grown to some fifteen hundred fenced acres, some of it "the best agricultural and hay land in the park," and MacGregor was grazing "over a hundred head of fine graded Shorthorn cattle [branded XIX], which he is now crossing with thoroughbred Hereford stock."[62] During this period MacGregor also owned a ranch in the valley stocked with Devon cattle.[63]

While living in Fort Collins, Alexander MacGregor became involved in local politics, using his office as a place to caucus about candidates for alderman and the state senate, as well as to organize a county bar. Clara continued her artwork, and both of them regularly took part in the town's social activities. One of these events was a masquerade ball, attended by two hundred, at which the petite Clara appeared in the "grand promenade" dressed as "Cherry Ripe"; Judge MacGregor's costume, unfortunately, went unreported.[64]

The MacGregors would continue to make Denver their home for the next decade, moving back to Estes Park in the late fall of 1894. A year and a half later, on June 17, 1896, Alexander MacGregor was killed by a bolt of lightning while doing assessment work on a mining claim near the Poudre Lakes at the edge of a cliff at the head of Forest Canyon. He was fifty-one. Though Clara completed the building of a new two-story, five-room home (their third home on the ranch), she herself returned to Denver. She died in 1901. Donald MacGregor, the second son, took charge of the ranch between 1899 and 1902, after which it was leased for a number of years to Charles and Edward Johnson and used almost exclusively for ranching and farming. In 1909 and 1910, Donald bought out his two brothers, George and Halbert, left his job as a pricing agent

Figure 6.6. Alexander MacGregor and family (c. 1892) in front of the "second" ranch house, or "A. Q. House," built in 1882 around one of the original homestead cabins. Courtesy MacGregor Trust.

Figure 6.7. Picking flowers in the Black Canyon. Courtesy National Park Service—Rocky Mountain National Park.

for Hendrie & Bolthoff, the Denver hardware and machinery company, and brought his wife, Minnie Maude Koontz, and his six-year-old daughter, Muriel, back to the Black Canyon to operate the ranch on a full-time, year-round basis. By this time, however, its days as a tourist resort were a thing of the past.

For many, if not most, visitors during these two decades, vacationing in Estes Park continued to mean erecting a tent in some scenic and secluded spot and taking full advantage of life lived out-of-doors at a leisurely pace that most of us have long since forgotten. Anna Gordon, who tented for a month on "a beautiful eminence of ground in Willow Park" with her husband and children in the late 1870s, has left us a marvelous account of her experiences, as well as a description of the world of the Spragues that lay before her. "At the foot of the hill on the east was a group of cottages, ever suggestive of the pleasures of home life," she wrote of Sprague's ranch; "and, promiscuously scattered, were the tents and canvas-wagons, dotting the camp grounds of transients. The former were often pitched at night and taken down in the morning, while their tenants moved to visit other points of interest." Food was

Figures 6.8, 6.9, 6.10, 6.11. Early day camping in Estes Park. Courtesy Lulabeth and Jack Melton; Fort Collins Public Library; City of Greeley Museums, permanent collection; National Park Service—Rocky Mountain National Park.

prepared over an open fire among the boulders and eaten while sitting on benches at a table beneath a small arbor of pine trees on one side of which was stretched a tent fly. "Our side-board, washstand, ottomans, têtes, etc.," she added, "were of solid mountain granite, hewn out by nature's artistic hand; though, from an occasional want of adaptability, we sometimes feared we had perverted their uses." At night, after the conviviality of the evening campfire, they peacefully retired to two tents, each of which slept four.[65] It could become crowded. "Some spots around the park," the *Rocky Mountain News* reported in August 1882, "resemble a military encampment, groups of tents, horses, wagons . . . gathered together in pleasant locations. . . ."[66]

Though Gordon's own equipage was modest, camping out did not have to be primitive. Period photographs reveal that campers brought with them a surprisingly large number of amenities: folding tables, chairs and stools, hammocks, cookstoves, dutch ovens, mess chests, portable sideboards for fixing food or washing dishes, and other comforts of home. Many campers from the valley towns (a species familiarly known as "sagebrushers") also brought with them not only springboard wagons, with their canvas tops and open sides, but four-wheel surreys, which made for enjoyable outings along "thirty-five to fifty miles of smooth, level and easy graded roads" winding through the park. Some campers chose to pitch their tents close to Sprague's or the Elkhorn Lodge in order to take their meals with the regular boarders. While most campers, aided by guidebooks,[67] brought their supplies with them, by the early 1880s a small number of stores were operating during the summer months, sometimes as branch outlets for enterprising shop owners from the valley.[68]

Throughout the 1880s and into the 1890s Estes Park was celebrated not only "for its unequal rural scenery" but for its "fine herds of Hereford cattle,"[69] clearly the breed of choice. William James, Hank Farrar and his partner and fellow hunter and guide, Caleb A. Cook, Horace Ferguson, and Alexander MacGregor all invested heavily in an industry that until the boom ended in 1885 in a glutted market and falling prices seemed to offer an almost certain return on invested capital. Theodore Whyte, with the financial backing of Dunraven and the Estes Park Company, led the way. In 1879 he brought in a number of prize Swiss cattle known for their ability to adapt to high altitudes and cool temperatures, which he preceded both to breed and show. As late as 1891, long after the cattle boom in Colorado had ended, Whyte maintained a herd of 375 Hereford cows and 20 bulls with their distinctive cross and bar (x) brand.

Several newcomers also interested themselves in the cattle business. One of these was Peter J. Pauly Jr. (1854–1935), the wealthy son of the founder of the Pauly Jail Building and Manufacturing Company of St. Louis. After graduating from St. Louis University, the younger Pauly spent three years as an architectural apprentice and then joined his father's company. In 1873 Pauly came west to Denver in search of mountain air and a better climate. He returned to St. Louis in 1875, but three years later was back in Colorado, where he spent a month at the Elkhorn Lodge, which then consisted of a main building (containing a living room, dining room, kitchen, and four small bedrooms), a smaller one-room log cabin, and a number of tents. In 1881, still suffering from poor health, twenty-six-year-old Peter Pauly came back, intending to stay.

Known to his friends as "P. J.," Pauly and his wife, Sarah, arrived at the James ranch on September 15, 1881, and were given a room in a small cottage set up on stilts called "the Rustic." They spent the winter of 1881–1882 at the James ranch, helping to replace the one-room cabin with a three-room cottage. By the following April, Pauly had completed a four-room house of his own with logs brought down from Horseshoe Park. It stood on the north side of Fall River opposite the Elkhorn Lodge, a site that Pauly had purchased from James even before his arrival. That fall, with apparently very little in the way of prior experience, Pauly entered the range cattle business, acquiring the government grazing privileges held by George Ragan at the foot of Devils Gulch, the future site of Glen Haven. (Ragan, like Griff Evans a one-time partner of Captain George Brown, had been running cattle since the 1870s.) The following spring, using lumber brought down from James's sawmill up Fall River, Pauly built a barn behind his cottage and a four-room cottage for Ragan, with whom he had made arrangements to look after his cattle. That same year Pauly purchased Frank Hyatt's land and cattle in Horseshoe Park, and in February 1884 Hank Farrar and "Cale" Cook's property along Cow Creek. There he built a barn, corrals, enlarged the original log house, and gave the place the name "Double Bar Y Ranch." Eventually, with the financial support of his father and partner, P. J. Pauly and Son would control some four hundred acres.[70]

Pauly stocked his ranches with white-faced Hereford cattle, many of them purchased in Iowa. In 1884 he imported four thoroughbred bulls from England, each of them fully recorded in the English herd book. Money was never a problem. In 1885 he paid eight hundred dollars for a single cow and heifer calf and added another bull to his herd, as well as forty-three head of high-grade cows and heifers from half to seven-eighths bred.[71] Pauly, to his credit, entered fully into the community life of Estes Park, serving as justice of the peace in 1884 and 1885, and willingly pitching in on local projects such as the maintenance of MacGregor's toll road. His major love, however, was ranching, and as late as April of 1886 P. J. and his father were looking to expand their operation by acquiring "property in the vicinity of Loveland . . . with the intention of establishing a blooded stock farm."[72] Pauly might well have remained in the ranching business indefinitely (his wife would later say that "the happiest days of our lives were spent in the Park"), but the steady decline in cattle prices finally induced him to return to St. Louis in the mid-1890s, where he became president of his father's company and for all practical purposes ended his formal relationship with Estes Park.[73]

We know rather less about two other early ranchers, William D. Ewart and Samuel B. Hart. What we do know is that Ewart, a Chicagoan, had come to Estes Park, together with his wife and daughter, for reasons of health and that on August 9, 1879, he purchased a quarter section in Horseshoe Park, where he briefly raised Herefords in partnership with William James.[74] That same year he built several cottages in the park. By 1883 the twenty-five-year-old Hart, a native of New York City, had joined Ewart as a resident of the park, and by 1884 they were doing business together, ranging Hereford cattle over 1,120 acres of land, which they presumably had leased. Included in the herd were at least four bulls, one of which had "taken numerous premiums at eastern fairs" and was said to be worth one thousand dollars.[75] A year later Ewart and Hart were numbered among the largest taxpayers in Larimer County.[76]

The year 1885 seems to have marked the zenith of cattle raising in Estes Park, as it did in many places in Colorado. Considering the limited size of the park, where open grazing land was constrained by recreating tourists and overgrazing posed a risk if the size of a herd became too large, the surviving figures are impressive. That year, in addition to Ewart and Hart, who had 225 head of cattle, Farrar and Cook had 97,[77] Horace and Hunter Ferguson 144, William James 120, Alexander MacGregor 60, Peter J. Pauly 250, and Theodore Whyte 319. These figures, which come from the *Fort Collins Courier*, do not include the small herd kept in the Tahosa Valley by Elkanah Lamb or, for that matter, any herd of less than 50. On a countywide basis, the figures for Estes Park become even more impressive. The number of cattle being raised in 1885 by ranchers with 50 or more head in Larimer County totaled 19,932; of these 1,215, or 6 percent, were being ranged in Estes Park.[78] The seriousness (and cost) of this commitment are further illustrated by the *American Hereford Record* for that year, published by the American Hereford Cattle Breeders' Association. Registered in this volume are 7 animals belonging to P. J. Pauly and Son, 4 belonging to William James, and 38 belonging to William Ewart and Samuel Hart.[79]

The ranging of cattle in Estes Park, and in fairly substantial numbers, persisted into the early years of the twentieth century. The largest herds continued to be those ranged on lands belonging to the Estes Park Company. During the summer of 1898, for example, William Golding-Dwyre, then managing Dunraven's holdings, was pasturing 1,000 head for two men named Thomas and Hammond.

The following winter, 1898–1899, proved, however, to be the kind that drove even veteran ranchers like Horace Ferguson to despair. Loss of stock in and around the park reportedly ran as high as 55 percent.[80] There were substantial snows in November ("the worst November I ever saw in the Park," Ferguson, now seventy-two, wrote on December 1st[81]), and they did not abate until the following April. Ferguson was living at the Highlands and keeping cattle both in the vicinity of Marys Lake and in Moraine Park, where he had harvested and stored substantial amounts of hay for winter feeding. During the months that followed he recorded his frustrations in a series of letters written to his son-in-law Charles Reed.

"The snow drifts are awful," Horace wrote Reed on March 21, 1899,

I have lost 8 cows & 4 calves. Have the poorest ones pretty well in hand. Have to go or send to Willow Park every day. Have 4 young calves. I have had the hardest time I ever had. The 4 last cows that died were caught in the last storm on the 5 & 6, got caught in a snowbank and died. I hope you are having better luck down there.[82]

Conditions had not materially changed by March 30. "I have been riding since the storm to see what the damage was," he wrote Charles that day.

Yesterday I was over [to the] Lake pasture, found 41 head. They looked very well. Today I went to W. Park Found 2 cows & 1 yearling dead & another down. . . . The snow was 22 inches in W. Park, 18 here. Sunday morn the thermometer registered 20 below here. . . . The snow banks are so bad you can't go where you want. . . . This is the hardest winter I ever saw anywhere. It does not look any more like spring than it did a month ago.[83]

Snows continued into April, forcing Ferguson to "haul down" another five hundred pounds of Hay in Moraine Park. "The way the roads are," he wrote on April 2, "I am kept busy hauling hay & still the cattle seem to get poorer. I can't see how they stand it."[84] Horace Ferguson was no stranger to the vagaries of nature. He had survived the winters and grasshopper incursions of the 1870s, and once again he found the fortitude to carry on. That winter he had ample company. Hugo Miller suffered "a heavy loss in cattle" at his ranch on Cow Creek, while the English Company reported the loss of forty-two head "by the hard winter and black leg. Some of their cows were seen by George McGregor [sic], dead—standing on their feet."[85]

Not all the open land in Estes Park was devoted to cattle and tourists. The record, though spotty, indicates that during these years, despite a growing season of less than a hundred days, substantial acreage was given over to farming, not only at the MacGregor Ranch, but throughout the park. Hay, wheat, oats, rye, barley, and vegetables were the preferred crops. "We saw crops of these in various parts of the Park," the *Longmont Home Mirror* reported in August 1881, "which were not surpassed by any in the lower valleys for quality or luxuriance of growth."[86] Not to be outdone, Elkanah Lamb brought in respectable crops of potatoes, radishes, lettuce, and other vegetables, and at an altitude of 9,350 feet.[87] In the potato department, however, the record clearly belonged to Henry M. Ely of Beaver Meadows, who in 1886 produced, and sent down to Fort Collins as proof, a potato weighing three pounds ("not a knob on it").[88] During the same period Ely's near neighbors and in-laws, the Hupps, had twelve acres under cultivation where they grew potatoes, oats, hay, barley, wheat, and garden vegetables with an annual cash value of two hundred dollars. Photographs of the day suggest that the areas placed under cultivation were sometimes substantial, as do such brief news items as one of 1883 indicating that Hubbell and Gilbert had sent a McCormick harvester up to the park by wagon to cut sixty acres of oats.[89]

One important source of information on the agricultural life of early Estes Park is the 1885 Colorado census, which collected a good deal of statistical information on both ranching and farming activity for the previous year. It shows, not surprisingly, that Theodore Whyte was not only the largest rancher in the park but the largest farmer as well, raising that year one hundred tons of hay and producing twenty thousand pounds of butter. Julian Johnson and William James each are listed as having harvested fifty tons of hay, while Peter Pauly harvested twenty. Pauly's land also produced five hundred bushels of potatoes, while his cows produced two hundred pounds of butter. Perhaps the most versatile farmer-rancher of that year, it turned out, was the postmaster, John Cleave, who is recorded as having used over thirteen hundred acres of land (presumably leased from his old employer, the Estes Park Company) to grow three hundred and twenty-five bushels of oats and one hundred and fifty bushels of potatoes and to raise cattle (his cows produced six hundred pounds of butter), horses, pigs, and chickens.[90]

Well before the turn of the century parts of Moraine Park, aided by irrigation ditches, were also under active cultivation. Horace Ferguson raised enough hay on his ranch there in 1903 to justify the purchase of

Figure 6.12. Haying in Moraine Park in the 1890s. Courtesy National Park Service—Rocky Mountain National Park.

a new baler. That same year he reportedly produced fifty bushels of potatoes from a single acre.[91]

As for Theodore Whyte, both he and the Estes Park Company managed to make a go of it through the 1880s and into the 1890s. Like his fellow ranchers, Whyte discovered after 1885 that cattle raising in Estes Park, even with the added advantage of the company's holdings along the North Fork, was at best a marginal undertaking. Nor was the rest of the Dunraven enterprise in much better shape. Several of the original stockholders, including the earl's brother-in-law, Arthur Pendarvis Vivian, pulled out of the company, leaving Dunraven to shoulder the major financial responsibilities. There were other problems as well. Various tracts of company land were seized for nonpayment of taxes and then redeemed, and lawsuits were filed, at least two by former hotel managers, and another by John Cleave.

Nor had Theodore Whyte's personal life been easy. He had come to Estes Park a bachelor, but shortly after the Estes Park Hotel opened in 1877 he met Ida Webster, a young woman from Massachusetts who was in the park that summer for her health. "Mr. Whyte and Miss Webster were seen together nearly every day on horseback," Abner Sprague recalled; "Mr. Whyte on one of the hunters; then is when he used the gates for hurdles."[92] The two were married in 1878. Ida Whyte bore her husband five children, all but the last, Beatrix, dying in infancy. She herself died shortly thereafter.

On October 12, 1886, at Trinity Episcopal Church in Greeley, Whyte married Lady Maude Josepha Ogilvy, the daughter of David Graham Drummond Ogilvy, eighth earl of Arlie, and his wife, Blanche Stanley. After a short wedding trip to Denver, Whyte brought his new wife and her maid, Jennie Henderson, back to his cottage in Estes Park. The two had met at the Crown Ranch near Greeley, which her brother, Lyulph Gilchrist Stanley Ogilvy (or "Lord Ogilvy," as he was known locally) had established with the help of his father in 1879. Whyte and Lady Maude, who was thirteen years younger than her husband, had four children, three of them while living in Estes Park. An able and astute man, Whyte made himself a valued part of the community, which he served as postmaster and as an elected justice of the peace. He also participated in Republican county politics. By the time of his marriage to Lady Maude, whatever hard feelings there might once have been between him and other valley residents had long since dissipated, leaving the *Fort Collins Courier* effusive in its praise: "Mr. Whyte has long been known as one of the most successful ranchmen in Colorado. His name is identified with the advancement of the state, and the vast interests he represents are of incalculable value to this part of the west."[93]

These were, nonetheless, difficult years with undercurrents of unhappiness, some of it, it was later said, resulting from Lady Maude's loneliness. The major causes, however, no doubt had to do with the financial pressures on Whyte himself, caused by problems in the cattle and hotel business, and by Dunraven's increasing reluctance to invest more in an enterprise that paid so little. For a time Dunraven leased the entire operation to Whyte, but without measurable improvement in anyone's fortunes. At length hanging on proved more difficult than simply letting go, and in 1895 or 1896 the Whytes left Estes Park for England, where Whyte managed a large estate near his native Devonshire. He died in 1903, at the age of fifty-seven.[94]

At the time of the Colorado census of 1885, some twenty families and 105 individuals were living in Estes Park. Though by 1900 the population reached two hundred, including the residents of the Tahosa Valley, major growth and development remained in check until midway through the first decade of the twentieth century, when two important exchanges of land—one John Cleave's one hundred and sixty acres at the confluence of the Big Thompson and Fall Rivers, the other the residual holdings of the Earl of Dunraven—altered the face of Estes Park forever.

Chapter 7

∽

Mountaineering in Colorado: The Peaks About Estes Park

When Frederick Chapin, a drug wholesaler from Hartford, Connecticut, first visited Estes Park in 1887 and turned his attention to the surrounding peaks, he made a number of discoveries. Perhaps the most interesting was the fact that most early visitors to Estes Park did not climb mountains. Longs Peak, then as now, was a magnet for the adventuresome, but for the most part the mountainous areas surrounding the park remained unchallenged and virtually unknown. Part of the problem was the lack of knowledgeable guides. Even Carlyle Lamb, who conducted Chapin to the top of Longs Peak that summer, and who had been guiding professionally since 1880, admitted that "he had never climbed any other elevation west of Longs Peak."[1] What the younger Lamb might have told them was that until Longs Peak had been mastered, and mastered again, there was little incentive to move on to other goals.

Though William Byers had failed in his first attempt in 1864, he was, of course, wrong in his statement that Longs Peak could not and would not be climbed. The summit could be reached, and by a variety of routes, as the one-armed Civil War veteran Major John Wesley Powell (1834–1904), then a professor of geology and natural science at Illinois State Normal University, would prove on August 23, 1868. Powell and his students were in Colorado that summer as part of the Colorado Scientific Exploring Expedition, a largely self-financed party of twenty-one, made up almost exclusively of amateur scientists and advanced students from Illinois State and nearby Illinois Wesleyan.[2] Their immediate object was to gather as large as possible a collection of specimens for the Normal Museum illustrating the geological history and natural resources of the Rocky Mountain West, whose status in 1868 "was still remarkably uncertain."[3] Though it was understood before they left home that the summer's agenda would include an attempt to ascend Longs Peak,[4] that feat, successful or not, was to be but a prelude for grander things to come. Powell's "great and final object"[5]—the target for the following year—was an exploration of the upper Colorado River and a descent through its uncharted canyon.

The members of the Powell Expedition, as it came to be known in the press, left Normal, Illinois, for Chicago on June 29, 1868. Some two weeks later the party had reached Denver, now outfitted with horses and mules, many of them untamed, that they had purchased and tried to educate to harness in Cheyenne. "Unused to riding, and our animals being untutored," one member of the party wrote home, "we could not have been mistaken for a scientific expedition."[6] From Denver, Powell and his companions proceeded through Bear Creek Canyon and up to Empire, where they were joined by the undaunted Byers, a guide named Jack Sumner, who happened to be Byers's brother-in-law,[7] and several other experienced mountaineers. Byers and Sumner accompanied the party on a leisurely reconnaissance across Berthoud Pass into Middle Park. From their base camp at Hot Sulphur Springs on the banks of the Grand River, where Sumner ran a trading and outfitting post and Byers dreamed of one day establishing a resort for tourists, the Powell party spent the next three months exploring the mountains, taking measurements, sketching geologic formations, collecting specimens, and documenting the natural history of the region. Not only was Powell in no hurry, he was thorough to a fault, and, as one biographer noted, his penchant for comprehensiveness "drove his packers and collectors until they groused and grumbled in their diaries."[8]

Just how the party to attempt Longs Peak was finally put together is uncertain. Besides Powell it consisted of William Byers; Walter H. Powell, the major's brother; Jack Sumner; and three of Powell's students from Illinois—Lewis W. Keplinger, Samuel M. Garman, and Ned E. Farrell. Byers and Sumner were there by prearrangement, and Lewis Keplinger by virtue of the fact that his assignment that summer was to measure altitude, latitude, and longitude with instruments provided by the Smithsonian. For Keplinger, that summer was a dream come true. "I was crazy for the opportunity to go," he later confessed, "and they gave it to me."[9]

The other two collegians, Sam Garman and Ned Farrell, needed little encouragement to accompany the major on his quest other than a break from routine and a chance for mountain sport. The Powell party left Hot

Sulphur Springs for Grand Lake on Wednesday, August 17, camping that night on Willow Creek, "half a mile from the mouth and fourteen miles from the Springs."[10] The next day they arrived at Grand Lake, where they made camp on the western shore to await the arrival of Major Powell, who had lagged behind hunting for lost stock. Nor were they alone. Byers counted twenty-five fishermen, including "an outfit of eight or ten from Denver, with two wagons, who expected to load back with fish."[11]

On August 20, Powell and his companions left for Longs Peak on horseback, leading a mule carrying ten days' rations. The terrain was unexpectedly rough. The next day, the horses and mule abandoned, the party proceeded on foot to the western base of McHenrys Peak near what is now Lake Powell. From there they climbed the sharp ridge that connects McHenrys Peak with Chiefs Head and Pagoda Mountain. The ridge grew narrower and narrower. Sumner, the veteran mountaineer, who had taken the lead, became exasperated and sat down. "By G———," he exclaimed, "I haven't lost any mountain."[12] Though Keplinger found the courage to go on, leading his companions across a narrow ledge not more than eighteen inches wide, they finally found themselves cut off from their destination "by impassable chasms." Retreat was now un-avoidable. Recrossing the Continental Divide, the party descended into Wild Basin on the south side of Longs Peak and established camp about 3:30 P.M. at the tree line above Sandbeach Lake to await the next day.

Twenty-seven-year-old Lewis Keplinger, or "Kep," as his compan-ions called him, was not content to wait. Over their objections, and leaving his blanket, barometer, and other gear behind, he set out alone to do some preliminary exploring in preparation for a new effort. Find-ing a couloir, or gully, winding up the south flank of the peak to a notch cut into the ridge south of the East Face, Keplinger succeeded in ascend-ing to within several hundred feet of the summit before returning after dark to his anxious comrades to report that "the ascent might be pos-sible." "The night was passed with little sleep by most of the party as only two had blankets," Ned Farrell wrote four days later.

> It was amusing to see the dodge that was played by the would-be sleepers; they would crowd close to the fire till some poor fellow would be entirely forced out, when he would throw on wood and scorch their backs so he could get an inside place. The cold wind howling, pine wood cracking, flames glowing, men growling, swearing, and snoring made a scene never to be forgotten.[13]

The ascent began about 7 A.M. on the morning of the twenty-third, with the party alternately climbing and crawling up the rocky gorge.

Two hours later they had reached the place where Keplinger had turned back the evening before. Here the party sat down and rested: "gazing on the forbidding cliffs above, which revealed no foothold from below, the word passed round that it was dangerous to attempt it. One remarked that no man could scale the point and live."[14] The defining moment had arrived. Then, Farrell wrote, apparently in reference to Jack Sumner, clearly the most experienced of the group, "one arose, tall, gaunt, but muscular, and said determinedly, 'I have come too far and worked too hard to give up: I shall go as far as fingers and toes will aid me.' With staff in hand he started up. . . ."[15]

After watching for a moment "anxiously," the others followed. By 10 A.M. the entire party, fittingly enough led by Keplinger, stood on the summit of Longs Peak, having achieved what Byers had predicted was unachievable only four years before. "The peak is a nearly level surface, paved with irregular blocks of granite," Byers told his readers a week later,

> and without vegetation of any kind, except a little gray lichen. The outline is nearly a parallelogram—east and west—widening a little toward the western extremity, and five or six acres in extent. On the eastern end are some large boulders, giving it an apparent altitude of ten or fifteen feet above the remainder of the surface. Along the northern edge, and especially at the northwest corner, the surface rounds off considerably, though the general appearance is almost that of a perfect level.[16]

There was no evidence, Keplinger later recalled, that anyone had preceded them.[17]

While most of the party relaxed and savored their accomplishment, Keplinger used his barometer to determine the altitude. The party then erected a monument to their achievement, inserting in its base a tin case into which they placed notes of the instrument readings together with a number of other mementos. Unfurling a small American flagstaff, which they left floating in the breeze, the major made a brief speech. Someone had brought along a bottle of wine in anticipation of the celebration. Some of the wine was splashed on the monument by way of christening, the remainder being consumed by five members of the party. "Two of us withstanding all entreaties did not drink on Longs Peak," one of the students, Sam Garman, a Quaker, reported to a female friend back home at Bloomington, "whatever the papers may say to the contrary."[18] After a stay on the summit of nearly three hours, Powell and his companions began a two-hour descent into Wild Basin on their way back to Middle Park.[19]

For nearly two decades, and until the time of Frederick Chapin, the conquest of Longs Peak remained an achievement worth recording, and in a number of cases worth writing about as well. Two of the most memorable of those early ascents were made by women—Anna Dickinson and Isabella Bird. The first, and nearly fatal, descent of the East Face was made by Elkanah Lamb in 1871.

Anna Dickinson's climb is remembered chiefly because it was made by a woman and has traditionally been regarded as a first.[20] Viewed from the perspective of the man who arranged it, Ferdinand V. Hayden, it was something of a promotional stunt as well. In the celebrated lecturer Anna Dickinson, a woman who took great delight in her mountaineering accomplishments, Hayden found a most willing accomplice.

Hayden had a cause to promote. As head of the Hayden Survey, or the United States Geological and Geographical Survey of the Territories, the largest of the three great western surveys launched between 1870 and 1880, his agenda was an extremely ambitious one. In 1873 and again in 1874 and 1875 Hayden's civilian scientists worked in Colorado, measuring and reading the geological history of the land, identifying its natural resources, collecting and classifying its flora and fauna, and recording and interpreting its indigenous Indian culture. The survey also put to good use men like William H. Jackson, whose brilliant photographs of the scenic wonders of the West captured the imagination of the nation. All this depended upon annual appropriations from the government, and to that end good publicity was always helpful.

Anna Dickinson (1842–1932) was no stranger to publicity, and by 1873 she needed it badly. However popular she had been during and immediately after the Civil War, her career as "Queen of the Lyceum" and her health were in fragile condition, and her prospects for the future were uncertain. Economic times throughout the United States were bad and worsening, and the lyceum movement was one of its victims. By the spring of that year Anna had become physically and emotionally worn out and anxious. Then came a letter from Ralph Meeker, the son of Nathan Meeker, the agricultural editor of the *New York Tribune* and the founder of the Union Colony at Greeley,[21] inviting her to restore her health by coming to Colorado. Anna accepted, providing she could "make it out in any right shape," scraped together the necessary funds, and that August set out to visit the Rocky Mountain West accompanied by her brother, the Reverend John Dickinson, a Methodist clergyman.

Anna Dickinson arrived in Denver on August 16 and immediately took to the mountains, conquering in rapid succession the summits of Pikes Peak, Grays Peak, Mount Lincoln, and Mount Elbert, fourteeners all. On the slopes of Mount Lincoln she dined with the miners at the Montezuma Mine, "the highest mine in North America." The *Denver*

Tribune recorded these exploits, reporting that as the first woman ever to ascend Mount Elbert "she will rank well in the annals of mountaineering."[22] Anna's health improved dramatically, and by early September, when she returned to Denver to deliver her two most famous and popular feminist lectures ("Joan of Arc" and "What Is to Hinder?"), Anna Dickinson had clearly recovered both her enthusiasm and her form. When she took the platform at Guard's Opera House on the evening of September 3, deeply tanned from her mountain excursions and "neatly dressed in black silk . . . with several costly and dazzling diamond rings, and a cross, blazing with the same jewels," "her appearance and address were both commanding."[23] Her performance a week later, before the "largest audience that ever graced Denver's Governor's Guard Hall,"[24] was one that left her audience "spellbound."[25]

On September 10 Anna Dickinson left again for the mountains, this time to meet up by prearrangement with one of the parties of Ferdinand Hayden's survey, to visit Estes Park "and Long's Peak also."[26] As the *Rocky Mountain News'* account of the events that followed indicates—events climaxed by Anna Dickinson's successful ascent of Longs Peak on the morning of September 13, 1873—the planned rendezvous occurred at 4 P.M. on the afternoon of the twelfth at Hayden's camp near the base of Longs Peak.

Hayden's group had come in by way of Middle Boulder Creek, Ward, and the St. Vrain. "Saturday we make the ascent of Longs Peak," James T. Gardiner, one of Hayden's principal assistants, wrote to his mother, obviously with a sense of anticipation. "Anna Dickinson goes up with us. She spent part of yesterday at our camp. She has pledged herself an advocate to our cause, and she is no mean power to enlist. Dr. Hayden seems to make friends everywhere and I do not wonder, for he is full of good feeling when his belligerent power is not aroused."[27]

The assembled group was made up of some eighteen people, the largest single party that had ever attempted to climb the peak. It included members of Hayden's expedition—Hayden, Gardiner, the topographer William Henry Holmes, and Hayden's executive officer, James Stevenson—William Byers of the *Rocky Mountain News*,[28] and the Dickinson party of nine, who had come up from Estes Park, guided by the ubiquitous Welshman Griff Evans. Evans's guiding that day evidently left something to be desired, for his party, it was later reported, "missed their way," took more than six hours to make it up from the valley to the point of rendezvous, and had to be rescued by Ralph Meeker.[29] By late on the afternoon of the twelfth Evans had his group encamped in the vicinity of the sheltered area now known as "Jim's Grove."

Anna Dickinson was impressed by her scientific companions, particularly Ferdinand Hayden and James Gardiner. "What a pair of heads had that party!" she wrote some six years later in her book *A Ragged Register* (1879):

> Hayden, tall, slender, with soft brown hair and blue eyes—certainly not traveling on his muscle; all nervous intensity and feeling, a perfect enthusiast in his work, eager of face and voice, full of magnetism. Gardner [sic], shorter, stouter, with amber eyes and hair like gold, less quick and tense, yet made of the stuff that takes and holds on.
>
> I remember that after supper when we were camping at timber line, Gardner took one of his instruments and trotted up the side of the mountain to make some observations. He expected to be gone half an hour, and was gone, by reason of the clouds, nearer three hours, "but," as he quietly said when he came back, speaking of the clouds, "I conquered them at last."[30]

The campfire that evening proved particularly memorable:

> We sat around the great fire that was kept heaped with the whole trunks of dead trees, and watched the splendors of sun-setting till they were all gone, and these vanished, still sat on by the blazing fire circled by the solemn stately majesties, talking of many things—strange stories of adventure in mountain and gorge, climbs through which a score of times life had been suspended simply on strength of fingers, or nice poise on a hand-ledge thrust out into eternity, wild tales of frontier struggles—intricacies of science, discussions of human life and experience in crowded cities, devotion and enthusiasm as shown in any cause—all things, in fact, that touch the brain and soul, the heart and life, of mortals who really live, and do not merely exist. A talk worth climbing that height to have and to hold.[31]

From this campfire discussion, tradition has it, came the decision to name Longs Peak's two companions: Mount Meeker, named after Nathan Meeker of the Union Colony, and Mount Lady Washington.[32]

The ascent of Longs Peak began at 6 A.M. on the morning of September 13, following the now familiar route across the Boulder Field and through the Keyhole. Byers was convinced that the path they traversed was actually more difficult and less satisfactory than the one taken five years earlier by Major Powell and his party. Anna Dickinson raised at least a few eyebrows by wearing trousers,[33] which before the day was out she had succeeded in splitting on a snowbank.[34] They made amazingly good time, with some of the party making the ascent from camp "in considerably less than three hours." By 1 P.M. that afternoon, Hayden, Dickinson, and party were on their way down, spending the night at their former base camp before returning to Griff Evans's ranch where the next evening Anna Dickinson was fascinated by Mountain Jim's fireside stories.

Anna Dickinson left Colorado wonderfully impressed, both by what she had seen and by what she herself had accomplished. "It was the grandest pleasure I ever experienced," she wrote. "I believe it has been said that I have been to the summits of more great mountains in America than any other woman alive."[35]

Isabella Lucy Bird's climb the following month, by contrast, was a seriocomic affair almost from beginning to end. Despite the lateness of the season and the discouragement of Griff Evans, Isabella Bird was determined to climb Longs Peak. Her account of that event in the company of Rocky Mountain Jim and his dog Ring, and wearing her thin Hawaiian riding dress and a pair of Griff Evans's boots, later became the central episode of her book. It was also clearly the highlight of her visit to Colorado. "I wonder how you will like the Longs Peak letter," she wrote her sister Henrietta on Sunday, November 30, 1873. "I like it almost better than any for it represents what I thoroughly liked."[36] Even before she left Colorado, Bird had drafted and sent off to J. E. Liller in Colorado Springs a brief article on her Longs Peak experience for the December–January, 1873–1874, issue of his small magazine *Out West*.[37]

Though the focus of her narrative is on Mountain Jim, they were, in fact, a party of four: Isabella Bird, Jim, and the two "rude young men" who had originally accompanied her from Longmont to Estes Park, Platt Rogers and Sylvester Downer.[38] Their guide, Mountain Jim, presented

a shocking figure; he had on an old pair of high boots, with a baggy pair of old trousers made of deer hide, held on by an old scarf tucked into them; a leather shirt, with three or four ragged unbuttoned waistcoats over it; an old smashed wideawake, from under which his tawny, neglected ringlets hung; and with his one eye, his one long spur, his knife in his belt, his revolver in his waistcoat pocket, his saddle covered with an old beaver skin, from which the paws hung down; his camping blankets behind him, his rifle laid across the saddle in front of him, and his axe, canteen, and other gear hanging to the horn, he was as awful-looking a ruffian as one could see. By way of contrast he rode a small Arab mare, of exquisite beauty, skittish, high spirited, gentle, but altogether too light for him, and he fretted her incessantly to make her display herself.[39]

The first night out was spent before a great fire in Jim's Grove, around which they ate their supper and then gave themselves over to the kind of evening that often becomes memorable: "One of the young men sang a Latin student's song and two Negro melodies; the other 'Sweet Spirit, hear my Prayer.' 'Jim' sang one of Moore's melodies in a singular falsetto, and all together sang, 'The Star-spangled Banner' and 'The Red, White, and Blue.' Then 'Jim' recited a very clever poem of his own composition, and told some fearful Indian stories."[40] It was a cold night. By 9 P.M. the temperature had dropped into the low twenties. Jim replenished the fire, and his dog Ring dutifully curled himself up at Isabella's back as if instructed to keep her warm. "I could not sleep," she wrote, "but the night passed rapidly. . . ."[41]

It was still cold the next morning. Breakfasting at 7 A.M., the party of four continued on horseback as far as the "Lava Beds" (Boulder Field), which they had to cross on foot to gain the Keyhole. Not only was Bird quickly affected by "the rarefied atmosphere," but the pair of boots lent her by Evans were too large to give her a proper foothold. Fortunately, she discovered a pair of small overshoes beneath a rock, presumably those recently discarded by Anna Dickinson, "which just lasted for the day."[42]

At the "Notch," as she called the Keyhole, "the real business of the ascent began." Bird, if she is to be believed, became almost paralyzed by fright as they made their way along the back of the mountain to the Trough, descending in the process some two thousand feet to avoid ice. She wanted to turn back, but Jim insisted otherwise, to the point of threatening to carry her. Her description is graphic: "Slipping, faltering, gasping from the exhausting toil in the rarefied air, with throbbing hearts and panting lungs, we reached the top of the gorge and squeezed ourselves between two gigantic fragments of rock by a passage called the 'Dog's Lift,' when I climbed on the shoulders of one man and then was hauled up."[43] This brought them to the Narrows. "'Ring' refused to traverse the Ledge and remained at the 'Lift' howling piteously." At the bottom of the Homestretch Bird froze: "As we crept from the ledge round a horn of rock I beheld what made me perfectly sick and dizzy to look at—the terminal Peak itself—a smooth, cracked face or wall of pink granite, as nearly perpendicular as anything could well be up which it was possible to climb, well deserving the name of the 'American Matterhorn.'"[44] In Bird's retelling it took her an hour, "crawling on hands and knees, all the while tortured with thirst and gasping and struggling for breath," to make the top, but "at last the Peak was won."

They did not remain long on the summit. After placing their names and date of ascent in a tin can within a crevice, they began the descent, with Jim insisting that the safest way to proceed was to once again drop deep into the Trough on the way back to the Keyhole. Bird's recollections are again marvelously graphic:

> I had various falls, and once hung by my frock, which caught on a rock, and
> "Jim" severed it with his hunting knife, upon which I fell into a crevice full of

soft snow. We were driven lower down the mountains than he had intended by impassable tracts of ice, and the ascent was tremendous. For the last 200 feet the boulders were of enormous size, and the steepness fearful. Sometimes I drew myself up on hands and knees, sometimes crawled; sometimes "Jim" pulled me up by my arms or a lariat, and sometimes I stood on his shoulders, or he made steps for me of his feet and hands, but at six we stood on the "Notch" in the splendor of the sinking sun, all color deepening, all peaks glorifying, all shadows purpling, all peril past.[45]

They reached the Evans ranch at noon the next day without further incident: "A more successful ascent of the Peak was never made, and I would not now exchange my memories of its perfect beauty and extraordinary sublimity for any other experience of mountaineering in any part of the world."[46]

Platt Rogers and Sylvester Downer, on the other hand, were anything but impressed by Rocky Mountain Jim's abilities as a guide. According to Rogers, who provided Enos Mills with a brief reminiscence in 1905, much of the fatigue that Miss Bird experienced resulted from Jim's incompetence:

> After passing through the notch[47] Downer and I had a controversy with Jim as to the best way to get over the side. He insisted on going to the bottom near the head waters of the Big Thompson, and then climbing again until the Keyhole was reached. Downer and I thought we could reach the Keyhole directly and without the long descent and arduous climb. Miss Bird attached herself to Jim and we went our respective ways, Downer and I reaching the Keyhole while Jim and Miss Bird were somewhere in the gulch below. This made a long wait, and when they finally came up with us she was so fagged that she was unable to make her way unaided up the last steep slope of the peak. By alternately pulling and pushing her and stimulating her with snow soaked with Jamaica ginger, we got her to the top. We were then so late that we could remain but a short time, and we started on our return in the early afternoon. Jim insisted on the miserable trail he had followed in coming, and consequently he and Miss Bird floundered in the depths of the gulch once more while Downer and I returned by the upper and more direct trail, which necessitated another wait on our part at the lava beds. When Jim got her to the top again she was unable to mount her horse. She was therefore lifted on and practically held on until we got to camp, where she was lifted off, in fact, she was completely "done."[48]

Jim's mountaineering notwithstanding, Isabella Bird's account of her ascent of Longs Peak climb remains one of the great documents in the annals of Estes Park.

Elkanah J. Lamb, who would become the preeminent guide to the peak in the late 1870s and into the 1880s, had a very different kind of experience to narrate. In August of 1871, while still an itinerant preacher for the United Brethren, Lamb made his first visit to Estes Park, where he not only climbed Longs Peak (ascending by means of the traditional Keyhole route) but then, in an act that almost cost him his life, decided to descend the peak's vertical, 1,630-foot East Face, "where man had never gone before."

Lamb recalled the details of his descent in 1906 in the volume of recollections he titled *Memories of the Past and Thoughts of the Future*, by which time, safely distant from the event, he could tell the story with a sense of wry humor and understatement. Just what possessed him that day is unclear. In the retelling Lamb talks in a convoluted, preacherly style about the need to circumvent "old roads, rules, grooves, and conventional codes" and to break away "from old, fossilized systems and moss-grown customs"[49]—hardly the kind of advice one would expect from a seasoned mountaineer. At the time he no doubt simply followed an impulse.

Though the exact route he took is somewhat unclear in Lamb's retelling, it apparently first led him some thousand feet below the Notch, to the cut in the ridge to the south of the East Face. At that point the six-foot-five Lamb realized his danger. Retreat was impossible. Traversing the ledge known as Broadway, Lamb reached the snowfield that from that day on has been called "Lamb's Slide." Hugging the niches in the adjacent wall, he then started across the ice, only to lose his balance and begin to fall. Fortunately, he was able to grab a projecting boulder with his right hand, which stopped his plunge but left him dangling some five feet from the mountain. Somehow Lamb managed to get a knife out of his pocket, which he opened with his teeth, and then began to dig a niche in the ice for a toehold. When his knife broke in two, there was no choice: "putting the tip of my left foot in the shallow niche I had cut (knowing that if my foot slipped I was a lost Lamb), then working my arm to the top of the rock, I gave a huge lunge, just managing to reach the foot of the mountain."[50] Even after almost a century Father Lamb's dramatic account loses little of its power to excite and terrify.

For many of those who climbed Longs Peak during those early years the chief delight of the trip seems to have been examining the cairns and exhuming the evidence of those who had gone before. In August 1870, for example, Donald Brown, a twenty-four-year-old Scotch-born resident of upstate New York, climbing alone reported that

> I found in the southeast point of the summit a small tower of stones erected by Prof. J. W. Powell, in August, 1868. Beneath the rocks was a tin box, con-

taining a photograph of Powell, a paper signed by him and his party, stating they were the first persons who had ever made the ascent, a two cent and a one cent coin, a carbine cartridge, two percussion caps, and a biscuit.[51]

Having boiled water and made coffee, Brown then proceeded to erect a monument of his own:

> I built a tower over the ashes of the fire, near five feet in diameter, in the center of which I set the post I brought up, with the inscribed board affixed. I put in my coffee box a nickle five cent piece, two wild roses, a little ringlet from the head of a favorite child at home, Ada Northrop, and a fish hook that saved my life on a former expedition, by enabling me to catch trout when I had nothing else to eat. I then secured the box in the top of the tower.[52]

The very next month, Griff Evans, having guided a party of eight to the summit, reported a similar discovery in an account published, like Brown's, in the *Boulder County News*:

> We were much interested in examining the contents of the tin box that Major Powell's party left here in 1868, safely protected in a stone tower. There were various coins, Powell's photograph, some bread of his own make in a perfect state of preservation; but the most interesting thing was the record of their expedition, to which the names of the party were appended. I give the scientific part of the record in the matter.
> "August 23, 1868—Day fine, with cumulus clouds from southeast, and light wind from same direction. Air clear, the mountain ranges visible in all directions for 200 miles. At 10:15 A.M. barometer is 100 inches; thermometer wet bulb, 39°; dry bulb 49. 2°."
> We found the tower and relics of the Scotchman's ascent, an account of which appeared in your columns last month. In conclusion, I would say that the impression that Long's Peak is very difficult and dangerous of ascent, is altogether a wrong one. From Este's [sic] Park the trip is safe, easy, and pleasant.[53]

The summer of 1870 was apparently a busy one, for there was at least one more climb by a party of men from Greeley. A member of that group, a man named Long, the *Greeley Tribune* reported, made a copy of the record left by the Powell party and brought it back with him.[54]

The next year, 1871, Ralph Meeker of Greeley—Anna Dickinson's future escort—climbed the peak with engineers from Clarence King's Fortieth Parallel Survey. Meeker reported finding the names of the Greeley party of 1870 as well as "those of the Kentucky visitors." He also reported the existence of three "memorial towers" near the top of the Homestretch. Though he was absent getting water when the Powell monument was opened, he did "see a piece of bread which was said to have been baked by Major Powell" and reported that others had found "a tin can, containing the names of the Powell party, some bread, coins, and Powell's photograph. There was also a memorandum, regarding the observations, the ascent and the bread, saying: 'Let no man eat this bread,' or words to that effect."[55]

Abner Sprague and his future brother-in-law, Alson Chapman, also exhumed the major's relics in July of 1874 when they made their first climb of the peak—a feat that Abner Sprague repeated on foot exactly fifty years later. (They approached the peak by the "most direct route," going up Wind River and the north side of Battle Mountain to timberline. From there they made the ascent in three hours and ten minutes, "which we thought good time.") Sprague, in the account he published in 1922, recalled finding the names of the Hayden party "pricked on a tin plate" nailed to a short stick and discovering a small box in which "was a lady's spring tape, the yard long kind, inclosed in a metal case, on which was scratched the name of Anna E. Dickinson, the only name of a woman we found among all the names."[56] Chapman, who had published his account of the trip years earlier in the August 12, 1874, edition of *Fort Collins Standard*, noted that

> the names of nearly all who have ever visited the peak are there making about fifty or sixty in all. We find in a tin can a photograph of Major Powell and his memorandum (he having been the first man who ever made the ascent) dated July 7, 1870. . . . the bulk of the names date from the summer of 1873. Marks of Prof. Hayden's geological survey are here, and many other items of interest, which we have not time to mention.[57]

When Sprague returned to the summit several years later, he could find nothing but "Major Powell's picture, where it had been used for a target by some vandal, shot so full of holes that you could only tell it had been a photograph." "It is a pity," Sprague concluded, "that there are so few accidents from carrying fire arms on such climbs. I mean it."[58]

Relics of Powell's historic achievement apparently remained on Longs Peak until 1935. That year Everett Long, during an outing of the Colorado Mountain Club, found some of the major's notes, which he retrieved and presented to the Colorado Historical Society. Time had taken its toll. "The only decipherable words," Long reported, "are Major Powell's name and a notation that he first climbed the peak in 1868 and again in 1873."[59] Interestingly enough, there is no mention by any of the early climbers of the peak of anything remotely resembling the large eagle trap that one of the 1914 Arapaho had recalled for Oliver Toll.

How many people actually made the summit of the peak between 1875 and 1900 is, of course, unknown, though we do know that the number grew each year, just as it has in more recent times. Elkanah and Carlyle Lamb built a "steep" and "very difficult" pony trail to timberline from their valley ranch in 1878, which they improved on by cutting a new trail with a much easier grade in 1882. But the lack of adequate overnight shelter unquestionably discouraged many, for as late as 1884, the year of Carrie Welton's death on the peak, the Lambs had limited facilities for guests. George Arthur Webb of Fort Collins, who climbed that summer, recalled in 1923 that accommodations at Lamb's Long Peak House were so limited that while the Lambs could sleep the two ladies of the Webb party, the men had to sleep outdoors under the wagon.[60] On August 21, 1888, Elkanah Lamb guided S. A. Windsor, a minister from Fort Collins, and a party of nine, including four women, on a six-hour climb to the summit. The next day, he told Windsor that "in the last five years a hundred and twenty-five ladies have ascended the peak" and "about one hundred ladies and gentlemen have already made the trip this year." And, Windsor concluded, "Parson Lamb is the best living authority."[61]

The year 1885, when Fred Sprague blazed a new trail to the Boulder Field up the west fork of Wind River through the basin at the head of Boulder Brook, greatly shortening the journey from that popular part of the park, was a record one. Elkanah Lamb noted that September "that the number who made the ascent of Long's peak this year is twice as large as in any former year in which he has acted as guide."[62] By then the climb itself—by the usual route at least—had long since become a rather pedestrian affair, so much so that in August 1880 six members of the Longmont Coronet Band actually played a special musical program on the summit. As early as 1874, in fact, the editor of the *Boulder County News* told his readers not to submit any more firsthand accounts of their Longs Peak adventuring, for "the subject itself is threadbare."[63]

When Carlyle Lamb took over the actual running of Longs Peak House in the 1890s, the facilities were expanded, and by 1895 a number of "neat cottages" had been built to rent. Further building took place in time for the 1898 summer season.[64] The surviving hotel register for the years 1891 to 1901 contains the names of 2,730 visitors,[65] many of whom left notes, or in some cases fairly lengthy accounts, of their visits.

Most of these visitors to Longs Peak House arrived by horse, wagon, or on foot. By the 1890s, the golden age of "wheeling" and "wheeling clubs," would-be climbers were also coming by bicycle. One such group, the Denver Ramblers, made Longs Peak House a stop on their second and third "annual tours" of 1891 and 1892 and left a record of both visits in the Lamb register. "The Denver Ramblers, always to the front," one of the five young men wrote on August 15, 1891, "having been first wheelmen to push wheels to summit of Pikes Peak, enjoying the glorious coast down the Cascade Toll road. Reached Lamb's at 5:00 P.M. after one of the grandest bicycle rides in the world consuming most of the day of Friday on the delightful roads of Estes Park."

Leaving Lamb's on foot at 4:15 A.M. the next morning, they encountered a "terrific wind" at the Keyhole, where they ate their sandwiches, and a "blinding sleet storm" in the Trough. "Brilliant electric flashes lighted the clouds and thunder crashed and roared. The scene was magnificent, yet terrible, but the party was composed of Denver boys, familiar with mountain storms, and expecting a sudden abatement climbed upward, with freezing hands and shivering bodies." Given the conditions, the stay on the summit of the "five shivering wretches" was brief.

Down the Trough and across the dangerous slope and again to the Key Hole, through which the wind had not ceased to blow with irresistible force. Several photos were taken from here, looking all directions, with a 4 x 5 Triad camera.

Figure 7.1. Cyclists at Lamb's ranch, 1892. Courtesy Colorado Historical Society.

Just at the north end of the Boulder Field the boys saw a covey of ptarmigans and after a couple of hours hunt bagged four, which was quite fair for revolver practice. These were photographed as a matter of record. Lamb's ranch was sighted just before another rain storm came on, at 3:40 P.M. . . .

"The day was thoroughly enjoyed," the writer ends his account, "with anticipation of an early supper, refreshing sleep, and best of all, a magnificent coast back down to Lyons on the victor cushions, the boys are now around the fire, telling how it was, etc., etc." Undaunted, a year later, on August 6, 1892, the Ramblers returned to Lamb's ranch "via Middle and North Parks by wheel." The next day they again climbed the peak. "Today's trip," one of their number recorded with satisfaction on the seventh, "was a very fine one and made up for the terror of last year's blizzard."[66]

Good guiding was appreciated—and praised: "The ascent from the key hole," reads an entry of August 22, 1891, from a member of a party of eight from Greeley, "was quite laborious owing to a fall of 2 to 3 inches of snow the previous day[,] but our guide knew how to persuade and quote poetry and so he got us all to the top." The guide that day was Carlyle Lamb's stepbrother, James Morger.[67] Another climber who showed appreciation of her guide (in this case Enos Mills) was thirteen-year-old Mildred Baldwin from Peoria, Illinois, who on August 27, 1899, climbed the peak with a party of seven, which included Elkanah Lamb and John Cleave's daughter, Virginia. "The above girls," Mildred wrote in the Lambs' book, "are both only thirteen and are believed to be the youngest that have ever set foot on the top of Long's Peak." Mildred then confessed "that the guide had to pull me (Mildred) up the 'home stretch' as I was completely fagged out (and could hardly fall down after I had been pulled up). . . ."[68] The Longs Peak House register also includes the names of many of the early residents of Estes Park, among them Madeline Whyte, the daughter of Theodore Whyte and Lady Maude, who on August 25, 1891, celebrated her fourth birthday at the Lambs with her parents, her mother's maid, Jennie Henderson, and her stepsister Beatrix.

The Lambs, father and son, were but the first of a distinguished line of Longs Peak guides that in the decades that followed would include Fred Sprague, Enos Mills, James Morger (the elder Lamb's stepson), Shep Husted, Warren Rutledge, Joe Mills, John Hubbard, Harold Dunning, and Jack Moomaw. Enos Mills and Shep Husted were both exceptional. Mills, who purchased Longs Peak House from Carlyle Lamb in 1901 and turned it into the world famous Longs Peak Inn, made his first climb in the younger Lamb's company in 1885, as a boy of fifteen. It

Figure 7.2. Enos Mills's first ascent of Longs Peak, 1885, at age fifteen. Courtesy National Park Service—Rocky Mountain National Park.

was an experience he would repeat 304 times, 257 of them while serving as a guide for others, an occupation that he perfected. Mills was blessed with catlike quickness and enormous energy. In August 1906 alone, the year he gave up his active career as a guide to pursue his developing interests as a writer, lecturer, and wilderness advocate, Enos Mills climbed Longs Peak 32 times, 6 of them by moonlight. Mills remained curiously reticent about his mountaineering accomplishments, even his most celebrated ones. Emerson Lynn, who for a time managed Longs Peak Inn for Mills, is doubtless correct in his statement that "Enos Mills, so far as I know, didn't claim to be an extraordinary mountaineer. Time and time again he said publicly that he had done nothing which others could not do; his objective was to lure others to the mountains, believing that they would be won as he had been, by the beauty and joys found in nature."[69] A case in point was Enos Mills's duplication of Elkanah Lamb's August 1871 descent in June 1903, using only an ice axe, a feat he left to journalist Earl Harding to describe.[70]

Shep Husted (1867–1942), to whom Mills turned over the reigns of guiding, went on to surpass not only Mills but Carlyle Lamb as well. Husted had come to Estes Park in 1893, built a homestead cabin out in Dry Gulch in 1896, and then, four years later, in 1901–1902 built the two-story Rustic Hotel on the crest of Devils Gulch, which he and his wife, Clara, ran for several seasons. Husted was, however, first and foremost a guide, winning even the admiration of the demanding Enos Mills, who chose Husted, "a prince on the trail," to be his successor. "In all respects," Mills wrote in the *Saturday Evening Post* in 1917, "he is the

Figure 7.3. Enos Mills, mountaineer. Courtesy National Park Service—Rocky Mountain National Park.

most capable guide I have known."[71] The novelist Edna Ferber, whom Husted took up to the peak during the summer of 1921, remembered him as "changeless and seemingly indestructible as Longs Peak itself. . . . He is tireless, dependable, cautious and wise in the ways of mountains." "He ought to be in a book," Ferber wrote in 1940. "I tried to sneak him into *Fancy Herself*, but he wouldn't fit. Too perfect. He left the imagination nothing to work on."[72]

Husted's record as a Longs Peak guide was simply remarkable. Carlyle Lamb had climbed the peak a total of 146 times, the first time in 1879, with his mother, father, and stepbrother, the year before he began guiding professionally. "My father didn't think I could do it," he later recalled, "and I could do it, and I had to show him."[73] Enos Mills outdid Lamb by more than a factor of two. But both men paled in comparison with Shep Husted, who during his career reached the summit on some 350 separate occasions—27 in August 1907 alone, and the last in 1936 when he was almost seventy.

~

When Frederick Chapin made his first visit to Estes Park in 1887, Longs Peak, of course, was an obligatory part of his itinerary. Chapin made the ascent, beginning on July 18, 1887, in the company of Carlyle Lamb, who had already climbed the peak 55 times. The first night was spent at Longs Peak House, "a charming mountain-inn" serving "a remarkably good supper," in whose sitting room before the rough stone fireplace Chapin sat and talked with Elkanah Lamb late into the evening. When they did turn in, Chapin lay awake until midnight. "Perhaps the stories of our host had something to do with it," he later wrote; "for the elder Lamb tells some very interesting ones of his many ascents of the mountain. . . ."[74]

Awake at three in the morning, Chapin and Carlyle had breakfasted and were on the trail by 5:05 A.M. It was an uneventful climb. "The difficulties of the ascent of Long's Peak are frequently exaggerated," Chapin wrote. "There is hardly a place on the mountain where the climber need use more than one hand to help himself up." "About a hundred people have climbed annually in recent years," he added, almost apologetically, "but this large number is made up by parties, sometimes as many as twenty . . . and all going up at once,—or trying to go up."[75] Carlyle assured him that many did not venture beyond the Keyhole.

Chapin, it turned out, was less interested in Longs Peak—though he enjoyed the climb and took several fine photographs from the summit—than he was in the as yet unnamed Chasm Lake below its east face.

The following year he visited the lake twice, once with Carlyle Lamb and again with a companion from the East, Frederick Ives Gilman. On those occasions Chapin thoroughly investigated the snowfield lying on the western side of the lake and attempted to measure its motion by laying out a series of cairns.

During 1887 Chapin also visited Hallett (now Rowe) Glacier lying in the cirque beneath Hagues Peak. In so doing he became fascinated with the wilderness area lying to the north and west of Longs Peak that would in 1915 become part of Rocky Mountain National Park. Here, he discovered, were mountains that were seldom, if ever, climbed: goals worthy of the veteran mountaineer. When he returned to Estes Park in 1888, bringing with him a number of New England friends, it was to these peaks—Hallett Peak, Flattop Mountain, Mummy Mountain, Mount Ypsilon, Hagues Peak and its glacier, and Stones Peak—to which he turned their attention. It is the stories of these climbs—a number of which turned out to be historic firsts and genuine explorations of discovery—that form the central narrative of Chapin's classic primer of 1889, *Mountaineering in Colorado: The Peaks About Estes Park*, which he illustrated with dozens of his own remarkable photographs.

Returning to Hartford, Chapin used the fall and winter of 1887–1888 to share his visit to Estes Park. He presented a lecture to members of the Appalachian Mountain Club in October on his visit to Hallett Glacier, "First Ascent of a Glacier in Colorado," and then published this account with accompanying photographs in the December 1887 issue of *Appalachia*. He and his Boston friend, George Thacher, then invited, or perhaps challenged, a number of their fellow Appalachians to vacation together in Estes Park.

The following July, Alice and Frederick Chapin, Mr. and Mrs. George Thacher (Mrs. Thacher and Mrs. Chapin shared a love for mountain flowers), Professor Charles Fay of Tufts, J. Raynor Edmands of Harvard, and Benjamin Ives Gilman, an ethnomusicologist, who had recently returned from Europe, all assembled at the Ferguson ranch. Alice Chapin was the pluckiest of all—suffering as she was through the final stages of consumption. As it turned out, Chapin had offered the easterners an incentive. "In extolling to Mr. Edmands and myself the charms of Estes Park for mountain lovers," Fay recalled years later, "he held out as a special lure the possibilities of at least one virgin climb."[76]

The first days of their stay at Ferguson's were given over, like the previous summer, to "minor walks and climbs" to nearby Prospect, Giganttrack, Rams Horn, and Lily Mountains. Then came longer excursions to Estes Cone and out along Wind River. Fay, on his own, but

Figure 7.4. Ferguson's ranch. Photograph by Frederick Chapin. Courtesy Appalachian Mountain Club.

doubtless at Chapin's suggestion, climbed the crest of Deer Mountain, from where he could obtain a spectacular view of Mount Ypsilon and its neighbors across Horseshoe Park. Other climbs followed, in which members of the larger group alternatively took part: Flattop Mountain, no doubt making good use of the new trail that Fred Sprague had opened that summer, Chasm Lake, Hagues Peak, Hallett Glacier, and Stones Peak.

It is doubtful that Chapin, knowledgeable as he quickly became, could have accomplished much of this on his own. Fortunately, the previous year he had met the rancher William Hallett, who since 1881 had been summering in a cottage next to Ferguson's and taking many of his meals at the ranch. Chapin could not have been more fortunate, for next to Hallett's own mentor, Abner Sprague, the long and lanky ranchman probably had more firsthand knowledge of the mountains surrounding Estes Park than any other living individual. Hallett proved a most willing participant. That first summer he took Chapin, Thacher, and the Boston climatologist Charles Osgood Otis[77] up Flattop Mountain by way of the Mill Creek trail to visit Tyndall Glacier and the peak that Chapin would name for Hallett himself. He also guided Chapin to the newly rediscovered Hallett Glacier west of Hagues Peak.[78]

The promised "virgin climb" turned out to be a three-day excursion to the summit of Mount Ypsilon, so named by Alice Chapin during

a ride with her husband along the borders of Wind River. Observing
the perfect Y, "my wife said to me, 'Its name shall be Ypsilon Peak.'" "So
it went forth," Chapin related, "and the name was accepted by the dwellers
in the valley and by the visitors at the ranch."[79] The trip was guided by
the ever-ready Hallett. Taking a wagon and two extra horses, which later
served as pack animals, they left Ferguson's ranch on August 9, 1888,
and rode to the end of the road in Horseshoe Park, where the wagon
was unpacked and sent home. Following an old trail along Roaring River
for a time, they then turned their faces toward their destination, forded
the mountain stream, and in the absence of a trail began to bushwhack.
"Mr. Hallett led the procession with axe in hand, and was obliged to cut
and hew right and left."[80] They spent the night in the open without a
tent.

Since Chapin, as usual, wanted photographs, their route the next
morning was anything but direct. Chapin carried the camera and tri-
pod, Hallett the sensitized plates. Both were heavy. Soon the party was
scattered all over the flanks of Mount Fairchild, which they intended to
climb. Chapin stopped to photograph Ypsilon, Hagues Peak, and the
west peak of the Mummy Range. The morning was now getting late.
Chapin, who had been suffering from a gimpy foot, together with

Figure 7.5. Benjamin Ives Gilman (left) and Carlyle Lamb on Mills Moraine,
summer 1888. Photograph by Frederick Chapin. Courtesy Appalachian Mountain
Club.

Figure 7.6. On Hallett [Rowe] Glacier; William Hallett in foreground. Photograph by Frederick Chapin. Courtesy Appalachian Mountain Club.

Thacher and Gilman decided to skirt Fairchild in favor of Mount Ypsilon. By 3:10 that afternoon they were standing on its summit. "Ypsilon," Chapin would write,

> from above is even finer than from below. The snow gullies which form the long lines converging together at the base, which gave the peak its name, cut deep into the mountain's flanks, and have formed miniature canons. Weird shapes of snow cling to nooks which are sheltered from the sun. One cornice had a big hole in it, as if a cannon-ball had passed through. But the great point of interest is the steep character of the whole northeastern face. Numerous lakes were visible below, between us and our camp; some were perched on high moraines far away from the base of the peak; while straight down and over two thousand feet below, immediately at the base of the cliffs, we saw two large ones which were walled in by dikes.[81]

That night, around the campfire, each man had a story to tell, Fay and Edmands about their chance encounter with two large cinnamon bears. "Our camp," Chapin concluded his wonderful narrative, "was also a merry one; we knew no sadness. We had been upon a beautiful mountain, had met with adventures and no mishaps, and were now safe around a blazing fire within the circle of whose rays neither bear nor

Figure 7.7. "We three": William Hallett, Benjamin
Ives Gilman, and Frederick Chapin and camera.
Courtesy Appalachian Mountain Club.

mountain lion would dare to venture."[82] Fortunately, anyone wishing to
measure old-time mountaineering in Estes Park has Frederick Chapin to
turn to.

As the summers in Estes Park came and went, others succeeded
Frederick Chapin and his colleagues. More and more remote places were
visited, and other landmark features received their names. Though by
1876 Black Canyon, Longs Peak, Hagues Peak, Estes Cone, Fall River, Lily
Mountain, and Muggins Gulch had appeared on Clarence King's and
Ferdinand Hayden's survey maps, most of the other naming opportunities fell to later visitors like Frederick Chapin. Chapin named not only
Mount Ypsilon but Hallett Peak. Abner Sprague named Alberta Falls on
the trail into Glacier Gorge after his wife Mary Alberta and Mills Lake

Figure 7.8. Ypsilon Camp. Photograph by Frederick Chapin. Courtesy Appalachian Mountain Club.

after Enos Mills. Mills then returned the favor by naming Sprague Lake. Sprague also named Andrews Creek (together with Andrews Glacier, Andrews Pass, and Andrews Tarn) after Edwin B. Andrews, his brother-in-law, and McHenrys Peak, near Longs Peak, after Benjamin F. McHenry, a professor from Indiana. William Hallett named Mummy Mountain, Mount Otis, and Bear Lake, the latter for his friend and neighbor Horace Ferguson, who had the courage, or wisdom, not to shoot a bear that he stumbled upon in that vicinity. In the next century Dr. William Workman, the builder of Fern Lake Lodge, named Marguerite Falls, Grace Falls, Notchtop Mountain, Little Matterhorn, Odessa Lake, and Lake Helene, while the brothers Julian and Albert Hayden, who arrived in Estes Park in 1906 and became avid mountaineers, named the trio of lakes above Forest Canyon: Arrowhead, Doughnut, and Hourglass.

～

One area of Estes Park that largely escaped attention during the nineteenth century was the watershed of the St. Vrain to the south of Longs Peak known as Wild Basin. The area, some thirty square miles, and roughly triangular in shape, is bounded on the west by the Continental Divide, on the north by Longs Peak and Meeker Ridge, and on the southeast by the irregular chain of mountains that form the divide between the north and middle branches of the St. Vrain. Deep, remote, and heavily wooded, it had been penetrated in August 1868 by Major Powell and his companions, who, coming from Grand Lake on their way to attempt Longs Peak, camped above Sandbeach Lake the evening before the ascent. For the next three decades, Wild Basin was largely left alone, untraversed, unmapped, and visited only by an occasional hunter or prospector. All this began to change with the turn of the century, or shortly before, when irrigationists, anxious to increase the water supply for farmers and ranchers along the Front Range, constructed reservoirs at Sandbeach, Pear, and Bluebird Lakes.[83] At about the same time, John B. Copeland, who owned valuable water rights on the North Fork of the St. Vrain, established a ranch on 320 acres in the vicinity of what is now Copeland Lake, where he permitted camping.

Wild Basin received its first significant attention during the summer of 1907, when Charles Boynton, editor of the *Longmont Ledger*, together with his photographer, F. H. Hildreth, visited Ouzel Falls and Ouzel Lake and then wrote about his trip.[84] Ouzel Lake itself was sufficiently remote so that when Fritz Withmiller wandered off from Allenspark on a drunken spree and encountered a blinding storm on October 1, 1903, his skeleton was not found there by hunters until October of 1910.[85] As late as 1911 there were, nonetheless, only three "well defined trails" leading into Wild Basin: the first leading to Pear Reservoir, the second along the North Fork of the St. Vrain to Ouzel Falls and Ouzel Lake, and the third, northwest of Copeland Park, to Sandbeach Lake. "Without these trails," one writer noted, "it would be somewhat difficult to travel on account of fallen timber and the roughness of the country."[86]

Enos Mills, who arrived in the Tahosa Valley in 1884, came to know the region early and well. Over the years he explored Wild Basin thoroughly, named a number of its most prominent features, including Ouzel Lake, and took special delight in introducing other mountain enthusiasts to its rugged beauty. Mills's most famous initiate was William Skinner Cooper (1884–1978), a young man from Michigan, who spent most of the summers of 1906 and 1908 as a guest at Longs Peak Inn. "Enos Mills had often spoken of Wild Basin . . . as having more natural beauty and greater variety than any other nearby area," Cooper later recalled.[87] In early September of 1906, the year before Editor Boynton wrote his story, Mills accompanied Cooper as far as Ouzel Lake, after which he left Cooper to explore on his own. For the next two days Cooper tramped the area, discovering and naming Mertensia Falls, climbing Mount Copeland to the Continental Divide, where he found bear tracks in the snow, and returned past two lakes that he would later name

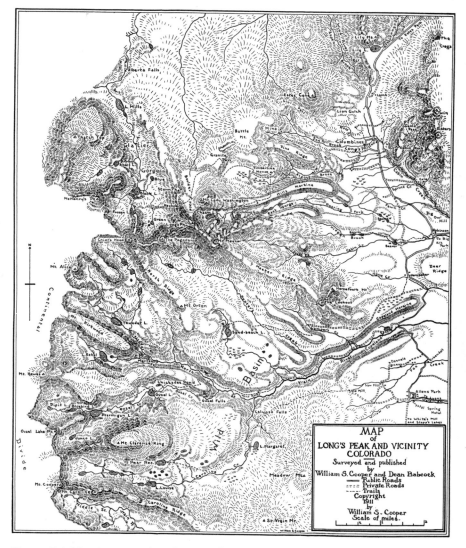

Figure 7.9. The Cooper-Babcock map of 1911. Courtesy David Cooper.

Pipit and Bluebird. Cooper returned to camp at Ouzel Lake the second evening where, to his surprise, he found Joe Mills waiting for him. "Evidently Enos had sent his brother to make sure that the tenderfoot adventurer was safe."[88] Cooper spent the next day collecting plants and taking notes, after which he and Joe rode leisurely back to the Inn. It was a treasured initiation. Cooper fell in love with Wild Basin, and, with

Enos Mills's enthusiastic blessing, decided that as a future project he would return to explore and map the entire region.

That opportunity came two years later, in the summer of 1908, when Cooper discovered the companionship of Charles Edwin Hewes, the subsequent owner of Hewes-Kirkwood Inn, who was working that summer as a stage driver and "flunky" at Longs Peak Inn. The two men immediately hit it off, and it was not long before they were hiking together. Their first journey was a memorable one: a circle trip up Longs Peak trail and down into Glacier Gorge, followed by a trek past Loch Vale, up Andrews Glacier and its frozen tarn, along the Continental Divide plateau to Hallett Peak and Flattop, down Tyndall Gorge, and home via Wind River trail. "Back to the Inn in time for dinner," Cooper noted with satisfaction; "two sets of tennis, then to bed."[89]

Their next venture, and Cooper's chief project for the summer, was an eight-day exploration and mapping expedition of Wild Basin. Taking sightings on Estes Cone, Longs, Meeker, and the Lookout in order to establish a base line, Cooper and Hewes plunged into the wilderness on June 16, taking along a burro named Pat, who turned out to be recalcitrant in the extreme. From Copeland Lake, as yet without a resort hotel, they pushed on to reach Ouzel Lake, which was to be their base camp. Though Cooper had taken the trail to the lake two summers before with Enos Mills, the two men soon lost their way in the fallen timber. The experiences that followed, which left both men feeling, Cooper said, "better than ever before in our lives," had their decidedly humorous moments, the most comic of which involved an attempt to put together a meal of chipped beef in cream by using self-rising flour, an experiment that ended, much to their disgust, with the frying pan being tossed into Ouzel Lake.

In the days that followed, Cooper and Hewes methodically worked their way over the area, climbing Mount Copeland and Ogallala Peak and visiting Eagle, Bluebird, and Finch Lakes, among others, all the while taking sightings and measurements. Though Cooper was called home prematurely to Detroit late in August by the illness of his father, he made arrangements before his departure with a young artist from Illinois named Dean Babcock to finish the fieldwork and coauthor the map.[90]

The ten-by-twelve-inch Cooper-Babcock map of 1911, "the first authentic topographical map of the Longs Peak region," is filled with the enthusiasm and audacity of youth. Many of the names chosen—Mt. Cooper, Mt. Hewes, Mt. Kirkwood, Mt. Caroline (together with Lake Caroline and Caroline Ridge), Lake Margaret, and Lake Ethel—were either Hewes and Cooper family names or, in the case of Lake Margaret, the name of Cooper's girlfriend of the season or, in the case of Lake Ethel, of the new wife of Enos Mills's younger brother, Joe. Enos Mills did not approve and, apparently as early as 1908, withdrew his offer to publish the map. Neither did the Colorado Geographical Board, which subsequently selected other, less idiosyncratic, names. Though the Cooper-Babcock map has long since been superseded, eleven of the natural features that Cooper and his companions named remain to commemorate their memorable summer journey of some ninety years ago: Ouzel Peak, Meadow Mountain, Mount Orton, Pine Ridge, Bluebird Lake, Junco Lake, Pipit Lake, Chickadee Pond, Calypso Cascades, Mertensia Falls, and Columbine Falls.

Chapter 8

⌒

"Alone amid the wind's mad revelry": The Strange Career of Carrie Welton

Shortly before twelve o'clock on the night of Tuesday, September 23, 1884, a forty-two-year-old woman from Connecticut named Carrie Welton became the first recorded death on Longs Peak. She died in darkness and alone, huddled against the rocks of the Boulder Field, a victim not only of exhaustion and exposure but of her own willfulness and love of adventure. In the years that followed there would be other deaths on the peak under circumstances ranging from the merely prosaic to the highly dramatic. The tragedy of Carrie Welton was no less remarkable, or improbable, than her life had been.

Carrie Welton's family was New England to the core, able to trace its roots in Waterbury back to at least 1679. Her father, Joseph Chauncey Welton, a highly successful man of business, had begun his career as a quintessential Yankee peddler, selling clocks and other merchandise throughout the antebellum South as a traveling agent. Returning north in 1839, he became a partner in the firm of William R. Hitchcock and took charge of the company's store in New York City. That same year Welton married Jane E. Porter, the youngest daughter of Deacon Thomas Porter, the original owner of the Waterbury Brass Company. Their daughter, and only child, Caroline Josephine, or Carrie, as they called her, was born three years later, on June 7, 1842.

By the time Carrie was eleven, the Weltons were back in Waterbury, where Joseph, a tireless worker who prided himself on never taking a vacation, purchased interests in both the Waterbury Brass and the Oakville Pin Company. Success and prosperity quickly followed, culminating a decade later, in 1863, in the purchase of Rose Hill Cottage, a handsome stone mansion with six acres of grounds on Prospect Street. Jane Welton, the social member of the family, spared little expense in furnishing her new home with such visible signs of wealth as thick oriental rugs, heavy carved chairs, and marble statues on pedestals. Under her hand Rose Hill Cottage soon became one of the centers of Waterbury society.

The Weltons were equally careful in securing their daughter's education, sending her off to Miss Edwards's School in New Haven and the Mears-Burkhardt School in New York City, after which she studied drawing and oil painting in New York with several well-known artists of the day. None of this, including the attention paid by Waterbury society and its eligible bachelors, seems to have mattered much to Carrie Welton. From the age of twenty, the center of her life was her beloved horse, Knight, a gift from her father in the spring of 1862. Carrie Welton loved animals (she kept dogs, cats, and rabbits), but Knight was her favorite. She installed him in a velvet-draped stall in the Rose Hill stables, equipped him with special shoes and tack trimmed with silver, and fed him his oats from a bone-china bowl hand-painted with pansies and patterning bearing his name in gold. Carrie and her spirited black horse became familiar figures to neighbors as they rode out into the woods, fields, and streets of Waterbury even in the most inclement weather. On horseback, Carrie Welton was fearless. It was said that she "would not hesitate to back any animal that could be saddled."[1]

Blue-eyed and brown-haired, Carrie Welton became a striking woman. A life-sized portrait now in Waterbury's Mattatuck Museum (she poses in a formal, closefitting, and clearly elegant evening dress) reveals her as tall and dark-complexioned with a bearing that is self-confident and almost regal. Long before she left home for Colorado, Carrie Welton had become known among her contemporaries as a woman of social graces "with a propensity to do uncommon things" and a "reputation for courage and physical endurance."[2] She was also impulsive and headstrong, used to having her own way, and confronting life on her own terms.

For the Weltons of Waterbury life changed forever on March 26, 1874, when Joseph Welton, by then president of Waterbury Brass, the firm founded by his father-in-law, was killed by a kick from Carrie's horse, Knight, which had somehow gotten loose late at night in the Rose Hill stables. For his two survivors, money was not a problem, for Joseph Welton had seen to it that both his wife and daughter were well taken care of. The distribution of his estate was odd in at least one respect, however, for Rose Hill was divided: Jane Welton was given the house, Carrie its grounds.

Both women initially sought consolation through travel, and 1875–1876 saw mother and daughter together in California, following which they attended the nation's centennial celebration in Philadelphia. By 1880, however, their relationship had significantly changed: there was a deep and lasting estrangement, and for reasons never entirely clear. Though "disagreements on money matters" was sometimes cited,[3] the causes were more likely rooted in their personalities. Jane Welton was known as "stern and majestic" and was as headstrong and determined to have her way as her daughter. Years later, for example, at the age of eighty-one, and despite the fact that she not only lacked previous training but had cataracts in both eyes, Jane Welton went to considerable effort to indulge her lifelong interest in art. Traveling to Europe, she visited the Louvre and the Prado, where she copied, in giant size, paintings by Murillo, Rubens, and Raphael, which she then displayed in gilt frames on the walls of Rose Hill Cottage.[4] Whatever the reason for their original quarrel, the two women were content to go each their separate ways. After 1880, Carrie Welton never returned to Rose Hill. In 1883 she removed her mother as executrix of her will.

By 1884 Carrie Welton had become a spinster, whose life was precariously balanced and plainly in transition. Again she turned to travel and physical activity, coming west that spring, first to Yellowstone Park, where she spent several weeks exploring, and then to Colorado Springs. There Carrie took up residence at the splendid new seventy-five-room Antlers Hotel on Cascade Avenue, which had just opened its doors to guests that June. Carrie and the hotel's manager, fellow New Englander Augusta A. Warren, were apparently friends of long standing. The two women shared a love of nature and the out-of-doors, and during the weeks following her arrival Augusta took Carrie to

Figure 8.1. Portrait of Caroline Josephine Welton. Courtesy photographic collection of Mattatuck Museum, Waterbury, Connecticut.

Bear Creek Canyon where she had a homestead log cabin and to other attractions in the vicinity, including Manitou.

For Carrie Welton this was a second visit. Though it would later be intimated that she suffered from a heart condition,[5] Carrie Welton had come to Colorado Springs the previous year, presumably staying with Augusta Warren, who then ran two popular boarding houses. The highlight of her visit was a climb of 14,109-foot Pikes Peak, which she completed despite encountering a severe storm. When she returned in 1884, Carrie Welton was determined not only to repeat her success but to make the first ascent of the season. The winter of 1883–1884 had been an exceptionally cold one, and well into summer the trail, clogged by deep snows, remained "almost impassable." An augur of things to come, Carrie Welton was warned "by everyone that the undertaking was a foolish and dangerous one." But having somehow obtained the services of two guides, she left the Barker House at Manitou at midnight and reached the summit after a "tedious" trip during which "the whole party suffered from the cold."[6] Arthur L. Bronson, a young man from Waterbury traveling in the West that summer for his health, duly reported Carrie's achievement to the editor of the *Waterbury Republican*.[7]

From Colorado Springs Carrie Welton went north by train to Denver, where she stayed with a group of friends. From there she journeyed westward into the mountains where (in the company of an artist named Mrs. Culver) Carrie rode to the top of 14,270-foot Grays Peak on horseback and visited the Chicago Lakes on the northern slope of Mt. Evans.[8] The lure of the mountains (reinforced, no doubt, by encouragement from Augusta Warren) next brought her to Estes Park, apparently during the week of September 14. Carrie took up residence at the Estes Park Hotel on lower Fish Creek Road, which since its opening seven years earlier had served as the fashionable centerpiece of Dunraven's Estes Park holdings. Her first days in the park were spent largely "on horseback riding and visiting the surrounding points of interest in the mountains."[9] Then, on Monday, the twenty-second, she announced her intention to ascend Longs Peak.

Climbing mountains had clearly become a reigning passion. In fact, Carrie had informed an acquaintance prior to her departure for Estes Park, "that she intended to have a gold band put around the handle of her pretty riding whip for every peak she had climbed."[10] Theodore Whyte, Dunraven's resident manager, tried to dissuade her. Whyte undoubtedly told her that the snows of the preceding winter that had left the peak unclimbable until late August, particularly on its north and west sides, still remained and that September weather, however warm and golden, was unpredictable.

Buoyed by her successful climb of Pikes Peak, Carrie Welton was adamant. On Monday afternoon, leaving behind a small package at the hotel but taking her jewelry with her, she engaged Henry S. Gilbert, a local livery operator, to take her up to Lamb's ranch. By 1884 Elkanah Lamb had turned the business of guiding over to his son Carlyle, and it was with the younger Lamb that Carrie Welton made arrangements to guide her on the eight-mile ascent of Longs Peak the following day. Gilbert left, but with orders to return for her at 8 A.M. on Wednesday morning.

After a night at the ranch and a "hasty breakfast," Carrie and Carlyle left the Lamb ranch at 5 A.M. on horseback. She was warmly, if somberly, dressed. Over a pair of black broadcloth riding pants she wore a black alpaca dress and a heavy black saque in addition to an elegant black dolman coat trimmed with astrakhan fur. Around her neck was a heavy cashmere shawl, on her hands a pair of heavy kid gloves. Carrie also carried with her a gossamer raincoat, which she would later put on against the weather. Wisely, she covered her face with a silk domino mask as protection against the intensity of the sun.[11]

Though the day broke "warm and pleasant," it took some five hours to make the first six miles. As on Pikes Peak, the snows of the preceding winter were still very much in evidence, at times obscuring and blocking the trail itself. Their horses, usually surefooted, kept breaking through snowbanks warmed by the sun. At length it proved so difficult for the horses that Carlyle and Carrie made a tactical decision to leave them at a spot above the tree line, but well below the usual tethering place on the Boulder Field. That decision, made in sunshine while the two climbers were still fresh, probably cost Carrie Welton her life.

Lamb and his companion then made their way on foot across the tumbled mass of boulders rising at a visible angle toward the Keyhole, the jagged opening with its rocky overhang on the northeastern side of the peak through which they must pass to reach the summit. At the Keyhole the weather began to turn against them. They encountered a "strong, chilling wind" and dark ominous clouds, a portend of worse weather ahead. Young Lamb, who had been climbing Longs Peak since the age of seventeen, wisely counseled retreat, telling Carrie that even if they did succeed in gaining the summit there would be no view. Carrie Welton would have none of it. She had heard such objections from her guides on Pikes Peak. Her response, Carlyle Lamb later told his father, was that "she had never undertaken anything and given it up." They went on.

Seasoned climbers know that it is best to be up and off Longs Peak by noon to avoid the possibility of afternoon storms. By the time that Carrie and her guide reached the summit it was very late—3 P.M. by the elder Lamb's account—and it was cold and chilly. Despite the fact that Carrie was tired, their stay was a short one. As Carlyle feared, dark clouds had moved in, a sign that a storm had already set in below. The clouds briefly lifted as they left the summit. But now, as they recrossed the Narrows and headed down the Trough, they found themselves caught in a blinding snowstorm, the heaviest, Lamb would later report, that "he ever saw in the mountains." Their descent became increasingly slow. Carrie began to complain of being weary, and by the time they reached the bottom of the Trough, she showed clear signs of exhaustion. Carlyle did the best he could. For the next two hours, during which time they covered no more than two-thirds of a mile, Lamb alternately led and carried his charge. Carrie Welton, fully dressed, weighed about 130 pounds, and Carlyle too began to tire. They finally made the Keyhole. By then Carrie Welton, who had grown more and more numb from the cold, had become "so utterly exhausted and chilled that she could not stand alone." The moment of crisis and decision had come. It was now ten o'clock at night.

Descending a short distance below the Keyhole, over terrain so rough and steep that it is almost impossible for one person to provide much help to, let alone carry, another, Carlyle Lamb called a halt. Sitting down, he confided to Carrie what he must have sensed for some time: he too was exhausted and so cold that he could scarcely walk. The only chance that either of them had for survival, he told her, was for him to hurry on ahead and seek assistance. At first Carrie objected to being left alone. Finally she agreed to remain where she was until he could return. Carlyle removed his vest and tied it around her feet, arranged her raincoat and shawl as best he could as protection against the cold and wind, and then plunged into the darkness in search of the horses tethered below.

The storm had by now lifted, and Lamb was aided materially in his descent by the light of the moon. Reaching the horses, he rode one and led the other down through the timber to the Lamb ranch, a distance of five miles. Lamb made good time. Rousing his father, who had retired for the night, and fortified by a quick cup of tea, the two men began the return trip. Elkanah Lamb, still strong at fifty-two and as experienced as any man alive in the ways of Longs Peak, took the lead. Carlyle, "almost completely exhausted" and plainly suffering from his ordeal, fell behind. As they reached timberline, "the wind was blowing a gale," making progress difficult as they continued up the moraine toward the Boulder

Field. Just before daybreak, the elder Lamb came to the edge of the rocky uplift. He would never forget the sight awaiting him. "Almost a mile across the Boulderfield," Elkanah would write years later,

> I came in sight of the tragic spot, where Carrie J. Welton lay at rest, having died alone amid the wind's mad revelry and dismal dirge, and which was yet holding high carnival over her body by blowing every section of her garments in its unrelenting fury, seemingly sporting with its victim in demoniacal triumph. I remember, with clear distinctness, my involuntary expression as I approached the body: "I fear, my young lady, that you are past saving."[12]

Carrie Welton had moved about ten feet from the spot where Carlyle left her, and had fallen over a rock, bruising both her head and wrist. She lay in a snowbank, still wearing the silk mask of the day before, covering a face whose features were now rigid but placid. Beside her was an ivory-handled riding whip bearing her name and address—the one she announced she intended to have banded to reflect her mountaineering achievements. In her belt was a five-cylinder Smith & Wesson revolver. A gold watch was fashioned to her dress with a black silk cord, and in her bosom, it was later discovered, she was carrying a small chamois-skin bag containing three elegant rings, one a solitaire diamond "of a very large size."

The Lambs worked as expeditiously as possible under the conditions. They placed Carrie's body in a double blanket, tied together by a small rope cut in sections. It took a full two hours to reach the horses. By 10:30 A.M. they were back at the Lamb ranch, where they found Gilbert's driver waiting, as previously instructed, to return Carrie Welton to the valley below.

Once at the ranch, Elkanah Lamb summoned the local justice of the peace, Estes Park rancher Peter J. Pauly Jr. Pauly had the remains placed in a box. He then accompanied them as they were taken down to Longmont by wagon to be embalmed and to await instructions from Carrie's family. Pauly left Estes Park at 6:30 P.M. on the evening of Wednesday, September 24, and by about 1:30 A.M. the next morning was in Longmont. Almost a half century later, Margaret Ross, who helped to lay out Carrie's body, would recall that "her hair was so beautiful and all her clothing so wonderfully neat and handsome; and her complexion was like velvet."[13]

Initially, there was confusion caused by the difficulty in contacting Carrie's relatives. Jane Welton had abandoned Rose Hill Cottage and was in Europe, and the first reports listed Carrie Welton as a resident of New York, not Connecticut. Pauly persisted and at length succeeded in contacting both Augusta Warren in Colorado Springs and Carrie's cousin, Joseph L. Porter of New York City.

Carrie Welton's airtight metallic casket, stained to represent rosewood and trimmed with silver, arrived by train in Waterbury on the evening of October 7, 1884. It was taken immediately by hearse, accompanied by friends in carriages, to Hall Memorial Chapel in Riverside Cemetery to await the return of Mrs. Welton. In preparation "the floor had been carpeted with evergreens, thus robbing the stone-covered floor of its sepulchral coldness."[14]

Ten days later, on Friday, October 17, a small private service took place at Rose Hill Cottage. Those that attended did so by special invitation. Following the hymn "Abide With Me," Carrie Welton's remains were interred in the family plot at Riverside.[15] Two thousand miles to the west, among the rocks of the Boulder Field on Longs Peak near the spot where Carrie Welton had lain down to die, Elkanah Lamb erected a small rude wooden slab: "Here Carrie J. Welton lay at Rest. . . . Died Alone . . . Sept. 23, 1884."[16]

By Friday, September 26, the dramatic story of Carrie Welton's death was picked up by the Colorado press, and then by such eastern papers as the New York Times, New York Tribune, New York Sun, Springfield Republican, and, of course, the Waterbury Republican. The Longmont Ledger and Denver Daily Times had the story first, the Ledger having talked with Carlyle Lamb himself.

Figure 8.2. The wooden marker that Elkanah Lamb placed on the Boulder Field. Courtesy James H. Pickering.

"Under the circumstances," it agreed, "Mr. Lamb could see no other way out of the difficulty but to leave Miss Welton and proceed with all practicable haste to his father's house for help."[17] Though the *Ledger* saw no reason to challenge Lamb's story, Carlyle's decision to leave Carrie, and the precise "circumstances" that surrounded it, would soon come under scrutiny and become a source of controversy.

The press, anxious to make the most of the story, pushed ahead with inquiries, and the next day follow-up stories appeared in both the *Denver Tribune-Republican* and *Colorado Springs Daily Gazette.* The *Tribune-Republican's* account was particularly detailed and quoted I. N. Rogers, the Denver undertaker who had been summoned to Longmont to embalm the body, as saying "that young Lamb ["a rough, good-hearted country boy"] "is not censured by the people living in the park, for he undoubtedly did what he considered the best thing to do when he abandoned Miss Welton and hurried on for assistance. Fault is found by some who think that Lamb could have kept the lady from freezing by gathering some dry wood when he had reached timber line and kindled a fire where he left her."[18] Rogers also squelched any rumor of foul play when he reported that Carrie Welton's money, mostly in the form of three large drafts against banks in New York, had been given by her to the proprietor of the Estes Park Hotel for safekeeping.

This story appeared on Saturday, September 27. By the next day the *Tribune-Republican* had focused its attention squarely on Carlyle Lamb. The thrust of the accusations, euphemistically described as "new developments," was carried in sensational front page headlines: "The Death on Long's Peak. Additional Facts in Regard to the Sad Fate of Miss Welton. Some Evidence of Gross Neglect. A Suspicion that She Was Deserted by the Guide When Most in Need of His Assistance." The source of this "evidence," it turned out, was Henry Gilbert, the liveryman, who had taken Carrie Welton up to the Lambs and then sent a team and driver to bring her back to the hotel.

The driver, Gilbert said, had driven that morning past the Lamb ranch and "up to timberline, five miles above the house." There at 10 A.M., Gilbert continued, he had met the Lambs carrying Carrie Welton's body. To be sure, the story of driving a team and wagon to timberline on Longs Peak under any conditions in 1884 is improbable, if not outright impossible. Yet once told, it yielded the conclusion "that it does not seem reasonable that it would take two men six hours to carry the body but one mile" and the accusation that the Lambs thus had not returned immediately for the body as claimed. Rather, the *Tribune-Republican's* special correspondent in Longmont rushed on,

Those who are best acquainted with the location and guide do not hesitate to charge young Lamb with cowardice in the matter. They think when he saw Miss Welton was first taken with a fainting fit in the dark, that he became frightened at the prospect of a night on the peak, and that he abandoned her to her fate, and that he and his father did not ascend the peak in search of her until after daylight the next morning.[19]

The next day, September 28, this same story was repeated in the Colorado Springs Daily Gazette, the Pueblo Daily Chieftain, and the New York Sun. By the twenty-ninth it had appeared in the Waterbury Republican.

Elkanah Lamb was naturally stung by the charges leveled against Carlyle. Not only did he have implicit faith in his son's veracity and courage, but as a seasoned mountaineer the elder Lamb knew all too well the vagaries and dangers of the mountains. On October 1, four days after Gilbert's comments first surfaced in the Times-Tribune, Elkanah told a reporter for the Fort Collins Express that

his son did everything that he could under the circumstances, that the extreme roughness of the path made it impossible to carry the lady any farther, she having become helpless. It is even difficult for a person unencumbered to pass over the route where she was left. . . . the day upon which the lady lost her life, was the coldest in the park that had been experienced in the past four weeks. Miss Welton made the ascent of the peak against the protestations of the Elder and his family. It seemed that these only made her the more anxious to make the attempt.[20]

The Express itself was convinced, for in a separate story in the same issue, it assured its readers that

the tragic death of Miss Carrie Welton, who perished on Long's peak one night last week, was the result of a foolhardy undertaking. Possessed of a venturesome spirit, the lady has often undertaken hazardous journeys, much against the wishes and advice of friends. One of her eccentricities was a desire to ascend mountain peaks at a season when more cautious people would shrink from such an undertaking. Her ambition proved her destruction.[21]

The Fort Collins Courier, the Express's cross-town rival, also came to the defense of the younger Lamb in its edition of October 2:

Later dispatches to the Denver papers attempted to convey the idea that Miss Welton's death was due to gross neglect on the part of Mr. Lamb. The Courier does not believe there can be any reasonable grounds for that supposition. Mr. Lamb is known to be one of the most faithful and trustworthy young men in the country, and the idea that he willingly neglected his charge in time of peril, is considered preposterous by all who know him best.[22]

The elder Lamb continued to press his side of the story, furnishing the following week's issue of the *Courier* with his own account of the events of September 23rd. It began, "In view of the many reports and some of them very exaggerated, that have been published, we think justice to ourselves and to the community at large demands an intelligent statement concerning the tragic fate of Miss Carrie J. Welton. . . ."[23]

By the time of Elkanah Lamb's letter, Carlyle had already received public support from an unexpected quarter: a letter to the editor of the *Denver Tribune-Republican* "in defense of young Lamb, the guide, who has been censured, to some extent, for leaving Miss Carrie Welton on Long's Peak." "I believe this to be entirely untrue, and unjust to a brave and faithful guide," wrote E. S. Darrow. Darrow then explained in his letter, published on the front page, that he and his two young daughters had made the ascent of Longs Peak the preceding year, guided by Carlyle Lamb. Having lost their way, and being late in returning, they were forced to spend

> the night on the mountain, a mile or two below the spot where Miss Welton perished and about a mile above timber line. We were overtaken by darkness before reaching the timber; a terrible thunder storm of hail and sleet coming on; it was impossible to regain the trail.
>
> Young Lamb was thoughtful and considerate and most faithful to his charge, building a fire from the gnarled roots and underbrush. He spent the night in watching the camp and looking for the trail, and was constant in his efforts to minister to our comfort and safety, and at the dawn of day, resuming our descent, he brought us to the hotel . . . a quiet and manly fellow, and fearless of danger.[24]

This journalistic exchange of late September and early October for all practical purposes brought to an end the public discussion of Carlyle Lamb's conduct. To the extent that a verdict was rendered, it was that Carrie Welton was a headstrong, adventurous young woman, who died because of her own recklessness. Perhaps the *Denver Daily Times* summarized the tragedy best by placing Carrie Welton's death in a larger context:

> Miss Welton seems to have been unusually romantic, or peculiarly persistent in her desire to behold the glories of the mountain world. Yet, after all, hers was in a woman something of the same spirit which in a man carries one off in search of the North Pole and the open sea of the Arctics; and, as so many of the men who have fallen under this influence have done, she surrendered her life in—shall we call it the satisfaction of her curiosity, the gratification of a whim?—or shall we say it was all an accident, and that it could not have been avoided? Call it what we may, there is something very sad in the thought of a

young woman, who had evidently been reared in the lap of luxury, breathing her last in the dark hours of the night on the side of a barren mountain so far above the haunts of life that the wild animals would not even lend their presence to the scene; with no hand except that of the icy blast to soothe her last moments, and no voice to cheer her in the dread ordeal except that of the shrill blast of the mountain wind. The place of her death should be marked. It will always be an object of interest to tourists.[25]

To this chapter of Carrie Welton's story there is only one additional note, and a disquieting one. Even before Carrie's remains returned to Waterbury, stories began to circulate in the eastern papers, and then in those in Colorado, that Rose Hill Cottage, abandoned in the quarrel between mother and daughter, had become haunted and that the "wraith" of Carrie Welton could be "seen nightly riding horseback in the front yard."[26] The reported specter of Carrie Welton and Knight proved prophetic.

Subsequent events began to unfold on December 8, 1884, with the presentation in probate court of Carrie Welton's will, whose assets totaled some quarter million dollars. After disposing of her jewelry, furs, and other apparel to two cousins, aged four and six at the time her will was made, her largest bequest was a gift to Henry Bergh and his Society for the Prevention of Cruelty to Animals. The second largest was the gift of an animal drinking fountain to the town of Waterbury, honoring Knight. Not surprisingly, the will was immediately contested—not, as it turned out, by Jane Welton, but by two cousins who saw in Carrie's bizarre conduct and the estrangement of mother and daughter an opportunity for themselves.

Carrie Welton's interest in Henry Bergh and the organization he had formed in 1866 was not new. For some years prior to her death, Carrie Welton had been giving a tenth of her income to charity, half administered by her rector, the other by Bergh himself. Jane Welton shared her daughter's enthusiasm. The SPCA was Jane Welton's favorite charity as well, and, according to family tradition, on at least one occasion Jane invited Bergh to come to Waterbury from New York City to be her escort at a charity ball at Rose Hill Cottage. In the midst of it all, the account continues, was "Aunt Jane refulgent in scarlet velvet, the tremendous diamond twinkling mischievously on her high forehead, leading off the grand march with the remarkable Mr. Bergh."[27]

Just when Carrie's interest in animals first led her to embrace Bergh and his society is not clear. It was well developed by 1878, the year when her will was first signed, for Bergh together with her mother were named executors of her estate. Two years later in a codicil Carrie then removed her mother's name in favor of Bergh's. Carrie also further thered Bergh's cause by helping to organize the Connecticut Humane Society, which was incorporated at Hartford on April 14, 1881. The two corresponded during Carrie's travels in the West. Carrie wrote Bergh from Colorado Springs, "asking if some means could not be devised to protect the animals on the plains from the severities of winter and the cruelty of man."[28]

The appeal from probate—"one of the most interesting will cases ever tried in New England"[29]—went to trial in New Haven on October 12, 1886, before Judge Morris Beach Beardsley of the Superior Court of Connecticut and in the days that followed was well reported in newspapers throughout New York and New England. The contesting relatives, George R. Welton and Mrs. Horace Johnson, her seventy-seven-year-old cousin (now deceased) and his half sister, focused, as expected, on Carrie's "monomania" and her mental condition at the time the original will was made. It was also charged that Bergh had exercised undue influence upon her.[30] The lead attorney for the plaintiffs, John O'Neill of Waterbury, announced during opening arguments that

> he meant to show that she had an inordinate fondness for animals, that she was intensely desirous of notoriety, and that she was insanely afraid that her mother was trying to poison her. . . . He also said that he expected to prove that she was forever talking about her mother, telling her neighbors how immoral, untruthful, and thoroughly bad she was. . . . The attorney stated that he would put witnesses on the stand who would testify that after Miss Welton ordered her favorite horse killed because he had heart disease, she had him interred with great pomp, having over $150 worth of blankets buried with him. Then, too, she had the horse's shoes taken off and gold plated.[31]

The courtroom contained a number of "noticeable figures . . . who attracted much attention." These included the tall, slender, mustachioed, and fastidiously dressed Henry Bergh ("a striking figure in any assemblage"[32]), referred to snidely by the *New Haven Morning Journal and Courier* as "the apostle of kindness to the brute creation,"[33] and Elbridge T. Gerry. Gerry, the grandson of one of the signers of the Declaration of Independence and since 1870 counsel for Bergh's society, who had drafted Carrie Welton's now contested will.

O'Neill followed his announced script closely. Carrie's cousin Ellen Johnson "testified that Carrie had suffered from the delusion that her mother wanted to do away with her and that she suspected her of trying to put poison in her food."[34] Mrs. Johnson explained that although before going off to boarding school Carrie had been "a very lively girl," she had become upon her return "very sedate and developed a great love of animals." Mrs. Johnson also told the court that during the year and a half that Carrie had lived with her in Waterbury beginning in November 1880, she had "kept almost altogether in her room" with the door locked, "kept a pistol with her all the time," refused to let anyone in to clean, sometimes for weeks at a time, and often sang "in a strange, monotonous and unmusical voice."[35]

The pomp and circumstance surrounding the death of the twenty-year-old Knight was easily established, and another relative pointed out that a memorial to Knight was an odd, if not perverse, bequest since the horse had kicked her father to death. It was also corroborated that during her travels in California Carrie had already raised a monument to Knight.[36] The appellants had prepared their case well. As the *Waterbury American* noted, the testimony elicited by O'Neill and his colleagues covered "about every thing the poor girl thought or did," culminating in a statement by Henry P. Stearns of the Hartford Asylum for the Insane that in his opinion Miss Carrie Welton was indeed insane.[37]

Timothy E. Doolittle scored points for the defense when he attacked the testimony of Carrie's cousin, Eleanor Hart of New Britain. "Gentlemen of the Jury," Doolittle solemnly intoned,

> Your attention was called to Mrs. Hart's hair, and you were told that because Carrie refused to call that hair beautiful she was insane. Is it true that Mrs. Hart has beautiful hair? If it had been hanging down her cheek, I should have been tempted to say that her hair hung down her damask cheek like seaweed down a clam. I do not believe that one man in this intelligent jury is going to say Miss Welton was crazy because she did not think that hair beautiful.[38]

At Doolittle's conclusion, the courtroom had to be cleared to allow the jurors and court officers to regain their composure.

To her credit Carrie herself had already provided most of the defense that her lead counsel, George E. Dewitt of New York, and his colleagues needed, for, as if anticipating efforts to defy her intentions, she had had the foresight at the time she drew up her original will and its codicil to be examined by two New York doctors, Charles McBurney and George A. Peters, each of whom certified her sanity. The defense also placed on the stand Dr. Allan Hamilton of New York, an expert on insanity, who "declared that while Miss Welton may have been eccentric she was not, in his belief, insane."[39]

The defense put on a parade of witnesses as well. These included James S. Elton, a former Connecticut state senator who had succeeded Carrie's father as president of Waterbury Brass, Greene Kendrick, who had just stepped down as mayor of Waterbury, and Mrs. John Kendrick, Greene Kendrick's mother, whose husband had also served as Waterbury's mayor. She testified that Carrie "was a decided favorite, very bright, very pretty and very much admired by the gentlemen." Carrie's uncle, Timothy H. Porter, spoke of his niece's "more than ordinary intelligence" and "love for the grand and beautiful in nature" and denied that she had ever "made any charges against her mother that were not strictly true."[40] Uncle Timothy's testimony was agonizingly slow. His long sentences led the reporter for the *New Haven Evening Register* to comment that "if all the witnesses had been like Mr. Porter, the case would have gone until Christmas."[41]

Another uncle, the New York banker Thomas Porter, called Carrie "the most exact and best business woman" he had ever known.[42] Porter told the court that his niece had been a frequent visitor to his house until the time of her departure for the West and that he had watched her "to see if there was any foundation for the reports that she had some delusion." His findings were quite to the contrary: "He had never been able to observe anything in her actions to indicate that she was insane or that her mind was impaired in any manner."[43] There was also the testimony of the two gardeners who took care of the grounds at Rose Hill. Both men said they "never saw anything in Carrie's actions, language or appearance which might give the opinion that she was insane."[44]

The emotional climax of the trial came on October 25 when, escorted by Attorney Doolittle, Jane Welton entered the courtroom and took her seat at a table near the counsel for the appellees. She was dressed in deep mourning, heavily veiled, and "used her black fan nearly all the time." Her testimony the next day occupied the entire afternoon. Up until 1880, Mrs. Welton told the court, there had been no change in Carrie's character ("She was always rather imperious and fond of having her way in everything"). Moreover, Carrie had plainly told her prior to making out her will in October 1878 that her heirs at law had plenty of money and that she intended to give half her property to the Society for the Prevention of Cruelty to Animals. Mrs. Welton testified further that the much cited estrangement between herself and her daughter took place during the latter part of 1879. At that time "her daughter said many disrespectful things about her," though she denied that Carrie had ever accused her of "poisoning her or deceiving her" or had ever charged her with "immorality."[45]

Doolittle finished his summation for the defense on the morning of the thirtieth, the thirteenth day of the trial. Judge Beardsley then charged the all-male jury and reviewed the testimony, "telling them that the question for them to decide was whether Miss Welton was of sound mind when she made the will."[46] To declare "this will and codicil invalid," he instructed them, "you must find that Carrie Welton was insane on October 18, 1878, and that the will was the outcome of that insanity."[47] In contrast to the trial itself, the jury's deliberations were brief. In three short hours they brought in a verdict: Carrie Welton's will was valid.

The trial over, Bergh and his society got their money, though the expected bequest had been reduced by the litigation to some seventy-three thousand dollars.[48] Two years later, on November 10, 1888, the Carrie Welton Memorial Fountain was completed at a cost of seven thousand dollars. Standing on what in earlier days had been the Waterbury village green, it consisted of an eight-and-a-half-foot-high block of Quincy granite surmounted by a twenty-five-hundred-pound bronze statue of Knight. The bronze horse was the work of the sculptor Karl Gerhardt of Hartford, who had previously designed the statue of the American schoolmaster-turned-patriot Nathan Hale that adorns the Connecticut state capitol. Affixed to the fountain's base is the plaque: "Erected 1888. A Gift to Her Native Town. By Caroline Josephine Welton. A Friend of Animals."

As for Carlyle Lamb, the survivor of their ordeal on the peak, he would take over the running of Longs Peak House from his father in 1890. Though Lamb would complete 146 ascents of Longs Peak, the last in 1935, when he was seventy-three, none would prove more harrowing or memorable than his climb of September 1884 with Carrie Welton. It would not be until January 1925, and under circumstances eerily familiar, that such high drama would return to Longs Peak, when another headstrong and adventurous woman, Agnes Vaille, would die after making the first winter climb of the precipitous East Face.[49]

Elkanah Lamb would retell the story of Carrie Welton in his 1913 memoirs, *Miscellaneous Meditations*, in which he confessed, apparently for the first time, that two days after Carrie Welton's death he had been visited by her apparition. Having sent his family to their winter home in Fort Collins, the elder Lamb had remained behind at the ranch to build two cottages to accommodate an increasing tourist trade. Understandably, his thoughts turned to Carrie Welton and the events so recently concluded. "I tried, by imagination," he later wrote,

> to conjecture her state of mind as she lay there alone, exhausted, and not able to travel, with the wild wind howling its dismal requiem as it swept over the Boulderfield; and knowing that in nature's realm of darkness and chilling night, there was no pity nor tears to shed over suffering humanity. . . .
>
> While musing thus the night following the departure of my family, I lay down upon my couch to rest and sleep, incidentally casting my gaze towards the window in my chamber; and there, under my startled gaze, and seemingly

as natural as life, stood Carrie J. Welton, looking directly toward the bed where I lay, the yellow silken mask over her features adding intensity to the uncanny presentation. Now I am not superstitious, and I do not believe in ghosts, spooks, or hobgoblins, but this ghostly appearance in the solitude of my lonely situation was the severest test of my equilibrium and courage ever before experienced in my life. Even while I was denouncing my superstitions, fears and feelings, a strange inexplicable fascination drew my eyes towards the window again, and there she stood gazing steadily towards me on the couch. Well, I leave the witchery of this peculiar mental phenomenon and experience to the expert psychologists to explain.[50]

Carlyle Lamb, by contrast, remained noticeably reticent on the subject, at least in print. Toward the end of his life, he did write at least one terse and elliptical comment on the episode. It came in a letter dated August 3, 1940, to James Rose Harvey. "Among some of the memories outstanding," the younger Lamb wrote, "the trip with Miss Carrie J. Welton on Sept–23rd 1884 when she lost her life from exposure do [sic] a weak heart."[51]

Chapter 9

1900–1915: The Coming of a Town and a Park

William Cooper, the future explorer and mapper of Wild Basin, was still an undergraduate at Alma College in Michigan when he first visited Estes Park with his parents during the summer of 1904. What they discovered was a small and peaceful hamlet numbering some two hundred year-round residents. Contemporary photographs show the future site of the town as little more than a dirt road bordered by pastures and barbed-wire fences, interrupted by a handful of buildings. These included John Cleave's frame house and, close by, his eight-by-twelve-foot post office; Sam Service's general merchandise store; a blacksmith shop run by Service's brother-in-law, Jim Boyd; William T. ("Billy") Parke's photo and curio shop; a small store run during the summer months by Elizabeth Foot and Jenny Chapin; William F. Cantwell's stage barn; George and Ben Johnson's meat market; and a forty-by-twenty-two-foot community building, the largest structure in town, which was capable of seating 150 and was alternately used as church, school, and meeting hall. West of the post office was a small cabin that since 1900 had been used by Henry C. Rogers, like John Cleave an Englishman from Cornwall, and the park's first resident photographer.[1] Dotting the valley beyond lay the guest ranches, working ranches, and farms, the Estes Park Hotel, and an increasing number of private homes and cottages, many of them occupied only during the summer season.[2]

Hidden from summer visitors like Cooper was the strong sense of community that held this world together. Well before the turn of the century, and despite its seasonal isolation, Estes Park enjoyed the kind of year-round life typical of most rural settlements. As Alexander

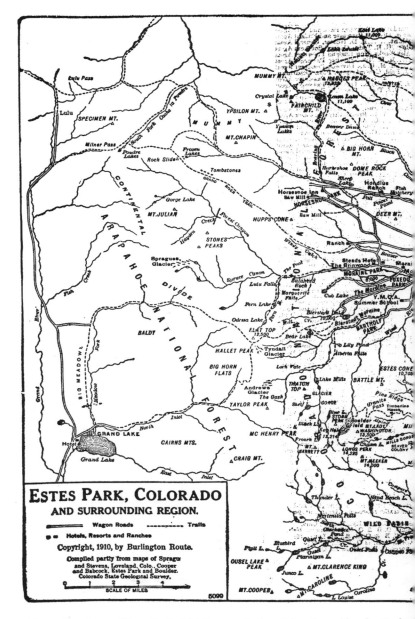

Figure 9.1. Map of Estes Park, 1910, compiled and distributed by the Burlin

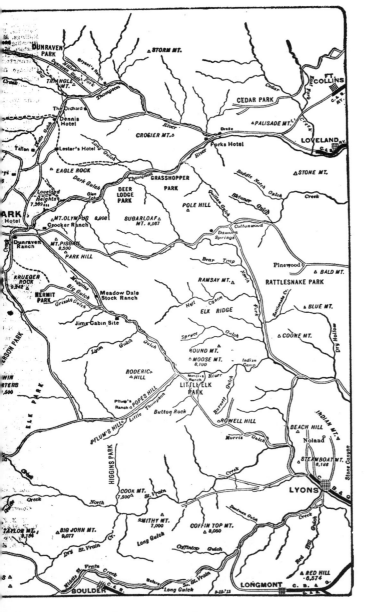

...oad. Courtesy Estes Park Area Historical Museum.

MacGregor's surviving diaries indicate, from the mid-1870s on there was a more or less constant exchange of goods, services, and sociability among the pioneer families. MacGregor writes about hiring local workers, like L. A. Mills and Walt Beach, buying elk meat from Israel Rowe, furnishing logs and lumber to the Spragues and Fergusons, helping Abner and Fred Sprague survey Hunter Ferguson's claim in Moraine Park, renting Theodore Whyte a cow to provide milk for his children, and visiting back and forth and sharing meals with Griff Evans, Horace Ferguson, Abner Sprague, and others. Where cash was lacking, early settlers provided labor or simply swapped for what they needed. The controlling ethos, which they shared with hard-working men and women throughout the West, was a hardheaded pragmatism softened by love and respect for the natural world around them.

Though the park lacked its own church building and a salaried minister, it enjoyed for many years the services of the Reverend Elkanah Lamb. Between 1895 and 1908, Father Lamb preached year-round at the community building, sharing the pulpit at times with the Reverend

Figure 9.2. The Elkhorn Lodge, summer 1904. Courtesy Colorado Historical Society.

Edward Baldwin and the Reverend Albin Griffith. In return for his labor, Lamb asked only for a dinner and freewill offering on his birthday in return. (In 1903 "this happy affair [fittingly described as "a donation party"] netted Mr. Lamb about $80."[3]) Lamb preached without notes, often wandering away from the pulpit while delivering sermons in a manner distinctly his own. Eleanor Hondius, the daughter of the founders of Elkhorn Lodge, remembered him vividly:

> He was of the United Brethren sect, and certainly a great believer in hellfire and damnation; his sermons were never less than an hour in length.
>
> He was at least six feet five inches tall, and he wore a long black frock on Sunday. On the table which served as a pulpit he would lay a snowy white handkerchief. As he preached, his voice would get louder and louder, and finally he was shouting. Suddenly, he would stop, pick up the handkerchief, and give his nose a violent blow. (I always thought this trumpeting would put Gabriel to shame.) Then Mr. Lamb would start the sermon again, and go back up the scale.[4]

Figure 9.3. The Reverend Elkanah J. Lamb. Courtesy Estes Park Area Historical Museum.

A small Sunday congregation apparently did not prove daunting. "As long as there are eight or ten people gathered together in the name of the Lord," she quotes Lamb as saying, "I will preach."[5] Elkanah Lamb, whose faith helped him to deal with a personal life marred by tragedy,[6] was also much in demand for weddings and so much a believer in the institution itself that one winter he offered "to marry at half price" any Estes Park resident so inclined.

In the months between tourist seasons the residents of Estes Park found ways to entertain themselves. There were community dances, oyster suppers (at which the Elkhorn excelled), bridge and High-Five parties (with prizes and booby prizes), moonlight serenading (particularly of newlyweds), wintertime skating, sleighing, and ice fishing, in addition to quiet visiting. There were also occasional theatricals. One such production, put on at the Elkhorn in November 1896 by a group calling itself the "Estes Park Amusement Committee," was titled "Ferret or the Lightning Rod Agent." It was "well received."[7] After the turn of the century there was a much-remembered Literary Society, featuring "performances" by such local residents as Johnny Adams, Enos and Joe Mills, and Warren Rutledge. Much of the fun, however, was impromptu. On a Saturday evening in March of 1904, for example, Charles and Edward Johnson, two bachelors who had leased the MacGregor Ranch, were interrupted during dinner by "about thirty-five good people of the park, laden with well filled baskets."[8] When time hung heavy in winter it was always possible for the men to find comradery around the wood stove in Sam Service's store where they could exchange news and stories or talk politics—the valley was almost to a person Republican in persuasion.

Holidays brought local residents together. Community Fourth of July celebrations began in 1897, when 150 people gathered near John Cleave's post office, raised the flag, and listened to an oration by the budding naturalist Enos Mills. In 1899 residents staged a daylong Independence Day celebration in Moraine Park, beginning at 11 A.M. with remarks by the president of the day, Abner Sprague, and featuring a Grand Basket Dinner at noontime, an address by Enos Mills, "Happy Hours" at 2 P.M., and fireworks at 8 P.M.[9] By 1908 these festivities had grown considerably more elaborate. That year a crowd estimated at 1,000 witnessed and took part in bronco busting, a pie-eating contest, greased-pig and burro riding, wheelbarrow races, and a surprise race in which a group of young men rode their horses three hundred yards, dismounted, changed into old clothes, and dashed back to the finish line.[10] There was also an annual Thanksgiving "reunion" dinner at the schoolhouse, usually followed by a program, to which everyone for miles around was invited. In 1902 92 people "brought their best cooking with them and had a happy feast together," after which they enjoyed a two hour program featuring piano music and an opening prayer by Elkanah Lamb, followed by his "Thanksgiving address." Enos Mills closed the day with yet another address, "occupying one hour."[11]

While the families of the pioneers of '75 remained at the center of Estes Park life, by 1900 they were sharing the scene with a variety of interesting and often talented newcomers. Among them were Johnny Adams, who came to the Elkhorn Lodge to work in 1889, and his brother, George, who followed, both of whom lived beyond the Elkhorn on Fall River; Shep Husted and Warren Rutledge, who would leave their marks as foresters and mountain guides; the Reverend Albin Griffith, who about 1890 homesteaded 160 acres on the Big Thompson below Ferguson's and later operated a sawmill and lumberyard; and Charles Lester, who came to the park in 1887 and for many years ran a small summer store in a log cabin a half mile north of the Estes Park Hotel on Fish Creek and later managed the hotel itself. There was also the Dutchman Pieter Hondius, who had come to the park seeking relief from chronic asthma in 1896. Hondius stayed on to ranch a large area in Beaver Meadows, married Eleanor James of the Elkhorn, and became a civic leader in his own right. Others included Hugo Miller, who in 1897 gained control of Peter Pauly's ranch on Cow Creek, which he enlarged and later sold to John J. McGraw; the architect-carpenter Al Cobb, who helped to build both the new schoolhouse and the Stanley Hotel; and the talented, if underappreciated, oil painter Richard Tallant, who first lived in the north end of the park but subsequently built a new home with an attached studio on Elkhorn Avenue.

During the short, but hectic, summer months owners of summer cottages helped to swell the population and added additional ambience to the festivities of the resorts. Among the better-known summer residents were the newspapermen William Allen White and Charles F. Scott, both of whom built in Moraine Park on land acquired from the Chapmans and Spragues. There was also the landscape artist Charles Partridge Adams, who rented a cottage for a summer studio during the early years of the century and then, in the fall of 1903, secured a quitclaim from Dunraven to a few acres on Fish Creek road. There he built a new studio with twenty-foot ceilings called the "Sketch Box," which enjoyed fine views of Longs Peak to both the south and the west. "It was the simple life," Adams recalled years later; "bracing air, beautiful scenery, flowering meadows, clear streams, plenty of wholesome food, good books and

papers to read, money enough for the necessities, friends often coming in, and good health."[12] Adams made enough that first summer to
pay for both house and land.

Throughout the first decade of the new century change was decidedly in the air. By the time young Cooper returned to Estes Park on his
own two years later, in 1906, he noted significant differences. Where
there had been a hamlet, there was now the beginnings of a town and,
within a decade, to the south, west, and north, where there had been
unkept wilderness, there would be a new national park "for all the
people." These two events defined the decade and a half between 1900
and 1915, and their impact was enormous. Not only did they dramatically alter the appearance of Estes Park and determine how and where
much of its future development would take place, but they introduced
and then magnified issues having to do with growth and progress that
would dominate much of the following century. In the 1880s and 1890s
Estes Park and its citizens had discovered, and exploited, tourism and
the recreational uses of scenery. In the years that followed they would
test and retest the thesis that tourism and recreation, if properly directed
and managed, could create and sustain both a local economy and a sense
of community. Behind these transforming events was the vision, entrepreneurial energy, and advocacy of four individuals: Cornelius H. Bond,
Burton D. Sanborn, Freelan O. Stanley, and Enos A. Mills.

~

Cornelius Bond (1854–1931) first visited Estes Park during the summer of 1879, when fresh from Ohio he camped near the Sprague ranch
in Willow Park and then crossed the Divide to visit Lulu City. Four years
later, in January 1883, the former schoolteacher came back to Colorado
to stay, settling at Loveland, where he married and went into business.
Bond's interest in the park and its opportunities developed over the next
two decades, particularly during the five years between 1895 and 1901,
when he served as elected sheriff of Larimer County, and in 1902, when
he was appointed to a three-member review committee, together with
J. B. Harbaugh, a former commissioner, and William L. Beckfield,
Loveland's former mayor and postmaster, "to see what could be done"
with the Bald Mountain road to Estes Park. As sheriff, Bond had traveled
over much of the region on horseback, observing at close hand the
condition of its roads and trails. The 1902 report of Bond and his associates confirmed what people had been saying for years. The existing
road with its three less than gentle hills was clearly inadequate: the
residents of Loveland, Fort Collins, and Greeley needed a more direct,

serviceable, and scenic access to the park. The most obvious choice was to construct a new road up through the Big Thompson Canyon, a route that had been under consideration for at least a decade.[13] Bond was one of five men asked to secure a preliminary survey.

"The assurance of a new, good road from Loveland . . . is about the best news that Estes park people have ever had," one resident wrote to the *Fort Collins Weekly Courier*. "For years the park has suffered annoyance and expense. On the toll road the rate was outrageously high, while the county road was so bad that no one, except the assessor and possibly a coyote, traveled it without a tincture of anarchy."[14] "The proposed route is through the big canon and then follows the Big Thompson and South fork into the park," the *Fort Collins Express* added.

> This will give a water grade all the way and make a net saving of about 2,000 feet of climbing. In addition it will make an attractive route by affording fine scenery, plenty of water, with good camping and fishing all the way. . . . To make Estes Park easily accessible to tourists the patronage of the park will soon double and to hold its business in Larimer County, where it belongs, will amply justify the expenditure to say nothing of public convenience.[15]

Getting the new road built turned out to be a more complicated affair than Bond and the Larimer County commissioners anticipated. The survey of early September 1902 showed that a route up the canyon was entirely feasible. The grade averaged 3 percent, in no place was more than 7 percent, and there was far less rock to be removed than had been originally thought. Accompanying the survey, as a further incentive, was a petition with a long list of signatures. The commissioners authorized $24,000 for the project, and at their meeting of November 28, 1902, after examining both plans and specifications, instructed the county attorney to prepare a contract and advertise for bids.

Eleven bids were received, but when they were opened on January 26, it was discovered that only two offered to complete the entire road, including bridges, and both were in excess of the $24,000 that had been authorized. The commissioners rejected all the bids. But anxious to move the popular project forward, they just as promptly entered into an agreement with one of the two bidders they had just rejected, Loveland contractor William American Riley, who agreed to trim the cost of the project through "minor changes" in order "to construct the road and bridges in compliance with specifications, for $24,000."[16] Riley was "assured" that "he'd not lose anything by signing."[17] It was a decision that both contractor and commissioners would soon regret.

From that point on there were problems. Riley, who had promised

completion by July of 1903, began work on January 31. By April he
had about 150 men on the road and still expected to meet his dead-
line. But as spring turned to summer, Riley discovered that his original
bid of $27,500 had probably been correct and that the price he had so
eagerly accepted the previous November was much too low. (Riley
would later tell Abner Sprague that he had based his bid on the speci-
fication for rock and earth removal provided by the county engineer
rather than his own.[18]) The commissioners, on their part, were also
becoming nervous, apparently fearing that given the available financing the road might never be completed. To complicate matters further,
Riley began to have problems with his workers. On September 12,
1903, with "about twenty miles of the road . . . already completed and
four miles remain[ing] to be done," most of his crew walked off the
job to go to work at the Loveland sugar factory. Contractor Riley
promptly laid off the rest until he could get a full quota. By then the
road had cost some $30,000, and it was estimated that its completion
would require an additional $3,000.[19]

Though in early December the *Loveland Reporter* pronounced the road
"complete" and praised Riley for having "done as he agreed in constructing a good road,"[20] by January of 1904 an impasse had been reached
between contractor and county. The county had by then paid him
$15,891, but Riley claimed that he was owed over $8,000 more, that
the commissioners would not settle, and that their aim was "to make

Figure 9.4. Stage on the Big Thompson Canyon road. Courtesy National Park
Service—Rocky Mountain National Park.

him throw down his tools and quit."[21] The commissioners, on their part, following the lead of the county engineer, cited the fact that Riley had deviated from the original survey. Riley sought legal counsel. He was told by his lawyer, Denverite Greeley Whitford, that until the road was paid for, he was its legal owner. Riley also discovered that the easements promised by property owners as a condition of building the road had never been executed or delivered. Riley's subsequent strategy, which some viewed as mere "bluff," was to up the ante. Not only did he instigate a lawsuit and secure an injunction against the county, but, with the help of seven partners from Denver and Loveland, he incorporated the Loveland and Estes Park Electric Railway, to which he promptly "gave a quit claim deed to the entire road." He also gave the new corporation the missing easements that he had now secured.[22]

In mid-January, to heighten the drama and, as he said, "to force some action," Riley closed and fenced the road at the mouth of the canyon and posted two shifts of guards. He also let it be known that he was acting on the advice of his attorney, who had told him "to stop all travel over the road"—even if he was forced to "use Winchesters."[23] To

Figure 9.5. Estes Park, c. 1906, looking southwest. New school at lower right; Sam Service's general store center left. Courtesy Lula W. Dorsey Museum, YMCA of the Rockies.

give additional reality to his projected railroad, Riley hired one of his new partners, Abner Sprague, to survey and map its route over the existing canyon roadbed.

The response of the county was anemic at best. During the second week of January, two of the commissioners, together with County Surveyor Emmet C. McAnelly, "went over the road and made a critical examination of the work done to determine what had been left undone." What they discovered, they claimed, was that Riley "had failed to do much that he had agreed to do and that the road lacked considerable of being completed according to contract." Among the work not yet completed was the construction of "some 60 turn-outs or passing points," each forty feet long and sixteen feet wide. Arguing that Riley had defaulted on his contract and that what had been completed belonged not to the contractor but to the county, the Larimer commissioners then directed Surveyor McAnelly "to employ a force of men and teams and go on and complete said public highway as the contract specifies it shall be done."[24]

The crew that McAnelly assembled was a small one, and when Riley encountered six men "tearing up the road where he said he had already completed the thoroughfare," he ordered them off. To discourage their return and underline his own determination, Riley removed the planking from the bridges in the lower canyon.[25] Though Riley later said that he had expected to be arrested, nothing happened, leaving him free to announce in April 1904 that "there will be no stages over this road this year—nor any other year. We do not propose to have our rights trampled upon. Unless the commissioners see fit to pay us what is just and right we don't propose to allow the public to travel over the road. We are going ahead with our electric road."[26]

At this point, for both parties, it appeared to be a matter of awaiting the outcome of a litigation process that promised to be both long and expensive. For the commissioners it also meant the passing of yet another tourist season without the long-promised road to the park. In June 1904, with Bond's help, the two sides reached an "amicable conclusion." For the sum of $1,500 and a subsequent payment of $8,165.80 "in full settlement," Riley agreed to drop his suit and give "peaceful possession of the road" to the county.[27] With the help of an additional $3,000 raised by Loveland businessmen the road to Estes Park was finally put through.

Though it would remain a dusty, narrow, one-track affair until 1919 when the state began to widen it, the Big Thompson road was a success from the beginning. By 1908 it had been extended from the hamlet of

Drake up the North Fork to Glen Haven, which since the summer of 1903 had been a summer encampment called the Presbyterian Assembly Association, sponsored by the Boulder presbytery, and consisted of a community numbering some twenty cottages.[28] The following fall and spring this road was further extended up Devils Gulch to enter the park near the Rustic Hotel.

With the new road a reality, Cornelius Bond moved quickly to take advantage of an increasingly accessible Estes Park. In March 1905, together with the help of three partners and longtime friends, Joseph R. Anderson, William L. Beckfield, and John Y. Munson, Bond purchased for eight thousand dollars the quarter section of land owned by the fastidious Englishman John Cleave at the junction of the Big Thompson and Fall Rivers. The location was ideal. Bond and his companions wanted to lay out a town, and the spot they selected with its intersecting roads and rivers, schoolhouse, and post office was already the center of community life. Most importantly, they found Cleave, a resident of the park for more than thirty years, and its postmaster for twenty, willing to sell and move on because "the danged place [was being] overrun by tourists."[29] On June 1, 1905, as a sign of his intent, Cleave resigned his position of postmaster in favor of C. H. Bond.[30]

Bond and his associates wasted little time. In May they hired Abner Sprague to survey and subdivide the land. The next step, which occurred on August 24, was to form the Estes Park Town Company as their vehicle for development and to plan for a two-inch waterline from Cleave's land to a small dam located on Black Canyon Creek, above MacGregor Ranch.[31] Installed the following spring, the 14,500-foot mainline covered the entire length of the property with a fall of more than four hundred feet. Twenty-five-foot lots fronting Elkhorn Avenue were offered for sale for fifty dollars; lots farther to

Figure 9.6. Guy Robert LaCoste. Courtesy Lula W. Dorsey Museum, YMCA of the Rockies.

the east for thirty-five. Activity was brisk, and by June twenty-five lots had been sold.[32] Bidders were so eager to purchase and get into the tourist business that a number of them actually camped out in tents while the company finished the platting so as not to miss out on the opportunity to purchase. One of the campers was Fred Clatworthy, the future world famous photographer, who purchased two lots for one hundred dollars. Clatworthy, who had to borrow the money, thought the price cheap. "A few capitalists," he recalled some years later with evident regret, "bought as many as four lots." Then construction began. "Our next step was to 'beg, borrow, or steal' enough money," he noted, "to build anything that would shed water and hold a business name or sign."[33] In Clatworthy's case it was a building to be used as a photography gallery, which was ready and open to the public by July 4, 1905—the beginning of a business that Clatworthy would conduct in the park for the next fifty years.

Figures 9.7 and 9.8. North-south and east-west views of the future village of Estes Park, 1903. Courtesy Colorado Historical Society; Lula W. Dorsey Museum, YMCA of the Rockies.

These new businesses—including Clatworthy's photography studio, a shoe repair shop, bakery, barber shop, laundry, butcher shop, and livery stable—sprang up almost overnight. A year later, in 1906, Josie Hupp opened her twenty-three-room Hupp Hotel at the corner of what is now Elkhorn and Moraine Avenues, featuring steam heat and hot and cold running water. By that summer Tena Boden, Ruth Cassady, Elizabeth Foot, John Jones, and John Manford, among others, were advertising cottages to rent. The expanded tourist capacity was clearly needed. On July 5, 1907, for example, the *Longmont Ledger* casually noted that "fifty students, five professors and a Chinese cook arrived from the Chicago University Monday evening, to stay all summer at the Elkhorn Lodge."[34]

Returning visitors were quick to note the escalating change. "There is lots of new buildings here in Estes Park since you were here," a young woman named Audra wrote her cousin on May 21, 1907.

They have moved the Post Office back towards Cantwell's barn, and have built a big Hotel on the corner where the P.O. was. They have also built a residence, a drug store, and a barber shop between the barn and where the Post Office used to stand. There are 8 or 10 new houses going up now and one steam laundry and one Livery Barn, right here on Main St. or rather Elk Horn Ave., as the people out here call it.

The man I am working for has also built this store since you was [sic] here. His name is Samuel Service. Do you remember him[?]. He is a tall, red headed, Irishman.[35]

By that October some 324 people were getting mail at the Estes Park post office, and the population of the town had reached an estimated five hundred.[36] Though Estes Park would not be incorporated for another decade, until 1917, the beginnings of its infrastructure were rapidly falling into place.

Almost simultaneously, there was a second, and equally momentous, transfer of property. This involved the residual holdings of the Earl of Dunraven and his remaining partner in the English Company, Lord Barrymore, some 6,400 acres in all (plus an additional 700 acres then in litigation), consisting of almost seventy separate parcels, the majority of them, like Cleave's, full quarter sections. Though the ability to obtain so much prime real estate, and at one time, was a developer's delight, the transaction itself proved anything but easy. Behind the sale there was a complex and fascinating story, for getting Dunraven's attention, let alone his signed agreement, took both time and talent.

~

That story began with the dreams of Guy Robert LaCoste (1875–1954), a young Denver newspaperman, who by the turn of the century had homesteaded 360 acres above Wind River (the future site of the YMCA of the Rockies), holdings that he would soon expand to almost 1,000 acres. Though not yet thirty, LaCoste was ambitious in the extreme. Within a few brief years LaCoste had determined not only to become a major landowner in his own right, but, working for and with others, to gain control of the entire valley and a monopoly over its tourist trade. LaCoste clearly knew what he wanted. He also knew, or thought he knew, how to proceed. During the 1890s he had worked in Denver for his father and the Hampton-LaCoste Investment Company, one of the largest investment companies in Colorado, where he learned both risk taking and the art of leveraging other people's money.

On December 16, 1901, together with two Denverites, businessman George D. Sullivan and Arthur B. West, a lawyer, LaCoste organized the Estes Park Land and Investment Company to serve as his vehicle for acquisition and development. The articles of incorporation made the company's purpose clear: "to buy, sell and lease real estate, lands and interests in landed property of every kind and character . . . to build, construct and maintain hotels, inns and other places of public entertainment upon such lands . . . and to operate such hotels, inns or other places of public entertainment and carry on the general business of a hotel or innkeeper. . . ."[37] Their first project fell well within this prospectus. By the following summer LaCoste had completed and opened to the public Wind River Lodge, consisting of a two-story, gabled main building and six adjacent cottages, built on the lower slopes of Green (now Emerald) Mountain. But this was only the beginning. By 1902 LaCoste and his partners had conceived a much larger plan: the acquisition of the Earl of Dunraven's hotel and properties.

Dunraven had long since lost interest in Estes Park. For all of Theodore Whyte's diligence, the cattle and hotel business had never been profitable, and following Whyte's return to England the situation showed little, if any, improvement. The expiration of Frank Bartholf's three-year lease in 1902 gave LaCoste and his friends their opportunity. Unable to work out an agreement through the Earl's Denver lawyer, Frank Prestidge, LaCoste decided to carry an offer directly to Dunraven himself. That meant the expense of a trip abroad, but the stakes were high and the cocky LaCoste had every expectation of success. Once in England, LaCoste still found Dunraven strangely elusive, and he spent weeks trying to contact the Earl through his solicitor. Finally a new lease arrangement was worked out, lacking only Dunraven's signature.

Confident that he had succeeded—that the Earl would sign the prepared documents once he returned from a visit to France—LaCoste sailed for home and his job at the *Denver Post*. On April 3, 1903, LaCoste then allowed (perhaps even arranged for) the news of his grand design to be published in the Colorado press, including the *Denver Republican*. The article is breathtaking in its sweep. Speaking with the absolute confidence and conviction of a man with a "done deal," LaCoste not only announced the consummation of an agreement that still lacked a signature, but spoke of his future intentions in a way that must have left knowledgeable readers shaking their heads in disbelief:

The Estes Park Company . . . has 11,000 acres of lands in the park, with above 30,000 acres of range lands, comprising the former holdings of the Earl of Dunraven and of the Estes Park Land & Investment company. On these two tracts are located the Wind River lodge and the Estes Park hotel. . . . The company is also negotiating for the Rustic Hotel with surrounding grounds, and Sprague's, which stands on another large tract. Practically all the cottages in the park not owned by non-residents and kept as their homes have also been bought by the syndicate, and it has acquired all the stage lines. . . .

It is the intention of the new owners to build roads to and through all parts of the park, to improve the stage service to make the park much more accessible from the railroad, and to build, on the Dunraven ranch, a modern high class summer hotel. . . . It will also conduct a big general store, and will also provide for the furnishing of nearly all supplies that the park can produce direct to the hotel and cottages. For example a creamery will be established, so that the best of milk and cream and butter may be obtained. Cattle fattened on the sweet grasses of the hills will be slaughtered, put in cold storage and provided instead of beef brought by wagon from the railroad. All the vegetables which will grow in the mountain valley will be obtained by the hotel keepers and cottagers.

Another building will be an immense summer sanitarium. . . . The general plan will be to make the park, not a fashionable resort, but a place where people may go to enjoy the comforts of civilized life, while wearing their old clothes, hunting, fishing, mountaineering or simply loafing.

The purchase price paid by a syndicate of unnamed men from Denver and Boston was given as some $400,000, with an additional $100,000 for "improvements."[38]

Whatever LaCoste thought he was accomplishing by publishing (or allowing others to publish) his future plans before he had even finalized them, he was soon disappointed. Dunraven returned from France and refused to sign the lease. In the meantime, several newspapers in the valley picked up the story and tried to verify, without success, the syndicate's purchase of "hotels and land."[39] Moreover, the press was becoming skeptical. When another story began to circulate during the summer of 1903 about the sale of Estes Park—this time involving seven thousand acres, a purchase price of $128,000, and plans even more elaborate than LaCoste's—the Loveland Reporter took pains to remind its readers this was "the third or fourth time this year" that such "paper deals" had been floated: "The plan looks very nice to those who are interested—but it is a question of moment whether or not the plans can be completed."[40] There was, however, at least one transaction by LaCoste's syndicate: five months after his April announcement, on September 17, 1902, LaCoste transferred for $250 his three-hundred-acre Wind River holdings to the Estes Park Land and Development Company.[41]

Guy LaCoste did, in fact, succeed. On April 21, 1904, acting as agent for others, he managed to negotiate a five-year lease, to run from April 15 of that year, "of all the property of the Estes Park Company Limited situate[d] in Larimer County," including sixty-six hundred acres and five hundred head of Hereford cattle.[42]

What happened next is not totally clear. What we do know is that eight months later, in December 1904, Guy LaCoste returned to England in a new attempt to negotiate directly with the Earl of Dunraven. Once arrived in England, LaCoste made a Christmas journey to Oxford University to visit a friend and fellow countryman, a thirty-one-year-old teacher named Anna Wolfrom. The two had met in Estes Park at the home of fellow Denver Post newspaperman Frank Lundy Webster, who had homesteaded above Wind River in 1896. Anna Wolfrom was then

Figure 9.9. Burton D. Sanborn. Courtesy City of Greeley Museums, permanent collection.

studying at Oxford, and over Christmas dinner, she recalled many years later, LaCoste calmly told her that he had come to England "to buy Estes Park" on behalf of Freelan O. Stanley and Burton Sanborn, whose own letters of offer Dunraven had refused to respond to. LaCoste returned to London on December 27. Several days later Wolfrom also came down to London, where she accompanied the young American to Parliament and saw Dunraven hand him some papers. About three weeks later Anna received a letter from LaCoste "saying that the sale of land in Estes Park had been consummated and he was sailing for America."[43]

Though Anna Wolfrom's recollection about the involvement of Stanley and Sanborn at this date is suspect,[44] what brought LaCoste back to England was an attempt to persuade Dunraven to change the terms of his April 1904 agreement. LaCoste and his partners were not content to lease the Earl's Estes Park holdings as others had previously done. They wanted the option to purchase them outright. This is precisely what LaCoste achieved. Acting on his own behalf and as agent for fellow newspaperman and Estes Park summer resident Al Birch, Denver surgeon William Bagot, Denver lawyer and financier Gerald Hughes, and J. C. Hoover of Hamilton, Ohio, LaCoste persuaded Dunraven to cancel the "old lease" of April 1904 and give him a new one. Under the terms of this "new lease," which went into effect on January 1, 1905, and ran for a period of seven years, LaCoste and his associates were to pay an annual rent of $1,850, and, beginning on January 1, 1906, to make at least $5,000 in preapproved, yearly "permanent improvements." Most significantly, the new lease contained an option to purchase the properties of the Estes Park Company for $50,000.[45]

LaCoste's new arrangement with the Earl of Dunraven, ironically, did not begin well. On the night of February 27, 1905, the building next to the Dunraven ranch house called "the Chapel" caught fire and burned to the ground. Asleep inside, and escaping unhurt, were none other than Guy LaCoste and Al Birch.[46]

The "new lease" gave LaCoste precisely what he needed to realize his plans, and he notified the press of his intentions. He would immediately invest $50,000 in remodeling and refurbishing the Estes Park Hotel and in turning Dunraven's cottage into a country club, with the work to be finished by July 1.[47] Once again something went wrong. Undoubtedly it had to do with money. The "new lease" that LaCoste negotiated said nothing about remodeling the hotel or cottage, though such changes, if approved, were allowable. It did, however, require the lessee to discharge "all the liabilities of the Estes Park Company Limited" and to "at once stock the demised land to its full capacity and push its development investing for this purpose not less than twenty five thousand dollars."

One can easily surmise, given LaCoste's inability to make good on earlier plans, that he was unable to arrange the required financing. Whatever the reason, on October 5, 1905, "for one dollar and other good considerations" LaCoste and his partners signed a quitclaim agreement relinquishing their lease. The dissolution itself was carefully planned and negotiated, for on the very same day (and under substantially the same terms) a lease with an option to purchase was given to Miller B. Porter, secretary and treasurer of the W. W. & Miller B. Porter Investment Company of Denver.[48] From that time on we hear little more about Guy LaCoste. In 1907 he sold his remaining interest in the Estes Park Land and Investment Company and two years later gave up the newspaper business in favor of becoming private secretary to United States Senator Charles J. Hughes Jr.

Like LaCoste, Porter also had partners and plans. And in February of 1906, together with Harry C. Bonsall and A. B. McGaffey, he incorporated the Estes Park Development Company with capital stock of $50,000 in order to pursue them.[49] (This was the corporate entity of which Burton Sanborn and Freelan O. Stanley subsequently purchased a controlling interest.) Shortly thereafter, presumably some time in the spring of 1906, Porter assigned the lease to the Estes Park Development Company. There the matter rested until January 19, 1907, when Sanborn, for a reported price of $80,000, arranged to purchase the Dunraven holdings,[50] a sale finally consummated by both Sanborn and Stanley a year later on June 16, 1908.[51] However complex and protracted the actual details of divestiture, the story became simple in the Earl's retelling: "The show could not be managed from home, and we were in danger of being frozen out. So we sold for what we could get and cleared out. . . ."[52]

~

Until the time of purchase, Burton Davis Sanborn (1859–1914), upon whom, together with F. O. Stanley, the ownership of Dunraven's property now descended, was chiefly known for his work as an irrigationist. Some years earlier, as president of the North Poudre Irrigation Company he had reconstructed a system of reservoirs known as the North Fork Ditch. He also organized the Seven Lakes Reservoir Company and almost single-handedly financed and built Boyd Lake Reservoir, the largest in Larimer County, completed in July 1908. A native of Vermont, Sanborn had come to Greeley from Ohio in 1870 as one of the original members of the Union Colony, where he subsequently became senior partner in the real estate, loan, and investment firm of Sanborn and Houston.

Sanborn first visited Estes Park in the late 1870s, and on August 20, 1879, made his first climb of Longs Peak in the company of Carlyle Lamb. From that time on Estes Park became something of a summer ritual. On one subsequent camping trip, Sanborn not only met a young woman named Carrie Bassett, who would become his wife, but gained an intimation that his own future and the future development of Estes Park were destined to become intertwined. The *Greeley Tribune* told the story in July of 1908:

> As the wagon swung out of the upper end of the canyon of the Big Thompson, and the tired, though happy crowd of campers beheld for the first time the grandeur of the scene that opened before them, young Burton had a fleeting mental glimpse of the future. Fleeting though it were [sic], it returned again

and again at brief periods during their stay there. He would catch it as he saw the tumbling waterfalls, the glaciers and the lakes, and in a crude way he measured their possibilities. Also in a vague way the thought was born that he would some day have to own all this, though how and why he had not the slightest idea.[53]

In subsequent years, Sanborn began to invest in the area, and by the time he turned his attention to Dunraven's holdings, he already owned Bear and Bierstadt Lakes, the water rights on Fall River, where he hoped to develop a hydroelectric plant, and two cottages.[54]

The initial response among Estes Park residents to the news of Sanborn's purchase was one of apprehension. Word quickly circulated that it was the new owner's intention to build a large storage reservoir in the main body of the park and thus "destroy it as a resort."[55] So persistent was the rumor that Sanborn sent a lengthy letter of disavowal to the Loveland Chamber of Commerce, which was then published in the *Loveland Reporter*. "I must say," Sanborn wrote, clearly betraying his annoyance,

> that I am complimented by the confidence that the Estes Park people have in my ability to carry out such a stupendous project. They must think I have "money to burn," as it is a certainty that an irrigation reservoir of this character would cost enormously and there is no unappropriated water to fill it. . . . The matter is an absolute impossibility unless the United States government or someone should spend millions of dollars in tunneling the range and bringing in additional supplies of water. I wish the Estes park people to give me credit for having common sense and I wish to advise them that I know of no one, unless it is Mr. Stanley, who is more interested in developing the Park and making possible the glorious future of this vicinity, than myself.[56]

He did allow, however, that "a large lake on which launches and row-boats might be placed would prove a valuable feature for the park."[57] Like his soon-to-be partner, Freelan Stanley, Burton Sanborn was clearly a visionary. His suggestions about "tunneling the range . . . bringing in additional supplies of water" and building "a large lake" prefigure the construction of the Alva Adams Tunnel and the damming of the Big Thompson to create Lake Estes some forty years later.

Where large irrigation projects were concerned, Burton Sanborn was clearly irrepressible. Within months of having disabused residents that he had a plan to turn part of the park into a reservoir, his name was linked to a project that would do precisely that. According to the September 19, 1907, edition of the *Loveland Reporter*, "B. D. Sanborn and other capitalists" proposed to build a three-mile-long, 125-foot-high dam for the generation of electricity, extending from the Dunraven ranch down into the Big Thompson Canyon to within about a mile of Loveland Heights. Three miles below the new dam the highway would be rerouted "up over the mountains on the north side of the river."[58] This time there was little or no public outcry, for we hear no more about the proposed dam and power plant until March of 1908, when Sanborn quietly announced that it had been put off "on account of the recent money stringency."[59]

~

Money was not a problem for Sanborn's new partner, Freelan Oscar Stanley (1849–1940), and that was, no doubt, precisely what attracted the irrigationist. Sanborn meant what he said about not having "money to burn"; in fact, part of his initial payment to Dunraven had taken the form of a section of land near Fort Collins and stock in the North Poudre Irrigation Company.[60] Stanley brought with him a ready supply of capital. Moreover, at the time of Sanborn's purchase of the Dunraven properties Stanley had already announced his plans for developing the park by building a first-class modern hotel and for introducing an auto stage line to and from the valley.[61] Though just when their partnership was struck is not clear, it was reported in the press at the time of Sanborn's purchase in January 1907 that the two men were "negotiating."[62] In his February 6 letter to the Loveland Chamber of Commerce Sanborn further noted that "I had the pleasure of an interview with Mr. Stanley yesterday and have hopes of cooperating with him in such a way that the best results can be reached."[63] Whatever the terms of their ultimate arrangement, when the final agreement with Dunraven was announced in June 1908, Sanborn and Stanley together were its recipients.[64]

Freelan O. Stanley and his identical-twin brother, Francis Edgar, were men of ingenuity, perseverance, and native shrewdness. Born in Maine, they were Down-East Yankees through and through. In the course of their lifetimes these two inventor-manufacturers not only developed and perfected two important new technologies, but were resourceful and farsighted enough to capitalize commercially upon them. When they turned to other fields, as F. O. Stanley did with his activities in Estes Park, they were equally successful.

Though both brothers were supremely talented, when it came to inventing, it was Francis (or "Frank," as F. O. called him), a "sort of all-around mechanical genius," who took the lead. Already one of the leading portrait photographers in New England, Francis Stanley began to experiment in the early 1880s with dry-plate photography, eventually developing a dry-plate coating machine that greatly increased productivity.

By November 1884 he and Freelan had become partners in the highly profitable Stanley Dry Plate Company, which they would later sell to their major competitor, George Eastman of Rochester's Eastman Kodak Company. Well before that sale the brothers had shrewdly moved their production plant from Lewiston, Maine, to Watertown, Massachusetts, in order to gain access to better railroad facilities and their suppliers and markets. It was there, in Watertown and adjacent Newton, that they achieved their second, and even more famous, success, the steam automobile.

By the time Francis began to tinker with steam-propelled locomotion, the technology itself was hardly new, and by the 1890s a number of American inventors—including Ransom Eli Olds—had successfully experimented with steam automobiles.[65] The Stanleys' involvement began in 1897, when Francis, having seen an operating model at a fair in nearby Brockton, set out to build a steam auto of his own. Within less than a year, and at a cost of only five hundred dollars, he had produced a two-seat prototype with a light-weight, two-cylinder, reversible engine, which he and Freelan were able to take for a trial run through the streets of Newton. By 1898 the brothers were beginning to produce vehicles with standardized parts at their Watertown plant and were on their way to becoming the first in the world to manufacture automobiles in commercial quantities. But they were also finding it increasingly difficult to operate two major manufacturing businesses. The next year, in a decision that they would soon regret, the brothers sold their automobile business (patents, manufacturing facilities, and goodwill) for $250,000. Fortunately for the Stanleys, the Locomobile Company of America, the successor company, almost immediately ran into problems. The purchasing partners, Barber and Walker, did not get along, a rift developed, and the firm was split, allowing the Stanleys to repurchase their original patents in the spring of 1901. Well before that date, the Stanleys, realizing their mistake, were back in the steam automobile business and had founded a new firm, the Stanley Motor Carriage Company, with Francis as president.

Fate then intervened. In late February 1903 Freelan Stanley was informed by his doctor that he had tuberculosis and his life was in jeopardy. That spring, at the age of fifty-three, Stanley, like so many before him, came to Colorado and then to Estes Park in search of his health. Though Stanley managed to keep up appearances, he was clearly a very sick man. His weight had fallen to 118 pounds. Yet when Stanley came west, he did so in the style befitting one of America's emerging auto giants, bringing with him not only his wife, Flora, but his personal automobile. Having decided to summer in Estes Park, Stanley was determined to do so, quite literally, under his own steam. On June 29, 1903, after several months in Denver, he arranged for Flora and her Swedish maid to travel to Lyons on the Burlington Railroad and then to the park by conventional horse-drawn stage. The same day, so the story goes, after waiting in vain at the Brown Palace until 3 P.M. for a young man who had agreed to accompany him and do the heavy work of carrying water, the impatient Stanley decided to go on alone, only to miss the road and find himself at sundown north of Boulder. Finally arriving in Lyons, Stanley made his way up the canyon to William ("Billy") Welch's North Fork Hotel, a mountain ranch resort on the St. Vrain River. Welch, who had attended Oxford and had studied law, was evidently bemused by his guest, for automobiles were still regarded as a rich tourist's amusement. The next day he refused to "sacrifice" a man to accompany him, leaving Stanley to continue on his own.[66]

Welch had every reason to be skeptical. A resident of the canyon since 1893, and knowledgeable about the condition of its road, Welch was doubtless aware that the first automobile trip from Lyons to the park in May of that year had not been particularly impressive. The vehicle was a big, twelve-passenger, gas-propelled automobile with a thirty-horsepower engine. Despite the condition of the road, which saw the auto "going into mud up to the axle in numerous places," the journey was completed. The problem was that it took some four hours, "more time," the *Lyons Recorder* pointed out, "than the present four-horse stage makes it in."[67]

If Stanley knew about his predecessor, he was undeterred. He fired up his kerosene-powered boiler and calmly drove his much lighter and more compact machine up the road to Estes Park, arriving in front of Sam Service's store in an hour and fifty minutes. Tradition has it that Stanley immediately put in a call to Welch, who refused to believe that he had arrived until Sam Service got on the phone to confirm the facts of Stanley's story. That moment, on June 30, 1903, Stanley's friend Enos Mills would later declare, climaxed the "epoch-making event in the history of the Park."[68] In terms of Stanley's subsequent financial investment alone, Mills was doubtless correct.

That summer the Stanleys spent three months in a cottage near the Elkhorn Lodge. Given the air and daily regimen of the mountains, Stanley's health and weight improved dramatically, so much so that he was soon able to return to Newton and the life of a New England industrialist. But the experience took. In 1904, he completed building the $7,000 Georgian-style home to the north of the future village that would become his summer residence for the rest of his life. The adjacent garage contained a turntable, so that Stanley, who apparently was reluctant to steer in reverse (or had trouble doing so), never would have to shift his auto out of forward gear.

That same year Stanley began to focus his energy and money on the condition of the roads to the park and the transportation that passed over them. With the new road up the Big Thompson now in use, Stanley turned his attention to improving the North St. Vrain road coming up from Lyons. His overtures were eagerly received. The people of Lyons and Longmont had watched the building of the rival road, with its notable "lack of hard hills and steep grades," with great consternation, fearing that easy access to Loveland's new Colorado and Southern depot and growing number of commercial establishments would cut into their own business. As a result, when Stanley proposed to improve "their road" to the park, the Lyons and Longmont business communities came forward at once, and with the help of like-minded individuals in Estes Park and Denver, Stanley was easily able to raise the necessary funds. Abner Sprague did the survey work, while John B. Hall of Lyons and five crews of men built what in effect was a new road from the point where it entered the foothills to its connection with the existing road at Little Elk Park (Pinewood Springs), a quarter mile above the Meining ranch. The incentive for Stanley and his fellow underwriters was that once the work was completed the road would be taken over and maintained by the county.[69]

This new and "improved" road to Estes Park still left much to be desired, particularly if, as Stanley clearly intended, the automobile was to compete with and eventually replace the horse-drawn stage. In 1907, with the construction of his new hotel in the park about to begin, he intervened again, this time to bring the road up to the standards of the heavy-duty auto. The state of Colorado appropriated $3,250 for the project, and Stanley subscribed $5,000, with other private subscriptions bringing the total to be expended to over $15,000. The specifications called for a road "no less than fourteen feet wide," one that would "give ample room for the machines and vehicles to pass each other."[70] To achieve this goal, major portions of the existing road needed to be upgraded. But new sections were also necessary, including one through Welch's resort, above Lyons, that made it possible to redirect traffic along the creek and away from Rowell Hill, whose twenty-two-hundred-foot gain in a matter of two miles was a perennial source of complaint and the scene of more than one accident.[71] This bypass was so critical to the road's success that Stanley personally negotiated the easement with Welch. As part of the project Stanley announced that he would put through a new telephone line from Lyons to Estes Park that could be connected, as needed, to individual automobiles. "This feature," the *Lyons Recorder* assured its readers, "will be a very valuable arrangement in case of a breakdown of any machines on the roads, which will enable the drivers to inform headquarters of their difficulty at once. . . ."[72]

During the period that Stanley was helping to reconstruct the North St. Vrain road, the South St. Vrain road from Lyons was also being improved for tourist travel. Begun as a toll road in 1892 with the financial backing of Longmont businessmen as a means of gaining access to the lumber of the St. Vrain watershed and to serve the mines at Jamestown, it was rebuilt in 1895 as a road for both wagon and stage travel. By 1903 this road, together with the road up the North St. Vrain, furnished an increasingly popular "circle route"—"one of the grandest drives in the Rocky Mountains"—beginning and ending in Lyons. The first part of the journey took passengers up the South St. Vrain by way of the South Fork toll road, which remained in private hands until 1910, when the county acquired it for eight hundred dollars. This road wound its way past the Big and Little Narrows and a series of other named rock

Figure 9.10. The Stanley Hotel during construction. Courtesy City of Greeley Museums, permanent collection.

formations as far as Charles Raymond's popular cottage resort on the
Middle St. Vrain, at the foot of Stanley Hill. (Both the hill and the road
that climbed it were named for G. B. Stanley, a pioneer on the lower St.
Vrain who in 1902 had homesteaded a three-room log cabin in the
vicinity.) Stanley Hill Road, as this mile-long stretch was called, for
years marked the steepest part of the journey, often forcing passengers
to get out and either push or walk.[73]

Once the crest of Stanley Hill was reached, it was on to Allenspark,
a small mountain community, which by 1903, thanks to the opening of
the Clara Belle Mine, a low-grade producer of gold, silver, and copper,
was witnessing a mining boom. By then the town contained a saloon
(for the miners), a general store, and George Phfeifer and Dan Slaughter's
Crystal Springs Hotel. (Phfeifer reported in May of that year that lots in
Allenspark were actually selling for the astronomical price of one hundred dollars.[74]) From Allenspark the road, until 1910 scarcely little
more than a trail, swung north through Copeland Park to Cabin Creek
Park, where rancher Harry Cole ran a resort, and from there past Longs
Peak Inn and down to Estes Park. By late May of 1906 the South St.
Vrain road had been sufficiently improved to allow the first auto-
mobile, a twenty-two-hundred-pound machine carrying six people,

Figure 9.11. The Stanley Hotel complex. Courtesy National Park Service.

to reach Raymond's, though it would be several years more before the road past that point would accommodate heavy automobile use.[75] The year 1906 also saw the building of a new road from Estes Park to the Tahosa Valley along the eastern side of Lily Mountain. Ten feet in width, with a grade no steeper than 7 percent,[76] it replaced the original Lambs road of 1875–1876, long considered "a terror to nervous drivers."[77] Looking back on that year in his memoirs, William Cooper recalled that the "automobiles that braved the mountain roads in those days, were thoroughly disliked by all horseback riders. Fortunately one could hear the approach of a car while it was still at a safe distance. One then made haste to leave the road, put a distance of a hundred feet or so between it and you, place your horse with its tail to the road, and wait until the sound of the iron monster had faded into the distance."[78]

Auto stages were first introduced on the road up the Big Thompson Canyon beginning in 1907, when the Loveland–Estes Park Automobile Company, managed by David O. Osborn, placed in service three five-passenger Stanley model F automobiles. The fare for the five-and-a-half-hour round trip was six dollars, and that summer an estimated three thousand people were transported by the new company to and from the park. Stanley was not directly involved in this venture, but the next year he took full advantage of the newly rebuilt North St. Vrain road by helping to establish the Estes Park Transportation Company. This stage line also made use of five-passenger Stanley red-and-yellow automobiles, able to complete the trip from Lyons to Estes Park in about an hour and a half. Powered by a thirty-horsepower steam engine, each machine carried a thirty-gallon water tank, capable of carrying the car about ten miles over good road and less over bad stretches. On the drive from Lyons to Estes Park that meant several stops to refill the water tank along the way. To further improve service at the Lyons end, the Burlington Railroad, at Stanley's request, agreed to have its trains reach Lyons by 10:30 A.M., an hour earlier than usual—Stanley guaranteeing to have passengers in the park "ready for a big dinner." Stanley made little attempt to conceal his self-interest. But when he made an offer to improve the road up the Big Thompson Canyon in 1907–1908 in exchange for an exclusive franchise to carry auto passengers, he was rebuffed. Stanley made yet another investment in roads in 1912, when he helped finance the old Bunce School road from Peaceful Valley to Allenspark to facilitate the transportation of tourists from the railroad depot at Ward to Estes Park.

The advent of the automobile in Estes Park was not without its perils. A single issue of the *Longmont Ledger* of August 14, 1908, for example, reported three separate accidents. In the first, an auto from Stead's resort, having run over "an old lady one mile west of Estes Park" and "knocked her clear out of the road," "did not even stop to see if she was hurt." The second involved two west-bound cars from Osborne's new Loveland–Estes Park Auto Company that collided with one another six miles east of the park. The first vehicle had blown a cylinder and stopped quickly, only to have the second, which had been following closely, run into it at full speed. "If the forward car had not lodged against some big logs," the *Ledger's* correspondent noted, "it would have turned turtle into the Big Thompson, and probably some one might have been hurt or drowned, as it was loaded with women and babies." The third reported accident did result in a fatality. A Mrs. Stover of Greeley was run over and killed at a bridge in the park. Out driving with her husband and baby, she was thrown from her two-seat buggy when an auto came up from behind and frightened the horse.[79]

While investing in roads and transportation, Stanley was busy in Estes Park with the building of the promised hotel and a small hydroelectric plant on Fall River to provide its electricity. Hotel construction began on October 10, 1907, and took two years to complete. For the hotel's site Stanley chose 143 acres of the old Dunraven estate transferred from the Estes Park Development Company, located on a gently sloping hillside above the village. The site was perfect, backing onto Lumpy Ridge and its famous Twin Owls and fronting to the south and west on Longs Peak and the Front Range. Stanley spared no expense to make his hotel, which cost some half million dollars, a replica of the classic resorts of his native New England.

The Stanley Hotel was simply stunning in its immensity.[80] Four stories and 88 feet in height (including a basement) and measuring 217 by 107 feet, the clapboard structure consisted of a high central gallery flanked to the east and west by wings, containing a total of 105 rooms. Most of the exterior lumber was cut locally, at Hidden Valley and at Bierstadt Lake. The sawmill at Bierstadt was operated by the Reverend Albin Griffith and his two sons, Dan and John, who had reached an agreement with the Forest Service to harvest trees killed by the Bear Lake fire of 1900. From both places the lumber was taken by wagon to the James' planing mill west of the village for finishing, before being transported to the hotel site.

Initially the hotel was to be called "the Dunraven" or "the new Dunraven." But when Estes Park residents objected and handed him a deerskin petition, Stanley agreed to allow the hotel to bear his own name.[81] The Stanley contained everything one could ask for in the way of elegance and amenities. Its 102-by-56-foot lobby, with formal grand staircase, was furnished with green leather chairs and settees and crimson-and-white carpets to match the walls. To one side was the formal 80-by-40-foot dining room capable of seating 250, to the other a drawing room and music room done up in Louis XVI decor of bright frost and gold. (The latter served in the mornings as a writing parlor.) The billiard room, smoking room, and bar were, by contrast, heavily masculine, featuring mahogany-paneled walls and beamed ceilings. The second and third floors contained eighty-eight guest rooms, each with its own bath and telephone, and each individually color-coordinated to match the hotel's yellow-and-red Georgian exterior. Along the front ran an open porch where guests could eat, chat, or simply look out at the mountains. Safely tucked away behind the scenes was Stanley's pride, a 52-by-24-foot all-electric kitchen, one of the first in the country.

In addition to the hotel the Stanley complex contained the Manor House (a smaller, thirty-three-room, fully winterized replica of the main building intended to handle extra guests), stables, a 96-by-44-foot Casino (capable of seating 600), a bowling alley, tennis courts, a croquet field, a golf course, and, later, even an airfield—everything, in short, that the well-to-do patron could desire or afford. With its opening on June 22, 1909, in time to host a convention of state pharmacists, luxurious and thoroughly modern accommodations for the gentry (those who could afford five dollars a day) had come to Estes Park.

~

Spurred on by the Bond and Sanborn-Stanley land acquisitions and the opening and improvement of roads to the park, there were other significant changes as well. A new schoolhouse was constructed in 1906, and a year later, as a special project of the Estes Park Protective and Improvement Association, a fish hatchery was opened on Fall River beyond the James property. In 1908, a year that saw the winter population reach five hundred,[82] the town's infrastructure was substantially increased with the organization and opening of the Estes Park Bank, the Estes Park Water Company, the Estes Park Electric Light and Power Company, and the development of a local telephone exchange (with a list of twenty-five subscribers).[83]

The need for the water company indicated just how quickly the village of Estes Park had grown. When the original pipe was laid down from the Black Canyon in 1906, "it was supposed that this would supply the demand for at least five or ten years." By 1908, just two years later, that source was clearly inadequate. At its July meeting the officers of the Estes Park Town Company decided to push ahead with the construction of two new reservoirs—one thirty by thirty feet above the Elkhorn, the other twenty by twenty feet north of the new Stanley Hotel—linked by a four-inch pipe. When completed, these reservoirs were to have a capacity of one hundred thousand gallons and make possible the distribution of six to seven thousand feet of new main throughout the town.[84]

Securing an enlarged water supply helped, but the town fathers soon had their hands full with respect to the sewerage being discharged into the Big Thompson and carried down to Loveland. Loveland sued, and the case went to the Colorado Supreme Court, only to have the matter resolved by compromise in January of 1911 when the City of Loveland agreed to give the town of Estes Park five hundred dollars toward the construction of a three-thousand-dollar sewer system.[85]

The year 1908 also saw the organization of the village's first church; the publication during the summer months of the park's first, if short-lived, newspaper, J. Gordon Smith's *The Mountaineer*; the opening of John Manford's thirty-room hotel diagonally across from the Hupp Hotel, "with four nice bath rooms and a spacious lounging room in front"; Fred Adams's bakery; Harry Boyd's new meat market; the Smith brothers' barber shop; George Johnson's new livery barn (the town's third); and a combination pool hall–confectionery shop that Raymond Wiles opened in Boyd's old building. Of particular importance to the local resort industry was the opening of Julian Johnson's new steam laundry, which freed managers "from the onerous task of washing bed clothes, towels and table linens themselves or hiring help for that purpose."[86] Not to be outdone, the Estes Park Hotel completed a thirty-five-by-fifty-foot addition, bringing its number of guest rooms to seventy-five, and Sam Service completed an addition to his new store. That same summer Enos Mills completed Timberline Cabin on the Longs Peak trail. Located below Jim's Grove and connected by telephone with Longs Peak Inn in the valley below, it provided food and overnight lodging for those heading up the peak. The only disquieting note in this period of "growth and progress" was the decision of the government, over the protest of Bond and other leading Estes Park citizens, to relocate the Forest Reserve office to Fort Collins. Amidst all this civic and commercial activity, and serving no doubt as a catalyst, there was increasing talk about the possibilities of a new national park.

~

Behind the "park idea" was the hard work and single-mindedness of another unusual man: Enos Abijah Mills (1870–1922), naturalist,

Figure 9.12. Enos Mills and his famous collie, Scotch, on the porch of Longs Peak Inn, c. 1910. Courtesy Colorado Historical Society.

writer-lecturer, and owner of the much-celebrated Longs Peak Inn. What made Mills even more remarkable was the fact that his beginnings had been distinctly unpromising. Born and raised on a farm in Linn County, Kansas, Mills's childhood was marred by a weak constitution (the result of digestive problems—he was said to be allergic to starch) that left him unsuited to the rigors of farm life. In 1884, apparently at the suggestion of the family doctor, Mills left Kansas for the mountains of Colorado, making his way alone to Estes Park and the Tahosa Valley ranch run by his father's cousin, the Reverend Elkanah J. Lamb.

Though Mills later tended to exaggerate the extent of his isolation and independence during his early years in Colorado, the fact of the matter is that, aside from whatever oversight the Lambs provided, from the age of fourteen on Enos Mills was left pretty much on his own. Whatever he could achieve in the way of health, education, and career would be largely up to him. That, in time, he achieved all three—and became in the process one of the better-known men of his generation—speaks directly to the energetic determination, the active and acquisitive intelligence, the uncompromising individualism, and the rigid Protestant discipline and work ethic that formed the bedrock of Enos Mills's character.

Having landed in Colorado, Enos Mills made the most of his new opportunities. That first summer he did odd jobs at the Elkhorn Lodge (where a surviving photograph has him posing), and though his whereabouts during the intervening winter are not entirely clear, by the following spring he was back in Estes Park, working for Elkanah Lamb at Longs Peak House. He also made his first ascent of Longs Peak under the watchful eye of Carlyle Lamb. The following fall he began work on a twelve-by-fourteen-foot homestead cabin roofed with corrugated iron on the lower slopes of Twin Sisters Mountain.

To a teenage boy, particularly one with an active imagination and an inclination toward what he would later call "the poetry of nature," the world of the Lambs was all that anyone could wish. Flanked by Longs Peak and its lofty neighbors Mount Meeker and Mount Lady Washington to the west and Twin Sisters Mountain to the east, this high, flower-filled upland valley, teeming with wildlife, was then a largely unspoiled and unexplored wilderness of closely gathered lodgepole pine forests intermixed with stands of aspen and willow. Here were lodges of active beaver, as well as mule deer, chipmunks, rabbits, martens, and chattering pine squirrels, together with every variety of mountain bird. There was also an occasional mountain lion, bighorn sheep, bear, and fox. Enough nature surely to pique the interest and occupy the time of any would-be outdoorsman and naturalist.

Summer employment in Estes Park was easy enough to come by, but a steady winter job with decent pay and the possibility of advancement posed a definite problem. Many, if not most, summer residents of Estes Park, the Lambs included, moved back to towns in the valley once the tourists departed in the fall. By 1887, having spent three winters doing odd jobs at ranches on the plains, Mills had decided that he, too, must move on. That fall, he traveled north to Butte, Montana, to become a tool boy at the Anaconda Copper Company. Mills proved to be a quick study. He was soon promoted to miner and then, in turn, to machine driller, compressor operator, night foreman, and plant engineer. In 1890 he would be offered a secretarial position in the front office. Butte also provided the other thing that young Mills needed most: the opportunity for a good education, or, to put it more accurately in Mills's case, the opportunity for self-education. Mills could learn a great deal in the masculine, wide-open mining community of Butte, but as preparation for the rest of the world, he needed books. Butte contained an excellent, free public library, and Mills became a frequent borrower and an eclectic reader.

Winters in Butte were more than compensated for by summers of freedom, first to explore the mountainous areas of Estes Park, then to range more widely. One journey—a trip to California in the fall of 1889—brought him into contact on a wind-swept beach with the naturalist John Muir, whose impact on Mills's subsequent career was profound. It was Muir who not only awakened Mills to his deficiencies as a writer, but, by giving him "a glimpse of a larger field of usefulness,"[87] served as the catalyst for transforming Mills's real, yet largely undirected, appreciation and understanding of nature into a commitment to follow Muir's emerging program of wilderness preservation. "You have helped me more than all the others," he would write Muir in 1913; "but for you I might never have done anything for scenery."[88]

The winter of 1901–1902 was Mills's last as a miner. The previous summer, on July 22, 1901, he had purchased Longs Peak House from Carlyle Lamb and embarked on a new career as mountain innkeeper. Under Mills's very personal supervision and exacting standards, Longs Peak Inn became one of the best-known mountain hotels in the nation. Undaunted by a fire that destroyed the sixteen-room main lodge and its recently enlarged dining room on June 4, 1906, Mills quickly began rebuilding to his own specifications and sensibilities. Employing, wherever possible, wind-killed or fire-killed trees, gnarled roots, and tree stumps, Mills gave the "new" Longs Peak Inn with its sixty-two-foot porch an unusual and distinctive appearance. Visitors quickly caught the spirit of the place:

> The reception room strikes one as being unusually unique and attractive with its trimmings of weathered pines, beaver cut logs, and old-fashioned fireplace with its iron tea kettles. The tables, the bases of which are the roots of old trees, and a screen in front of the dining-room door, a cross section of an immense root, being about 16-feet square, and forming a most beautiful lattice work, is very odd in appearance. The only finished wood one senses is the door and window casings.[89]

The dominant mood at the inn was one of rustic austerity, projecting at every turn the personality and convictions of its owner-proprietor. The rules of this "non-tip house" were fastidious. Activities like drinking, dancing, music, card playing, and flower gathering, though part of the daily routine at other resorts, were either frowned upon or prohibited at Longs Peak Inn. "What Do You Want With an Armful of Wild Flowers?" read one sign. Mills wanted his patrons, whom he greeted each morning with a cheery "Glad you're living?" to be outdoors, enjoying the natural world that lay all about them. Tradition has it that those who were unwilling to cooperate with Mills's program, whether guests or staff, were simply asked to leave. The unappreciative were summarily dismissed with a dose of Mills's dry humor. "I hear there is some fine scenery up here," one newly arrived tourist reportedly said. "Where do I go to see it?" To which Mills responded, "You must have been misinformed."[90] Despite the inn's popularity, Mills's impulse was to keep the place relatively small and its prices reasonable. Though the new Longs Peak Inn was larger than the old, and Mills doubled its capacity in 1916 in response to the increased number of visitors lured by the new national park, the inn's beginning weekly rate was among the lowest and its guest capacity among the smallest of any of the major resort hotels in Estes Park.

Mills would probably have remained little more than a local celebrity, had it not been for two events that, together with his writings, provided him with the audience, reputation, and influence he needed to achieve larger goals. In 1902, he was appointed Colorado's official state snow observer. For the next three winters Enos Mills traversed the high country, recording the depth of the snowpack at the head of streams and other data of concern to ranchers and farmers. It was a romantic, if lonely, calling, but one that caught the public imagination. "The Snow Man," they called him, and Mills emerged from the experience with the disarming and engaging sort of public persona of which reputations are made. "Enos Mills Faces Death in Mountains. State Snow Inspector Caught in Severe Blizzard Recently," read the front-page headline of the *Loveland Register* in October 1904. The blizzard that caught Mills in the Uncompahgre Mountains west of Lake City was real enough, and Mills subsequently explained that "only his exact knowledge of the mountains and his ability to stand hunger, cold and fatigue . . . pulled him through the trying trip."[91]

Enos Mills's second reputation-enhancing assignment of the decade began in January 1907, when he went to work as a lecturer for Gifford Pinchot's new Forest Service at an annual salary of twenty-four hundred dollars plus expenses. Only two years old, and struggling to consolidate and expand its role, the Forest Service had embarked on a nationwide campaign to publicize the need for "wise use" conservation. Though Mills would later repudiate the Forest Service and its motives, in 1907 he was clearly comfortable enough with Pinchot's program to become the perfect advocate. From Mills's perspective, the appointment elevated his platform from a regional to a national one and allowed him to fine-tune a growing preoccupation with conservation and the recreational and aesthetic uses of nature. For the next two years the peripatetic Mills took his message to the nation. Between October 1908 and May 1909 alone, Mills made some 140 appearances in thirty-six states, speaking to educational and civic groups on "the practicality and poetry of forestry," offering up a most palatable mixture of personal experience, forest history and science, and the physical and moral value of getting outdoors to enjoy "the spell" of nature. Clad in a brown sack suit, the athletically built Mills seemed unpretentious to the core: a happy, enthusiastic, down-to-earth man of the West. Mills projected the same image in his writings. From 1902 on Mills began to make a name for himself as a popular writer on nature and conservation topics, placing his essays in such big-circulation magazines as the *Saturday Evening Post*, *Atlantic*, *Colliers*, *Country Gentlemen*, *American Boy*, and *Youth's Companion*. Beginning in 1909 Mills began to gather his essays together for republication in such miscellanies as *Wild Life on the Rockies* (1909), *The Spell of the Rockies* (1911), *In Beaver World* (1913), and *Rocky Mountain Wonderland* (1915).

Enos Mills left the Forest Service in May of 1909, without fanfare and without much in the way of explanation. The truth of the matter was that he had decided to move on to a new and larger interest: the possibility of a new national park in the Estes Park area. The germ of the idea came from a suggestion made at the October 1907 meeting of the Estes Park Protection and Improvement Association by Herbert N. Wheeler, head of the Medicine Bow National Forest. "If you want to draw tourists," Wheeler told his audience, "you should establish a game refuge where tourists can see the wild life."[92] By way of illustration, he then produced a map covering four townships. It showed an area of over one thousand square miles extending from the Poudre River along the foothills through Estes Park and west toward North Park.

The preserve idea drew a positive response. Many of Estes Park's more farsighted residents had grown increasingly concerned about the scarcity of big game and the treatment of fish, wildlife, and the wilderness in general. The Estes Park Protection and Improvement Association had been founded in 1895, partly "to prevent the destruction of the fish in the rivers of the Park, the illegal killing of game, and the destruction of the timber by camp fires."[93] Its concern was justified. Dunraven, his friends, and those who followed him (including many of the park's first settlers) had heavily hunted the area, for reasons having to do with subsistence and income as well as leisure and sport. By 1880 indigenous elk had been reduced to the point of extinction and would need to be reintroduced in the new century into an area where they had once roamed freely.[94] As Abner Sprague put it with his usual succinctness, and with a tinge of bitterness:

> Our elks only lasted about three years. They came down from their high range just before Christmas, in 1875, by the thousands and were met by hunters with repeating rifles and four horse teams; hauled to Denver and sold for three or four cents per pound. In 1876, fewer came down; in 1877 very few were seen on this side of the Divide. In 1878 I killed my last elk, and to get him had to go over Flat Top. [95]

Such systematic and indiscriminate destruction of wildlife, it should be noted, was found throughout the West. During the winter of 1874–1875, between 1,500 and 2,000 elk were slaughtered within a fifteen-mile radius of Yellowstone's Mammoth Hot Springs solely for their skins—which fetched between $2.50 and $3.00 on the open market.[96]

Other large animals, particularly bears and mountain lions, though not infrequently killed or captured,[97] were also becoming scarce, and this in a county praised in 1874 as raising "the best crop of mountain lions of any county in the Territory."[98] Both animals, of course, had their trophy value. In October of 1883, for example, a mountain lion shot by a resident of the Larimer County town of Virginia Dale was sold to a collector for $60.00, who promptly brought the carcass to Fort Collins and put it on display at Evans and Thomas's butcher shop.[99] The posting of state and countywide bounties on bears, mountain lions, wolves, and coyotes further served as encouragement for hunting. During the two years ending in November 1892, the state of Colorado paid out $66,869.88 in bounties on these animals and reported the killing of 2,263 bears, 926 mountain lions, and 20,606 wolves and coyotes. The state bounty on bears and mountain lions was $10.00, on wolves and coyotes $1.00.[100] Wolves in Estes Park, on the other hand, were rare. In fact, Abner Sprague told Fred M. Packard in 1939 that he had seen two wolves on the east side of the park in 1875, but none since.[101] Game laws were one solution. In 1897 the Longmont Ledger noted that "there are notices up in various places in Estes Park forbidding fishing or hunt-

Figure 9.13. Front page of the *Denver Post*, January 20, 1915.
Courtesy National Park Service—Rocky Mountain National
Park.

ing without permission," adding, perhaps by way of wishful thinking,
that "the penalty is large enough to cause anyone to hesitate."[102]

The size of the local trout population also demanded attention.
Stories of large catches in the streams and lakes of Estes Park were le-
gion and well publicized. For years the park's resorts had encouraged
their guests by handing out prizes for those who caught the most fish
in a single day, regardless of size. The press did not hesitate to celebrate
manic feats like the one accomplished by William Hallett's friend, the
Reverend George Spinner of Cleveland, who in a single day in August
1882 caught 197 trout, easily surpassing William James's total of 150
the previous week.[103] Trout were not particularly cheap—in 1876 trout

from the park were selling in Boulder for twenty-five cents a pound. But trout, unlike mammals, could be reseeded by human hands, a fact that led to the establishment through local subscription of a good-sized fish hatchery, which opened in July 1907. During its first five years of operation the hatchery, under its superintendent Gaylord H. Thompson, placed some six million trout in the park's major streams and tributaries.[104]

Fishing, as well as hunting, had been a favorite pastime for such early residents as William and Howard James, Abner Sprague, and Horace Ferguson, who presumably made good use of the large hauls they reported in the dining rooms of their resorts. It was thus fitting that these same resort owners, or their heirs, should take a leadership role in the Estes Park Protection and Improvement Association, an organization that, as its first order of business, pledged an end to such profligacy. When the association elected its initial set of officers in 1895, Abner Sprague was chosen president, Ella (Mrs. William) James, treasurer, and James Ferguson, Horace's son, who was then operating the Highlands, secretary.

Though Mills did not attend the 1907 meeting, Wheeler's pro-

Figure 9.14. *Left to right:* Enos Mills, F. O. Stanley, Colorado Senator Edward Taylor, and Mary K. Sherman, "The National Park Lady," at the park dedication. Courtesy Colorado Historical Society.

posal struck a resonant chord, and he subsequently wrote him to inquire about where the boundaries for such a preserve might be located. There the issue rested until the June 1909 meeting of the association, when a committee of two, consisting of Enos Mills and Freelan O. Stanley, was appointed to study the matter further.[105] From that point onward Mills more or less took things into his own hands. Within days of the association's September meeting, at which the membership voted unanimously to seek the creation of the Estes National Park and Game Preserve along the lines of Wheeler's original suggestion,[106] Mills issued for publication his own proposal calling for a national park. Engaged and then consumed by the idea, Mills then went to work enlisting support for his project, using both the lecture platform and his own expanding reputation as a writer. These efforts were aided considerably in January 1913 by the release of the enthusiastic report and endorsement of Robert Marshall of the United States Geological Survey.

Mills's major problems were tactical and political.[107] It required, above all, the establishment of an effective coalition of regional and national groups that would lobby for a park bill and monitor its progress through Congress. Mills received a great deal of help: from J. Horace McFarland and his powerful American Civic Association, from James Grafton Rogers and the Colorado Mountain Club, and from a variety of other groups including the National Federation of Women's Clubs, the Daughters of the American Revolution, the Colorado legislature, the state Democratic and Republican organizations, the Denver Chamber of Commerce, and local business and civic organizations in Boulder, Larimer, and Grand Counties. With some exceptions Colorado's press was supportive. Mills's old friend, the ever-dependable John Muir, came aboard early. "I'm heartily with you in your plan for a National Park in Colorado," he wrote Mills on February 21, 1910. "Will call attention of the Sierra Club to the proposed new park."[108]

There was, as might be expected, opposition, chiefly from mining, grazing, timber, and water interests, who argued against restricting still further the amount of public land available for commercial use. The only major local objection of a vocal sort came, interestingly enough, from a group of Mills's Tahosa Valley neighbors, the so-called Front Range Settlers League,[109] who thought they saw in Mills's advocacy a threat to their own property. Mills also discovered early on that the position of the Forest Service, whose policy of "preservation through use" included grazing and lumbering on public land, was far from clear. At the very least the Forest Service was guilty of foot dragging, if not, as Mills suspected and later openly charged, being an active, if covert, opponent out to sabotage, delay, and, if possible, kill the Estes Park project. "Scratch any old Forest Service man," he wrote to his friend and ally McFarland in March 1911, "and you will find a Tartar who is opposed to all National Parks."[110]

Enos Mills's personal involvement proved critical and decisive. During the six years of the park campaign, which Mills called "the most strenuous and growth-compelling occupation I ever followed,"[111] he made more than three hundred appearances. It was fatiguing work. "This campaigning annihilates me," he wrote McFarland on April 24, 1912, "and on arrival home I felt so aged."[112] In the end it was the tediously slow, but inexorable, political process that carried the day. Between February 6, 1913, when Congressman Atterson Walden Rucker of Aspen introduced the first bill, and the date of final passage on January 18, 1915, it took three separate park bills and five major revisions to get the measure through Congress and onto the desk of President Woodrow Wilson. By that time the 700-square-mile park that Marshall had recommended was reduced to 358.5 miles, far short of Enos Mills's original proposal, which had called for 1,000.

The official dedication of Rocky Mountain National Park on the

Figure 9.15. William Ashton's Horseshoe Inn. Courtesy National Park Service—
Rocky Mountain National Park.

afternoon of September 4, 1915, was a festive holiday throughout the Estes Park region. It also marked the high point of Enos Mills's public career. Never again would this naturalist-innkeeper turned lobbyist enjoy so much goodwill, influence, and wide acclaim as a major figure in America's preservation movement.

All that morning streams of cars, carriages, wagons, and horses made their way through Estes Park village and out along Fall River Road to the western end of Horseshoe Park. There (near what is now the Lawn Lake trailhead) they were greeted by a banner, strung between two pines and flanked by Colorado flags, announcing the spot where the formal ceremonies were to take place. The crowd of visitors—estimated at between two and three thousand—came from Denver, Loveland, Boulder, Fort Collins, and other towns along the Front Range as well as from Estes Park and its surrounding hotels and cottages, drawn by what was clearly a historic moment. A band from Fort Collins entertained early arrivers, while the Estes Park Woman's Club distributed coffee that was much appreciated, for the day was cool and the skies glowering. At 2 P.M. the formal ceremonies began with a chorus of "America the Beautiful" from an assembled group of schoolchildren.

Then Enos Mills, chair of the "celebration committee" and the day's master of ceremonies, approached the impromptu rostrum. Close by his side, clutching a small American flag, stood his friend and supporter F. O. Stanley. They made a somewhat incongruous-looking pair, these two, the sixty-six-year-old bewhiskered Stanley and the wiry, ruddy-faced Enos Mills. Appearance and age notwithstanding, they had much in common. Not only had each accomplished a great deal for Estes Park and the region they had come to love, but each was a quintessential American—inventive, industrious, and determined, used to having his own way and willing to stake out strong positions and champion causes that many found reason to oppose.

Mills proceeded to read congratulatory messages from President Woodrow Wilson and Secretary of the Interior Franklin Lane and to introduce the attending dignitaries. In addition to Stanley, later known affectionately as "the grand old man of Estes Park," they included Stephen Mather, assistant secretary of the interior, who a year later would become the first director of the new Park Service; Colorado's governor, George A. Carlson; Representative Edward T. Taylor, who had shepherded the park bill through Congress; and Mary Belle King Sherman, chairwoman of the Conservation Department of the General Federation of Women's Clubs, whose advocacy of preservation would earn her the title of "the National Park Lady."

But the day and the hour belonged to Enos Mills. For as Frank Lundy Webster of the *Denver Post*, himself a summer resident of the park, reminded his readers, "This was Enos Mills day in Estes Park."[113] Cheered by the crowd as the "Father of Rocky Mountain National Park,"[114] Mills responded in kind. "This is," he told his audience, "the proudest moment of my life. I have lived to see the realization of a great dream come true. It means great things for Colorado and for the nation."[115] As he spoke, thunder and a light rain began to descend upon Horseshoe Park. This day, however, nature would not be denied a celebration of her own. By the time that Governor Carlson had finished speaking, "the clouds parted . . . and the sun of Colorado broke forth in rain-tinged splendor from across the newly laid snow on Longs Peak and made a new fairyland of the dazzling land of bewilderment."[116]

～

Talk of the new park, and increasing signs that Mills and his colleagues were likely to succeed, led to yet another expansion of Estes Park's guest facilities and summer residences. Though none of the new hotels could rival the Stanley in size or appointments, the decade between 1905 and 1915 saw the construction of a number of new resorts. Although Enos Mills's reconstructed Longs Peak Inn was probably the most unique, he was by no means alone in attempting to erect a rustic structure that seemed to complement and reflect its natural setting. Among the most

Figure 9.16. Stanley Steamers on Elkhorn Avenue, c. 1915. The Hupp Hotel (far right) had been sold to C. H. Bond in 1913, who renamed it the Park Hotel. Directly across the street, on the corner of Elkhorn and Moraine, is E. M. A. Foot's "Utility and Curio Shop." Courtesy Lula W. Dorsey Museum, YMCA of the Rockies.

successful was Willard H. Ashton's Horseshoe Park Inn, built in 1908 on land at the mouth of Endovalley that he had acquired a year earlier. The inn, which featured a huge granite fireplace on the front veranda, where a cheery fire burned each evening, could accommodate fifty guests in its main building, four cabins, and dozen tent cottages. Ashton also operated a small summer campground and lodge on the eastern shore of Lawn Lake, by now dammed as an irrigation reservoir, a hike of more than six miles from the inn. It could take care of up to fifteen guests and was a favorite place for fishermen. That same year Fred Sprague built a similarly rustic resort on the upper North Fork above Dunraven Glade, consisting of eleven cabins, a large dining hall, barn, dairy house, and icehouse—a site long since known as the Deserted Village.

Four new tourist accommodations were opened in 1910 and 1911. The first, built in Moraine Park, where the Spragues and later James Stead long enjoyed a monopoly over the tourist business, was Moraine Lodge, owned and operated by the colorful Mary Imogene "Mother" McPherson, who in 1903 had purchased a homestead relinquishment of 160 acres above Sprague's. There, two years later, she built a summer cottage that became the nucleus of a resort. Opened to the public in 1910, and then added to over the years, Moraine Lodge eventually consisted of forty buildings—of which the single survivor is the recreation and assembly hall completed in 1928, which since the summer of 1935 has housed the Park Service's Moraine Park Museum. July of the next year saw the opening of another new resort in Moraine Park, the Brinwood. Located to the west of Stead's Ranch and Moraine Lodge, the Brinwood Hotel was erected by Charles Reed Sr. and his brother-in-law James Ferguson on two quarter sections of land purchased in 1908 for seven thousand dollars. The owners came to the new enterprise with experience. James Ferguson and Sallie Reed were the children of Horace Ferguson, the founder of the old Highlands Hotel, which both had taken turns running in the 1890s and into the first years of the new century. As finally completed, the Brinwood, which would remain in the Reed family for forty-seven years, consisted of twenty-nine log-and-frame buildings on 290 acres of land, capable of entertaining ninety guests.

These years also saw Abner Sprague's reentry into the tourist business in Glacier Basin, where for some years he had held property. Though by no means of the scale of his former resort in Moraine Park, Sprague's Lodge on Glacier Creek (then known as the South Fork) was both isolated and intimate and located in an area that in 1910 was fresh and inviting. Much the same thing was true of Fern Lake Lodge, a smaller and even more remote group of cottages in Odessa Gorge, built by Dr. William Workman, which could be reached by foot or horseback over a four-mile trail. The lodge, which was nestled in the woods close to the lake's outlet, consisted of a central building (containing living room, dining room, and kitchen) as well as a series of log cabins. It was built entirely of logs, with wooden pins replacing nails. Rather than planking the floor of the lodge in the traditional way, Workman laid down a series of smooth and compact cross sections of logs, connected by compacted dirt. An additional feature of the place was a large Lazy Susan built into the dining room table, making every meal a family-style affair.

With these new resorts came an interval of trail building, both by Estes Park civic groups and by a Forest Service anxious to prove itself friendly to the recreational uses of nature. The civic projects included the construction of a trail up Prospect Mountain, extending to Marys Lake beyond, built by the Estes Park Improvement and Protective Association in 1907, and new trails to Loch Vale (which lacked a "well defined trail which could be followed with assurance by the average tourist") and up and over Deer Mountain in 1913. The former was financed by the Business Men's Association, the latter by the Estes Park Woman's Club.

The Forest Service, on its part, gave the new resorts in the Moraine Park–Odessa Gorge–Flattop Mountain area special attention. In September of 1914, having that summer already completed trails up the Twin Sisters, from Glacier Creek to Bierstadt Lake and Storm Pass and across the northeastern saddle between Estes Cone and the peak, the Forest Service began work on a new trail from Fern Lake to Flattop where it could connect with the old Estes Park–Grand Lake trail. Stead's, the Brinwood, the Moraine Park Livery, and Workman's Fern Lodge chipped in an additional fifty dollars' worth of work to improve the trail between Moraine Park and Fern Lake, which included both repairing and rebuilding the old trail, particularly the section between Fern and Marguerite Falls, with the intention of limiting the two-mile section of the trail from the Pool to Fern Lake to a 10 percent grade.[117] Ever suspicious of the Forest Service's motives, Enos Mills was not impressed. He warned the *Estes Park Trail* that this "deep interest in the roads and trails in the Estes Park region" is little more than an attempt to discourage support of the park bill. "Let no one," he added, "be deceived by the hypocrisy of this political machine—the Forest Service."[118]

The 1914 season, which opened against the gathering clouds of war in Europe, saw a final flurry of resort and hotel building, with the opening, on July 4, of both Joe Mills's Crags Hotel on a twenty-one-acre tract on the shoulder of Prospect Mountain, overlooking the village; and the Hewes-Kirkwood Hotel, Ranch & Store in the Tahosa Valley behind Enos Mills's Longs Peak Inn. The two resorts were very different. The Crags was a traditional twenty-room frame hotel with a big and comfortably furnished lobby and reading room. Hewes-Kirkwood, by contrast, was as rustic as its location. It consisted of a group of six single and three double cabins and a series of tent platforms and other outbuildings surrounding Mary Kirkwood's original homestead cabin built in 1907, "Bleak House," which her two sons, Charlie and Steve Hewes, had enlarged to provide an office, living room, dining room, and kitchen. That same summer Burns Will completed his eleven-bedroom, five-cottage Copeland Lake Lodge at the mouth of Wild Basin, and Enos Mills purchased the old Richard Tallant property on the rim of Devils Gulch, added a dining room, bathroom, and kitchen and a number of cottages, and opened it to the public as the "Horizon." Demand was such that summer that A. D. "Gus" Lewis, cashier of the Estes Park Bank, and his wife opened their attractive home, located on a bluff overlooking the village, to tourists. Enlarged over the years, the Lewis bungalow eventually became the three-story stone-and-wood Lewiston Hotel, with a capacity for 150 guests.

The arrival of Rocky Mountain National Park was, of course, a watershed development and encouraged the building of still more tourist facilities and summer residences. In 1916, the year after its dedication, some 51,000 visitors entered the park. By 1917, that number had more than doubled, and by 1919 the total reached 170,000. A year later, with the completion of Fall River Road, making it possible for automobilists to drive to Grand Lake and complete a circle trip from and to Denver,[119] the number of visitors jumped to 240,996. So great was the increase that as early as 1917 Lewis Claude Way, the park's second superintendent, could boast to his superiors in Washington that Rocky Mountain National Park had attracted more visitors that year "than the combined tourist patronage of Yellowstone, Yosemite, Glacier, and Crater Lake Parks." How best to deal with that fact would try the patience and ingenuity of Way and his successors as well as of the citizens of Estes Park for many years to come.

Afterword

~

If the preceding history of Estes Park has a theme, that theme has to do with change—or, perhaps more correctly, with change *and* continuity. In little more than half a century Estes Park evolved from a hunting ground and ranch land for the few into a summer resort and vacation spot for the nation. But, as its residents and returning visitors were quick to point out, the transformation was leisurely and slow and took place within the context of a mountain world whose features seemed as fresh and unspoiled as that day in October 1859 when Joel Estes first gazed upon them.

For much of this we have the Earl of Dunraven to thank. As Abner Sprague pointed out more than seventy years ago, "We all began to see that the holding of so much of the Park by one company, even if it had been secured unlawfully, was the best thing for the place. . . ." Dunraven's dream, it has often been said, was of a vast reserve teeming with wildlife that he and his friends could enjoy. Rocky Mountain National Park, in one sense, is Dunraven's dream turned upside down. Instead of a monument to aristocracy, privilege, and exclusivity, the park is a treasure held in trust by the government for all the people. Fortunately, the Earl's failure was almost immediately followed by Enos Mills's success. At the very time that Dunraven relinquished his holdings, thereby making possible the rapid expansion of Estes Park as a resort community, Mills, and those who shared his dream, were making sure that to the north, west, and south 358.5 square miles of wilderness would be set aside forever and spared the kind of indignities that have overtaken so much of nature in America.

Since the dedication of Rocky Mountain Park almost a century has passed, and both park and town have witnessed many memorable events, some of them tragic. One thinks of the death of Agnes Vaille, who died on the Boulder Field in January of 1925, not far from the lonely spot where Carrie Weldon perished; the extensive loss of life and damage that marked the flash flooding of the Big Thompson in July 1976, the worst natural disaster in Colorado history; and the widespread destruction unleashed upon the town of Estes Park with the breaching of the dam at Lawn Lake in August 1982. Other events, equally momentous, have the happier ring of "progress" about them: the final, if delayed, opening of Fall River Road in 1920, making possible direct traffic with Middle Park to the west, and a one-day scenic-circle tour beginning and ending in Denver; the completion of Trail Ridge Road—the highest continuously paved highway in the world—in 1932; and the confirmation of Burton Sanborn's dream: the holing-through of the seventeen-mile Alva Adams Tunnel across the Continental Divide to the eastern slope in 1944 and the damming of the Big Thompson to create Lake Estes in 1949.

If the world of the MacGregors, Jameses, Fergusons, Spragues, and Lambs often seemed changeless and suspended in time, the years since 1915 have been marked by accelerated growth. How best to properly manage this growth while sustaining the economic viability of both park and town (or, conversely, to decide whether growth is a goal worth pursuing at all) has long since emerged as the single most important challenge for both and, not surprisingly, has been the catalyst for discussion and controversy.

For Rocky Mountain National Park the controversy began early. The new park had scarcely consolidated its operations when it was consumed by heated debate over a new Park Service concessions policy relating to access. In May 1919, without public discussion or competitive bidding, Superintendent L. C. Way implemented a directive from Washington and granted an exclusive franchise to Roe Emery's Rocky Mountain Parks Transportation Company that banned from park roads rental-car drivers who operated on their own or on behalf of local hotel and resort owners. Though intended to improve service and eliminate confusion, Way's action met quick and stiff local opposition from none other than Enos Mills, who, having fought to create a park, now battled to keep it open to automobiles from resorts like his own. Once aroused, Enos Mills proved a pugnacious opponent. Having decided that the park's new transportation policy and the monopoly it created were wrong, a violation of the principle of free competition as well as of his belief that parks should be as accessible as possible, he deliberately provoked a confrontation by dispatching a car, driver, and three passengers into the park. When Superintendent Way, a former military man, personally intercepted the vehicle on Fall River Road near Chasm Falls and ejected it, Mills filed a lawsuit in the U.S. District Court of Colorado, claiming that the Park Service had interfered with "his common rights as a citizen of the State of Colorado in traveling over the Park roads."

Before the issue could be resolved in the courts, it became subsumed in a much larger issue challenging the right of the federal government to regulate traffic over roads built with state funds that had never formally been ceded to the jurisdiction of the United States. This so-called Cede Jurisdiction Controversy, which was not finally resolved until February 1929, almost seven years after Enos Mills's death, showed just how difficult it could be—and would be in the years ahead—to balance the claims of those who demand unrestricted park access and usage and those who seek to limit both in the name of conservation and preservation. In more recent times this debate has been framed most often in environmental terms by critics such as Karl Hess Jr., who views Rocky Mountain National Park as "a landscape in crisis," and their concern over the degradation of the park's fragile high-elevation ecosystems. More often than not the park administration has found itself on the defensive, caught between servicing the needs of three million annual visitors in an era of declining federal support and the uncontested fact that overuse by both visitors and an overexpanded elk population, which has outstripped its winter range, directly threatens the biological diversity and vitality of the park itself.

For the town the terms of the ongoing debate are much the same: how to accommodate growth and its economic benefits while retaining what residents are fond of referring to as the "character," "unique charm," and "tone" of "the village." Though such a formulation oversimplifies what is obviously an extremely complicated and complex issue, it is roughly these two opposing views—each driven by its own set of values, aesthetics, economics, public policy implications, and rhetoric— that have framed much of the twentieth-century history of the town of Estes Park.

A case in point is the 1985 controversy over the development of Stanley Village, Estes Park's first major shopping center, and the even longer debate over the appropriate use of the thirty-five-acre Storer or STT Ranch property in Dry Gulch off Route 34. The issue in both cases is the classic one: the right of an owner (or owners) to develop property commercially as well as residentially versus the insistence by adjacent property owners (and other "concerned citizens") on their right to an aesthetically pleasing environment unmarred by commercial development.

The debate over these issues (which has included court action, the intervention of both the Colorado Historical Society and the state's governor, as well as years of heated exchanges in the *Estes Park Trail Gazette*) has introduced into the local vocabulary such terms as "open space," "view corridors," "conservation easement," "land trust," "housing density," "Urban Renewal District," "zoning and rezoning standards," "growth control," and "affordable housing." What gives new impetus and urgency to such discussions is the fact that the permanent, year-round population of the Estes Park valley at mid-decade passed nine thousand and, by the estimate of one recent "Comprehensive Master Plan," may reach thirty thousand in the early years of the new century.

These concerns, and the values that inspire and animate them, are real. Yet viewed dispassionately and historically, this debate, like so many others that have occupied the town's attention, is not without its overriding irony: for almost a century and a half the residents of Estes Park have found ways—and justification—to tolerate and support growth, not only in the form of resorts, liveries, shops, and restaurants, but in "catch your own" trout ponds, amusement park rides, arcades, miniature golf courses (there were three on Elkhorn Avenue by 1930, not to mention a four-hundred-yard driving range at Beaver Point), an aerial tramway, and, most recently, a replica of Noah's ark, which surely must closely approximate the original in size. Though the debate over "growth" and "progress" will continue (and in many respects is a sign of community vitality), the results will likely be much the same.

For those who resent such monuments to tourism and entrepreneurial energy, it is well to remember that in future days many of these "attractions" will be replaced just as others before them have been. There is no longer a Riverside Dance Hall with its famous Dark Horse Tavern (much to the regret of many longtime residents who remember with nostalgia the 1920s, 1930s, and 1940s when they danced there to the music of Ted Jelsema's Romancers, Hub Else's Jayhawkers, Eddie Jungebluth's Nebraskans, and other "big name" bands from Denver and beyond). Gone, too, is Phil "Casey" Martin's train ride and Ripley's Believe It Or Not Museum (which itself replaced the old National Park Hotel). Most of the other early landmarks along Elkhorn Avenue are also gone or have been so transformed, as is the case with several original shops, as to be no longer recognizable.

There is perhaps more to regret in the demolition of many famous resort hotels within the park itself ("those castles of wood" as one historian has called them), the result of a deliberate attempt by the Park Service to eliminate in-holdings and thereby restore the park to a

condition that the 1914 Arapaho and their forebears could easily recognize. One by one those hotels and lodges have disappeared: the
Brinwood, Horseshoe Park Inn, Stead's Hotel, Sprague's Lodge, Forest Inn,
Fern Lake Lodge, Moraine Lodge, Fall River Lodge, Deer Ridge Chalet.
Almost gone and badly deteriorated is the old Peter Pauly–Hugo Miller–
John McGraw Ranch down on Cow Creek, now being restabilized for
future use by the Park Service. Other old-time and much-remembered
resorts have suffered a similar fate, the victim of fire: Dunraven's Estes
Park Hotel in 1911, Cascade Lodge in 1939, the Lewiston Hotel in
1941, Enos Mills's Longs Peak Inn in 1946, the Estes Park Chalets in
1978, and Copeland Lake Lodge (the original Wild Basin Lodge) in
1980. Still other landmark hotels and lodges have lost their names and,
in some cases, their identities. Up in the Tahosa Valley the Columbines
Lodge survives as High Peak Camp (like Longs Peak Inn the property
of the Salvation Army), and Hewes-Kirkwood Inn as the Rocky Ridge
Music Center. Josie Hupp's hotel, at the corner of Elkhorn and Moraine
Avenues, shorn of its porches, for many years has been an Indian curio
shop, while the lower level of the Hupp Annex, diagonally across the
street (the old Manford Hotel), has been converted to shops. Further
down Elkhorn the hotel she named the Josephine is now one of Estes
Park's better-known bars and restaurants, and the National Park Hotel,
once Ripley's "museum," is now a mall. Out Dry Gulch, Shep Husted's
Rustic Hotel with its panoramic view of Longs Peak and the Front
Range (though amazingly well preserved) has become a youth hostel.
Bear Lake Lodge still exists, but has been moved from its original site
to adorn one of Estes Park's private campgrounds.

There are, fortunately, some notable survivors. The Elkhorn Lodge
looks much the way it did (minus, perhaps, its tent cottages) when Edna
James and her sons enlarged it early in the century. The Macdonald Book
Shop, since 1928 a landmark farther east on Elkhorn Avenue, is the original home that the merchant James Edward Macdonald erected shortly
after his arrival in Estes Park in 1908. Though "Joe Mill's Pond," at the
foot of Prospect Mountain, has been replaced by a fast-food restaurant,
his hotel, the Crags, has been tastefully maintained and looks much the
way it did in 1935, the year of Mills's death. The same thing is true of
Gordon Mace's Elizabethan stick-style Baldpate Inn with its three-story
central wing, observation deck, and world famous Key Room, which
fronts on the original road to the Tahosa Valley cut out of the mountainside
by the Lambs in 1875–1876. Also surviving and in use as a summer
home is the octagonal Queen Anne cottage that John Cleave built for the
Earl of Dunraven above Fish Creek Road. And, of course, there is the still

magnificent Stanley, without its original yellow paint, standing above the town and framing the Twin Owls and Lumpy Ridge just as F. O. Stanley erected it in 1907–1909. The Stanley, to be sure, has had a rough go of it in modern times. Patterns of leisure have changed, and with those changes many of America's grand old hotels in the tradition of the Breakers, the Grand on Mackinaw Island, and the Greenbriar have become an endangered species. Fortunately for all of us who cherish the past, magnificent resort hotels like the Stanley have somehow managed to survive to remind us of the way the affluent once spent their summers.

The changes and the passage of time, as sketched so briefly here, have scarcely dimmed or diminished the popularity of Joel Estes's valley. Estes Park remains, as in Griff Evans's day, a magnet for the nation and, increasingly, for the world. To understand why one need only to reread Isabella Bird's *A Lady's Life in the Rocky Mountains* and Frederick Chapin's *Mountaineering in Colorado: The Peaks About Estes Park*. Doing so, one discovers that even at the distance of more than a century, and despite all the changes that worry so many, the Estes Park of Isabella Bird and Frederick Chapin in its most essential and enduring ways is still very much our own.

To be sure we will not ride up to the Longs Peak trailhead on horseback as they did. We will make the nine-mile journey by car over a new road cut into the eastern slope of Lily Mountain and do so in less than half an hour. At the foot of the peak, as we register our names at the ranger station, we may well lament the fact that we will not, as Chapin and Carrie Welton did, have a chance to spend the night before our climb in front of Father Lamb's cheerful fire, listening to his stories of mountaineering in an even earlier day. But once on the trail itself, the ranger station and parking lot left behind, we have begun a journey in which the passage of the years scarcely seems to matter. At the Keyhole, we will look down (as Griff Evans, Mountain Jim, Isabella Bird, Anna Dickinson, Frederick Chapin, Carlyle Lamb, Carrie Welton, and Enos Mills all did) upon the lakes nestled deep in Glacier Gorge. With the good fortune of a fair day and willing body, we will eventually crawl up the Homestretch and reach the summit—the same summit on which Major Powell unfurled his flag, toasted his companions, and made his speech. Here in "this blue hollow," removed as we are from a world whose defining characteristic seems to be relentless change, there are, fortunately, still to be found such moments in the midst of nature's grandeur—moments that remind us of the common humanity we share with those who in other, earlier days also passed this way.

Endnotes

~

CHAPTER 1

1. Milton Estes, "Memoirs of Estes Park," *Colorado Magazine* 16, July 1939, 121.

2. Though trappers had probably visited the area, their presence in any numbers over any extended period of time is doubtful, for Abner Sprague is surely correct that "the same fur bearing animals were plentiful at lower altitudes, and could be secured with less effort nearer the plains and lines of travel" (Abner Sprague, "The Estes and Rocky Mountain Parks: An Historical Reminiscence," *Estes Park Trail*, April 21, 1922, 8).

Enos Mills himself was apparently the source of the story linking Kit Carson (1809–1868) with Estes Park. While conducting guests at Longs Peak Inn to the beaver ponds on nearby Cabin Creek, Mills enjoyed pointing out fire-smutted stones and the ruins of an old log cabin above which he had erected a wooden sign bearing the words "Kit Carson Cabin Site." Unfortunately, however, according to Harvey L. Carter, coauthor of *Kit Carson: A Pattern for Heroes* (1984), the story is without substance. "I have never found any evidence to support the story of Kit Carson in Estes Park," Carter wrote the author in a letter dated January 19, 1985.

No doubt some abandoned primitive cabin once occupied the site you mention and speculation was that it dated back to the era of the trappers. Since Carson was the most well known of these it would be an easy step to attach it to him. But it may have dated only from the post-trapping era when Mariano Medina, Nick James, & others lived in the general area in the 1850s and 1860s. As you know, Carson left the mountains in 1841 and came to Bent's Fort. During the forties he was with Fremont much of the time and in the Taos vicinity otherwise, so that it can not be at all probable that he was trapping anywhere near this location at any time after 1840–41.

Charles Edwin Hewes, who came to the Tahosa Valley in 1907 and presided over Hewes-Kirkwood Inn near Longs Peak Inn, clarifies the matter further. "I asked Mills as to the authenticity of the Kit Carson cabin site," Hewes recorded in his journal on November 23, 1919,

> and he said that some very old man, a former witness of the Colorado-Kansas Water case, had claimed to be here with Kit in the winter of 1853–54; but that he had drawn a sketch for him which readily identified the spot so that Mills felt certain, at least as to his having been there. He said that old man [the Reverend Elkanah J.] Lamb knew of the place but did not know who occupied it. The cabin was standing until burned by some careless campers. It had a door to the south, was built of logs, and [had] a pole and gravel roof. (Hewes, "Journal, 1912–1944," unpublished manuscript, Estes Park Area Historical Museum, p. 429).

Kansas's suit against Colorado over control and use of the Arkansas River reached the Supreme Court in May of 1901.

3. The most intriguing of these accounts is the one by Rufus Sage, a native of Connecticut, who visited the West between 1841 and 1844 during the heyday of the fur trade. On September 25, 1843, Sage left Fort Lancaster on the Platte and made his way west in the direction of Longs Peak on a hunting excursion. Sage speaks in his *Rocky Mountain Life*, first published in 1846, of coming upon "a large valley skirting a tributary of Thompson's creek." "The locality of my encampment," Sage wrote,

> presented numerous and varied attractions. It seemed, indeed, like a concentration of beautiful lateral valleys, intersected by meandering watercourses, ridged by lofty piles of precipitous rock, and hemmed in upon the west by vast piles of mountains climbing beyond the clouds, and upon the north, south, and east, by sharp lines of hills that skirted the prairie; while occasional openings, like gateways, pointed to the far-spreading domains of silence and loneliness.

It was a hunter's paradise, and Sage remained a month before returning to Fort Lancaster by way of the St. Vrain on October 30. If the valley that Sage describes was, in fact, Estes Park, his arrival preceded that of Joel Estes by sixteen years. Rufus Sage, *Rocky Mountain Life; or, Startling Scenes and Perilous Adventures in the Far West During an Expedition of Three Years* (Lincoln: University of Nebraska Press, 1982), p. 344.

Abner Sprague, on the other hand, believed that the valley Sage entered was Allenspark: "He did not range far enough to the west or north to see or discover Estes Park" (Abner Sprague, "Early History of Estes Park Region," *Estes Park Trail*, July 19, 1940, 12).

4. The Cudahy-Norwall Mine, whose shaft extended some fifteen hundred

feet, operated until about 1918. Charles Edwin Hewes speaks in the unpublished autobiography, which he completed in May of 1916, of having encountered "relics, an old fireplace and decayed cabin logs, of a miner and prospector generation visiting the Vale from five to ten years previous to the advent of the Lambs. And another and later generation of prospectors, about five years previous to our coming, erected a couple of cabins and dug a shaft and started two short tunnels on the west side of the Vale." These two tunnels, he tells us in a November 1933 journal entry, were called the Big Indian and the Pack Rat—the former located on the old Longs Peak trail about a mile west of Longs Peak Inn; the latter on the northern bank of Alpine Brook, a quarter mile upstream from the Longs Peak campground. See "The Autobiography of Charles Edwin Hewes," unpublished manuscript, Estes Park Area Historical Museum, p. 217; Hewes, "Journal," 911.

The early mining activity referred to by Hewes would belong to the period between 1870 and 1875; the latter to the turn of the century. Newspaper accounts from 1898 to 1903 confirm a number of efforts to discover what the *Longmont Ledger* referred to in August 1898 as "the long lost rich vein on Long's Peak" and mention several claims on the peak as high as the timberline (*Longmont Ledger*, August 19, 1898, 2).

Known mining properties in the vicinity of Longs Peak during the same period include the Columbia, belonging to the Genoa Mining Company. Further to the south of Meeker Park on Cowbell Hill was the Clara Belle Mine, which fueled the mining boom at Allenspark in 1903. Abner Sprague recalled that years earlier, in the fall of 1875 or 1876, a party of hunters from Boulder, which included a man named Barber, found ore-bearing rock in the Wind River and Glacier Basin drainage, and that Barber returned for several years trying in vain to locate the spot. He also remembered being told that the artist Albert Bierstadt had picked up a piece of quartz "shot through with free gold, until it was almost a nugget" during one of his excursions into the Loch Vale region. See Abner Sprague, "Lost Mines," *Estes Park Trail*, March 3, 1922, 7.

5. See James B. Benedict, *The Game Drives of Rocky Mountain National Park* (Boulder, CO: Johnson Publishing, 1996). Benedict indicates that the largest of the nine overlapping drive systems on Flattop Mountain alone would have required the cooperative efforts of at least fifty men, women, and children. Frederick Chapin had noted such structures on Flattop during the 1880s. "An old moraine among the rocks near where we saw the ptarmigan," he wrote, "was distinctly traceable for several hundred feet down the mountain, by rounded stones piled in a curving row about two feet high, reminding one of a stone-wall in the Berkshire hills" (Frederick H. Chapin, *Mountaineering in Colorado: The Peaks About Estes Park* [Boston: Appalachian Mountain Club, 1889], p. 76).

6. Though most of the artifacts on the Oldman Mountain site were recovered during the 1930s, their interpretation is the work of James Benedict, as reported in his *Old Man Mountain: A Vision Quest Site in the Colorado High Country*, Research Report No. 4, Center for Mountain Archaeology, Ward, CO (Boulder, CO: Johnson Publishing, 1985). Benedict and teams from his Center for Mountain Archaeology have done similar pioneering work documenting ancient Indian activity in Estes Park and at a number of sites in the high country of Boulder County. Ranger Jack Moomaw was the area's premier early and inveterate collector of Indian artifacts, claiming to have found "flint relics of a long vanished people" at more than twenty separate sites. See Jack Moomaw, "Arrowheads," *Estes Park Trail*, October 19, 1928, 12; Dorr Yeager, "Nature Notes from Rocky Mountain National Park," *Estes Park Trail*, December 18, 1931, 10; Dorr Yeager, "More Indian Material," *Estes Park Trail*, March 17, 1933, 5.

7. Vaille herself was apparently responding to a suggestion made by Enos Mills during a lecture given the previous year before the Mountain Club at which he "proposed naming the many peaks of the range which now have no designation" by using their original Indian names (*Estes Park Trail*, July 25, 1914, 4).

8. *Longmont Ledger*, July 17, 1914, 1.

9. Oliver W. Toll, *Arapaho Names and Trails: A Report of a 1914 Pack Trip* (n.p.: Oliver W. Toll, 1962), p. 10. See also Harriet Vaille Bouck, "Arapaho Hunting Grounds Revisited," *Trail and Timberline* 558, June 1965, 105–7. In forwarding her project, Harriet Vaille and her friend, Edna Hendrie, had followed the advice of Livingston Farrand, then president of the University of Colorado, by traveling by train and wagon to the Wind River Reservation where they sought out and interviewed "old Arapahos who knew our mountains," then hastened back to Colorado where they raised the needed funds and made arrangements for the visit to Estes Park. Harriet and Edna did not, however, join the pack trip: in 1914 "young ladies just did not do that."

10. Sprague, "Historical Reminiscence," *Estes Park Trail*, April 21, 1922, 8.

11. Abner Sprague, "Prehistoric Trails," *Estes Park Trail*, August 1, 1930, 20.

12. In subsequent years Francis Marion Estes (1846–1911), the second youngest child of Joel and Patsy Estes, would claim that he was with his father at the time of the discovery of Estes Park. He recounted his version of events in a September 13, 1909, article that appeared in the *Rocky Mountain News*, a typescript copy of which is found in the Colorado Collection, Pamphlet File, Estes Park Public Library.

13. Milton Estes, "Memoirs of Estes Park," 124–25.

14. Abner Sprague, "Roads and Trails," *Estes Park Trail*, December 8, 1922, 3. See also Abner Sprague, *Estes Park Trail*, June 8, 1934, 8.

15. Dunham Wright, "A Winter in Estes Park with Senator Teller," *The Trail*

13, July 1920, 9. See also Teller's interview with a reporter from the *Denver Post*, May 26, 1911, 12.

16. Dunham Wright, letter to the Estes Park Chamber of Commerce, April 26, 1927, Joel Estes Collection, Colorado Historical Society.

17. Dunham Wright, letter to the Estes Park Chamber of Commerce, c. 1927, Joel Estes Collection, Colorado Historical Society. Teller wrote Wright on March 19, 1921, that "I have always remembered our trip to Estes Park, including the trip from Central to Boulder and getting lost in the woods" (Henry Teller, letter to Dunham Wright of March 1912, Joel Estes Collection).

18. Dunham Wright, letter of September 2, 1920, Joel Estes Collection.

19. Ibid.

20. "Extract From Verbatim Dictated Statement of John T. Prewitt Who Visited Estes Park in 1864, From a Manuscript, the Property of Mrs. C. A. Garfield of San Francisco, California," Colorado Collection, Pamphlet File, Estes Park Public Library.

21. Wallace Stegner, *Beyond the Hundredth Meridian: John Wesley Powell and the Second Opening of the West* (Boston: Houghton Mifflin, 1954), pp. 26–27.

22. William M. Buehler, *Roof of the Rockies: A History of Colorado Mountaineering* (n.p.: Cordillera Press, 1986), p. 35.

23. Ibid. According to Buehler, "Using a barometer to determine elevation, he [Parry] made the most accurate measurements up to that time of a number of peaks, including Pikes, Grays, Evans, James (13,294), Audubon (13,223), Parry (13,391), Flora (13,132), and Guyot (13,370); any of the last five might have been firsts, unless Indians or miners got there first."

24. William N. Byers, "Ascent of Long's Peak," *Rocky Mountain News*, September 23, 1864, 2.

25. Ibid.

26. Charles C. Parry, "Excursion to Long's Peak," in *King of Colorado Botany: Charles Christopher Parry, 1823–1890*, ed. William A. Weber (Niwot, CO: University Press of Colorado, 1997), p. 120. Parry's account originally appeared in the September 18, 1864, issue of the *Chicago Evening Journal*.

27. Ibid., 121.

28. Byers, "Ascent of Long's Peak," 2. Just who the five successful climbers of Mount Meeker might have been has never been established.

29. Ibid.

30. *Colorado Sun*, August 14, 1873, 1.

31. Milton Estes, "Memoirs of Estes Park," 127. Hearst, or "Muggins," also apparently operated a sawmill. See Neil C. Sullivan, "An 1892 Camping Party at Estes Park," *Estes Park Trail*, February 5, 1926, 6.

32. Though nearly sixty years old, Joel Estes's wanderings were not over. From New Mexico, Joel and Patsy, Milton and his family, and eighteen-year-

old Joel Jr. continued east across Texas to take up ranching near Fayetteville, Arkansas. In 1868 both families returned to the West, Joel Sr. and Milton taking up new ranches near Raton, New Mexico, while Joel Jr., now married, established a ranch of his own near Farmington. During the early 1870s, according to Francis Marion, his mother and father also engaged in farming to the north in Huerfano County, Colorado. Sometime later Joel and Patsy apparently went to live with Joel Jr., for it was there that Joel suffered a stroke that paralyzed him. Joel Estes died on December 31, 1875, at the age of sixty-nine. His place of burial is unknown. After Joel's death, Patsy made her home with her daughter, Sarah, in Sidney, Iowa. Patsy Estes died at Sidney on August 6, 1882, at the age of seventy-six, where she is buried in the town cemetery.

CHAPTER 2

1. Enos A. Mills, *The Story of Estes Park* (Denver, CO: Outdoor, 1905), p. 9. One of the sources of Mills's information may have been an article on Hollenbeck in the July 24, 1904, issue of the *Lyons Recorder*, which states that Joel Estes's "need for oxen induced him to trade his interest in Estes park to our friend Hollenbeck, for one 3-year-old steer. Hellenbeck [sic] helped him to move out, to boot" (*Lyons Recorder*, July 21, 1904, 2).
2. *Rocky Mountain News*, August 26, 1874, 4.
3. For both the federal census of 1880, when he was living in the Pella district of Boulder County, and the Colorado census of 1885, by which time he was in Jamestown, Griff listed his occupation as "miner."
4. Arthur Pendarves Vivian, *Wanderings in the Western Land* (London: Sampson Low, Marston, Searle, & Rivington, 1879), pp. 140–41.
5. Reprinted in the *New Lyons Recorder*, July 9, 1987, 6.
6. Isabella Bird, *A Lady's Life in the Rocky Mountains* (London: Virago, 1982), pp. 128–29. The text cited here and throughout is the third edition, published in London by John Murray in 1880.
7. Isabella Lucy Bird, *Letters from Colorado, October 23, 1873–December 4, 1973*, transcribed by Louisa Ward Arps and Alex Warner, Western History Department, Denver Public Library, p. 4. These are what remains of the original, unedited letters that Isabella Bird wrote home to her sister Henrietta.
8. Vivian, *Wanderings in the Western Land*, 141. Evans told an English visitor in August 1873 that during the preceding winter "he [had] shot 128 deer, sold most of it for ten cents per pound, and the fine heads for three dollars each" (*The Field*, September 13, 1873, 279).
9. Bird, *A Lady's Life*, 94–95.
10. Ibid., 127–28.
11. George M. Brown (1840–1929), a native of Leominster, Massachusetts, came to Burlington, Colorado, in the fall of 1865, having served with the Army of the Potomac until mustered out in July 1864. Brown, often re-

ferred to as "Captain" because of his Civil War experience, settled on the North St. Vrain on a ranch he called "The Hermitage" and began raising cattle. His operations soon extended to Estes Park, where he and his partner, Wilbur C. Lothrop (1845–1900), entered into a working relationship with Evans. His interest in cattle and cattle raising was a serious one, for in 1872, when the Colorado stock growers organization was formed, Brown served as a member of its executive committee. That same year Brown further diversified his interests by contracting to provide several thousand railroad ties. Once cut, the logs were floated down the St. Vrain River to where it forked and formed an island near Burlington. From there they were hauled to Erie, ten miles away. In 1876, Brown added a brick and tile business to his holdings. Wilbur Lothrop had come to Denver in 1865 and become chief clerk in the United States Collector's Office. In 1870, he became territorial superintendent of public instruction, a position he would hold until 1873.

12. *Colorado Press*, March 13, 1872, 3. Two months later Evans corrected slightly this account, with respect both to the size of the herd and its self-sufficiency: "Mr. G. J. Evans, of Estes' Park, made us a call to-day. He wintered six hundred cattle and a number of horses in the park last winter, and the entire number fed but twenty-five tons of hay" (*Colorado Press*, May 22, 1872, 3).

13. *Boulder County News*, June 7, 1872, 3. The *Greeley Tribune* had earlier reported, without mentioning Evans, that "Estes' Park . . . has furnished feed for cattle all Winter, though they had to seek it first in one place, then in another" (*Greeley Tribune*, March 27, 1872, 2).

14. *Central City Daily Register*, September 2, 1874, 3.

15. Reprinted in the *Greeley Tribune*, July 12, 1876, 1.

16. *Boulder County News*, June 17, 1876, 1. Very little is known about James McLaughlin (b. 1825) other than that he occupied a squatter's claim farther up Fish Creek where he both ranched and farmed. Occasionally referred to as "James McNasser," his name is linked with Evans's in several contemporary newspaper articles. See *Colorado Press*, June 19, 1872, 3; October 23, 1872, 3; and October 6, 1872, 3. Though McLaughlin was one of those who subsequently challenged Dunraven's purchases before a grand jury in 1874, he did not stay. In 1878 he sold out his Fish Creek property to the Dunraven interests and moved to the newly organized town of Alpine, southwest of Buena Vista.

17. *Chicago Tribune*, August 15, 1871, 3.

18. *Colorado Press*, April 17, 1872, 2.

19. Ibid.

20. *Fort Collins Standard*, April 22, 1874, 3.

21. Henry Adams, *The Education of Henry Adams*, ed. Ernest Samuels (Boston: Houghton Mifflin, 1973), pp. 310–11.

22. *Chicago Tribune,* op cit.
23. Ibid.
24. *Greeley Tribune,* September 13, 1871, 2.
25. Ibid., May 17, 1871, 2.
26. *Larimer Press;* subsequently published in the *Greeley Tribune,* August 27, 1873, 2.
27. *The Field,* September 13, 1873, p. 279.
28. This young woman seems to have made her home with the Evanses periodically. She is identified in the 1880 census as Katie. One source suggests that she was the daughter of Jane Owen's brother Will, who lived in Denver.
29. Bird, *A Lady's Life,* 131.
30. *Denver Tribune,* November 23, 1873, 4. Cavanaugh's name appears in Bird's original letters as "Mr. Kavanagh" and in *A Lady's Life* as "Mr. Kavan." Buchanan appears in Bird's book as "Mr. Buchan," Allen as "Mr. Lyman." Buchanan may well be the John Buchanan who on June 21, 1874, married the niece of Griff Evans, Mary Jane Roberts. In a letter written in 1925, Mary recalled that she had arrived at the Evans ranch in June 1873 and was in residence at the time of Isabella Bird's visit. On May 22, 1874, her birthday, Rocky Mountain Jim named Marys Lake in her honor. After their marriage Mary and John Buchanan filed on a quarter section of land half a mile south of Marys Lake (*Estes Park Trail,* June 5, 1925, 21).
31. *The Field,* September 13, 1873, p. 279.
32. *Colorado Press,* June 19, 1872, 3.
33. Alexander Q. MacGregor, letter to John A. Jones, July 23, 1881, MacGregor Trust, Estes Park.
34. Sprague, "Historical Reminiscence," *Estes Park Trail,* May 5, 1922, 3.
35. Horace W. Ferguson, "Mr. Ferguson's Story (As Told to Mary E. Stickney)," typescript copy, Colorado Collection, Pamphlet File, Estes Park Public Library, p. 5.
36. In support of MacGregor's date is the following comment by Mr. Painter from the August 14, 1873, edition of Greeley's *Colorado Sun* that Evans "has sold partial interests to other parties, but still makes the Park his home, and has lately taken in a partner by the name of Edwards. Mr. McLaughlin also resides in the Park, and with Messrs Evans and Edwards are the only parties having an actual residence there" (*Colorado Sun,* August 14, 1873, 1). If Painter is correct, then the sale took place the previous month, for the English visitor, "G. W.," who visited in mid-July, was told by Evans that the park was then for sale.

  By the spring of 1873 Evans found himself with money in his pocket—either through Dunraven or through his own enterprise. In May of that year he hired Fernando C. Willett of Denver as a tutor for his children. Willett, who had coauthored "a valuable pocket compendium" of the territory titled *Handbook of Colorado*, came to the park in the company of his uncle John Hubbell, of New York City, who expected to go into partnership with Evans. They rented the Denison house at the base of Mount Olympus for six months, but left the park before Isabella Bird's arrival because Mrs. Hubbell disliked the loneliness and remoteness of the place (Roger W. Toll, "Notes on a Conversation with Mrs. E. E. [Emma Hubbell] Shumway, September 7, 1928," Colorado Collection, Pamphlet File, Estes Park Public Library, p. 1).

On the other hand, the purchase by Whyte of Brown and Lothrop's herd of cattle (an event that it is generally asserted came at about the same time that Evans disposed of his holdings) apparently did not occur until after Estes Park had been surveyed and opened for entry on May 1, 1874. The *Boulder County News* of that date contains the following item: "Geo. W. Brown, Esq., who wintered several hundred head of cattle in Estes' Park during the past winter tells us they have come through in good condition, and without feeding. The loss is about one out of a hundred" (*Boulder County News*, May 1, 1874, 3).

37. *The Field*, September 13, 1873, p. 279.

38. *Fort Collins Standard*, November 4, 1874, 3. The two-story frame St. Vrain Hotel located on Main Street in Longmont, where Isabella Bird stayed going to and from the park, had been operated by Captain William Beach Sigley (1833–1889), a Civil War veteran who came to Longmont from Chicago in search of better health in June 1871, found the hotel under construction, and became its manager. "The bluff and hearty" Sigley had the reputation of making "every guest his friend." Sigley operated the hotel until 1874, and, as the *Longmont Ledger* explained in announcing Sigley's death, "during that time the house became deservedly popular, not only with its regular boarders but with the traveling public as well, and there was a feeling of universal regret when Captain Sigley decided to retire from its management" (*Longmont Ledger*, March 15, 1889, 2). After passing out of Evans's hands, the hotel was destroyed by fire on September 8, 1879 (*Boulder County News*, July 18, 1873, 2; *Fort Collins Courier*, September 11, 1879, 2).

39. *Colorado Business Directory and Annual Register, For 1875* (Denver: J. A. Blake, 1875), p. 189.

40. *Fort Collins Standard*, November 4, 1874, 3.

41. The St. Vrain Hotel register ("G. J. Evans, Prop.") was subsequently passed on to Griff Evans's descendants. A microfilm copy is part of the Special Collections of the University of Colorado, Boulder.

42. The *Greeley Tribune* reported that Evans's house and post office were destroyed by fire in late November of 1877 (*Greeley Tribune*, December 5, 1877, 2). If so, I have been unable to corroborate the fact from other contemporary sources.

43. According to the historian Dave Hicks, these 160 acres, which Evans sold to Dunraven's company on November 7, 1878, for five hundred dollars, "[were] not, however, the ranch property where the Earl spent his first night in the Park. That deed was not found among the records" (Dave Hicks, Estes Park From the Beginning [Denver: A-T-P Publishing, 1976], p. 19).

44. Sprague, "Historical Reminiscence," Estes Park Trail, April 28, 1922, 3.

45. See Edward S. Lyon, letter to Lillie Lyon Thorne Smith, January 2, 1922; Lyons Recorder, January 26, 1922, 1.

46. Longmont Ledger, September 22, 1882, 3. This injury was compounded when the next year Evans was thrown From a horse and broke his leg (ibid., June 29, 1883, 3).

47. Ibid., February 16, 1883, 2.

48. Jann Gurnsey, Barbara Heaton, and Jean King, Mountain Memories: A History of Jimtown (n.p.: 1976), p. 16.

CHAPTER 3

1. For studies of British travelers and entrepreneurs attracted to the American West, see Robert G. Athearn, Westward the Briton (New York: Charles Scribner's Sons, 1953); John I. Merritt, Baronets and Buffalo: The British Sportsman in the American West, 1833–1881 (Missoula, MT: Mountain Press, 1985); Lawrence M. Woods, British Gentlemen in the Wild West: The Era of the Intensely English Cowboy (New York: Free Press, 1989); and Maurice Frink, W. Turrentine Jackson, and Agnes Wright Spring, When Grass Was King: Contributions to the Western Range Cattle Study (Boulder: University of Colorado Press, 1956). For an account of the attractiveness of the cattle industry as a place to invest British capital, see William A. Baillie-Grohman, "Cattle Ranches of the Far West," Fortnightly Review 38, September 1880, 438–57.

2. Though Theodore Whyte's father, Colonel John James Whyte, owned estates in both Devon and in County Leitrim, Ireland, his elder brother, Charles Cecil Whyte, born a year earlier, stood first in line of succession. Thus, like so many younger sons of the landed gentry, Theodore Whyte had to make his own way in the world. His decision to come to Canada resulted, no doubt, from the fact that his mother, Mary Ann Jesse de Montenach, was a French Canadian heiress, who could trace her roots in Canada back to 1641. Whyte came to Colorado because he had friends there, among them J. E. Liller of Colorado Springs, the editor of Out West.

3. Sprague, "Historical Reminiscence," Estes Park Trail, April 28, 1922, 3. The filers did in fact have names. The first survey of January was requested by Benjamin A. Williams, George Robinson, and Thomas C. Carpenter; the February survey by James L. Daly, John W. Dogherty, and William Haines. All of these individuals subsequently filed claims, and, as the list of filers clearly indicates, they filed together.

4. Alexander Q. MacGregor, letter to John A. Jones, July 23, 1881, MacGregor Trust, Estes Park.

5. Part of the difficulty in detecting false claims can be explained by the pressure under which the land office worked. The Denver office was particularly active. In 1872 it had to handle filings on 174,098 acres; in the first nine months of 1873 alone, the number of acres filed upon rose to 395,235 (*Denver Tribune*, December 5, 1873, 4).

The Estes Park filers made no pretense to comply with the law in proving up on their land. In some instances these entrymen (or perhaps Whyte, acting in their stead) laid down four logs in the form of a square constituting a "claim shanty." A number of these structures, though almost rotted away, were visible as late as 1910 (*Denver Post*, October 15, 1916, sec. 2, p.14).

6. *Greeley Tribune*, December 27, 1871, 2.

7. *Fort Collins Standard*, October 28, 1886, 6.

8. *Denver Tribune*, December 6, 1872, 2.

9. *Pueblo Daily Chieftain*, June 17, 1874, 3.

10. *Colorado Springs Gazette*, August 1, 1874, 2.

11. *Rocky Mountain News*, June 24, 1874, 3.

12. Though Dunraven spent most of his youth at Adare Manor in Limerick on the Manque River, there was a Dunraven Castle in Glamorganshire in southeastern Wales, overlooking the Bristol Channel.

13. *Rocky Mountain News*, July 22, 1874, 4. Dunraven was not the only early visitor to Estes Park to have an encounter with a mountain lion. A year earlier, in July of 1873, Griff Evans told an English visitor that he "nearly got in a mess with one. He saw its head just over some rocks, and being a very good shot, blazed away at it, and missed. The animal at once charged; Evans luckily had a large pine tree near, behind which he dodged, and every time the beast sprang at him he ran round the tree. After shooting at it seven times, hitting it twice, it retired" (*The Field*, September 13, 1873, p. 279).

14. *Fort Collins Standard*, August 12, 1874, 3.

15. See *Fort Collins Standard*, August 26, 1874, p. 3; *Greeley Tribune*, September 2, 1874, 2.

16. *Greeley Tribune*, August 26, 1874, 2, citing the *Denver Tribune*.

17. Securing such indictments in the Colorado Territory, where land speculation and its attendant charges of "land-grabbing" were frequent, was not easy, even for a veteran prosecutor like Alleman. At the very time he was attempting to secure indictments against the filers in Estes Park, he found himself embroiled in a controversy over his efforts to secure similar indictments for fraudulent claims made at Las Animas in southeastern Colorado. One of those indicted in the Las Animas case was David H. Moffat Jr., a cashier at the First National Bank of Denver "and a citizen of

high character, standing, and worth." When editor William Byers rushed to Moffat's defense, and editorialized in the *Rocky Mountain News* that the Las Animas indictments were "obtained without authority of law, and without even a decent regard for the sanctity of established usages, to serve a base foolish purpose," Alleman not only defended himself in a letter to the *News* but sued Byers and his managing editor, W. R. Thomas, for libel. (Thomas was subsequently arrested on a warrant; Byers, fortunately, was away in Middle Park.) It is worth noting that David Moffat and his bank subsequently became the conduit through which Dunraven funded his Estes Park operations. See *Rocky Mountain News*, July 22, 1874, 2.

18. See *Rocky Mountain News*, September 23, 1874, 4; *Greeley Tribune*, September 26, 1874, 2.

19. While Byers made no attempt to defend fraudulent entry or "land-grabbing," there were at times extenuating circumstances, as he pointed out in an article on July 15 headlined "Whose Titles Are Safe?":

> The defects of the pre-emption and homestead laws and the difficulties of their administration, have been known and recognized during the settlement of the whole western country. . . . And doubtless in many instances, all over the country, false swearing has been resorted to, for the purpose of effecting entries. So notorious has [*sic*] these violations and evasions of those laws become, that their practice had almost ceased to attract attention. In tracing the titles of lands, and also in making purchases, buyers never thought of examining to see how the certificates of entry, and patents had been obtained—such certificates and patents being regarded as conclusive evidence of good title. . . . While we have no word of apology for the irregularities or frauds referred to, and will go as far, and do as much as any one, to prevent their perpetration and punish the actual guilty parties, we believe this raid upon government titles . . . is . . . the opening of an endless source of evil to the whole country by creating a vast want of confidence in the titles given by the government, and a general insecurity in real property . . . (*Rocky Mountain News*, July 15, 1874, 2).

Interestingly enough, Byers himself was not above bending the spirit, if not the letter, of the land law where valuable Colorado real estate was concerned. To obtain title to Hot Sulphur Springs in Middle Park, which Byers had surveyed for the government in October and early November of 1868, Byers made use of so-called Sioux Half-Breed Scrip. This scrip, originally issued to certain half-breeds chiefly in Minnesota, gave the holder the preferential right to claim up to 480 acres of surveyed public domain without payment. For an account of how Byers came by this scrip and then used it to obtain property he had long coveted, see Robert C. Black, *Island in the Rockies: The History of Grand County, Colorado, to 1930* (Boulder, CO: Pruett, 1969), pp. 62–73.

20. The *Fort Collins Standard*, for example, left no doubt that it deserved full

credit for driving the inquiry:

> The Attorney General has at last been prevailed on to look into the Estes Park
> land steal, and the *Tribune* claims all the credit of the expose in head lines that
> would mar the appearance of those bills issued by horse men in spring time.
> Other papers claim the same credit. Perhaps it is creditable to get some of
> the carpet-baggers that rule our Territory to attend to their business, besides
> it is so natural for the *Tribune* to be "ahead of all contemporaries as usual,"
> that we are not astonished at its claiming the withholding of the patents to
> the land in Estes' Park as a *Tribune* victory. The *Standard* published the first
> expose of the land grab, and in doing so only did its duty by the people of
> Larimer county (*Fort Collins Standard*, August 16, 1874, 3).

Denver's *Rocky Mountain Herald* made much the same point: "The Estes
Park land grab is busted. The *Tribune* claims to have done it with its little
hatchet, and as it was never known to tell a lie, we are bound to believe
it" (*Rocky Mountain Herald*, September 26, 1874, 1).

21. *Greeley Tribune*, September 23, 1874, 2.
22. Ibid., August 19, 1874, 2.
23. Ibid., September 26, 1874, 2.
24. *Fort Collins Standard*, August 12, 1874, 3.
25. *Rocky Mountain News*, July 29, 1874, 4. See also *Greeley Tribune*, August 5,
    1874, 2; *Central City Register*, July 30, 1874, 3; *Georgetown Colorado Miner*, August
    22, 1874, 8; *Pueblo People*, August 1, 1874, 3. The *Boulder County News* ex-
    panded on these ambitious plans in a story in mid-August. Its source is
    David Gray, a correspondent for the *Chicago Inter-Ocean*, who had just re-
    turned from Estes Park and seems to have learned the facts from Griff
    Evans himself.

> I spoke in my former letter of the purchase of Estes' Park by Earl Dunraven,
> and on my arriving at Longmont I learned more of his plans. He has rented
> it for twenty years to Mr. G. J. Evans, an experienced mountain resident and
> guide who has lived in the park for a long time. Evans goes right to work
> this fall on the following improvements: He builds a large hotel in the park,
> together with a number of cottages for the use of families. He also improves
> the road, and will upon the completion of his work upon it, collect tolls
> from all who use it. A half-way house is to be built at a point where a
> general view can be had of the plains, as well as a large and commodious
> hotel at Longmont. A cottage is to be erected as near to Long's Peak as one
> can go with ponies, so as to render it as comfortable as possible for all the
> adventurous persons who wish to risk their necks and bones in climbing
> that exalted summit. These things are all to be accomplished, as notes some-
> times read, "on or before" the first day of June next.

The story concludes with the opinion that Evans will be "as good as his word" (*Boulder County News*, August 14, 1874, p. 1). The statement that Dunraven had rented the park "for twenty years to Mr. G. J. Evans" is obviously erroneous, but does hint of an arrangement struck between the two.

26. The *Fort Collins Express* reported on September 12, 1885, that "government agents have been looking up the land question in Larimer county. They have been looking over the entries in Estes Park, and it is said four-fifths of the entries and patents will be revoked as they were not legally obtained" (*Fort Collins Express*, September 12, 1885, 1).

27. S. Nugent Townshend, *Colorado: Its Agriculture, Stockfeeding, Scenery, and Shooting* (London: The Field Office, 1879), p. 7. Townshend authored regular columns for the British gentlemen's newspaper *The Field* under the name "St. Kames."

28. *Rocky Mountain News*, July 15, 1874, 2.

29. One reason may be that by the summer of 1874 the proposed site, said to be in the vicinity of Big Elk Park, had been taken up by others. The *Boulder County News* reported in August that Colonel E. A. Selkirk and H. C. Colson had located a claim of a thousand acres there for a D. T. Charles of Albany, New York, who planned to use the land to run a thousand head of cattle and was in the process of building cabins (*Boulder County News*, August 7, 1874, 3). By 1881 there was a halfway house in operation (presumably in the St. Vrain Canyon above the future town of Lyons), where the horses were changed and travelers could "stop and eat a dinner with that keen relish that only mountain air can bring" (*Rocky Mountain News*, August 23, 1881, 2).

30. On January 9, 1877, the *Rocky Mountain News* reported that on the previous day Dunraven, his cousin W. Montagu Kent, and Bierstadt had returned from Estes Park where the artist "has been making sketches for pictures of Colorado winter scenery." Bierstadt, the *News* continued, "returns home to begin work upon the picture of Long's Peak and the park will doubtless be one of his grandest works." Returning east, Bierstadt wrote on October 9, 1877, that his monumental canvas *Long's Peak, Estes Park, Colorado* was nearly finished. Shortly thereafter it was exhibited in Boston and then sent back to Bierstadt's New York studio for retouching on February 27, 1878. From New York the painting was shipped to London, where it was exhibited at the Royal Academy before being taken to Glin Castle (*Rocky Mountain News*, January 9, 1877, 4).

31. *Rocky Mountain News*, July 11, 1877, 4.

32. Daniel Pidgeon, *An Engineer's Holiday; or, Notes of a Round Trip from Long. 0o to 0o* (London: K. Paul, Trench, 1882), p. 119.

33. *Longmont Ledger*, October 13, 1911, 5. The *Ledger* had earlier reported that Charles Lester, who for a number of years had managed the hotel under lease, "has purchased the site of the Estes Park hotel, lately burned, and

will commence rebuilding about September 1st" (*Longmont Ledger*, September 3, 1911, 7). The hotel, of course, was never rebuilt, and for years—until 1936—all that remained on the site was its stone chimney. It was torn down that year by Carl Sanborn, the son of Greeley developer Burton D. Sanborn, as a condition of his sale of the property to Dana X. Bible, the head football coach at the University of Nebraska. At the time of the fire, the Estes Park Hotel may have been owned by F. O. Stanley, for the *Longmont Ledger* had reported its purchase in July of the preceding year. See *Longmont Ledger*, July 3, 1910, 8.

Channing F. Sweet, who as a boy of thirteen was staying in a small yellow cottage near the hotel with his mother that summer, recalled the fire vividly. "It was like tinder," Channing wrote in 1967. "Many guests living in the hotel lost all their possessions since, from beginning to end, the fire lasted for only about twenty minutes." Mother and son promptly moved to the Rustic for the remainder of the summer. Channing F. Sweet, *A Princeton Cowboy* (Colorado Springs: Dentan-Berkeland, 1967), p. 45.

34. Earl of Dunraven, letter to the Honorable Bernard Fitzpatrick, Friday, October 4, 1879. Copy in Colorado Collection, Pamphlet File, Estes Park Public Library.

35. The *Fort Collins Courier* noted on July 30, 1885, that "the Earl of Dunraven, who owns the greater portion of Estes Park and who has been absent several years is expected to visit his property this year" (*Fort Collins Courier*, July 30, 1885, 8).

36. Sprague, "Historical Reminiscence," *Estes Park Trail*, May 5, 1922, 3.

37. Earl of Dunraven, *Past Times and Pastimes* (London: Hodder and Stoughton, [1922]), 1:142–43.

CHAPTER 4

1. S. Anna Gordon, *Camping in Colorado* (New York: Authors' Publishing, 1879), pp. 106–7.

2. Isabella L. Bird, *A Lady's Life*, 90–91.

3. Ibid., 92.

4. Ibid., 93.

5. Ibid., 92 n.

6. Ibid., 241.

7. Ibid., 145.

8. Bird, *Letters from Colorado*, 50.

9. *Rocky Mountain News*, July 11, 1871, 1.

10. This is not for lack of trying. Dave Hicks, in an effort to verify Jim's story for the brief history of Estes Park that he published in 1970, searched, without success, parish records in Montreal, the records of the Hudson's Bay Company, the records of the Kansas State Historical Society, and the records of two historical societies in Missouri. (See Hicks, *Estes Park From*

the Beginning, 32–33.) I have attempted to verify, without success, the statement by Abner Sprague that Nugent was born in Concord, New Hampshire. According to the New Hampshire Bureau of Vital Records there is no record of the birth of a James Nugent between 1840 and 1900.

Although one would like to believe that James Nugent was yet another example of the well-educated prodigal son fled to the frontier (Dunraven claimed that Nugent declaimed in Greek and Latin when drunk), I am now inclined to look for a simpler answer to Jim's identity. Closer to home in Colorado, one finds two unclaimed letters advertised in the *Rocky Mountain News* (one for a "J. Nugent," the other for a "James Nugent") on September 11, 1865, and July 24, 1867, respectively. Perhaps more significantly, the 1860 Colorado territorial census lists a James Nugent, age 22, a miner born in New York, as a resident of Gold Hill, a mining camp in Boulder County dating from 1859. The age is approximately right, and the location is right, but whether James Nugent the Gold Hill miner is Rocky Mountain Jim the hunter-trapper of Estes Park we probably will never know. It is possible, of course, that Nugent, like so many of those who escaped to the frontier, simply changed his name in the process of creating a new identity to close out the past.

11. *Colorado Sun,* August 14, 1873, 1.

12. Bird, *A Lady's Life,* 240.

13. Ibid., 241–42.

14. George Henry Kingsley, *Notes on Sport and Travel,With a Memoir by His Daughter Mary H. Kingsley* (London: Macmillan, 1900), p. 175.

15. Quoted in Enos A. Mills, *The Story of Estes Park* (1917 edition), pp. 29–30. In April 1917 Rogers made many of the same comments in a public address. See *The Trail* 9, May 1917, 25–28.

16. Sprague, "Historical Reminiscence," *Estes Park Trail,* May 12, 1922, 3.

17. Abner E. Sprague, "An Early Camping Trip," *Estes Park Trail,* March 10, 1922, 7.

18. *Central City Register,* August 5, 1871, 4. The author of this article is presumably the *Register's* owner and editor, D. C. Collier. It may well be that editor William Byers (mentioned specifically by Jim here) was the author of the *Rocky Mountain News* story of July 11 of Nugent's encounter with the bear. Byers had extensive interests at Hot Sulphur Springs in Middle Park, and the story in question begins with an account of the July 4 celebration at the Springs during which a June 6, 1871, letter from Governor William Bross to Byers was read to the assembled party by Byers himself. Bross, the lieutenant governor of Illinois, who also sent a flag for the occasion, had been in Middle Park with Byers, Schulyer Colfax, and other notables during the summer of 1868.

The substance of this paragraph from the *Register* subsequently found its way into John Tice's *Over the Plains, on the Mountains; or, Kansas, Colorado, and the*

Rocky Mountains (1872), where it is disingenuously described as an "extract" from "a private letter from Central." See John H. Tice, *Over the Plains, on the Mountains; or, Kansas, Colorado, and the Rocky Mountains; Agriculturally, Mineralogically and Aesthetically Described* (St. Louis, MO: Industrial Age, 1872), pp. 214–15.

19. *Rocky Mountain News*, August 5, 1871, 1. The *Caribou Post*, in its issue of August 12, 1871, also took note of Jim's recovery.

20. See Milton Estes, "Memoirs of Estes Park," 121–32.

21. Earl of Dunraven, "A Colorado Sketch," *Nineteenth Century* 8, September 1880, 450.

22. Anna E. Dickinson, *A Ragged Register (of People, Places, and Opinions)* (New York: Harper and Row, 1879), pp. 270–71.

23. *Boulder County News*, August 26, 1873, 3.

24. *Colorado Sun*, October 11, 1873, 4.

25. *Boulder County News*, October 17, 1873, 3.

26. Bird, *Letters from Colorado*, 67.

27. Ibid., 70.

28. Ibid., 45–46.

29. Ibid., 54.

30. Bird, *A Lady's Life*, 296.

31. Bird, *Letters from Colorado*, 73.

32. Bird, *A Lady's Life*, 295–96.

33. Ibid., 295 n.

34. *Boulder County News*, November 14, 1873, 3.

35. *Greeley Tribune*, August 9, 1871, 1.

36. Ibid., December 3, 1873, 1.

37. Ibid., December 31, 1873, 2.

38. Ibid.

39. Ibid., December 9, 1874, 1.

40. Quoted in Mills, *The Story of Estes Park*, 59–60.

41. Bird, *A Lady's Life*, 254.

42. Bird, *Letters from Colorado*, 51.

43. Ibid., 67.

44. Ibid., 43.

45. *Denver Daily Times*, September 1, 1874, 3.

46. Sprague, "Historical Reminiscence," *Estes Park Trail*, May 26, 1922, 3.

47. Bird, *A Lady's Life*, 287 n.

48. Ansel Watrous, "An Early Day Tragedy in Estes Park," *Estes Park Trail*, June 2, 1922, 5.

49. *Fort Collins Standard*, September 2, 1874, 3.

50. *Greeley Tribune*, July 8, 1874, 2. The long-standing grudge between the two men was also cited in *The People* (Pueblo), July 11, 1874, 1, and in the *Colorado Miner* (Georgetown), July 11, 1874, 2. All three papers give credit

for their stories to the Longmont *Inter-Ocean.* The *Tribune*'s immediate source was the *Boulder County News.*

51. *Fort Collins Standard,* September 2, 1874, 3. Florence Barr, who was staying at the Evans ranch, recalled at a distance of more than half a century that while Evans was away, hunting up the Black Canyon, Jim rode up to the house, made his horse stand on its hind legs so that he could look in the window, and "frightened us so, that we barricaded the doors." When Griff Evans returned, Barr recalled, he said that he would "go to Fort Collins and swear out a warrant to make Jim keep peace." Before he could do so, the shooting occurred (*Estes Park Trail,* August 8, 1930, 19).

52. Sprague, "Historical Reminiscence," *Estes Park Trail,* May 26, 1922, 3.

53. Dunraven, *Past Times and Pastimes* (London: Hodder and Stoughton, [1922]), 1:140; Rogers, quoted in Mills, *The Story of Estes Park,* 60–61.

54. Elkanah J. Lamb, *Miscellaneous Meditations* (n.p.: The Publishers' Press Room and Bindery, [1913?]), pp. 130–31.

55. "Rocky Mountain Jim's Story," *Fort Collins Standard,* August 12, 1874, 3.

56. *Pueblo Daily Chieftain,* August 30, 1874, p. 4. See also *Colorado Sun,* August 22, 1874, 3.

57. Kingsley, *Notes on Sport and Travel,* 178. It should be recalled that, to add to this difficulty, Jim's left thumb had been bitten off during his encounter with the bear.

58. *Fort Collins Standard,* August 12, 1874, 3. Other accounts of the shooting are found in the *Fort Collins Standard,* July 8, 1874, 2; the *Central City Register,* July 2, 1874, 3; and the *Colorado Sun,* July 11, 1874, 2.

59. Kingsley, *Notes on Sport and Travel,* 175–76. The Earl of Dunraven, in his autobiography, also recalled the event. "One fine day I was sitting by the fire, and Evans asleep on a sort of sofa," Dunraven later wrote,

> when some one rushed in shouting, "Get up; here's Mountain Jim in the coral [*sic*], and he is looking very ugly." Up jumped Evans, grabbed a shot gun, and went out. A sort of duel eventuated, which ended in Jim getting all shot up with slugs; no casualties on our side. He was not dead, but refused to be carried into Evans' house. We carried him down to the creek, and fixed him up as well as we could, and he made a solemn declaration, as a man who would presently be before his Maker, that he had not begun the scrap, and that it was sheer murder (Dunraven, *Past Times and Pastimes,* 1:140–41).

60. See the *Central City Register,* July 17, 1874, 3; and the *Greeley Tribune,* July 22, 1874, 2, citing the Longmont *Inter-Ocean.*

61. *Boulder County News,* July 3, 1874, 2.

62. *Fort Collins Standard,* September 9, 1874, 1.

63. Ibid., July 22, 1874, 3.

64. Ibid., September 2, 1874, 2.

65. Ibid., September 2, 1874, 3.

66. Ibid., August 12, 1874, 1.

67. Ibid.

68. Ibid., August 12, 1874, 3.

69. Ibid., September 16, 1874, 3.

70. Ibid., August 26, 1874, 3. The *Standard* reprinted the story from the *Denver Tribune*.

71. Ibid., September 2, 1874, 2. See also the *Colorado Sun*, September 5, 1874, 3.

72. *Denver Daily Times*, September 1, 1874, 3.

73. If one wishes to take the measure of Jim's contemporary reputation, one could probably not find a better barometer than Dr. James Stratton Harlow. Harlow (1840–1875), a New Yorker, had come to Fort Collins in February 1874 in an attempt to regain his health (he was tubercular), and by the following summer was handling emergencies for the popular Fort Collins doctor Timothy Smith, whose wife was in the final stages of consumption. One of their patients was James Nugent. Harlow kept a diary of his two years in Colorado in which he recorded his impressions about life in the West. Significantly, the diary is silent on the subject of Rocky Mountain Jim, despite the fact that Harlow attended Nugent during his final days and then, following his death, performed the autopsy. See *Diary of James Stratton Harlow*, copy, Fort Collins Public Library.

74. *Fort Collins Standard*, September 16, 1874, 3.

75. Ibid., September 23, 1874, 3.

76. Hicks, *Estes Park From the Beginning*, 32.

77. *Fort Collins Standard*, August 26, 1874, 3; Watrous, "An Early Day Tragedy in Estes Park," 5.

78. Hicks, *Estes Park From the Beginning*, 32.

79. *Fort Collins Standard*, September 16, 1874, 2.

80. Sprague, "Historical Reminiscence," *Estes Park Trail*, May 12, 1922, 3; and May 26, 1922, 3.

81. Pat Barr, *A Curious Life for a Lady* (London: Macmillan and John Murray, 1970), p. 195.

82. *Fort Collins Express*, May 8, 1886, 1.

83. Ibid.

84. Ibid., May 15, 1886, 1.

85. Edmund Gurney, Frederic W. H. Myers, and Frank Podmore, *Phantasms of the Living* (London: Kegan Paul, Trench, Trubner, 1918), p. 345.

86. Ibid., 346.

87. Quoted in Gurney, Myers, and Podmore, *Phantasms*, 345–46.

88. Ibid., 346.

89. Ibid. Edmund Gurney added in a footnote that "before this diary was recovered, Miss K. wrote to me, 'I distinctly remember that on my going into her room in the morning she told me immediately what she has

related to you.' "
90. Ibid., 347.
91. Ibid.
92. Ibid., 346.
93. Ibid.
94. Ibid.
95. Barr, *A Curious Life*, 98. Anna Stoddart, Isabella Bird's first biographer, had reported the farewell episode at St. Louis and its sequel at Interlaken without comment and without reference to the society's subsequent investigation:

> From Hospenthal an almost immediate move was made to Interlaken, and there one morning as she lay in bed, half unnerved by the shock of his death and half expectant, she saw "Mountain Jim," in his trapper's dress just as she had seen him last, standing in the middle of her room. Then one of her friends came into her room and she told her what had just occurred. When exact news of his death arrived, its date coincided with that of the vision (Anna M. Stoddart, *The Life of Isabella Bird* [London: John Murray, 1908], p. 84).

96. Others, closer to the historic events, have come to similar conclusions about Bird's portrait of Rocky Mountain Jim. For example, in 1900, A. T. Richardson, a resident of Nebraska City, perhaps prompted by the death of Griff Evans, set out to investigate what old-time residents recalled of Jim. In a story titled "Mountain Man," published in the December 6, 1900, issue of the *Lyons Recorder*, Richardson reported his findings:

> The writer who is a sincere admirer of Estes Park and of Miss Bird as well . . . took some pains, in the course of a recent visit to the park, to learn what was remembered of him there; with the result that is in the nature of a disillusion. . . .
> The stories of Jim differ, as may be expected, but they all agree that he was not such a bad man as he persuaded Miss Bird. Ask the natives whether he was not a desperate murderer and you will get a good natured laugh. He might have killed somebody before he came out there, they say, but he never gained any right to that reputation in that neighborhood. There was no harm to be approached from old Jim, by their account, unless his pistol went off by accident when he was drunk and got to swinging it around and blowing, as was his custom. "I've told him to his face he was a thief," says one informant, "when I had no gun and Jim was armed. I didn't consider there was any more risk in telling him what I thought of him than in talking to you now." (*Lyons Recorder*, December 6, 1900, 2)

One of these old-timers was Mrs. E. E. Shumway, the daughter of John Hubbell, whose family rented a house at the foot of Mount Olympus in May 1873. Mrs. Shumway recalled in a conversation with Park Superintendent Roger Toll a half century later that "Mountain Jim was a good neighbor, brought them venison, was a well read man, presumably of a good family" (Roger W. Toll, "Notes of a Conversation with Mrs. E. E. Shumway, September 7, 1928," Colorado Collection, Pamphlet File, Estes Park Public Library).

CHAPTER 5

1. Abner Sprague, "Historical Reminiscence," *Estes Park Trail*, May 5, 1922, 3.
2. *Fort Collins Daily Express*, October 27, 1883, 2. The *Express*'s biographical sketch of MacGregor was written and published at the time he was running for county judge on the Republican ticket.
3. As a lawyer MacGregor certainly knew how land was acquired in Colorado. As a resident of Denver he may well have learned about the impending survey and acted accordingly. If so, this would explain the sense of outrage he expressed when he discovered what Whyte had done, as well as his subsequent attempts to have the original patents nullified.
4. According to the MacGregor's granddaughter Muriel,

> This homestead extended southward to take in the property where the Stanley Hotel is situated now, but for the purpose of keeping the property unified, my great-grandmother in '76 traded Lord Dunraven the southern part of her homestead for a tract of similar size lying along Black Canyon Creek. Later my great-grandmother made use of her homestead right by living on her claim a half-mile west of her daughter's home, midway up the meadow. Later, too, my grandfather exercised his preemption right, and that claim cabin became, in the 80s, one room of a lath and plastered frame house, still standing, which was my grandparents' true ranch home (Muriel MacGregor, "Tales of Pioneer Days on MacGregor's Ranch," *Estes Park Trail*, April 19, 1935, 1).

The original nine-page typescript is in the possession of the MacGregor Trust. Additional information on the MacGregors can be found in Clare Arthur, *The MacGregors and Black Canyon: Three Generations of Tradition* (Estes Park, CO: Rocky Mountain National Park, 1984), and Glenn Prosser, *The Saga of Black Canyon: The Story of the MacGregors of Estes Park* (n.p.: 1971).
5. Much of the land that MacGregor subsequently obtained resulted from the simple expedient of paying the back taxes due on individual parcels of land. Between December of 1883 and March of 1893 Alexander MacGregor purchased fourteen such claims. Only two of the approximately twenty pieces of land that he acquired between February 5, 1878, and his death on June 17, 1896, were acquired from the U.S. government (Arthur, *The MacGregors and Black Canyon*, 4).
6. Incorporation Records, State of Colorado, book E, pp. 433–34. A second, amended charter of incorporation for the Estes Park Wagon Road Company was filed by Alexander MacGregor, Georgianna Heeney, and Henry

C. F. Jensen on March 13, 1875 (Incorporation Records, State of Colorado, book E, pp. 546–49).

Muriel MacGregor described the route taken by her grandfather's road in her 1935 article:

> To learn the course followed by the toll road, reference must be had to newspaper clippings in my grandparents' scrapbook. To summarize, . . . there was no town of Lyons, but the huge red sandstone formation was named Steamboat rock, then as now, and around its base came the roadway. For three miles the road followed the North St. Vrain, but then turned to the right through a narrow, rocky defile and climbed for three miles. From the mountain top thus attained, the Little Thompson was to be seen on the north, flowing through deep canyons, and southward, the sparkling waters of the St. Vrain, as well as the multicolored hogbacks in the east. As the road continued westward along the mountain tops, it reached high summits and then dropped into deep ravines. A pretty valley, Musk Park, was passed through, and then the road climbed to a particularly high point from which the plains and the far away Platte River came into view. The road then descended to the canyon of the Little Thompson near the present site of the Mining [sic] ranch house [in Pinewood Springs]. From that point, the present North St. Vrain highway practically follows the course of the toll road (Muriel MacGregor, "Tales of Pioneer Days," 27).

On March 22, 1879, MacGregor, Clara, and Georgianna Heeney filed articles of incorporation for still another toll road, the Estes Park Toll Road Company, "for the purpose of constructing a toll road to the park to connect with another road from Larimer county [presumably the road that came over Bald Mountain]" (Rocky Mountain News, March 30, 1879, 1; Incorporation Records, State of Colorado, book I, pp. 288–90).

The toll road statute authorized by the legislature was clearly designed to encourage the building of wagon roads for public use by private entrepreneurs like Alexander MacGregor. To protect the public interest the charges were regulated by county commissioners.

7. Arthur, *The MacGregors and Black Canyon*, 3. At their meeting of April 2, 1880, the county commissioners approved a new rate schedule for the Estes Park Toll Road Company. For each wagon or vehicle drawn by one span of horses, mules, or yoke of cattle the charge was fixed at ten cents per mile; each additional span cost two and a half cents more. Individuals riding or packing a horse or mule were to be charged one and a half cents per mile; horses, mules, cattle, or sheep being driven loose were charged one cent (County Commissioners Records, Larimer County, book 2, p. 257). That these new rates fueled at least part of the subsequent controversy over the MacGregor toll road can be inferred.

8. According to Abner Sprague, in the fall of 1875 Rowe killed in a single day three bears that he found feeding on grasshoppers at the foot of the

glacier (Abner Sprague, "Reminiscences of a Pioneer," typescript, Abner Sprague Collection, Colorado Historical Society, pp. 54–55).

9. Rowe sold this 160-acre property to Theodore Whyte for five hundred dollars on May 5, 1876. His homestead claim on 160 acres below Mount Olympus was filed on April 16, 1877.

10. After the Rowes moved to Longmont in 1882 so that their two children, by then ages nine and twelve, could be better schooled, Israel Rowe continued in the role of hunter and guide. During the summer of 1883 he also ran a freight wagon between Longmont and the park. On a hunting trip into Wyoming in the fall of 1884—a trip undertaken following a three-week siege of pneumonia in September—Rowe recontracted the disease, dying in November at a ranch several miles from his camp at Shirley Basin, south of Casper.

Rowe's expertise as a guide was in much demand during the late 1870s and, like his fellow hunter Hank Farrar, his fame reached as far as England. A British sportsman, writing a column entitled "Shooting in the Rocky Mountains" for the April 7, 1877, edition of *The Field* under the name "Jungli Oonth," describes a hunt of late August 1876 led by Rowe that lasted for more than two weeks. The invitation had come from Theodore Whyte, who made the arrangements. They were a party of three, and on the morning of the thirtieth they left the Estes Park Hotel (which had not yet formally opened for business) on horseback, taking with them a hound named "Queen." Their route led "up the Black Canon" where they encountered "tents pitched here and there with pleasure seekers from the plains on a holiday, and a wooden shanty or two." Camping at Lawn Lake ("a lovely little lake among the pine trees, in a valley of about 10,000 elevation"), where Rowe "made excellent bread," the party then made its way across the Divide in the direction of North Park. Thanks to Rowe, the two Englishman soon encountered enough mountain sheep, bear, deer, and wapiti to make any hunter envious, returning with the heads of several "stags" to serve as mementos of their visit (*The Field*, April 7, 1877, 392; and April 14, 1877, 422).

11. *Boulder County News*, reprinted in the *Greeley Tribune*, July 12, 1876, 1.

12. MacGregor, "Tales of Pioneer Days," 28.

13. Quoted in MacGregor, "Tales of Pioneer Days," 28. Muriel MacGregor's historical sketch of her grandparents (see chap. 5, note 4) was based in part on two diaries kept by Alexander and Clara MacGregor, covering the years 1875, 1876, and 1877, as well as scrapbooks into which they pasted newspaper clippings. The first diary covers the period of January 2 to October 4, 1875; the second, October 15, 1876, to May 2, 1877. The missing year hints at the existence of a third diary. Both extant diaries are the property of the MacGregor Trust. According to Abner Sprague, the post office had become "a bone of contention" between "the English

interests" and those who "wished the office to remain at MacGregor's" (Abner Sprague, "Alexander Q. MacGregor," *Estes Park Trail*, April 20, 1923, 3).

14. The McClintock cabin, located to the east of the ranch buildings, was first occupied during the summer of 1877 (*Fort Collins Courier*, June 30, 1881, 1. The Yale-educated McClintock (1845–1910), who prospered in Denver real estate, came to the park in 1875, seeking relief from asthma.

15. *Rocky Mountain News*, February 17, 1881, 4.

16. Carrie Adell Strahorn, *Fifteen Thousand Miles by Stage* (Lincoln: University of Nebraska Press, 1988), 1:66. Robert Strahorn, who advertised himself as the "Alter Ego" "of the western press," also took note of "the McGregor [sic] house, an excellent mountain hostelry," in his 1878 travel narrative, *To the Rockies and Beyond*. See Robert E. Strahorn, *To the Rockies and Beyond; or, A Summer on the Union Pacific Railway and Branches* (Omaha, NE: Omaha Republican Print, 1878), pp. 43–44.

17. *Boulder County News*, August 10, 1877, 1.

18. *Boulder County News*, reprinted in the *Greeley Tribune*, July 12, 1876, 1.

19. Ferguson, "Mr. Ferguson's Story." (As told to Mary E. Stickney, Unpublished typescript, Colorado Collection, Pamphlet Files, Estes Park Library.)

20. "Hank Farrar passed through Valmont, last week," the *Boulder County News* noted in December 1871, "loaded with 10 deers and 2 Mountain sheep, for Denver. The Farrar boys [Hank and his two brothers, Clint and Ike] have killed, thus far this season, forty deer and three sheep, on the Thompson" (*Boulder County News*, December 8, 1871, 3). A decade later the trio was still at it: "The three Farrar brothers, Clint, Ike, and Henry," the *Larimer County Express* of Fort Collins reported on December 1, 1881, "brought to town 20 elk which they killed in eight days, in the neighborhood of Gray Rock, on the Lone Pine. Henry Farrar has just returned from a hunting expedition in North Park, where he killed eight elk and fifty antelope. He brought out a pair of elk horns having eight prongs on one side and seven on the other. He sold them to J. H. Fletcher" (*Larimer County Express*, December 1, 1881, 4).

21. Sallie Ferguson Reed, "Reminiscences of an Early Estes Park Pioneer," *Estes Park Trail*, April 26, 1946, 60.

22. Ibid.

23. *Boulder County News*, May 4, 1877, 2.

24. Chapin, *Mountaineering in Colorado*, 18.

25. John Monnett, "Lewis B. France, Pioneer Outdoor Writer of Colorado," *Colorado Heritage* (summer 1993), 17. France also authored *Mountain Trails and Parks in Colorado* (1886), *Mr. Dide, His Vacation* (1890), *Over the Old Trail* (1894), *Pine Valley* (1897), and *Scraps* (1899) and was a regular contributor to outdoor magazines, including the Denver-based magazine *Western World*, for which he wrote a regular column titled "Scraps" under the pen name

"Bourgeois."

26. "Bourgeois" [Lewis B. France], "The Lure," in *Fishing With the Fly; Sketches by Lovers of the Art, With Illustrations of Standard Flies*, ed. Charles F. Orvis and A. Nelson Cheney (Manchester, VT: C. F. Orvis, 1883), p. 134. Orvis was the founder of the famous fly-fishing company; Cheney, the angling editor of *Shooting and Fishing*.

27. Ibid., 141.

28. "Bourgeois" [Lewis B. France], *With Rod and Line in Colorado Waters* (Denver, CO: Chain, Hardy, 1884), p. 151.

29. Eleanor E. Hondius, *Memoirs of Eleanor E. Hondius of Elkhorn Lodge* (Boulder, CO: Pruett, 1964), p. 6.

30. Betty D. Freudenburg, "Facing the Frontier: From Black Earth to Black Canyon," in *The Annals of Estes Park, A Colorado Reader*, ed. James H. Pickering, unpublished manuscript (Houston, TX, and Estes Park, CO, 1996), p. 29.

31. Hondius, *Memoirs of Eleanor E. Hondius*, 7.

32. "Historical Memorandum for the Files. Rel: Mrs. Chapman" (Notes of a visit to the Charles Chapman home in Moraine Park, December 22, 1931), Merrill J. Mattes Collection, Colorado Historical Society.

33. Strahorn, *Fifteen Thousand Miles by Stage*, 68.

34. *Fort Collins Courier*, July 23, 1886, 4.

35. *Longmont Ledger*, September 4, 1891, 2.

36. Abner Sprague, "Roads and Trails," *Estes Park Trail*, January 5, 1923, 5. See also Abner Sprague, "My First Trip as a Guide," *Estes Park Trail*, April 6, 1923, 3; and April 13, 1923, 3.

37. Elkanah J. Lamb, *Memories of the Past and Thoughts of the Future* (n.p.: United Brethren, 1906), pp. 124–25.

38. See Carlyle Lamb, "Original Settlement at Long's Peak Inn," *Trail and Timberline* 80, May 1925, 2. The road, as constructed, was as narrow in places as it was steep, making it necessary for some or all of the passengers to alight before reaching the top in order to relieve the horses. Lamb's road, with all its faults, would serve as the principal means of access to the Tahosa Valley until 1906, when a new road ascending the east slope of Lily Mountain was begun.

39. Incorporation Records, State of Colorado, book A, pp. 372–74. According to the articles of incorporation, the toll road was to run "up the valley of Lilly Creek to Lilly Lake; thence south by the most practicable route to the Ranch known as Lambs Ranch; thence south by the most practicable route to the North St. Vrains Creek; with a branch from Lambs Ranch by the most practicable route towards the top of Longs Peak, to or above timber line on said mountain; together with toll-gates as may be necessary."

40. Sprague, "Roads and Trails," *Estes Park Trail*, December 15, 1922, 3.

41. Lamb, *Memories of the Past*, 166.

42. *Longmont Ledger*, July 21, 1882, 2.
43. Lamb, "Original Settlement," 2.
44. Ibid., 2.
45. Abner Sprague in his historical reminiscences provides the fullest first-hand account of Whyte's treatment of would-be settlers. See "Historical Reminiscence," *Estes Park Trail*, May 5, 1922, 3; May 12, 1922, 3; May 19, 1922, 3; May 26, 1922, 3; June 2, 1922, 3; June 9, 1922, 3; and June 16, 1922, 3.
46. Ferguson, "Mr. Ferguson's Story," 6.
47. That Hupp and Ferguson were friends as well as business associates is indicated by the fact that John and Eliza Hupp named their eighth child, the son born at Otterville in January 1867, William Horace. No doubt it was from Horace Ferguson that the Hupps subsequently learned of the opportunities of Colorado and Estes Park.
48. James J. Daly had sold his 160 acres to Whyte on June 27, 1874, for twelve hundred dollars.
49. Sprague, "Historical Reminiscence," *Estes Park Trail*, June 2, 1922, 3.
50. Ibid.
51. Kellogg sold his 160 acres to Whyte on July 10, 1874, for twelve hundred dollars. This was Farrar's second cabin; the first, close to Alexander MacGregor's homestead cabin in the Black Canyon, was constructed in February 1875.
52. We know very little about George Bode, for his stay in Estes Park was brief. Before moving up to the park, he apparently had a small ranching operation in a small valley in the wooded foothills of the Little Thompson. One member of a party of Greeleyites, including five women, on their way to Estes Park to climb Longs Peak in August 1874, recalled making camp the second night out "in a beautiful meadow or park, where a German by the name of Bode has built a log cabin, and keeps a number of cows" (*Greeley Tribune*, September 16, 1874, 2).
53. County Commissioners Records, Larimer County, book 2, pp. 23–24. Sprague reported to the commissioners at their meeting of April 1, 1876, "that he had notified all the land owners along the line" of the proposed roads. Those landowners of course included Theodore Whyte as surrogate for Dunraven. The commissioners tabled the three petitions until their next regular meeting. Though two meetings later, on June 1, the matter was again "laid over," no action was taken in July for Whyte had already capitulated.
54. The practice of allowing the English Company's cattle to roam the park at will (or to drive them into pasturage adjacent to, or even on, the unfenced lands of homesteaders like Abner Sprague) proved to be something more than just an annoyance, for company cattle inevitably became intermingled with those belonging to others. Such a situation could not,

of course, be tolerated for long. In the fall of 1877, when William Miller, Abner Sprague, Horace Ferguson, and four others found their cattle branded with the distinctive cross and bar of the Estes Park Company, they took their complaints directly to Larimer County officials. That October a county grand jury delivered up a nine-count indictment against Griff Evans and Theodore Whyte, one of which found that Dunraven's surrogates "did feloniously brand and mark or cause to be branded and marked with a certain brand, not the brand of the owner, two cows . . . and two calves . . . the property of one William Miller, farmer . . . with the intent . . . to steal the cattle."

The indictment itself apparently proved sufficient, for there is no record in the court files of Larimer County (or in newspapers of the day) that either trial or verdict was forthcoming. See Hicks, *Estes Park From the Beginning*, 40.

55. Sprague, "Historical Reminiscence," *Estes Park Trail*, June 16, 1922, 3.

56. *Boulder County News*, June 17, 1876, 2.

57. Sprague, "Historical Reminiscence," *Estes Park Trail*, May 5, 1922, 3.

CHAPTER 6

1. *Estes Park Trail*, April 22, 1938, 28.

2. See, for example, *Fort Collins Courier*, March 1881, 5.

3. *Fort Collins Courier*, August 14, 1879, 3.

4. Quoted in G. Edward White, *The Eastern Establishment and the Western Experience: The West of Frederic Remington, Theodore Roosevelt, and Owen Wister* (New Haven, CT: Yale University Press, 1968), p. 48.

5. See Edwin S. Solly, *The Health Resorts of Colorado Springs and Manitou* (Colorado Springs, CO: Gazette, 1883). For a broader discussion see Billy M. Jones, *Health-Seekers in the Southwest, 1817–1900* (Norman: University of Oklahoma Press, 1967), particularly pages 88–149 on climatology and consumption.

6. *Harper's New Monthly Magazine* 60, March 1880, 544. For a history of the evolution of Colorado Springs and its sister resort Manitou Springs see Marshall Sprague, *Newport in the Rockies: The Life and Good Times of Colorado Springs* (Denver, CO: Sage, 1961); Jane Furey, "Tourism in the Pikes Peak Area, 1870–1880" (master's thesis, University of Colorado, 1958); and Bettie Marie Daniels and Virginia McConnell, *The Springs of Manitou* (Denver, CO: Sage, 1964).

7. Pidgeon, *Engineer's Holiday*, 140.

8. Francis M. Wolcott, *Heritage of Years: Kaleidoscopic Memories* (New York: Milton, Balch, 1932), p. 132.

9. Quoted in Daniels and McConnell, *Springs of Manitou*, 19.

10. Hattie Carruthers, "Overland to Estes, 1874–1914," *Estes Park Trail*, July 4, 1914, 5.

11. *Greeley Tribune*, October 13, 1875, 2. The petition for the road submitted

to the county commissioners by A. K. and E. B. Yount, W. C. Stover, and twenty-two others had requested an appropriation of three hundred dollars. County Commissioners Records, Larimer County, book 2, p. 4.

12. *Fort Collins Express*, August 24, 1895, 1.

13. Ibid., July 29, 1893, 1.

14. Ibid., August 24, 1895, 1.

15. Ibid., July 29, 1893, 1.

16. Sprague, "Roads and Trails," *Estes Park Trail*, December 15, 1922, 3. The journey remained a long and tiring one. When Clara MacGregor returned to Fort Collins from the park in June of 1883, where she had taken her sons and mother to spend the summer, the fifty-mile trip took a full twelve hours (including an hour and a half for lunch) (*Fort Collins Express*, June 25, 1883, 4).

17. *Longmont Ledger*, July 21, 1882, 3.

18. Peter J. Pauly Jr., "Undated letter to Abner E. Sprague," typescript copy, Colorado Collection, Pamphlet File, Estes Park Public Library.

19. *Fort Collins Daily Express*, January 22, 1883, 1. See also *Daily Express*, January 23, 1883, 4. The *Fort Collins Courier* took particular pleasure in the outcome, reporting on March 8, 1883, that it deserved "full credit of having influenced the cessation of toll collection," referring to its article of three weeks earlier, which carried the headline "The Rist Canon Road: The Calcium Light of Truth Exposes the Rottenness of the Toll Road Scheme" (*Fort Collins Courier*, February 15, 1883, 1; and March 8, 1883, 4).

20. *Fort Collins Courier*, July 3, 1884, 5.

21. Incorporation Records, State of Colorado, book 10, pp. 325–26.

22. Sprague, "Roads and Trails," *Estes Park Trail*, December 8, 1922, 3.

23. *Denver Times*, June 13, 1899, 3.

24. Ibid., April 27, 1900, 3; *Longmont Ledger*, April 27, 1900, 3.

25. Ibid., June 20, 1900, 3.

26. *Lyons Recorder*, July 5, 1900, 3.

27. *Loveland Register*, July 4, 1900, 1.

28. Ibid., September 16, 1900, 2; *Fort Collins Weekly Courier*, August 16, 1900, 6.

29. *Lyons Recorder*, September 6, 1900, 2.

30. Ibid., December 13, 1900, 3. See also the *Loveland Register*, December 12, 1900, 1.

31. Sprague, "Roads and Trails," *Estes Park Trail*, December 15, 1922, 3.

32. *Fort Collins Courier*, September 24, 1885, 5.

33. *Loveland Register*, May 1, 1900, 1.

34. "Nearly every day there are inquiries by visitors here as to how they can reach Estes Park," the *Loveland Register* noted on July 4, 1900. "There was a regular stage last summer, but so far this year none has been started, although we understand that a prominent business man here offers to

contribute $10 a month to whoever will run a stage during the season." By mid-September, however, the *Register* was confidently predicting "a first class stage line" for the 1901 season (*Loveland Register*, July 4, 1900, p. 1; and September 19, 1900, 5).

35. Ibid., May 17, 1905, 5.

36. *Lyons Recorder*, August 29, 1901, 1.

37. Incorporation Records, State of Colorado, book 10, pp. 325–26.

38. *Fort Collins Courier*, April 15, 1880, 3.

39. *Fort Collins Express*, August 5, 1893, 5. See chapter 9, note 13, for additional information on the People's Toll Road.

40. *Fort Collins Weekly Courier*, January 13, 1904, 1; Sprague, "Roads and Trails," *Estes Park Trail*, December 29, 1922, 5. Abner Sprague himself was one of the incorporators.

41. *Lyons Recorder*, July 21, 1900, 2.

42. Abner Sprague, "Early Day Transportation in the Estes Park Region," *Estes Park Trail*, February 10, 1928, p. 3.

43. *Longmont Home Mirror*, no. 8, August 1881, 6.

44. *Longmont Ledger*, July 21, 1882, 2; and April 17, 1885, 3.

45. *Rocky Mountain News*, August 27, 1882, 7.

46. *Longmont Ledger*, July 26, 1895, 3.

47. *Rocky Mountain News*, August 27, 1882, 7.

48. Ibid.

49. *Fort Collins Weekly Courier*, February 18, 1903, 6.

50. *Fort Collins Courier*, June 30, 1881, 1. William L. Hallett (1851–1941), a graduate of MIT, first visited Colorado and Estes Park in 1878 when he and his mother stayed briefly at Dunraven's one-year-old Estes Park Hotel. That winter Hallett married Vena Sessions of New York City and the following summer introduced her to the Estes Park region by taking her on a thirty-day camping trip to Grand Lake and Hot Sulphur Springs, guided by Abner Sprague. The trio, to the surprise of everyone, managed to survive nicely in a ten-by-ten-foot tent, divided down the middle. That same summer Hallett also made the acquaintance of Horace Ferguson. The two men hit it off; so much so that three years later, in 1881, Hallett erected a summer cottage, Edgemont, on three acres of land that Ferguson provided just east of the Highlands, where he and his family took many of their meals. The two men subsequently became joint owners of a stock ranch located about four miles northwest of Berthoud. On February 27, 1886, and March 5, 1886, Hallett and Ferguson purchased from Lyman A. White and William Walsh two quarter sections of land along Wind River that comprise part of what is now the YMCA of the Rockies, which they presumably used for ranching.

The Hallett cottage received its christening on the evening of August 7, 1881, when his friends gathered at Edgemont to celebrate his birthday.

For the occasion the porch was "hung round with Chinese lanterns," forming "for many an apartment more attractive than the interior." The evening featured "social talk," games and music, ventriloquism by the Reverend Mr. Spinner of Cleveland, and singing by Hallett's subsequent Wyoming ranching partner, James Marston, and his wife. After ice cream and cake, the company dispersed at "a reasonable hour" (*Longmont Ledger*, August 12, 1881, 4).

To further honor his friend and neighbor and commemorate the occasion, Horace Ferguson had printed a special "Highland Edition" of the *Longmont Ledger*, dated September 14, 1881. Included among the lengthy description of the evening's events was an ode composed and read by Mr. Buckman, which ended:

> In songs we'll raise our voices high
> And gaily sing this happy night,
> With joy perform our simple rite
> And "Edgemont" christen thee for aye.

"As the plaudits died away," the account continued, "Mrs. Hallett advanced to the entrance, bearing a silver chalice, and with its contents sprinkled the threshold, while repeating the following: 'In the presence of these assembled friends, I christen thee, Edgemont.' " Returning to center stage, Mr. Buckman then announced an encore event. There was to be " 'yet another christening to-night. . . . The place which for so long we have known and loved as "Ferguson's," is to have a new name. . . .' The address ended, all assembled on the ranch house porch and Miss Sallie Ferguson stepping forward, proceeded with becoming ceremony to bestow the appropriate name 'Highlands.' " Following the ice cream and cake reported above, "all assembled once more upon the lawn where a grand display of fireworks, provided by Mr. Hallett for the occasion, ended the evening's festivities" (*Longmont Ledger*, September 14, 1881, Extra Farewell Echo Highland Edition).

During the years that followed William Hallett left his mark on both the history as well as the topography of Estes Park. Though Hallett is most often remembered for the peak above Bear Lake that bears his name, as well as for his prowess as Frederick Chapin's guide, Hallett was also extensively involved in the cattle business. Hallett is best known as a cattleman, however, for his role in the Powder River Live Stock Company, which operated on five thousand acres in the Powder River country in Johnson County, Wyoming, near old Forts Reno and McKinney, and later on twenty-five hundred acres purchased in Nebraska's Elkhorn valley. The Powder River Company was incorporated on March 4, 1882, with three thousand head of cattle and paid-up capital of $140,000. James L. Marston of Colorado Springs served as president and William Hallett as vice-president.

By the spring of 1886, the company had increased its capitalization to $700,000 and was running upward of twenty-four thousand head of cattle, only to suffer a dramatic setback the following winter, among the worst ever recorded on the northern plains, which dispersed or killed fully two-thirds of its herd. Despite these losses, the company carried on for some years, finally closing its books in 1893. See Agnes Wright Spring, "Powder River Live Stock Company," *Colorado Magazine* 28, January 1951, 32–36; *Fort Collins Courier*, December 18, 1884, 1.

51. *Rocky Mountain News*, August 27, 1882, 7.

52. *Fort Collins Courier*, June 16, 1881, 2.

53. White remembered that summer vividly and years later devoted a chapter of his celebrated autobiography to his experiences in Moraine Park. "If I ever grew up and became a man," he wrote, "it was in the summer of 1889, in Colorado, in a little log cabin filled with a dozen boys on the Big Thompson River" (William Allen White, *The Autobiography of William Allen White* [New York: Macmillan, 1946], p. 175). White would return to Estes Park on his honeymoon in June 1893. In 1912 he bought an eighteen-by-twenty-four-foot cabin on the slope of Eagle Cliff Mountain overlooking Moraine Park, which would serve as his summer home for many years. See also Charles J. Bayard, "A Kansan's Vacation in Colorado: William Allen White in the Rockies," *Essays and Monographs in Colorado History*, no. 1, 1983, 39–52.

54. *Rocky Mountain News*, August 23, 1881, 2.

55. *Fort Collins Courier*, August 19, 1880, 2.

56. This quotation and those that follow are from a series of typescript letters from Sallie Ferguson Reed to her husband, included in Edward B. Reed, "Moraine Park Boyhood" (Fort Collins, CO, 1996), unpublished manuscript, Colorado Collection, Estes Park Public Library.

57. Carl Abbott, Stephen J. Leonard, and David McComb, *Colorado: A History of the Centennial State*, rev. ed. (Boulder: Colorado Associated University Press, 1982), p. 222.

58. *Longmont Ledger*, August 5, 1892, 3.

59. Ibid., July 28, 1893, 2. By 1880 such cautionary notes—a badly needed antidote to the early literature, which had pronounced Colorado's effect on diseases of all kinds to be little short of miraculous—were being widely circulated. In March 1880, in an article titled "Vacation Aspects of Colorado," *Harper's* warned its readers not to "delude themselves in expecting to discover paradise": invalids "should . . . on no possible account (and this caution is disregarded every day) think of coming until they have sent to some respectable, responsible, and experienced physician, resident in Colorado, not their own crude ideas of their condition, but a diagnosis prepared by a doctor who knows them well" (*Harper's New Monthly Magazine* 60, March 1880, 545).

60. Pidgeon, *Engineer's Holiday*, 114.

61. Ruedi (b. 1848), who is listed in the *Colorado Business Directory* under Estes Park for the years 1894 to 1897, was a celebrated English physician. He had come to Denver in the early 1890s from Davos, in southeastern Switzerland, where he operated a sanitarium for those with consumption and other respiratory problems. Among his patients was the Scottish writer Robert Louis Stevenson. Ruedi subsequently wrote a paper comparing the effects of the climates of Davos and Estes Park upon consumption. See Carl Ruedi, "A Comparison of the Winter Health-Resorts in the Alps with Some Places in the Rocky Mountains of Colorado," *Transactions of the American Climatological Association* 10, 893–1894, 28–42. Given its climate, Ruedi hoped that "in time we shall be able to found a sanatorium and have as good accommodations in Estes Park as the best health-resorts in Europe."

62. *Fort Collins Courier*, October 9, 1884, 4.

63. Ibid., April 8, 1886, 1. During the years in Fort Collins and Denver, MacGregor leased the ranching and farming operations to J. J. McCabe for a five-year period beginning in 1882. McCabe lived in the original ranch house, while the MacGregors, when in residence, occupied the "second house," or "A. Q. House," built that year.

64. *Fort Collins Daily Express*, February 22, 1884, 1.

While living in Fort Collins Clara had continued her painting and her work soon attracted a measure of local attention. "Mrs. A. Q. MaGregor [sic], wife of our county judge," the *Fort Collins Daily Evening Courier* reported on December 16, 1882, "is an excellent floral artist with the brush, and specimens of her work for holiday purposes have been placed on sale at the [drug and stationery] store of L. W. Welch." Two years later, in June 1884, a collection of Clara's oil paintings were included in the Fort Collins Woman's Christian Temperance Union's Art Loan Exhibition: "Among the display were noted: *Boulder Valley, Long's Peak, Above Estes Park, Grand Lake, Fort Collins in 1865*—all of which were true to life and handsomely executed." A number of Clara's paintings survive at the MacGregor Ranch (*Fort Collins Daily Evening Courier*, December 16, 1882, 4; and June 5, 1884, 8; *Fort Collins Daily Express*, February 22, 1884, 1).

65. Gordon, *Camping in Colorado*, 142–43.

66. *Rocky Mountain News*, August 27, 1882, 7.

67. See, for example, Charles Denison's *Rocky Mountain Health Resorts* (Boston: Houghton, Osgood, 1880), which contains in its chapter on "Camping Out" a table estimating on an item-by-item basis "one month's provisions for one person" (including summer 1879 prices furnished by "Saloman Bros. and Wolfe Londoner, grocers, Denver").

68. "Our fellow townsman, M. H. Sammis," the *Longmont Ledger* noted in August 1881, "seems to be doing a thriving business at his stand near the [Dunraven] ranch" (*Longmont Ledger*, August 12, 1881, 4). Sammis was "one

of Longmont's enterprising grocerymen."

69. Ibid., March 30, 1888, 2.

70. P. J. Pauly, undated letter to Abner Sprague, Colorado Collection, Pamphlet File, Estes Park Public Library. See also William Hyde and Howard L. Conard, eds., *Encyclopedia of St. Louis*, vol. 3 (New York: Southern History Company, 1899), pp. 1709–11; and P. J. Pauly, undated letter to Abner Sprague, *Estes Park Trail*, April 17, 1936, pp. 24–25.

71. *Fort Collins Courier*, June 18, 1885, 4. Like many cattleman of the era, Pauly had little or nó previous experience and had to learn by doing. In the fall of 1884 he attended the National Cattle Growers' Convention in St. Louis "to learn all he can of the stock business for his and his neighbor's good" (ibid., October 23, 1884, 8).

72. Ibid., August 29, 1886, 3.

73. Pauly retained some of his Estes Park property into the twentieth century and in 1909 donated two small ponds toward the enlargement of the town's fish hatchery.

74. According to his daughter, James came to Estes Park with very little money and got his start in the cattle business through a dying friend, "who left a little legacy with which Mr. James bought his first herd of cattle" (Eleanor E. Hondius, "William E. James," *Estes Park Trail*, July 13, 1912, 5). Ewart was evidently in Estes Park the preceding summer, for on August 10, 1878, he and George Petit requested a survey of some 4,100 acres in Horseshoe Park and Beaver Meadows. In April of 1879 Ewart requested an additional survey of 480 acres further to the west at the mouth of Endovalley.

75. *Fort Collins Courier*, July 3, 1884, 5. "The Herefords rule here in Estes Park," the *Courier* noted. "There are some as fine thoroughbred cows and heifers as can be found in Colorado." Later the same month the *Longmont Ledger* noted that "Mr. S. B. Hart has taken his fine Hereford cattle to New Mexico, where there is a demand for them" (*Longmont Ledger*, July 18, 1884, 3).

76. Ibid., March 26, 1885, 5. Their taxes of $200.25 were almost twice Alexander MacGregor's $109.40. Near the top of the list was Theodore Whyte and the Estes Park Company at $524.40.

77. This 1885 number may well represent a scaled-down operation, for the *Fort Collins Courier* had reported the previous year, on July 3, 1884, that "Messrs. Farrar & Cook leave Tuesday with their cattle for a new range on Brush creek. They take with them over 100 head of graded cattle, including two fine year old Hereford bulls. These gentlemen have sold a part of their range here to P. J. Pauly, Jr." (*Fort Collins Courier*, July 3, 1884, 5).

78. *Fort Collins Courier*, March 26, 1885, p. 5.

79. *The American Hereford Record and Hereford Herd Book*, vol. 5 (Beecher, IL: Breeders Journal Steam Print, 1886), pp. 3, 73, 252–53, 514, 529–33.

80. *Loveland Register*, April 19, 1899, 4.

81. Horace Ferguson, letter to Charles L. Reed, December 1, 1898, type-script copy, in Edward B. Reed, "Moraine Park Boyhood." Other old-timers agreed. Elkanah Lamb and Abner Sprague reported in early February that "this is by far the worst winter they have ever known up here" (*Longmont Ledger*, February 10, 1899, 2).

82. Ferguson to Reed, March 21, 1899. In a column dated the same day a correspondent for the *Longmont Ledger* noted that "Mr. Ferguson of Estes Park is still losing cattle. His loss will be very heavy if the weather doesn't get decidedly warmer soon." In the same issue John Cleave reported "73 inches as the snow fall for this winter, up to date for Estes Park" (*Longmont Ledger*, March 24, 1899, 2).

83. Ferguson to Reed, March 30, 1899.

84. Ferguson to Reed, April 1, 1899.

85. *Longmont Ledger*, May 5, 1899, 2; and April 21, 1899, 2.

86. *Longmont Home Mirror*, no. 8, August 1881, 6.

87. *Larimer County Express*, June 18, 1880, 2.

88. *Fort Collins Courier*, November 4, 1886, 8. Ely had married Nancy Maria "Nanna" Hupp (1864–1944), the youngest daughter of John and Eliza Hupp, the original homesteaders of Beaver Meadows, on November 1, 1882.

89. *Longmont Ledger*, September 7, 1883, 2.

90. Colorado State Census, *Schedule 2—Productions of Agriculture in the County of Larimer, State of Colorado, on the First Day of June, 1885*, pp. 19–20.

91. *Fort Collins Weekly Courier*, October 7, 1903, 6. That same summer Ferguson experimented by putting in an acre of broom grass (ibid., June 3, 1908, 8).

92. Sprague, "Historical Reminiscence," *Estes Park Trail*, May 12, 1922, 3.

93. *Fort Collins Courier*, October 28, 1886, 6. As time permitted, Whyte, like the other resort owners in the valley, "was indefatigable for the amuse-ments of his guests." Daniel Pidgeon noted of his visit in July 1880 that

> yesterday he drove a party of us round the park in his four-in-hand, and the journey was interesting as much from the superb driving over roadless hill-sides as from the wild beauty of the scenery. To-day he gave a picnic in Clear Creek, when the toilettes were as pretty and the lunch as good as if we had been under the trees of Cliefden Woods. To-morrow, a fishing party starts for the Big Thompson, where if any fishermen are as lucky as ourselves, they may take, as we did, a hundred and twenty trout in a short afternoon. In the evenings the saloon was full and the piano never idle, while flirtation flour-ished on verandah [*sic*], as rapid and rank of growth as on the stairs of a London House in the season (Pidgeon, *Engineer's Holiday*, 115).

94. According to a letter written in 1950 by the Whytes' daughter, Madeline,

Lady Maude returned first, taking the children to Scotland while her husband stayed on "to see if the tide would turn." Leaving Estes Park, Madeline wrote in March 1950, "broke my father's heart" (Madeline Whyte, letter to June Elizabeth Carothers, March 18, 1950, in June Elizabeth Carothers, "The Early History of Estes Park" [master's thesis, University of Denver, 1950], 165).

CHAPTER 7

1. Chapin, *Mountaineering in Colorado*, 30. "Very few people that come into Estes Park, and even those who ascend Longs Peak," Lamb told the editor of the *Loveland Register* in August 1892, "have any idea of the wildness of the scenery that lies immediately west of the peak, high up under the Continental Divide. In fact, I did not know of it myself until a few years ago" (*Loveland Register*, March 25, 1892, 8).
2. Though President Andrew Johnson, in a congressional bill signed on June 11, 1868, had authorized the secretary of war to furnish supplies for Powell's expedition, Powell had persuaded his own university and the Board of the Illinois Natural History Society in Bloomington to furnish "small sums of money" (the latter gave $750). To this the Smithsonian Institution contributed some instruments and the board of education of the state of Illinois gave $400. All personal expenses, however, were borne by the participants.
3. Stegner, *Beyond the Hundredth Meridian*, 374.
4. The previous summer Powell had come to Colorado at the head of an expedition of eleven during which time he climbed Pikes Peak and Mount Lincoln, visited Middle and South Parks, assembled a sizable collection of specimens to take back to Illinois, and first made the acquaintance of William Byers, who, in turn, introduced him to Jack Sumner. The Major had heard about Sumner from the eastern writer Bayard Taylor, who had employed him as a guide during his tour of Colorado in 1866. The decision to attempt to climb Longs Peak originated either before Powell left Colorado or over the intervening winter.
5. The exploration of the Colorado River was Powell's goal from the beginning. It was, however, "the part about which he had apparently said least when lining up his backing among the universities and museums. Collecting was never a major aim, but an excuse" (Stegner, *Beyond the Hundredth Meridian*, 32).
6. "The Exploring Expedition," *Chicago Tribune*, August 2, 1868, 2. The *Tribune*'s correspondent, who signed himself "Historicus," was the Reverend W. H. Daniels of the Congregational Church in Bloomington.
7. Stegner, *Beyond the Hundredth Meridian*, 26. Jack Sumner (1804–1907), who had closed his trading post to join the Powell expedition, complained as well about the lack of activity. He found his new eastern colleagues "about

as fit for roughing it as Hades is for a Powder House."

8. "Powell's Exploring Expedition," *Chicago Tribune*, August 22, 1868, 2.

9. Quoted in "Story of the First Ascent of Longs Peak," *Estes Park Trail*, January 26, 1923, 7.

10. William N. Byers, "The Powell Expedition," *Rocky Mountain News*, September 1, 1868, 1.

11. Ibid.

12. Lewis Walter Keplinger, "The First Ascent of Long's Peak," *Collections of Kansas State Historical Society* 14, 1918, 343.

13. Ned E. Farrell, "The Powell Expedition: The Ascent of Long [sic] Peak," *Chicago Tribune*, September 10, 1868, 2. Lewis Keplinger remembered that evening as well:

> That night we camped under a shelving slab or rock leaning to the south. It was quite cold. We spread our blankets under the incline and kept fires burning in front. There was not room for the entire party under the rock. When those on the outside got tired of being out in the cold they replenished the fires so as to make it too hot for those under the rock. In this way there was more or less alternating between those within and those without during the night (Keplinger, "First Ascent of Long's Peak," 344–45).

14. Farrell, "Powell Expedition." Farrell made the most of his Colorado experiences, publishing that same year a brief seventy-two-page guidebook to the state, constructed of materials that, he freely admitted, "I have borrowed largely from others." See Ned E. Farrell, *Colorado: The Rocky Mountain Gem, As It Is in 1868, a Gazetteer and Handbook* (Chicago: Western News, 1868).

15. Ibid. Sumner was six feet tall and of slender build.

16. Byers, "Powell Expedition."

17. Keplinger, "First Ascent of Long's Peak," 345.

18. Samuel Garman, letter to Gertrude Lewis. Quoted in Stegner, *Beyond the Hundredth Meridian*, 28.

19. Byers's diary entries for August 20–23 were characteristically factual and brief:

> August 20 Fine day. Started for Long's Peak. Traveled about ten miles over very rough country—fallen timber and rocks—and camped at timber line.
> August 21 Fine day. Made only a mile—could find no route further for stock. Camped at timberline.
> August 22 Fine day. Started for the Peak on foot. Very rough traveling. Climbed two very high peaks. Camped at south foot of the peak.
> August 23 Fine day. Started at 6 oclock [sic] & reached the summit at 10. Difficult climbing but made without accident. Erected a monument & unfurled a flag. Camped on western waters of St. Vrain (1868 Diary of William N. Byers, Western History Collection, Denver Public Library).

20. The honor of being the first woman to climb Longs Peak may belong to
    Addie M. Alexander. The Boulder County News reported on August 26, 1871,
    that "Al Dunbar from Estes Park, last week, piloted a party to the summit
    of Long's Peak, among whom were Misses Alexander and Goss of St. Louis,
    the first ladies who ever made the ascension" (Boulder County News, August
    26, 1871, 3). Two years later, on August 14, 1873, the editor E. R. Painter
    of the Greeley Colorado Sun reported that he had observed during his own
    climb of Longs Peak a number of cairns left by preceding climbers: "The
    names of two ladies—Addie Alexander and Henrietta Goss—are recorded
    in one of the monuments as having ascended, but parties who have every
    opportunity of knowing state emphatically that only one of them accom-
    plished the feat, while the other gave up in despair within a few hundred
    feet of the summit" (Greeley Colorado Sun, August 14, 1873, 1). The story of
    Mr. Painter's ascent was echoed by the Rocky Mountain News on August 9,
    1873: "There are also records of two ladies, only one of whom—Addie
    Alexander—made the summit. Henrietta Goss' name is on the summit,
    but she failed to reach the top when only a few hundred feet from the
    desired goal. Both these women deserve praise for their muscle and their
    perseverance" (Rocky Mountain News, August 9, 1873, 4). Of Addie Alexander
    little is known other than the reference in Gould's St. Louis Directory for 1878,
    p. 71, which identifies her as a teacher boarding at 1549 Papin.
21. Ralph Meeker had come west with his parents in 1869 and then be-
    come secretary of the Union Colony and a subeditor for his father's news-
    paper, the Greeley Tribune. He also became one of Dickinson's unrequited
    suitors. Quite unasked, young Meeker had traveled east from Colorado to
    visit the Dickinson home in Pennsylvania and later tendered her a formal
    proposal of marriage. Though Meeker passionately idealized her, accord-
    ing to Giraud Chester, Dickinson's biographer, "Anna was never more
    than amused by his ardor" (Giraud Chester, Embattled Maiden: The Life of Anna
    Dickinson [New York: G. P. Putnam's Sons, 1951], p. 114).
22. Denver Tribune, September 18, 1873, 2. The Colorado Springs Gazette had previ-
    ously reported her successful ascent of Pikes Peak: "Miss Dickinson made
    the whole trip in the saddle, being the first person, we believe, who has
    ever ridden clear to the summit of the Peak" (Colorado Springs Gazette, August
    23, 1873, 3).
23. Ibid., September 4, 1873, 4.
24. Rocky Mountain News, September 10, 1873, 3.
25. Ibid.
26. Ibid.
27. James T. Gardiner, letter dated September 10, 1873. Roger W. Toll, ed.,
    "The Hayden Expedition to Colorado in 1873 and 1874: Letters from
    James T. Gardiner," Colorado Magazine 4, July 1929, 149. Toll explains that

Gardiner (1842–1912) spelled his name in two different ways, one with and one without the i. Though during his years with Hayden the i was omitted, he reverted to the original spelling after his second marriage.

28. Byers reported the Dickinson climb in a column titled "The Hayden Expedition," *Rocky Mountain News*, September 21, 1873, 2. Byers's surviving diary of 1873 unfortunately provides no additional details, though it does contain Anna Dickinson's name and Philadelphia address.

29. Ibid. Byers's comment that the party guided by Evans "missed their way" prompted the *Longmont Press* to counter that "Evans did not lose his way, but that Ralph Meeker did, and that he afterward apologized for it." In rebuttal, the *Greeley Tribune* offered up a brief article, possibly authored by Ralph Meeker, the gist of which was that Evans, though he professed to know the route well, had indeed lost his way, "confessed that he had lost it," and was rescued from his confusion by Ralph Meeker, who located "the proper place" at the upper timberline and then directed Evans and the rest of the party up (*Greeley Tribune*, October 1, 1873, 2).

30. Dickinson, *Ragged Register*, 268–69.

31. Ibid., 269–70.

32. Louisa Ward Arps and Elinor Eppich Kingery, *High Country Names: Rocky Mountain National Park* (Estes Park, CO: Rocky Mountain Nature Association, 1977), p. 52. Dickinson apparently named 13,281-foot Mount Lady Washington for New Hampshire's Mount Washington, which she had climbed on many occasions.

33. "Anna Dickinson purchased a pair of those things, at Longmont, for the purpose of riding up Long's Peak, which allows a lady to ride on both sides of a horse at once" (*Boulder County News*, August 19, 1873, 3).

34. The *Boulder County News* was once again the source of the gossip:

> Were you ever a boy? and did you ever slide down hill and burst open your unspeakabouts, where the burst forced you to know what a cold and cheerless thing is snow? If you never was [sic] a boy, and never did such a thing, then you are to be commiserated for being a woman not like Anna Dickinson. She enjoyed this peculiar and interesting experience the other day when she ascended Long's Peak in a singular and sensible costume. But please don't tell anybody about it (*Boulder County News*, September 26, 1873, 3).

35. Quoted in Chester, *Embattled Maiden*, 152.

36. Bird, *Letters from Colorado*, 66.

37. Bird's article was picked up and republished by other Colorado papers, including the *Boulder County News*, which wondered whether her mountain climbing heroics were not "a type of the to-be woman of the period. . . . We tremble to think what the effect of such an example upon the progressive portion of the sex may be" (*Boulder County News*, March 6, 1874, 2). Bird's account, "The American Matterhorn," appeared a week later, on

March 13, 1874. It was also published in various versions by other Colorado papers. See, for example, *Fort Collins Standard*, March 18, 1874, 1.

38. Rogers (1850–1928), the older of the two, was the son of the eminent New York lawyer and Democratic congressman Andrew J. Rogers, and an 1871 graduate of Columbia Law School. In 1872 he had come to the new town of Evans, Colorado, on the west bank of the South Platte south of Greeley to begin the practice of law. There, earlier that spring, he had met Downer (1853–1922), a native of Zanesville, Ohio, who after finishing his junior year at Denison University had come west to restore his health. Both men were destined to become major figures in Colorado's legal community. In January of 1874 Rogers opened a law office in Boulder, as the town's youngest lawyer. Two years later he was joined by Downer, who had meanwhile returned to New York to earn a law degree at Columbia. After several years in joint practice, Downer became county judge of Boulder County, a district attorney, and then a district judge, before returning to private practice. Rogers, on the other hand, moved on to Denver in the early 1880s, where he played a leading role in municipal affairs, built a twenty-two-room mansion on East Colfax at Washington, and in 1887 went into a highly successful legal partnership with John F. Shafroth, later Colorado's governor and U.S. senator. Elected mayor of the City of Denver in 1901 by a "splendid majority," Platt Rogers gained the reputation as "the hard-handed" political leader who got things done, including the first paving of the city's streets and the planning for a civic center and Denver's park system.

Both Rogers and Downer (who at the time, Bird felt, "had little idea of showing even ordinary civilities") lived long enough to do right by Isabella Bird and that brief moment in time that brought them so unexpectedly together. Unfortunately, Bird died in 1904, the year before Mills published Platt Rogers's account, and thus was denied knowledge of the compliments that he paid her, albeit at a distance of thirty years. "Downer and I looked upon her somewhat in the light of an encumbrance," Rogers wrote,

> though when her book was published we realized that we had had the great good fortune to travel with a woman whose ability to describe the manifold beauties of Estes Park has never been excelled. She was a thoroughly disciplined and observant traveler, although of too light a build to perform of her own strength the task she set for herself. Her physical unattractiveness, which so influenced us when we first met her, was really more than compensated for by a fluent and graphic pen, which made the mountains as romantic and beautiful as doubtless were her own thoughts.

Sylvester Downer was more fortunate. If his granddaughter is correct, he had the opportunity to encounter Isabella Bird again face to face: "Many years later my grandfather . . . was playing golf at St. Andrews in Scotland and found she lived nearby. Whereupon he sent her a note and said, 'One of the "rude young men" would like to call on her,' which he did and they had a very nice time together." Mills, *The Story of Estes Park*, 23–24; transcript of interview of Charlotte Ball Seymour, August 25, 1985, Colorado Collection, Pamphlet File, Estes Park Public Library.

39. Bird, *A Lady's Life*, 99–100.

40. Ibid., 105.

41. Ibid.

42. The two women, fortunately, were about the same size. Anna Dickinson apparently had a problem with her shoes that summer. Georgetown's *Colorado Miner* (citing the *Central City Register*) reported tongue-in-cheek on October 30, 1873, that she "left a pair of shoes at the Teller House which being too large for any one in Central, were deposited in the rubbish pile" (*Colorado Miner*, October 30, 1873, 4).

43. Bird, *A Lady's Life*, 111.

44. Ibid., 113.

45. Ibid., 115.

46. Ibid., 118. In retrospect, Bird was able to put the difficulty of her undertaking in perspective and added the following note to her account: "Let no practical mountaineer be allured by my description into the ascent of Long's Peak. Truly terrible as it was to me, to a member of the Alpine Club it would not be a feat worth performing" (ibid., 113 n).

47. Rogers is referring to the top of the Trough where the climber enters the Narrows.

48. Mills, *The Story of Estes Park* (1917 edition), 61–62.

49. Lamb, *Memories of the Past*, 130.

50. Ibid., 132. According to Captain George Brown, who had located on the North St. Vrain in 1869, and who climbed Longs Peak with Clarence King and ten others in 1872, Elkanah Lamb's descent followed the route subsequently taken by the Princeton professor James Alexander in making the first recorded ascent of the East Face on September 7, 1922 (*Longmont Ledger*, September 29, 1922, 1).

51. There seems to have been a consistent fascination over the biscuit reportedly baked by Major Powell. Yet Lewis Keplinger, in his account (albeit one written years after the fact) raises doubts about whether a biscuit was actually deposited in the tin box. Keplinger wrote:

> Major Powell, though one-armed, insisted on doing his stint the same as the rest, even in "packing." At the camp where we left our horses he said, "This is my time to make the bread." I insisted on taking his place, but he would not consent. I carried with me always the picture of the major paddling with his one hand the sticky dough. But he made the biscuits, such as they were. When we put our names in the can, one of these biscuits was put in also, with

the statement that this was placed in the can "as an everlasting momento [sic] of Major Powell's skill in bread making." As we were about to leave the major thought that was hardly up to the dignity of the occasion, and the biscuit was taken out. We insisted that his real reason was he did not want future generations to know how poor a bread maker so good a mountain climber was. The biscuit was of the kind which when cut with a sharp knife would show a fine-grained, smooth, dark-colored surface (Keplinger, "First Ascent of Long's Peak," 345).

52. *Boulder County News*, August 24, 1870, 1.
53. Ibid., October 5, 1870, 2.
54. *Greeley Tribune*, August 30, 1871, 2.
55. Ibid.
56. Abner E. Sprague, "My First Ascent of Longs Peak," *Estes Park Trail*, March 31, 1922, p. 5. Perhaps Abner Sprague did not search hard enough, for that very same month one member of a party of nine from Greeley (five of them women) reported that "a number of cans were found containing the names of parties who had made the ascent, and among them the names of several ladies" (*Greeley Tribune*, September 16, 1874, 2).
57. Alson C. Chapman, "Ascent of Long's Peak," *Fort Collins Standard*, August 12, 1874, 1. Chapman's dating of Powell's ascent of Longs Peak is, of course, wrong—and by almost two years.
58. Sprague, "My First Ascent of Longs Peak."
59. *Denver Post*, September 7, 1935, 9.
60. Charles Edwin Hewes, "Journal of Charles Edwin Hewes," entry of June 3, 1923, 591. By July of 1887, the month and year of Frederick Chapin's first visit, the Lambs were able to accommodate forty-six, "of which forty slept in Lamb's home and six in the guide's [Carlyle Lamb's] cabin" (*Fort Collins Courier*, July 21, 1887, 1).
61. *Fort Collins Daily Evening Courier*, August 25, 1888, 2.
62. *Fort Collins Courier*, September 24, 1885, 5. Sprague later improved this trail at its lower end by going on the west side of Green (now Emerald) Mountain, through Glacier Basin, and over the Wind River moraine to connect with his first trail.
63. Quoted in Alexander Drummond, *Enos Mills: Citizen of Nature* (Niwot: University Press of Colorado, 1995), p. 43.
64. *Longmont Ledger*, July 1, 1898, 2.
65. An earlier ledger, Carlyle Lamb wrote in 1940, "got lost in our changes during the 1880s."
66. Ledger, 1891–1901, Longs Peak House, Carlyle Lamb Papers, Colorado Historical Society, pp. 7–10, 22–23. See also James H. Pickering, "Biking and Climbing with the Denver Ramblers, 1891," *Trail and Timberline* 919, August 1996, 474–76. The "Ramblers," which historian James Whiteside

describes as "the first resoundingly successful Denver cycling club," by the mid-1890s boasted a large clubhouse of their own at 1642 Larimer Street (James Whiteside, "It Was a Terror to the Horses! Bicycling in Gilded-Age Denver," *Colorado Heritage*, Spring 1991, 2–16).

67. Ledger, Longs Peak House, 13.

68. Ibid., 121–22.

69. Emerson N. Lynn, "The Minister's Son" (1959), in *The Scottage*, typescript copies in the Rocky Mountain National Park Library and in the Colorado Collection, Pamphlet File, Estes Park Public Library.

70. See Earl Harding, "Climbing Long's Peak: Sketch of a Coloradan," *Denver Times Friday Magazine*, October 7, 1904, 11–12. As Harding explained, "I arrived at the Long's Peak Inn just as the mountaineer was returning from this adventure."

71. Enos Mills, "Guides Wanted," *Saturday Evening Post*, January 6, 1917, Enos Mills Papers, Western History Department, Denver Public Library.

72. Edna Ferber, *A Peculiar Treasure* (New York: Garden City, 1940), p. 243.

73. Quoted by Roger Davidson, *Fort Collins Coloradan*, August 22, 1958, 12.

74. Chapin, *Mountaineering in Colorado*, 30.

75. Ibid., 35.

76. Charles E. Fay, "Professor Fay Recounts Visit in Rocky Mountains in 1888," *Estes Park Trail*, July 23, 1926, 3.

77. Otis (1848–1933) was a member of the surgical staff of the Boston Dispensary and a specialist on pulmonary diseases. Of all the New Englanders whom Chapin introduced to Colorado, Otis alone seems to have found the Highlands and Estes Park wanting, at least in terms of creature comforts. Estes Park, he remarked several years later, then "possessed very inferior accommodations and very poor board, and the arrangements for obtaining provisions were very inadequate." Otis nonetheless evidently enjoyed his Colorado experiences, for he soon joined Chapin and the others as a member of the Appalachian Mountain Club. See Ruedi, "A Comparison," 41.

78. Hallett Glacier (now Rowe Glacier after Israel Rowe, who had originally discovered it while guiding a party from Dunraven's Estes Park Hotel in the late 1870s or early 1880s) had been visited by William Hallett in 1883. Exploring alone, Hallett had suffered a near fatal fall into a glacial fissure. In November 1887 he wrote the editor of the *Longmont Ledger* about that experience and about Chapin's visit of July. See *Longmont Ledger*, November 25, 1887, 2.

79. Chapin, *Mountaineering in Colorado*, 121.

80. Ibid., 125.

81. Ibid., 129–30. In 1922, the two lakes at the base of Mount Ypsilon were named the Spectacle Lakes by Roger Toll, the superintendent of Rocky Mountain National Park, who thought they resembled a pair of eye-

glasses.

82. Ibid., 135.

83. When the original dam was built, Sandbeach Lake was known simply as Supply Reservoir No. 1. That dam broke in 1902 and was rebuilt. The same year Frank Arbuckle and J. P. Billings filed on five reservoirs in Wild Basin and promptly built dams on two of them, Pear (Arbuckle #4) and Bluebird (Arbuckle #2). These filings were subsequently sold to a group of Longmont businessmen, who formed the Arbuckle Reservoir Company.

84. *Longmont Ledger*, September 20, 1907, 1. Editor Boynton, writing two weeks earlier, on September 6, dates the discovery of Ouzel Falls as 1903, when a party of four men, including the Cabin Creek rancher Harry Cole, stumbled across it "in their mountain rambles." An earlier article in the *Ledger* moves that date back to 1895 and credits a man named Holmes as discoverer (ibid., September 6, 1907, 4; and August 30, 1907, 1).

85. *Lyons Recorder*, October 20, 1910, 1.

86. *Longmont Ledger*, July 28, 1911, 4.

87. William S. Cooper, "Mountains," unpublished manuscript, dated Christmas 1971, University Archives, Walter Library, University of Minnesota, p. 21.

88. Ibid., 22.

89. Ibid., 41.

90. Dean Babcock described the Wild Basin area, including many of the features that Hewes and Cooper named, in a brief essay, which he published in 1912. See Dean Babcock, "A Glimpse of Wild Basin," *Estes Park Trail*, August 31, 1912, 2–6.

CHAPTER 8

1. *Denver Tribune-Republican*, September 28, 1884, 1.

2. Ibid.

3. Many explanations for the estrangement were offered, then as later. Typical is the story reprinted in the September 28, 1884, issue of the *New York Sun*:

> The devotion of mother and child was very marked until there came disagreements on money matters. The daughter thought that her rights were being infringed, and then she heard that her mother thought her insane and was about to have her taken to an asylum. This so alarmed and enraged the daughter that she forthwith took her departure without stopping for personal effects. The night before she left she had the coachman and his wife come in and sleep by her door so that she could not be surprised. Her mother's grief at her departure increased, and she sought a reconciliation, but the daughter would have no intercourse with her. At length the mother went to Europe, the mansion was rented, and the daughter began to travel in the

West for her health where her tragic fate overtook her (*NewYork Sun*, September 28, 1884, 1).

Four days later the same story appeared in the *Tribune-Republican*, October 2, 1884, 2.

4. Dorothy Moreton, "Emerald Velour in the Kitchen," *New England Galaxy* 10 (Winter 1969): 21.

5. Several suggestions that Carrie suffered from heart disease were made at the time of the trial (see *Waterbury American*, October 22, 1886, 4; and October 27, 1886, 4). Elbridge Gerry testified that Carrie had told him in 1878, at the time her will was drawn, that she "had a touch of heart disease" (*New Haven Evening Register*, October 21, 1886, 1). See also Henry Bergh, "Tribute to Carrie J. Welton." This manuscript is located at the New York offices of the Society for the Prevention of Cruelty to Animals.

6. *Colorado Springs Daily Gazette*, September 28, 1884, 1.

7. *Waterbury Republican*, September 29, 1884, 1.

8. *Waterbury American*, October 29, 1886, 4.

9. *Colorado Springs Daily Gazette*, September 28, 1884, 1; *Tribune-Republican*, September 27, 1884, 1.

10. *Tribune-Republican*, September 28, 1884, 1.

11. This information and the information as to what happened during the next twenty-four hours can be found in the *Denver Tribune-Republican*, September 27, 1884, 1; and September 28, 1884, 1; the *Denver Daily Times*, September 26, 1884, 1; the *Colorado Springs Daily Gazette*, September 27, 1884, 1; and September 28, 1884, 1; the *Fort Collins Courier*, October 2, 1884, 8; the *Longmont Ledger*, September 26, 1884, 3; and October 3, 1884, 3; the *Waterbury Republican*, September 29, 1884, 1; the *NewYork Sun*, September 27, 1884, 1; and September 28, 1884, 1; and the *New York Times*, September 27, 1884, 2. Also see Elkanah J. Lamb, *Miscellaneous Meditations*, 78–92.

12. Lamb, *Miscellaneous Meditations*, 80–81.

13. "Journal of Charles Edwin Hewes," entry of July 16, 1933, 900–1.

14. *Waterbury Republican*, October 3, 1884, 1.

15. Ibid., October 18, 1884, 1.

16. The single known photograph of Father Lamb's plaque (reproduced here) is found in Merrill Tileston's *Chiquita* (1902). The following year, Carlyle Lamb reported to the *Fort Collins Courier* that "many friends of the unfortunate girl from her former home, Waterbury, Conn., have made the ascent to visit the scene of her death" (*Fort Collins Courier*, November 5, 1885 1).

17. *Longmont Ledger*, September 26, 1884, 3. Ironically, Carlyle Lamb had apparently not been Carrie's first choice for a guide. That honor belonged to Fred M. Dille, who at the age of nineteen had become Estes Park's second schoolteacher. Dille, who began guiding for the Lambs during the

summer of 1883, recalled late in life that while working in a hayfield on the MacGregor Ranch he had been asked to take Carrie Welton up the peak. He declined because he "did not like to leave the hay shocks and Carlyle Lamb took her up" ("Reminiscence," undated typescript, Colorado Collection, Pamphlet File, Estes Park Public Library).

18. *Tribune-Republican*, September 27, 1884, 1.

19. Ibid., September 28, 1884, 1.

20. *Fort Collins Express*, October 1, 1884, 3.

21. Ibid.

22. *Fort Collins Courier*, October 2, 1884, 8.

23. Ibid., October 9, 1884, 4.

24. *Tribune-Republican*, September 29, 1884, 1.

25. *Denver Daily Times*, September 27, 1884, 2.

26. *Tribune-Republican*, October 8, 1884, 2. See also *Denver Daily Times*, October 6, 1884, 3; and the *New York Sun*, September 28, 1884, 1.

27. Moreton, "Emerald Velour in the Kitchen," 20.

28. *Tribune-Republican*, September 28, 1884, 1. "She received an answer from Mr. Berg [sic]," the article continued, "but its contents are unknown."

29. *New Haven Evening Register*, October 12, 1886, 1. Carrie Welton's bequest to Bergh's society was not the first to be challenged in court. Nine years earlier, in 1877, the gift of a benevolent Frenchman named Louis Bonard, amounting to more than $100,000, "was contested on the grounds that Mr. Bonard was not mentally sound; that he believed in the transmigration of souls, and that his motive in making the legacy was for his self-protection in the future stage of what he supposed his existence might be, should his soul become absorbed in the body of an animal" (Roswell C. McCrea, *The Humane Movement: A Descriptive Survey* [New York: Columbia University Press, 1910], pp. 152–53).

30. *Waterbury American*, October 12, 1886, 4.

31. *New York Times*, October 13, 1886, 1. The headline read: "She Loved Animals. And Now Her Heirs at Law Say She Was Insane."

32. *New Haven Evening Register*, October 12, 1886, 1. Bergh, whose face was long and thin, was said to much resemble "the picture of Don Quixote, with sunken eyes and prominent cheek bones" (McCrea, *Humane Movement*, 155 n).

33. *New Haven Morning Journal and Courier*, October 13, 1886, 3.

34. Patricia L. Joy, "Turned Into a Family Circus," *Waterbury American*, February 20, 1985, 7.

35. *New Haven Evening Register*, October 13, 1886, 1; *Waterbury American*, October 14, 1886, 4.

36. *New York Times*, October 15, 1886, 1.

37. *Waterbury American*, October 21, 1886, 4.

38. *New Haven Morning Journal and Courier*, October 22, 1886, 4.

39. *NewYork Times*, October 28, 1886, 1.

40. *New Haven Evening Register*, October 26, 1886, 1.

41. Ibid.

42. Joy, "Turned Into a Family Circus," 7.

43. *New Haven Evening Register*, October 27, 1886, 1.

44. *New Haven Morning Journal and Courier*, October 22, 1886, 4.

45. *Waterbury American*, October 27, 1886, 4; *NewYork Times*, October 27, 1886, 1.

46. *NewYork Times*, October 31, 1886, 14.

47. *Waterbury American*, October 30, 1886, 4.

48. Court costs and legal fees consumed thirty-two thousand dollars of the estate.

49. See James H. Pickering, "Tragedy on Longs Peak: Walter Kiener's Own Story," *Colorado Heritage*, no. 2, 1990, 18–31.

50. Lamb, *Miscellaneous Meditations*, 90–91.

51. Carlyle Lamb, letter to James Rose Harvey, August 3, 1940, Carlyle Lamb Papers, Colorado Historical Society.

CHAPTER 9

1. The history of photography in Estes Park is, in itself, a subject worthy of exploration. That history begins with the photographs taken by William H. Jackson in 1873 and includes those of Frederick Chapin, Henry C. Rogers, J. R. Riddle, William Tenbrook Parke, Enos Mills, Joe Mills, and Fred Clatworthy. The list also includes F. E. Baker of Greeley, who by July of 1895 had established a store near the post office where he offered his photographs for sale. Baker pursued his art aggressively. As he noted in the Lambs' Longs Peak House register on August 2, 1895, "I made views of four different parties on the snow banks at timberline today." By the next year Baker was signing himself in the register as "The Park Photographer."

2. Cooper's 1904 visit is recounted by Cooper himself in James H. Pickering, "Summertime in the Rockies: Estes Park in 1904," *Colorado Heritage* (spring 1992): 42–47. The first decade of the twentieth century saw the founding of a number of new companies dedicated to the development of Estes Park and its tourist industry. Among them was the Estes Park Cottage Company, founded on March 25, 1902, and headquartered in Fort Collins, whose principals included Frank P. Stover, Frank A. Somerville, Frank G. Bartholf, and Thomas H. Robertson. Its purpose was "to acquire land by purchase, lease, or otherwise, to build, construct, lease or obtain houses, cottages, blds, and places of abode . . . maintain, operate and conduct hotels, boarding houses, resorts and like places for the accommodation of tourists and the general public."

3. *Fort Collins Weekly Courier*, August 26, 1903, 6. At that year's event Lamb was

also given a suit of clothes and a tribute (delivered in church) that read in part: "The residents and summer visitors in Estes park desire to express in a tangible way their appreciation of your zeal and faithfulness in upholding services for the worship of God in this place" (ibid., September 2, 1903, 6).

4. Hondius, *Memoirs of Eleanor E. Hondius*, 16.

5. Ibid.

6. The resilient Lamb buried two young daughters by his first wife and then lived long enough to bury an adult son, the Reverend Lawrence Lamb, in 1903, and the twenty-two-month-old daughter (and only child) of another son, Carlyle, and his wife Emma, in 1896. But his greatest personal tragedy—one that he dismisses in his writings in a single short and elliptical paragraph—involved his daughter Jennie (1872–1904) and his nine-year-old grandson Donald, who were murdered in February 1904 by their husband and father, Azel D. Galbraith, in a lonely cabin in Russell Gulch near Central City where they had been living since 1899. The bodies of mother and son lay undiscovered for some seven weeks. The couple, who were high-school sweethearts, had been married on October 25, 1892. Galbraith, once "the pride of the Fort Collins high school," was said to have been brooding over money problems and to have gone "from drink to fast women, gambling and forgery." Jennie Lamb, "a young lady whom [it was said] any man might be proud to win," was Fort Collins's "honors graduate for 1892," and had given up a four-year tuition scholarship at the University of Denver in favor of marriage. Galbraith pleaded guilty and was sent to the gallows at Canon City on March 6, 1905, the first man to be legally hung in Colorado in almost a decade. The story received front-page coverage throughout Colorado.

7. *Longmont Ledger*, December 4, 1896, 3.

8. *Fort Collins Weekly Courier*, March 16, 1904, 10. "Their coming was a complete surprise to the boys, but they made every one feel welcome. The evening was spent playing games. Everyone pronounced the boys splendid entertainers."

9. *Fort Collins Express*, June 24, 1899, 6. The Reverend William H. McCreery, writing to the *Estes Park Trail* in 1923, maintained that a Fourth of July observance was held as early as 1876. That event, a picnic, which also celebrated the entrance of Colorado into the Union (on July 1 Coloradans had adopted a new state constitution), was held in "a small grassy cottonwood grove on Fall River." Picnic arrangements were handled by Mrs. Griff Evans and Mrs. William E. James (*Estes Park Trail*, November 9, 1923, 3). Fireworks were commonplace. The correspondent for the *Longmont Ledger* reported in 1893 that the daylong celebration began at 4 A.M. when visitors and residents were awakened by the explosion of blank cartridges. The "tumult was kept up through the day" and was climaxed in the

evening "with a grand exhibition of fireworks." "After the fireworks a huge bonfire was kindled, by the light of which the celebration closed with a game of tennis" (*Longmont Ledger*, July 14, 1893, 3).

10. *Longmont Ledger*, July 10, 1908, 8.

11. *Fort Collins Weekly Courier*, December 10, 1902, 6. In 1899, the program, put on by the schoolchildren, was a "literary" one (*Loveland Register*, December 6, 1899, 3).

12. Charles Partridge Adams, "Go West, Young Man," typescript manuscript, Western History Department, Denver Public Library, p. 12.

13. In May of 1892 the People's Toll Road Mining and Manufacturing Company was chartered with a capital stock of fifty thousand dollars to build a road "up the main channel of the Thompson to the north fork; thence to Estes Park; from Estes Park to Lulu, and from there to Grand Lake, Middle Park" (*Loveland Leader*, May 27, 1892, 1). In June a party of men, including John Stuyvesant from Estes Park, set out on a trip over the proposed road and subsequently reported its progress back to the *Leader* in a series of letters. They explained that the route would go up through Fall River. Even Abner Sprague, who had helped locate the route, got into the act, writing the *Leader* that "I think no investment of money could be made that would be of more benefit to Northern Colorado." The projected road was to be completed to Estes Park by July 1, 1893. See *Loveland Leader*, June 3, 1892, 1; June 17, 1892, 1; July 8, 1892, 1; July 15, 1892, 1; November 25, 1892, 1; and December 23, 1892, 5; *Loveland Reporter*, May 26, 1892, 1; and *Fort Collins Courier*, December 22, 1892, 8.

14. *Fort Collins Weekly Courier*, February 18, 1903, 6.

15. *Fort Collins Express*, September 17, 1902, 7.

16. *Loveland Reporter*, February 12, 1903, 9; *Fort Collins Express*, January 28, 1903, 6. Riley, an Arkansas-born rancher and contractor, had operated the Estes Park stage over the Bald Mountain route in 1899.

17. *Loveland Reporter*, January 29, 1903, 15.

18. Sprague, "Roads and Trails," *Estes Park Trail*, December 29, 1922, 5.

19. *Longmont Ledger*, September 18, 1903, 2; *Lyons Recorder*, September 17, 1903, 2.

20. *Loveland Reporter*, December 10, 1903, 1.

21. *Loveland Register*, January 6, 1904, 1.

22. *Loveland Register*, January 6, 1904, 1; January 13, 1904, 1; and January 13, 1904, 1; *Fort Collins Weekly Courier*, January 13, 1904, 1; *Fort Collins Express*, January 31, 1904 1. Directors of the corporation were Riley, Frank G. Bartholf, Greeley W. Whitford, Abner E. Sprague, Andrew J. Houts, Dewey C. Bailey, and Frank S. Tesch.

23. *Loveland Reporter*, February 4, 1904, 7; *Loveland Register*, January 13, 1904, 1.

24. *Fort Collins Weekly Courier*, January 20, 1904, 12; *Longmont Ledger*, January 22, 1904, 1.

25. *Loveland Register*, February 3, 1904, 1.

26. *Loveland Reporter*, April 21, 1904, 6.

27. *Loveland Reporter*, June 9, 1904, 8; and July 14, 1904, 8.

28. *Fort Collins Express*, July 8, 1903, 1; *Loveland Reporter*, December 3, 1908, 1. By the spring of 1909 there were about twenty cottages in Glen Haven. That May Abner Sprague was hired to subdivide the land to encourage additional building (*Loveland Reporter*, May 13, 1909, 1).

29. The only problem, it turned out, was with Cleave's title: the land on which he had been living since about 1888 and to which he gave a quit-claim deed was not legally his own. Cleave (1840–1925) had originally come from England in response to a call for workmen following Chicago's disastrous fire of 1871. He then made his way to Colorado and by the spring or early summer of 1875 had arrived in Estes Park to help Theodore Whyte with his construction activities, including the building of the Estes Park Hotel. In 1882 he married Margaret May, the nurse of Theodore Whyte's young children. Some years later Cleave and Dunraven swapped parcels of land, Cleave giving up his original claim of November 16, 1883, behind the Estes Park Hotel on Fish Creek for this unoccupied quarter section. Bond wisely followed the suggestion of Frank Prestidge, Dunraven's attorney, who took up the matter directly with the Earl him-self, though, Cleave's daughter Virginia recalled in 1935, it took two trips to England (and until March of 1906) to persuade Dunraven to honor his old commitment and provide Cleave with a quitclaim deed. Various rea-sons for the original exchange have been offered: one is that the noise from the hotel bothered the Englishman and his family, another that Cleave's original property had a spring that the hotel's water system needed. Cleave's relationship with the English Company apparently was not al-ways a cordial one. On April 10, 1883, he won a judgment against the company for $184.00 plus $18.35 in costs before judge and acting clerk Alexander MacGregor.

   Cleave did not leave Estes Park at once. In 1905 he erected a new house on a lot obtained from George D. Reid. The next year, in the late winter of 1906, for reasons not certain, unless they had to do with the original sale, the Estes Park Company deeded Cleave another lot for the sum of one dollar. The Cleaves subsequently moved to Fort Collins and then to Mancos, Colorado, before returning to Estes Park, where they made their home with their daughter, Virginia Griffith. Both John and Margaret Cleave are buried on the original Albin Griffith homestead (*Loveland Register*, April 26, 1905, 8; *Fort Collins Weekly Courier*, April 4, 1906, 4; *Estes Park Trail*, April 19, 1935, 3).

30. *Loveland Reporter*, July 6, 1905, 8.

31. The three surviving MacGregor brothers (Donald, George, and Halbert) granted an easement in May 1906. The holding tank installed by the Estes

Park Town Company provided the MacGregor Ranch with its first running water.

32. *Denver Republican*, June 2, 1905, 1.
33. Fred P. Clatworthy, "Pioneer Business Men Made Estes Park History," *Estes Park Trail*, April 23, 1943, 36.
34. *Longmont Ledger*, July 5, 1907, 1.
35. Unsigned manuscript, Estes Park Area Historical Museum. Service (1860–1937) had come to Estes Park from Lyons in 1902, where he had operated a store and quarry and briefly served as mayor. In Estes Park he purchased Billy Parke's grocery and then in 1905 bought a corner lot on Elkhorn Avenue from the Estes Park Town Company, where a year later he built both a home and a store.
36. Charles E. Lester, *Longmont Ledger*, October 25, 1907, 4.
37. Incorporation Records, State of Colorado, book 91, pp. 163–65.
38. *Denver Republican*, April 3, 1903, 12. A far less detailed announcement of LaCoste's plans—dated Estes Park, February 27, 1903—had already appeared in both Fort Collins papers a month earlier, on March 4. See *Fort Collins Express*, March 4, 1903, 6; *Fort Collins Weekly Courier*, March 4, 1903, 9.
39. See, for example, *Fort Collins Weekly Courier*, April 22, 1903, 10; April 29, 1903, 10; and May 27, 1903, 10.
40. *Loveland Reporter*, August 6, 1903, 2; *Longmont Ledger*, July 31, 1903, 1. This "scheme," put together by Thomas J. Milner of Denver on behalf of "eastern parties," projected an "enormous power plant . . . that will furnish electricity for all the northern towns, including the city of Denver," trolley lines from Loveland and Lyons to the park, and "an attempt . . . to run the trolley to the summit of Long's peak."
41. *Fort Collins Express*, September 17, 1902, 2.
42. *Loveland Register*, May 25, 1904, 3; *Fort Collins Evening Courier*, May 2, 1904, 1.
43. These few meager details come from an article that Anna Wolfrom wrote for the *Estes Park Trail* almost forty years later and from an unpublished manuscript by John Reichardt, which contains extracts from her diary. The diary does confirm LaCoste's Christmas visit to Oxford and her own arrival in London on December 30, 1904, but some of the details of her later recollections are suspect, particularly the suggestion that he had come to England in 1904 as the agent for Stanley and Sanborn. See Anna Wolfrom Dove, "Account of the Purchase of Estes Park," *Estes Park Trail*, April 25, 1941, 22, 43; John Reichardt, "Anna Wolfrom Dove," unpublished manuscript, Colorado Collection, Estes Park Public Library.
44. Given the fact that LaCoste's plans apparently subsequently collapsed over the availability of capital, it seems unlikely that either man, let alone both, were yet involved. That involvement would come later, when, as the record shows, they were able to achieve their goals without hesitation or delay.

45. *Longmont Ledger*, April 21, 1905, 4. The "new lease" was filed in Larimer County on June 13, 1905.

46. *Loveland Register*, March 1, 1905, 8.

47. *Denver Post*, reprinted in the *Longmont Ledger*, April 21, 1905, 4.

48. *Fort Collins Evening Courier*, October 16, 1905, 1; *Loveland Reporter*, October 19, 1905, 1. Miller Porter, whose firm was involved in the buying, selling, and trading of real estate, came naturally to his calling. His grandfather, I. B. Porter, was a principal of the firm of Porter, Raymond and Company from 1885 to 1888, which during those boom years "probably bought and sold more real estate in Denver . . . than any other firm in Colorado" (*Denver Times*, December 31, 1899, 11).

   In addition to the land, Sanborn reportedly received "the Dunraven hotel, the Earl's cottage, quite a number of summer cottages, all in first-class condition, well-furnished, and most of them supplied with new furnishings the past year. Other property consists of a fine ranch house, stables and barns, thirty horses, fifteen milch cows, also the country club house and pavilion." The dance pavilion had been added by Frank Bartholf during the summer of 1900 (*Longmont Ledger*, January 25, 1907, 1).

49. Incorporation Records, State of Colorado, book 115, pp. 88–91.

50. *Greeley Tribune*, January 24, 1907, 1. The sale involved taking over the stock of Porter's Estes Park Development Company and then, apparently, invoking the "option to purchase" clause in the lease.

51. *Greeley Tribune*, July 1, 1908, 1; *Loveland Reporter*, July 2, 1908, 1. The purchase price reported by the press was apparently incorrect, for the actual quitclaim deed of June 16, 1908, between Frank Prestidge as attorney for the Estes Park Company, Limited, and the Estes Park Development Company records a price of fifty thousand dollars—the same price that LaCoste and his partners had negotiated for three years earlier.

52. Dunraven, *Past Times and Pastimes*, 1:143.

53. *Greeley Tribune*, July 1, 1908, 1.

54. At Bierstadt Lake (which originally had no inlet) Sanborn had utilized his irrigationist skills by diverting water into the lake from Mill Creek. He was also one of those responsible for digging a 1½-mile to 2-mile ditch bringing water from the western drainage of Flattop Mountain over to the Fern Creek drainage, from where it eventually entered the Big Thompson. Some time prior to March 14, 1907, Sanborn organized the Bierstadt Reservoir and Power Company, for on that date he bought Fred Sprague's half share in the company for one thousand dollars. *Loveland Reporter*, March 14, 1907, 1. See also Don Griffith, "The Griffith Family in Estes Park" (January 20, 1977), typescript, Estes Park Public Library Oral History Project, Colorado Collection, Estes Park Public Library.

55. *Longmont Ledger*, February 15, 1907, 6.

56. *Loveland Reporter*, February 14, 1907, 1. Sanborn's letter was dated Febru-

ary 6, 1907.

57. *Longmont Ledger*, February 15, 1907, 6.

58. *Loveland Reporter*, September 19, 1907, 1.

59. Ibid., March 12, 1908, 1.

60. *Greeley Tribune*, January 24, 1907, 1.

61. See, for example, *Longmont Ledger*, January 25, 1907, 1; *Fort Collins Weekly Courier*, January 23, 1907, 1.

62. *Longmont Ledger*, January 25, 1907, 1.

63. *Loveland Reporter*, February 14, 1907, 1. The previous month, in reporting the purchase, the *Longmont Ledger* had noted that "Mr. Sanborn is undecided as to what he will do with the property, but that it will be continued as a summer resort is a settled fact. He is at present negotiating with Stanley, of Denver, manufacturer of the Stanley steam automobile, the greatest hill-climber of the world" (*Longmont Ledger*, January 25, 1907, 1).

64. According to an article reporting the death of Burton Sanborn's son, Carl, in 1960, Sanborn and Stanley divided the Dunraven property, with Stanley agreeing to build a hotel and power plant in return for a half interest. Sanborn's share lay along Fish Creek and included the hotel and ranch (*Estes Park Trail*, December 2, 1960, 9). Carl Sanborn had taken over from his father as president-manager of the Estes Park Development Company. See also Carothers, "Early History of Estes Park," 124.

    Stanley's agreement with the Estes Park Development Company lasted until February 13, 1917. On that date, in consideration for ten dollars and cancellation of stock, Carl Sanborn transferred to Stanley by warranty deed much of the original Dunraven holdings spread across the northern part of Estes Park from Dry Gulch to Tuxedo Park and totaling some 1,350 acres.

65. For a concise history of the steam automobile, including the Stanley Steamer, see John Bentley, *Oldtime Steam Cars* (New York: Arco, 1953). See also John B. Rae, *The American Automobile: A Brief History* (Chicago: University of Chicago Press, 1965).

66. See *Estes Park Trail*, April 7, 1933, 10.

67. *Lyons Recorder*, May 14, 1903, 1.

68. Mills, *Story of Estes Park* (1914 edition), 91.

69. *Lyons Recorder*, May 12, 1904, 2.

70. *Lyons Recorder*, April 18, 1907, 1.

71. Stories about Rowell ("Roll Over") Hill, named for the rancher James Rowell (1850–1910), who operated the halfway house for several years, were sometimes spectacular enough to find their way into the press. "Last Tuesday," the *Longmont Ledger* graphically reported in August 1898, "the Estes Park stage overturned, and injured some of its passengers. It was on the down trip, the stage having nine passengers was descending Rowell's hill, when the break [sic] broke, the leading horses became de-

tached, the driver jumped from his seat, the stage struck the right bank and then the left and upset." Fortunately, while there were fractures, gashes, and bruises, there was no loss of life (*Longmont Ledger*, August 19, 1898, 3).

72. *Lyons Recorder*, November 21, 1907, 1.

73. The upper part of the road from Stanley Hill to the North St. Vrain belonged to the county and was a constant source of irritation to its users. "In the last 8 years that we have lived here," a correspondent for the *Longmont Ledger* wrote in June 1899, "there hasn't been $15 worth of work done on that 6 miles of road, excepting the work done by the residents here, and it has always been in horrible shape. Maybe if we had a 'stand in' with the county commissioners it would be different" (*Longmont Ledger*, June 9, 1899, 2). The next spring, when Henry Cole struggled up Stanley Hill on his way back to his ranch on Cabin Creek, "it took six large horses to pull them . . . and three men to keep the wagon from turning over" (ibid., May 11, 1900, 2).

74. Ibid., May 7, 1903, 1.

75. For a history of the South St. Vrain road and other roads in the Allenspark region, see Lorna Knowlton, *Weaving Mountain Memories: Recollections of the Allenspark Area* (Estes Park, CO: Estes Park Area Historical Museum, 1989).

76. *Loveland Reporter*, July 5, 1906, 2.

77. *Longmont Ledger*, October 6, 1905, 1; and August 10, 1906, 1.

78. Cooper, "Mountains," 25.

79. *Longmont Ledger*, August 14, 1908, 8.

80. Just how big, the Estes Park correspondent for the *Longmont Ledger* tried to point out to readers on Christmas Day 1908 by disaggregating the whole. The building, he noted, contained 466 windows, 378 doors, and 289 rooms; used up 32,500 yards of lathing and 36,500 yards of plastering, 120 yards of sand, 2,200 sacks of cement and a car of lime, 156,000 shingles (or 624 bales of 150 shingles each), 25 miles of telephone wire, 6 miles of gas and plumbing pipe, and 1 mile of picture molding; and required 345 acres of flooring, 20,000 pounds of paint, 40,000 feet of siding, and 596,718,916 nails ("figuring kegs and nails to the pound"). "According to the time put into the construction of this hotel and the number of men employed," the article concluded, "it would take one man twenty-one years, nine months and twenty-six days, providing, of course, that he could handle all the heavy timbers and steel by himself, that has been put into it" (*Longmont Ledger*, December 25, 1908, 1). Though some of the figures—most notably the number of rooms and number of nails—seem exaggerated, the writer's point is made.

81. "The name Dunraven," *The Mountaineer*, Estes Park's summer newspaper, explained to its readers in August 1908, "does not call up pleasant memories. About the only thing Dunraven suggests is a land-grabber who tried to convert the Park into a game preserve for his own use." On the other

hand, "Mr. Stanley's name will always be associated with the upbuilding of the Park, making it a place delightful for all the people" (The Mountaineer, August 13, 1908, 6).

82. Longmont Ledger, February 28, 1908, 1.

83. Telephone communication to and from Estes Park did not come easily. Though service by way of Loveland had been talked about for years, it was delayed by the fact that the Colorado Telephone Company of Denver refused to connect its lines to the Loveland exchange. In January of 1900 a group of Loveland citizens decided to take matters into their own hands. A committee was appointed, and within days "various dealers in telephone apparatus" had been contacted, and twelve miles of poles had been donated, "to be delivered along the route where needed." The seriousness of these efforts attracted the attention of Colorado Telephone, which almost immediately agreed to take over the project. By the fall of 1900 telephone service had arrived in Estes Park. This arrangement lasted until May 1907, when a group of park businessmen headed by Pieter Hondius and James D. Stead purchased the Estes Park exchange from Colorado Telephone. "Owing to the fact that the Colorado Telephone company could not afford to keep a man in the Park to look after its business, claiming that the work to be done was not enough to keep a man employed, it became necessary for the Park company to take a hand," the Loveland Reporter explained to its readers. "Two copper wires will be stretched to the Park from Loveland by way of the new [Big Thompson] road and this will mean that everyone will have a chance to talk into the Park without being told that the line was busy, as has been the case heretofore" (Loveland Register, January 24, 1900, 1; and April 25, 1900, 5; Loveland Reporter, May 9, 1907, 1).

84. Loveland Reporter, July 16, 1908, 1; and September 24, 1908, 1.

85. Loveland Herald, January 19, 1911, 1. On January 19, 1911, the Estes Park Sewer Company was incorporated (Incorporation Records, State of Colorado, book 152, p. 198).

86. Reed, "Moraine Park Boyhood," n.p.

87. "The Friend of the Rocky Mountains," Literary Digest 55, July 14, 1917, 44–45.

88. Enos A. Mills, letter to John Muir, January 31, 1913, Muir-Mills Correspondence, Pacific Center for Western Historical Studies, University of the Pacific, Stockton, CA. Hereafter cited as Muir Papers.

89. Estes Park Trail, August 15, 1914, 9.

90. Enos Mills Papers, Western History Department, Denver Public Library.

91. Loveland Register, October 19, 1904, 1.

92. "Memoirs of Herbert N. Wheeler," typescript copy, Boulder Public Library, p. 55.

93. Longmont Ledger, June 21, 1895, 2.

94. The idea of reintroducing elk to Estes Park, like so many others, probably originated with C. H. Bond, who as early as the spring of 1909 took an option "on a bunch of elk that he is going to try and get parties interested in and have them kept in a private preserve here in the park" (*Loveland Register*, April 15, 1909, 6). Bond's timing, unfortunately, was premature.

In 1913 local citizens raised enough funds to purchase and transport twenty-nine elk from the Jackson Hole region of Wyoming. The herd was shipped from Gardiner, Montana, by railroad car to Lyons and from Lyons to Estes Park by Stanley Steamer automobiles equipped with special cages. They were unloaded at Frank Grubb's livery corral on Elkhorn Avenue and then moved to pasture east of the Stanley Hotel. "One of the interesting sights for tourists in Estes Park, which will be new even to former visitors," noted the *Estes Park Trail*, "is a herd of about twenty-five elk, which can be observed any day grazing in what has been rechristened the Stanley Elk Park" (*Estes Park Trail*, June 21, 1913, 4). An additional herd of twenty-four elk was introduced into Little Horseshoe Park in 1915. Interestingly enough, pasturing the elk in Stanley Park was not for the benefit of tourists. As Frederick Morrell, the acting district forester, explained to Pieter Hondius in a letter of February 21, 1913, "By feeding the elk in the deer park in Estes Park it will tend to locate them, and they will undoubtedly return to that point during severe storms, making it possible to feed them during severe winters, should such conditions occur" (Frederick Morrell, letter to Pieter Hondius, February 21, 1913, Colorado Collection, Pamphlet File, Estes Park Public Library).

F. O. Stanley, however, was not impressed. He was also prophetic. As he wrote Pieter Hondius from Newton, Massachusetts, on March 20, 1913, "From what I learn about the elk, I am afraid Estes Park will be overrun with animals of that kind, and we may have to get Roosevelt up there to help reduce the number" (F. O. Stanley, letter to Pieter Hondius, March 20, 1913, Estes Park Area Historical Museum).

95. Abner Sprague, *Estes Park Trail*, June 5, 1925, 7.

96. Richard A. Bartlett, *Yellowstone: A Wilderness Besieged* (Tucson: University of Arizona Press, 1985), p. 34.

97. When Howard James, an avid sportsman, who had been trapping bears in Horseshoe Park for years and would do so as late as 1907, caught an "immense cinnamon bear" in one of his traps there in the late spring of 1902, the *Longmont Ledger* remarked that "this is the first bear caught here for two years." The bear had attacked and killed one of James's cattle (*Longmont Ledger*, June 8, 1902, 2). During the first week of June the following year Joe Mills "in one cluster of traps, caught a cinnamon bear, two cubs and a fox." Mills kept the two cubs, which he named Johnnie and Jennie, and that October presented them to the Denver Zoo (ibid., June 26, 1903, 2; *Fort Collins Weekly Courier*, October 16, 1903, 8). The two

bears grew to maturity in a compound known as the "stockade," which housed wolves, coyotes, and bears. Johnnie died in 1925; the six-hundred-pound Jennie lived until 1936.

98. *Daily Denver Times*, August 24, 1874, 2.

99. *Fort Collins Express*, October 12, 1883, 2.

100. *Longmont Ledger*, December 2, 1892, 1.

101. Fred M. Packard, "Notes of a Conversation With Abner Sprague," Merrill Mattes Collection, Colorado Historical Society. The extinction of these animals in Colorado and elsewhere in the West was, of course, an extension of the ranching frontier. That it also upset the balance of nature did not become obvious in the Estes Park region until after elk were reintroduced in the second decade of the twentieth century and began to multiply unchecked because their natural predators were gone. Six years earlier, in 1933, Sprague told the park naturalist Dorr Yeager that he saw his last wolf the second day of his first visit to Estes Park in April 1868 (*Estes Park Trail*, November 10, 1933, 8).

102. *Longmont Ledger*, July 16, 1897, 3.

103. *Rocky Mountain News*, August 27, 1882, 7. By 1887 game laws limited catches to twenty pounds of fish per day per man.

104. *Estes Park Trail*, July 6, 1912, 3.

105. *Loveland Reporter*, June 17, 1909, 1. By the fall of 1908 Mills's name had become linked with the idea of "A National Game Preserve for Colorado." See *Loveland Reporter*, October 15, 1908, 1.

106. Ibid., September 23, 1909, 1.

107. The two most detailed accounts of the campaign to create the Rocky Mountain National Park are found in Patricia Fazio's "Cragged Crusade: The Fight for Rocky Mountain National Park, 1909–1915" (masters thesis, University of Wyoming, 1982), and Alexander Drummond's *Enos Mills: Citizen of Nature*, 222–47. For other accounts see C. W. Bucholtz, *Rocky Mountain National Park: A History* (Boulder: Colorado Associated University Press, 1983), pp. 126–37, and Lloyd K. Musselman, *Rocky Mountain National Park: Administrative History, 1915–1965* (Washington, DC: U.S. Department of the Interior, National Park Service, 1971), pp. 17–27.

108. John Muir, letter to Enos A. Mills, February 21, 1910, Muir Papers.

109. The Front Range Settlers League was made up entirely of Enos Mills's own neighbors: Charles Edwin Hewes, Elkanah Lamb, Charles Levings, Dean Babcock, Harry Bitner, and Rosa and Harry Cole. On June 28, 1910, they published a protest in the *Denver Republican* under their own names: "We fear that the prominent part he [Enos Mills] is taking in said movement may be thought to entitle him to a place in the administration of said park, if created, and we feel that any authority he may acquire over our property or the surrounding region will be used to our detriment" (*Denver Republican*, June 28, 1910, 11).

110. Enos A. Mills, letter to J. Horace McFarland, March 20, 1911, Papers of J. Horace McFarland, Division of Public Records, Pennsylvania Historical Museum Commission, Harrisburg, PA. Hereafter cited as McFarland Papers.

111. Enos A. Mills, "Who's Who—and Why: Enos A. Mills Himself, by Himself," *Saturday Evening Post*, September 1, 1917, 9.

112. Enos A. Mills, letter to J. Horace McFarland, April 24, 1912, McFarland Papers.

113. Frank Lundy Webster, *Denver Post*, September 5, 1915, 1.

114. Ibid.

115. Ibid.

116. Morris Legg, *Rocky Mountain News*, September 5, 1915, 1.

117. *Estes Park Trail*, September 12, 1914, 12.

118. Ibid., August 15, 1914, 20.

119. By the early summer of 1913, following a petition presented by Estes Park residents Pieter Hondius, Dan and Minnie March, Carl Piltz, and Lottie Holden, all of whom owned land on the proposed right of way, the Larimer County commissioners agreed to build a road up Fall River to connect at long last Estes Park with Middle Park. Work began in August with the arrival of thirty-eight convicts from the Colorado state prison ("Tom Tynan's Boys"), who were housed in cabins built in Endovalley. There were numerous delays in the road's completion for reasons including the difficulty of the job itself and the availability of funds to complete a project whose cost, as usual, outstripped what had been appropriated.

Index

~

Estes Park From the Beginning (Hicks), xii

Estes Park–Grand Lake trail, 234

Estes Park Hotel, 50, 91, 97, 108, 119, 126, 127, 138, 189, 195, 205, 241; described, 49; invalids at, 128; photo of, 47, 48; refurbishing, 208, 220 site for, 46–47; Welton at, 174, 179

Estes Park Improvement and Protective Association, trails by, 234

Estes Park Land and Investment Company, 204; LaCoste and, 205, 208

Estes Park Past and Present (Carothers), xii

Estes Park Protection and Improvement Association, 225–26, 228; schoolhouse and, 219

Estes Park Road Company, changes by, 114

Estes Park Sewer Company, 300n85

Estes Park Toll Road Company, 268nn6, 7

Estes Park Town Company, 201, 296nn31, 35; reservoirs by, 220

Estes Park Trail, 293n9, 298n64; on elk reintroduction, 301n94; Mills in, 234; Sprague in, xiii; Wolfrom in, 296n43

Estes Park Trail Gazette, 240

Estes Park Transportation Company, Stanley automobiles for, 217

Estes Park Wagon Road Company, 268n6

Estes Park Water Company, 219

Estes Park Woman's Club, 231; trails by, 234

Evans, Evan, 21; photo of, 21

Evans, Florence Isabella, 21–22

Evans, George, 21; photo of, 21

Evans, Griffith J., xii, 17, 29–30, 35, 39, 40, 87, 96, 104, 134, 149, 192; Bird on, 20–21; death of, 31,

266n96; Dunraven and, 28, 29, 256n43; Estes Park and, 18, 24, 28, 242; Haigh and, 72, 74; hunting by, 22; land grabbing and, 42, 43, 45; Longs Peak and, 146, 147, 148, 152; photo of, 19; ranch of, 22 (photo), 23, 99; removal of, 19–20; Rocky Mountain Jim and, 30, 41, 53, 60, 62, 63, 67, 69–72, 74–76; St. Vrain Hotel and, 46; trial for, 73, 75, 106

Evans, Jane Owen, 19–20, 24, 30, 254n28, 293n9; Bird on, 21; Clara MacGregor and, 86; death of, 31; photo of, 20; Rocky Mountain Jim and, 62

Evans, Jennie, 21, 44; photo of, 21; Rocky Mountain Jim and, 71

Evans, Katherine Ellen, 21; photo of, 21

Evans, Llewellyn, 21; photo of, 21

"Evans of Estes Park" (*Rocky Mountain News*), 18

Evans ranch, 150; photo of, 49

Evans Townsite and Quarry Company, 31

Ewart, William D., 111, 279n74; cattle business and, 135

Fall River, 3, 92, 94, 139, 164; hydroelectric plant on, 218; road up, 303n119; water rights on, 210

Fall River Lodge, 241

Fall River Road, 231, 239; opening of, 235, 238

Fancy Herself (Ferber), 159

Farrar, Clint, 90, 270n20, 272n51

Farrar, Hank, 30, 48, 73, 81, 133, 134, 269n10, 270n20; Evans and, 44; Ferguson and, 89, 90; MacGregor and, 85; road petition and, 105; Whyte and, 104